Handbook of Asian
FINANCE

VOLUME 1

Handbook of Asian
FINANCE

Financial Markets and
Sovereign Wealth Funds

VOLUME *1*

Edited by

DAVID LEE KUO CHUEN
GREG N. GREGORIOU

Amsterdam • Boston • Heidelberg • London • New York • Oxford
Paris • San Diego • San Francisco • Singapore • Sydney • Tokyo
Academic Press is an imprint of Elsevier

Academic Press is an imprint of Elsevier
525 B Street, Suite 1800, San Diego, CA 92101, USA
225 Wyman Street, Waltham 02451, USA
The Boulevard, Langford Lane, Kidlington, Oxford, OX5 1GB, UK

Notice
No responsibility is assumed by the publisher for any injury and/or damage to per-sons or property as a matter of products liability, negligence or otherwise, or from any use or operation of any methods, products, instructions or ideas contained in the material herein. Because of rapid advances in the medical sciences, in particular, independent verification of diagnoses and drug dosages should be made

British Library Cataloguing in Publication Data
A catalogue record for this book is available from the British Library

Library of Congress Catalog in-Publication Data
A catalog record for this book is available from the Library of Congress

ISBN: 978-0-12-801287-1 (SET)
ISBN: 978-0-12-800982-6 (Vol. 1)
ISBN: 978-0-12-800986-4 (Vol. 2)

For information on all Academic Press publications
visit our website at books.elsevier.com

14 15 16 17   10 9 8 7 6 5 4 3 2

CONTENTS

David Lee Kuo Chuen is a Professor of Quantitative Finance at the Singapore Management University and the owner of Ferrell Asset Management Group. He is also Director of the Sim Kee Boon Institute for Financial Economics. Ferrell has been a specialist fund manager in hedge funds, direct investment, property portfolio, and development since 1999. He obtained his Ph.D. from the London School of Economics and Political Science in 1990. His Ph.D. thesis focused on Applied Semiparametrics. He was a pioneer in Hedge Fund investments in Singapore and founded Ferrell Asset Management in 1999. His deep involvement within the Singapore business community led to his appointment as the Managing Director of two publicly listed companies, namely, Auric Pacific Limited and Overseas Union Enterprise Limited. He was also the former Chairman of MAP Holdings Limited and a member of the SGX Security Committee. He has been sought after speaker at conferences and frequently quoted in the media. Currently, he is the Independent Director of several listed companies including HLH Group Limited and a member of the Monetary Authority of Singapore Financial Research Council. He is also a Council Member of the Economic Society of Singapore, and a Board Member of the Kwong Wai Shui Hospital as well as the Yueng Ching Foundation. He is a member of Investment Committee for several charitable, professional, and endowment funds. He was adjunct faculty in National University and Nanyang Technological University. He has published numerous books and papers in Statistics, economics, and finance journals with special interests in asset allocation, hedge fund, and portfolio management. His recent publications have appeared in Journal of Wealth Management and Journal of Investing.

Greg N. Gregoriou is a native of Montreal and of Greek decent. He obtained his joint Ph.D. at the University of Quebec at Montreal in Finance, which merges the resources of Montreal's four major universities UQAM, McGill, Concordia, and HEC. He has published 50 books, 60 refereed publications in peer-reviewed journals, and 22 book chapters since his arrival at SUNY (Plattsburgh) in August 2003. His books have been published by McGraw-Hill, John Wiley & Sons, Elsevier-Butterworth/Heinemann, Taylor and Francis/CRC Press, Palgrave-MacMillan, and Risk Books. Three of his Wiley books have been translated into Chinese and one published by Elsevier in Russian. His articles have appeared in the Review of Asset Pricing Studies [with Professor Stephen J. Brown the David S. Loeb Professor of Finance at NYU and Professor Razvan Pascalau at SUNY (Plattsburgh)], Journal of Portfolio Management, Journal of Futures Markets, European Journal of Operational Research, Annals of Operations Research, Computers and Operations Research, etc. He has also been quoted several times in the New York

Times and the Financial Times of London. He is hedge fund editor and editorial board member for the Journal of Derivatives and Hedge Funds, as well as editorial board member for the Journal of Wealth Management, the Journal of Risk Management in Financial Institutions, Market Integrity, IEB International Journal of Finance, The Journal of Quantitative Methods for Social Sciences, and the Brazilian Business Review. His interests focus on hedge funds, funds of funds, and CTAs. He is an EDHEC Research Associate in Nice, France and Research Associate at the Caisse de dépôt et placement du Québec Endowed Chair in Portfolio Management at the University of Quebec at Montreal as well as Lecturer in the School of Continuing Studies at McGill University. In addition, he is Senior Advisor to the Ferrell Asset Management Group in Singapore.

Raj Aggarwal is the Sullivan Professor of International Business and Finance at the College of Business Administration, University of Akron, USA. He has authored or co-authored over a dozen books/monographs and over a hundred scholarly papers in the finance and international business areas. Before the University of Akron, he has been a faculty member at Harvard, Michigan, South Carolina, Kent State, and John Carroll. He has won university-wide Distinguished Scholar and Distinguished Faculty awards for excellence in teaching and in scholarship. His scholarly leadership is widely recognized and he has been elected as one of the few Fellows of the Academy of International Business. He has been a Fulbright Research Scholar for South-east Asia and has been a Visiting Scholar at Universities in Australia, Japan, Singapore, and Sweden. He has been the finance area editor for the Journal of International Business Studies and is the editor in chief of the Journal of Teaching International Business. He has held many elected and appointed leadership positions in academia and in business. For example, he has been the elected president of the Eastern Finance Association and serves on selected business and non-profit boards including Manco Inc (Duck, LePage, and Loctite brands), Ancora Mutual Funds, Financial Management Association, the Cleveland Council on World Affairs, and the Financial Executives Research Foundation. He has been a consultant to the UN, the World Bank, US SEC, Fortune 100 companies.

Jonathan A. Batten is a Professor of Banking and Finance at Monash University. He has numerous publications in financial market development, financial econometrics, fixed income markets, and non-linear dynamics. He is the editor of Emerging Markets Review, Associate Editor of Journal of Banking & Finance, Journal of the Asia Pacific Economy, and Research in International Business and Finance, and special issue editor for International Review of Financial Analysis.

Jane Binner is Chair of Finance in the Accounting and Finance Department at the Birmingham Business School, University of Birmingham, UK. She was formerly Head of Accounting and Financial Management, The University of Sheffield, UK. She serves as an advisor to the Federal Reserve Bank in St. Louis on monetary aggregate construction. Her research interests primarily include the construction and interpretation of Divisia monetary aggregates and the application of artificial intelligence techniques in Business and Economics.

Kym Brown is a lecturer at Monash University specializing in banking. Her Ph.D. undertaken at Monash University examined the financial development of 12 economies across the Asia Pacific, and bank cost and profit efficiency allowing for regional differences. Her research includes bank performance, financial system architecture in developing countries, Islamic finance, corporate governance, bank liquidity, and syndicated loans.

Chia-Ling Chang is a postdoctoral researcher in the Department of Economics, Chen-Chi University, Taiwan. In 2011 August, she was awarded a Ph.D. in Economics from the National Chen-Chi University, Taiwan. She specializes in agent-based modeling and computational economics. Her key publications are in the area of agent-based computational macroeconomics and agent-based computational finance.

Helena Chuliá is a lecturer in the Department of Econometrics and Statistics at the University of Barcelona. She holds a Ph.D. in Quantitative Finance and she was Visiting Research faculty at the Erasmus University of Rotterdam in 2006 and at Humboldt University in 2011. She has published in refereed journals such as the Journal of Banking and Finance, the European Journal of Finance, the Journal of Futures Markets, European Financial Management, and Energy Economics. Her current areas of interest are on applied econometrics, portfolio management, and international finance.

Gemma Esther B. Estrada is an Economics Officer in the Macroeconomics and Finance Research Division of the Economics and Research Department at the Asian Development Bank. Her recent research has been on structural change, old-age security, and trade and economic integration. She also works on the *Asian Development Outlook,* an annual flagship publication of ADB.

John W. Goodell is currently an Assistant Professor in the Department of Finance at the University of Akron. His research interests focus particularly on the impact on financial systems of national culture and institutions. In 2011 he received the Stockholm School of Economics/Women in the Academy of International Business Award for Increased Gender Awareness in International Business Research. His recent work has been discussed in numerous media outlets including the *Washington Post, PBS NewsHour,* and *Bloomberg Businessweek.* He is currently the Assistant Editor of Journal of Teaching in International Business and serves on the board of the Southwestern Finance Association.

Wolfgang Karl Härdle obtained his Ph.D. in Mathematics at University of Heidelberg in 1982 and in 1988 completed his Habilitation at the University of Bonn. He is currently chair and Professor of Statistics at Humboldt-Universität in Berlin, and Director of Ladislaus von Bortkiewicz Chair of Statistics and Center for Applied Statistics and Economics (CASE). He is also coordinator of the Collaborative Research Center "Economic Risk." His research focuses on dimension reduction techniques, computational statistics, and quantitative finance. His papers have appeared in top statistical, econometrics, and finance journals. He is one of the "Highly cited Scientist" according to the Institute of Scientific Information.

Kin-Yip Ho is currently an Assistant Professor at the Research School of Finance, Actuarial Studies, and Applied Statistics in The Australian National University. He has held visiting positions, including a fellowship from the Korea Institute of International Economic Policy (KIEP) to work on a research project involving the Chinese financial markets. He has published articles in Thomson Reuters SSCI/SCI journals, such as China Economic Review, Japan and the World Economy, Journal of Applied Econometrics, Mathematics and Computers in Simulation, North American Journal of Economics and Finance, and World Economy. His current research interests lie in international finance, financial econometrics, and time-series analysis. He graduated with a Ph.D. in Economics from Cornell University and an Associate Diploma in Piano Performance from London College of Music.

Yuwei Hu is currently China Representative (Pensions and Insurance) of BBVA Group in Beijing. Prior to BBVA he was briefly with European Commission as Visiting Fellow. Between 2006 and 2009 he worked as Economist at OECD and, was responsible for advising Chinese government on various economic and regulatory matters, including sovereign and pension fund issues. He received his Ph.D. in Economics from Brunel University, UK, and was a post-doctoral researcher at Oxford University in 2005. As China expert, he has provided technical assistance to various international organizations, including ASEAN, IMF, and World Bank among others. He is also special research fellow to the Chinese Academy of Social Sciences.

Logan Kelly is an Assistant Professor of Economics and the director of the UWRF Center for Economic Research at University of Wisconsin-River Falls, USA, and is a research affiliate at the Halle Institute for Economic Research, Germany. His research interests include applied macroeconomics, monetary economics, and measurement theory.

Heeho Kim, Ph.D. is a Professor of Economics at Kyungpook National University, Korea, and his main research areas are economic development, international economics, and finance, and econometrics. His book entitled and Markets of Slaves and Land in the 17th–19th century Korea was awarded the best academic book in 2006-2007 in Korea by the Ministry of Culture. In addition, Heeho has published several books in the fields of international economics and economic history of Korea. He earned a Ph.D. in Economics from North Carolina State University and worked as a program manager for the Korea National Research Foundation. He was invited as a research fellow to the Institute of Finance and Economics, which is part of the Chinese Social Science

Institute (CSSI) based in Beijing, China. He sits on several boards of academic journals, including the Eurasian Economic Review and the Korean Journal of International Economics. He has published more than 50 articles and books in well-known international journals.

Francis Koh is a Professor of Finance (Practice) at the Singapore Management University (SMU). He received his MBA from the University of British Columbia and Ph.D. (Finance) from the University of New South Wales. He is a Chartered Accountant of Singapore and a Fellow of the Chartered Institute of Management Accountants in UK. Between 1994 and 2002, Francis was employed by the Government of Singapore Investment Corporation. In 2003, he was appointed Associate Dean and Director, MSc in Wealth Management Programme in the Lee Kong Chian School of Business. In November 2012, he assumed the post of Vice Provost (Special Projects) at SMU. In the same year, Francis was awarded an Honorary Doctorate in Economics by the University of St. Gallen in Switzerland. He has been active in consulting, executive development, and public service. He has also published in numerous academic journals, including the Journal of Financial Economics.

Robert W. McGee teaches accounting at Fayetteville State University in North Carolina, USA. He has published 58 books and more than 600 articles and book chapters in the fields of accounting, taxation, economics, law, philosophy, and ethics. He has several doctorates, including a Ph.D. in Applied Ethics from Leeds Metropolitan University and a Ph.D. in Philosophy from the University of Bradford.

David R. Meyer is a Senior Lecturer in Management at Olin Business School, Washington University in St. Louis, teaching international business, with a focus on Asia. Prior to this he was Professor of Sociology & Urban Studies at Brown University. He received his Ph.D. from the University of Chicago. His research examines financial networks, Asian economic development, global business centers, Asian business networks, and urban-industrial growth in the United States. This has been published in five books and monographs and about 50 articles and book chapters. His recent books on economic development in the United States included The Roots of American Industrialization and Networked Machinists: High-Technology Industries in Antebellum America. For the past 20 years he has studied Asian business, and his book, Hong Kong as a Global Metropolis, interpreted that city as the pivot of Asian business networks. His current research focuses on the network behavior of leading international financiers and has been funded by the National Science Foundation.

Heather Montgomery is a Senior Associate Professor in the Department of Economics and Business at International Christian University (ICU) in Tokyo, Japan.

Prior to joining ICU, she worked at JP Morgan Securities and the Asian Development Bank Institute, also both in Tokyo. While completing her Ph.D. dissertation research at the University of Michigan, she held visiting positions at the Federal Reserve Board of Governors in Washington, DC, the Bank of Japan, Japanese Ministry of Finance, and Japanese Ministry of Economy, Trade and Industry, among others.

Edward H. K. Ng runs his own business specializing in architecting and developing risk management systems for banks according to Basel II and III requirements. He spent more than two decades as a fulltime academic at the National University of Singapore. His client banks come from Singapore, China, India, Thailand, and Indonesia. He trains finance professionals and continues to teach and research in risk issues. Edward graduated with a Ph.D. in Finance from the Ohio State University and has published in Journal of Finance, Global Finance Journal, Pacific Basin Finance Journal, Journal of Asian Real Estate Research, Banks and Bank Systems, Hanil Institute of Finance and Banking Journal, and Global Portfolio Diversification. He continues to be an adjunct faculty at the National University of Singapore and Singapore Management University.

Yen N. Nguyen is currently a Ph.D. student at Monash University. She is about to finish her Ph.D. thesis about financial development and economic growth titled "Interaction effects between financial system components and the finance-growth relationship: a cross-country study."

Donghyun Park is currently Principal Economist at the Economics and Research Department (ERD) of the Asian Development Bank (ADB), which he joined in April 2007. Prior to joining ADB, he was a tenured Associate Professor of Economics at Nanyang Technological University in Singapore. He earned a Ph.D. in economics from UCLA, and his main research fields are international finance, international trade, and development economics. His research, which has been published extensively in journals and books, revolves around policy-oriented topics relevant for Asia's long-term development, including the middle-income trap, Asia's services sector development, and Asia's population aging. He plays a leading role in the production of Asian Development Outlook, ADB's flagship annual publication.

Sae Woon Park is a Professor of Finance at the Changwon National University, Korea. His research topics focus mainly on Asian housing markets. He teaches real estate economics and finance, and serves as a Director of the CNU Central Library. He received his Ph.D. from Myungji University, Korea. He has written numerous papers on the Korean real estate market, including "Price Run-up in Housing Markets, Access to Bank Lending and House Prices in Korea," published in Journal of Real Estate Finance and Economics. He was given an award in 2009 by the Korean newspaper "Maekyung" for his paper entitled "The Value of Outside Directors: Evidence from Corporate Governance" which was published in Journal of Financial and Quantitative Analysis.

Kok Fai Phoon is Associate Professor of Finance (education) and co-director of the M.Sc. in Applied Finance program at the Lee Kong Chian School of Business at Singapore Management University. He holds a Ph.D. in finance from Northwestern University. He was executive director of Ferrell Asset Management and also worked with the Yamaichi Research Institute and the Government of Singapore Investment Corporation.

Dedy Dwi Prastyo received his bachelor and master degree from the Department of Statistics, Institut Teknologi Sepuluh Nopember (ITS), Indonesia in 2006 and 2008, respectively. He is a researcher and lecture assistant in ITS since 2008. He is currently working toward the Ph.D. degree at the Institute of Statistics and Econometrics, Humboldt-Universität zu Berlin. His research interest includes credit risk modeling, computational statistics, and financial markets.

Tayyeb Shabbir currently teaches at the Wharton School's Department of Finance as well as at the College of Business and Public Policy at the California State University, Dominguez Hills. He is also the Director of the Institute of Entrepreneurship, Small Business Development and Global Logistics, CBAPP. He has vast teaching, research, and consulting experience that has been acquired internationally. In the past, he has also served as a faculty member in the doctoral as well as MBA programs at the LeBow College of Business, Drexel University as well as the Pennsylvania State University, University Park, and in the Economics Department of University of Pennsylvania. His areas of expertise include prediction, management, and prevention of financial crises, Entrepreneurial Finance, Microenterprises, Emerging Capital and Financial Markets and human capital investments. He has scores of publications and competitive research grants to his credit and he has also served as a consultant to the World Bank, the United Nations Development Program and the Asian Development Bank. Recently, he co-edited a book with Professor Lawrence Klein, Nobel Laureate in Economics and Benjamin Franklin Professor of Finance and Economics at the University of Pennsylvania. The title of the book is, "Recent Financial Crises: Analysis, Challenges and Implications" and it has been published by Edward Elgar, an international academic publisher.

Chandan Sharma is Assistant Professor of Business Environmental at Indian Institute of Management, Lucknow, India. He teaches Macroeconomics, International Economics and Finance, and Panel Data Econometrics. His research focuses on Industrial Economics, Infrastructure, Development Economics, Political Economy, and Shadow Economy. He has worked extensively on firm-level productivity, R&D, Infrastructure and growth nexus, Optimum currency Area (OCA), and International reserves. He has recently completed a crucial research and policy project on Unaccounted Income/Wealth both within and Outside India (Black Economy) sponsored by Ministry of Finance, Government of India. He is also a member of Expert Committee on developing Infrastructure Index for India constituted by Central Statistical Organization, Ministry of Statistics and Program Implementations, Government of India. He received a Ph.D. from University of Delhi.

Yanlin Shi is currently a Ph.D. candidate in Statistics at the Research School of Finance, Actuarial Studies and Applied Statistics at The Australian National University (ANU). His dissertation focuses on volatility modeling of high-frequency time series. He has published an article in the Thomson Reuters SSCI journal *North American Journal of Economics and Finance*, and presented papers at several international conferences, such as the 19th International Congress on Modelling and Simulation, of which the conference proceedings are included in the Thomson Reuters CPCI. He received two Master's degrees from ANU in the fields of Applied Statistics and Business with the highest distinction. In 2009 and 2010, he was awarded the ANU Chancellor's Letters of Commendation for Outstanding Academic Achievements.

Sunny Kumar Singh is a Fellow candidate at Indian Institute of Management (IIM), Lucknow, India. His research focuses on Macroeconomics, Monetary Economics, and International Finance. He has also worked in the area of remittance economy. Before joining IIM Lucknow, he completed his MA (Economics) from Gokhale Institute of Politics & Economics, Pune, India and worked at Indian Institute of Management, Ahmedabad, India as an Academic Associate. He has also qualified UGC-NET in 2012.

Michael Skully holds the Chair of Banking at Monash University. He is a Senior Fellow and director of the Financial Services Institute of Australasia as well as a trustee director of UniSuper Limited. He teaches and has published widely in the areas of financial institutions and corporate finance both in respect to Australia and the Asia Pacific region.

Yuki Takahashi is a Ph.D. student of economics at State University of New York at Stony Brook. His fields of concentration are industrial organization and finance.

Peggan Tan is an assistant wealth manager at DBS Private Bank. She received her Bachelor of Business (Hons) degree in Banking & Finance from the Nanyang Technological University and the MSc in Wealth Management from Singapore Management University. She has worked as an Analyst and Associate in the front, mid, and back-offices in the wealth management industry.

Yi-Heng Tseng is an assistant professor in the College of Management, at Yuan Ze University, Taiwan. In 2008 Aug, he was awarded a Ph.D. in Economics from the

National Taiwan University, Taiwan. His research interests include international trade and international finance. His key publications are in the area of applied macroeconomics, financial economics, energy economics, and tourism.

Natàlia Valls is an analyst of the Market Risk Department at CaixaBank, S.A. She is currently working on her Ph.D. thesis on Volatility in Financial Markets and has published the first part of the thesis in the refereed journal Global Economic Review. Her current areas of interest are applied econometrics, financial market risk, portfolio management, and international financial markets.

Yeomin Yoon is a Professor of Finance & International Business at the Stillman School of Business of Seton Hall University. He teaches international finance at both undergraduate and graduate levels and global business at undergraduate level. His research has been widely recognized, achieving some of the largest number of downloads from the Social Science Research Network.

Zhaoyong Zhang obtained his Ph.D. in economics from the Catholic University of Leuven (Belgium) in 1991. He is currently an Associate Professor of Economics and Deputy Director of FEMARC at Edith Cowan University (ECU) in Australia. Previously, he was Professor of Economics at NUCB Graduate School of Commerce and Business in Japan, and Associate Professor and Director of CSTE at National University of Singapore (NUS). He held several visiting professorship positions at ECU, Yokohama National University (YNU), ICSEAD (Japan) and KIEP (Korea), and was also a visiting fellow/adjunct (Associate) Professor at University of Western Australia, University of South Australia, University of Macau as well as several universities in China. He also held several consulting positions with international institutions including OECD, IDRC, and Hanns Seidel Foundation (Germany). He has been included in the 2000 Outstanding Intellectuals in the 21st Century by Cambridge International Biographical Centre in 2008; and in *Who's Who in the World* in 2007–2012. His major research interests are International Trade and Finance, East Asian Financial Crisis, East Asia Monetary and Economic Integration, Foreign Exchange Policy and Reform in China. He has published one book manuscript, 26 books chapters, and 46 articles in international journals, as well as co-edited four special issues for the international journals including Papers in Regional Science published in 2003 and The World Economy in 2006 and 2012, respectively.

ACKNOWLEDGMENTS

We would like to thank all the contributors and many others who expressed interest in this project one way or another. We would like to thank the handful of anonymous referees that helped in selecting the papers for this book. We thank Dr. J. Scott Bentley, Melissa Murray, and Jason Mitchell at Elsevier for their suggestions and continuing support throughout this process.

In addition we would like to thank both the President of Barclay Hedge (http://www.barlcayhedge.com) Sol Waksman and Beto Carminhato (IT manager) for providing hedge fund data as well as helpful comments and suggestions. Furthermore, we thank Finance Professor Maher Kooli the Head of the CDPQ Chair in Portfolio Management at the University of Quebec at Montreal for his helpful suggestions. Finally, we thank Evestment (http://www.evestment.com) for their database and PerTrac software.

We would also like to express our appreciation to our respective universities, namely, Singapore Management University and State University of New York (Plattsburgh). In particular, the President, the Provost and the Deans for their strong support. We thank Lim Chee Onn, Chairman of the Sim Kee Boon Institute for Financial Economics and the Advisory Board for their strong support. We thank Dr. Stephen Riady, Magnus Bocker, and Raymond Lim for their constant support. PhD supervisor Peter Robinson is a source of constant inspiration and role model for David Lee Kuo Chuen for this project even though he has graduated for more than 23 years. Colleagues at the Lee Kong China School of business especially Wolfgang Karl Härdle, Francis Koh, Benedict Koh, Lim Kian Guan, Christopher Ting, and Kok Fai Phoon are always supportive and instrumental in David Lee Kuo Chuen's research. We would like to express our appreciation to Colin James Tan for his assistance in research during his examination. Our colleagues at Ferrell Group of Companies were always in the background assisting and remained invisible. Of course, we would never forget the support of family members. Last but not least, to thank God for His plan in arranging the meeting of minds of the two editors for a meaningful project.

Asia Finance: The Emergence of Asia Economy and New Development in Finance

David Lee Kuo Chuen[a] and Greg N. Gregoriou[b]
[a]Singapore Management University, Lee Kong Chian School of Business, 50 Stamford Road, Singapore 178899, Singapore
[b]State University of New York (Plattsburgh), 101 Broad Street, Plattsburgh, NY 129 01, USA

This Handbook of Asian Finance provides an overview of the diverse financial developments in Asia that are of interest to both practitioners and academics. The Asian economies and related financial sectors have both shown great resilience and have undergone significant transformation over the last two decades. These economies have recovered miraculously from the 1997 Asian Crisis. In the decade spanning the years 2000–2010, the total GDP of eight East Asian economies (China, Hong Kong SAR, Indonesia, Malaysia, South Korea, Philippines, Singapore, and Thailand) has more than doubled in size. Economic growth has attained an even higher plateau when compared with the pre-crisis level and has allowed many Asian economies to build substantial foreign reserves, providing buffers against the vagaries of the global environment.

Problems and issues associated with Asian finance and banks are not of particular interest to many academic journals. The main reason is that these issues are deemed to be only specific and relevant to financial institutions operating in Asia. As trade, foreign exchange and other transactions and income from Asia increase over time, many global financial institutions and especially banks are likely to increase their participation in the Asian financial sector along with a greater share of profits from the Asian operations. By then, these Asian centric issues will be of great interest to the global financial industry. Another often cited reason is the lack of reliable data. However, with higher volume of transactions and more reliable maintenance of historical records, which were both not available previously, there is now scope for more meaningful empirical analysis and discussions.

There is always an overwhelming response of researchers to the idea of a project on Asia finance. We are not surprised that we have gathered many expert practitioners and respected academics that supported our work on Asia. While we are appreciative of the support, we had a tight timeline and we were not able to accommodate many who were interested in participating. We hope to initiate further projects in specialized topics in Asia finance in the near future. As a consequence of the excellent response, we have edited two volumes consisting of 20 chapters in the Volume 1 and 24 chapters in Volume 2. We have given a summary of the chapters below.

BANKING

With the transformation in relationship and increased linkages between real estate and banking sectors, interest to better understand the systematic risk of the bank's exposure to new alternative instruments has grown. Whether it is systematic risk, default risk, litigation risk or other enterprise risks, banks are in a new era with regard to managing risk in an ever changing and uncertain environment. Asian banks are buffered by different types of risk along with changes in their business models that are required to adapt to such volatile conditions. For those who are interested to find out more, there are eight chapters in this book to address various issues that Asian banks are facing.

MARKET DEVELOPMENTS AND GOVERNANCE ISSUES

Many of the concepts such as tax evasion, market manipulation, and corporate governance are distant and alien to the financial market participants in emerging Asian markets before the Asian Crisis. The transition from the status as an emerging to that of a developed market will naturally draw attention to these important issues once investors become more sophisticated. Given Asia's rapid growth, there will not be the luxury of time in dealing with such issues and attitude change will need to change quickly or to be time compressed. However, as human nature and along with it behavior takes time to change, significant tensions between the various players in Asian markets are expected with many issues and lessons having surfaced. There are eight chapters in the book to capture the more important issues in this area and they are by no means exhaustive.

SOVEREIGN WEALTH FUNDS

With the lessons learnt from the previous crises, Asian governments have improved the resilience of their economies to external shocks. They have increased their foreign reserves and have reduced their dependence on short-term loans denominated in foreign currencies. These short-term foreign loans were used to finance domestic borrowings for domestic economic growth. Supported by strong economic growth and trade surpluses, many Asian economies have been able to build up huge foreign reserves managed by sizable sovereign wealth funds. Sovereign wealth management issues including the setting of investment objectives, constraints, horizon, liquidity needs, allocation, and uses have drawn attention. This is mainly because of the increasing impact such sovereign wealth funds can have when deploying their funds in investments overseas. Given this increasing importance of Asian sovereign wealth and their global influence, we have included seven chapters in the book to discuss various issues surrounding these new trends in sovereign wealth fund management.

SUMMARY OF INDIVIDUAL CHAPTERS IN VOLUME 1

In the first chapter, Edward H.K. Ng proposed the use of transactional behavior model, which was both simple and flexible, instead of PIT (Point-In-Time) credit scoring model. His suggested approach for Asian banks could be a significant enabler in their quest to produce internal credit ratings for the requirements for Basel II. He uses 4 years of credit card delinquency data from a large Asian bank and demonstrates the advantages of the proposed approach to overcome the data challenges faced by banks. One very practical issue that has caused great difficulties is the practice of applying consumer credit scoring methods developed outside Asia to use universally in Asia, which is known as diverse in culture. Given that cost is not an issue with higher revenue and with big data, it is easy to develop more complex and adaptive behavioral model for risk management. While these models are deemed to be more realistic and resemble the behavior of the Asian markets, there are also scopes for such models to be used in the main stream. There is a possibility of reversing the earlier trend of intellectual flow from the developed markets to Asia, dictating the use of risk management technology and methodology.

In Chapter 2, David R. Meyer discusses the rapid growth of private wealth management business in Asia. While Asia Pacific High Net Worth Individuals (HWNIs) accounts for 27.7% of the total HNWIs in 2007, this percentage has grown to 31% in 2012 according to World Wealth Report 2013. The amount of investable wealth has grown from 23% to 26% in just 5 years. It is interesting to note that Singapore and Hong Kong are among the top five centers of private wealth management, along with Switzerland, London, and New York. Japan, with the most wealth in Asia, is not among the top. The author notes that the most important trend in global private wealth management is Asia's climb to equality with the US and Europe, with the view that it may grow to be the primary center of HNWIs and of their investable wealth over the next couple of decades.

In Chapter 3, David R. Meyer examines the history of the banking networks of Asia's financial centers in relation to British colonies such as Singapore, Hong Kong, India, and other locations like Shanghai and Japan. He looks at the banking functions of each center and the network of activities originated from each individual center. While Singapore and Hong Kong remain high on the ranking as international financial centers, South Korea and China are catching up, with India remaining stagnant in terms of ranking. The China growth phenomena as the leading stock exchanges in Asia is highlighted.

In Chapter 4, Heeho Kim and Sae Woon Park study the correlation between housing prices, bank lending and other macroeconomic factors. While the short-run relationship was ambiguous, there appear to be long-run positive relationship between bank lending and house prices.

In Chapter 5, Heather Montgomery and Yuki Takahashi investigate and uncover differences in the effect of bank mergers on shareholder value and bank performance. Consolidation in the financial sector is common after the crisis and bank failures. Few countries with a well-developed financial sector have experienced what Japan has gone through since the 1990s. Japan provides a very good case study since its economy and financial sector have seen a balance sheet recession. Using Japan data from 1996 to 2010, they discover that banks entering into a mega-bank enjoy large and significant excess returns at or around the merger announcement but disappear 1 year after the announcement. They conclude that action of the shareholders is merely a reflection of a flight-to-safety to banks which are perceived to be too big to fail.

In Chapter 6, Kin-Yip Ho, Yanlin Shi, and Zhaoyong Zhang examine the impact of announcement on bank stocks on a more general setting. They examine firm specific and macroeconomic announcements and their impacts on twenty bank stocks in Japan, China, Hong Kong, Korea, and Singapore using date from 2000 to 2012. They find that the announcements have predictive power for future stock returns. Both negative and positive news are positively correlated with the announcements and the impact is almost symmetric.

In Chapter 7, Wolfgang Karl Härdle and Dedy Dwi Prastyo employ an interesting technique to simultaneously select the default predictors and estimate the parameters. Rating agencies' core business is default risk estimation and financial institutions, in particularly banks, need to monitor the default risk of their counterparties. But most approaches will treat the identification of variables with good predictive power as independent from the estimation of the default risk. However, default analysis and predictor selection are two related issues. This chapter offers a new and reliable approach that unifies both using data from Indonesia, Malaysia, Singapore, and Thailand from 1998 to 2012. This chapter is extremely useful to practitioners in the field of credit risk analysis and provides an overview of currently used estimation methods and their shortcomings. In addition, they also apply, with very high accuracy, a regularized Logit model to estimate and select default predictors.

In Chapter 8, Chandra Sharma and Sunny Kumar Singh investigate the determinants of international reserves for seven emerging Asian countries and assess adequacy of reserves in these countries. Interestingly, international reserves in emerging Asia increased more than ten folds from USD139 billion in 1997 to USD4100 billion in 2011. The shares of emerging Asia to world's reserve increased from 34% in 2003 to 59% in 2011. Using data from 1980 to 2011 and dynamic models, Sharma and Singh analyze the determinants of international reserves. Given the buffer, the authors conclude that the probability of a repeat of the Asian Crisis of 1997 is greatly reduced and that the motivation is mainly for self-insurance.

In Chapter 9, David Lee Kuo Chuen and Kok Fai Phoon trace the history of development of Singapore's financial markets and discuss the challenges, future, and prospects. Singapore has a good track record of its policy makers having a good under-standing of how markets function and having the ability to create and maintain an eco system for growth. This chapter also looks at the challenges facing the Singapore markets given the current volatile trading environment with potential problems caused by voluminous capital flow in a time compressed manner. The authors conclude that the bet for long-term investors is still one way and very much in a real-estate based finance sector.

In Chapter 10, Francis Koh and Peggan Tan analyze the role and competitiveness of Switzerland, Singapore, and Hong Kong as wealth management centers. They note that Credit Suisse had identified five broad categories, namely, people, business environ-ment, market access, infrastructure, and general competitiveness, as success factors for international financial centers. Despite the challenges facing Switzerland with a slower economy in Europe and from legacy issues, they conclude that Singapore and Hong Kong will not replace but complement Switzerland as a wealth management center.

In Chapter 11, Natàlia Valls and Helena Chuliá analyze the effect of US macroeco-nomic news releases on the returns and volatility of Asian stock prices and their cor-relations with the US market. Using data from 2003 to 2012 for 10 different countries, they conclude that the financial crisis did not increase the sensitivity of Asian markets to US macroeconomic news releases. They also find that the more developed the country was, the less the influence of US macroeconomic news announcements.

In Chapter 12, Logan Kelly, Jane Binner, Chia-Ling Chang, and Yi-Heng Tseng advocate that the measure of money constructed using the Divisia index number for-mulation is superior to simple sum counterparts as indicators of monetary conditions. The simple sum approach may produce a time series that is much smoother and may give the impression that the correlation between monetary aggregate and inflation has decreased. Using data from 1970 to 2013 for Taiwan, they conclude from their results that future research into improved construction of monetary aggregates is promising and a worthwhile route to pursue.

In Chapter 13, Kym Brown, Jonathan A. Batten, Michael Skully, and Yen N. Nguyen examine the financial system development of Asia-Pacific countries from prior to the Asian financial crisis to the present. Using data from China, Hong Kong, Indonesia, Japan, Malaysia, Philippines, Singapore, Korea, Taiwan, and Thailand, the authors analyze the financial sector features relevant for economic development. They conclude that lessons from Asian Crisis had been learnt resulting in a more resilient market structure.

In Chapter 14, Raj Aggarwal and John W. Goodell produce evidence from corporate activities in 60 countries in regard to self-dealing transparency. Self dealing is the act of an agent acting in their own interest rather than in the interest of shareholders, ben-eficiaries or clients at the time of the transaction. Contrary to general belief, they con-clude that high self dealing transparency is positively associated with the Asian region. They also document that governance disclosure is negatively related with uncertainty avoidance and positively related with an English legal origin and superior economic inequality.

In Chapter 15, Robert W. McGee and Yeomin Moon surveys the theoretical and empirical literature on the ethics of tax evasion. The author also examines the opinions of 1199 South Koreans on the same issue. The South Korea dataset was collected from the individuals over 1982, 1990, 1996, 2001, and 2005. He concludes that the South Koreans were firmly opposed to tax evasion. The opposition was not uniform and there were differences in attitude.

In Chapter 16, Robert W. McGee summarizes the theoretical and empirical literature on the ethics of bride taking. He then examines the opinions of sample populations from China, Taiwan, and Hong Kong and finds that Taiwan's Chinese population is most opposed to bride taking than those in China and Hong Kong.

In Chapter 17, Donghyun Park and Gemma Esther B. Estrada note that the foreign exchange reserves of Asian countries have expanded rapidly to a point beyond optimal based on economic intuition. Using (1) the ratio of reserves to short-term external debt as the measure of an economy's financial vulnerability, (2) the ratio of reserves to M2 as the measure of confidence, (3) the ratio of reserves to the number of months of imports as the measure of vulnerability to adverse account shocks, and (4) the ratio of foreign reserves to GDP, the authors analyze if the optimal point had been crossed. They note that there was pressure for a strategic shift from passive liquidity management to active profit-seeking management of foreign reserves.

In Chapter 18, Yuwei Hu examines the organization structure and investment strategy of China Investment Corporation (CIC). The two subsidiaries of CIC, CIC International and Central Huijin operate in parallel and independently. While CIC International invests abroad, Central Huijin invests in the local market. With discussions on the problems and issues confronting the organizations, the author proposes various reform options.

In Chapter 19, Tayyeb Shabbir examines the asset allocation strategies of CIC with respect to types of investments, geographical destination of funds and its investment goals. He concludes that CIC's approach to these issues has significant implications for China's domestic economy as well as the global capital flows, financial stability, and economic growth.

In Chapter 20, Kin-Yip Ho and Zhaoyong Zhang review Sovereign Wealth Funds (SWFs) and provide an account of the investment strategies and recent development of three Asian SWFs, namely, China Investment Corporation, Korean Investment Corporation, and Vietnam State Capital Investment Corporation. The authors conclude that transparency remains an issue and propose that a set of guiding principles be developed. It is often argued that undervalued exchange rates and exchange rate manipulations in East Asia have contributed to the global imbalances and led to the accumulation of foreign reserves in the hands of SWFs. This chapter assesses the unique features of

Asian SWFs and their performance. The authors empirically investigate how SWFs can be effectively used as a means of stabilizer in the financial and foreign exchange markets and how SWFs impact the exchange rate volatility dynamics by taking into account the degree of East Asian economic integration.

RE-EMERGENCE OF ASIA

When one has finished reading the chapters in this book, one will begin to question how important Asia will become and what role will Asia finance play in the future. The re-emergence of Asia is a very important and interesting phenomenon to follow and to experience. We cannot leave the readers without highlighting the potential of Asia. We refer the readers to how analysts and economists forecast for Asia over the next 40 years. Many interesting references are provided in the list below.

Asia's share of Global GDP was around 60% before the start of the Industrial revolution in the 1700. The share gradually dropped to a low of 15% in the 1950s, before it climbed back to today's 28% in the past decade. Japan and Newly Industrialized Countries (NICs) led the growth in the 1950s, followed by the emergence of China and India in the 1980s.

Currently, Asia accounts for 58% of world population with 20% of total land. While 2050 is sometime away, analysts are forecasting that the population will double from 3 billion in 2010 to 6 billion by 2050. Asia's cities are expected to account for 80% of GDP with urbanization rates increasing from 40% to 63%. In the convergence school, analysts have forecasted that Asian GDP should reach USD174 trillion accounting for 52% of world GDP with GDP per capital growing to USD40,800. According to HSBC Global Research, China's per capital income is projected to grow 800% between 2012 and 2015. But, this ratio of China's income per capital to the US is still only 32% in 2050 as compared to 7% in 2012.

In short, the focus is now on Asia given the growth prospect of many Asian countries. Many of these countries are growing above 6%; some have even achieved double digits growth immediately after the 2008 crisis. Inter- and intra-regional trade with Asia will increase to 50% of world trade in the very near future, driving the demand of financial services and stimulating further financial innovations in Asia. We have attempted in this book to cover the more interesting issues closer to the heart of financial practitioners, academics, and participants. We are certain that by the time this book is published, there will be more areas in Asian finance that have caught the attention of many. For the time being, this book will give a perspective of what is going on in Asia and to bridge the gap caused by the fact that there remain few publications on Asia in academic journals. We are satisfied that we have started the process of collating a handbook of value to many for years to come and we hope this project will not be the last.

DISCLAIMERS

Neither the editors nor the publisher can guarantee the accuracy of each chapter nor are the editors or publisher responsible for the content of each chapter. Each author is solely responsible for his/her own chapter.

PART One

Banking

CHAPTER 1

Risk Rating in Asian Banks

Edward H.K. Ng
Dren Analytics Pte Ltd., 4 Burgundy Rise, Singapore 658855, Singapore

1.1 INTRODUCTION

Asian banks have longed relied on scoring models for consumer credit risk. Before Basel II, such models can be very simple as they are needed only for internal decision-making purposes. An actual Asian bank model assigns the values 1, 2, or 3 to a prospective customer based purely on the credit officer's personal judgment on the person's credit worthiness. No guidelines were issued on the basis by which credit quality should be assessed. Other banks turn to vendor-supplied (practically all of Western or Australian origin) credit scores. These are almost certainly generated using heuristics, a common one of which is that higher income is associated with lower credit risk. Unfortunately, such heuristics are increasingly invalidated by empirical evidence that disproves a not only linearity but even monotonicity in association. Besides, few or none of the models have been calibrated for Asian economic conditions.

Since the implementation of Basel II, Asian banks have been compelled to reconsider the reliability of their consumer credit scoring models as the outputs of such models like expected loss (EL), loss given default (LGD), and probability of default (PD) are necessary inputs into the risk-based capital requirement. Any attempt to develop robust models that can be defendable to the regulator is almost certainly met with the realization that data adequacy and quality is an almost insurmountable challenge. Some banks have resorted to a convenient but not necessarily reliable solution made possible under Basel II. Under this regime, consumers are categorized under retail together with small businesses. Retail exposures have to be credit risk rated using exposure pools. For these pools, PD can be derived as EL divided by LGD or vice versa. Once derived, the PD which is the obligor risk rating (ORR) akin to a consumer credit score is assigned to all obligors in the same pool. Since exposure pools are meant to be sub-portfolios of homogeneous PDs and LGDs, banks reason that pools formed using credit products satisfy the requirements. All car loans, for example, can be treated as one pool. Relying on estimates of historical EL and LGD, the PD of the pool can be derived. This PD then becomes the credit rating of all car loan borrowers.

While the PD derived using EL/LGD may satisfy Basel II requirements for retail exposures, it adds little value to a bank's consumer credit risk assessment. First, there is no reason to conclude that the PDs within an exposure pool are homogeneous if they are inferred from the EL and LGD. For banks hoping to leverage on the risk quantifications on product pricing and cross-selling, a pool PD is at best faulty and at worst misleading. In fact, every pool PD is likely to mask a range of credit risks just like the average of any natural measure like weight or height of an exogenously defined grouping. Second, the PD derived in this manner is possible for only existing customers. Although Basel II reasons that any single consumer credit exposure is too small to make a material impact on a bank's solvency, credit scoring has other implications for a bank. Advanced risk management has emphasized the importance of economic capital which is a function of risk level. Decisions like capital allocation, risk-based pricing, profitability, cross-selling, up-selling, etc., are dependent on reliable credit risk assessment.

Banks that do not resort to the PD = EL/LGD approach often despair at the state of internal data available for modeling. Deficiencies include missing, invalid, unreliable, and outdated data values. The range of problems is documented in Ng (2004). In his personal consultancy experience with banks, the author has estimated a surprisingly consistent estimate of about 17%[1] adequacy in bank data needed for consumer credit scoring which essentially is point-in-time (PIT) modeling. Such a low level of data availability will not meet with any standard of reliability of a statistical model.

This chapter proposes a relatively easy way for an Asian bank to enhance its consumer credit risk assessment through modeling transaction behavior. The main advantage of this approach is its almost universal feasibility since no modern bank is devoid of such transaction data. With further investigation, the results obtained from such behavioral scoring can even be exploited to refine any PIT model developed.

Section 1.2 explains how transaction behavior analysis or behavioral scoring as termed by some differs from credit scoring or PIT modeling. Section 1.3 describes the actual implementation of this approach in a bank that needed to improve its card credit assessment for both Basel II and business development purposes. The last section briefly demonstrates that behavioral scoring can improve credit risk assessment even where no PIT model was possible and discusses the advantages of the proposed approach especially in view of the data challenges faced by banks.

1.2 PIT VERSUS BEHAVIOR MODELING

Conventional credit scoring involves the use of PIT data to develop a risk profile. For consumer credit, such data are demographics like age, gender, education level, income, asset ownership, etc. It is quite obvious that such data are likely to change over time. Age, for instance, will certainly not remain constant for any individual bank customer.

PIT modeling attempts to identify intrinsic attributes that determine credit quality and the nature of the relationship if any. Once developed, the model provides an ex-ante

---

[1] This is a residual percentage after accounting for missing and invalid data values.

indication of credit risk that remains valid until the attribute values have changed. A fundamental assumption in such models then is that credit risk is dependent on a profile derived at the beginning of the exposure or holding period.

Unlike for corporations, consumer data are often riddled with deficiencies. For a start, individuals generally do not want to disclose more about themselves than they really need to. In most developing Asian countries, banks require consumers only to provide proof of employment or steady income and little else for regulatory compliance. Any form of consumer credit scoring prior to Basel II was largely for internal reference.

Another difficulty with consumer data is that many variables are non-numerical in nature. Education level may still be forced into an ordinal order but job or employment cannot be readily quantified to be used in a statistical method. If qualitative or categorical variables are not employed, precious little is left for modeling.

Even in the best of times, developing PIT models for consumer credit risk assessment poses many challenges. Again unlike for corporations where default can reasonably be assumed to be a rational wealth-maximization decision, consumers do not necessarily optimize on only one dimension. Avery et al. (2004), for instance, find that local circumstances influence an individual's propensity to default on a new loan. Temporary economic or personal shocks affect payment performance even after accounting for the individual's intrinsic credit quality. Their analysis can be easily extended to across Asian countries where cultural imperatives like the shame of defaulting can be a significant determinant in individual decision-making. It is questionable, therefore, if a "universal" consumer credit scoring model is even possible and if those developed by vendors originating in one geographic region can be applied to another.

Aside from conceptual issues, the paucity of good PIT data renders the development of robust consumer credit scoring models close to infeasible. By and large, Asians prefer secrecy and bank customers would grudgingly provide the bare minimum of what is required for a loan application. Unfortunately, such models are still needed as evidence of sound credit risk assessment. Transaction behavior analysis or behavioral scoring to some provides a possible mitigation of the problem.

A final and known issue for PIT models is non-stationarity. In the realm of social science, any model developed with PIT data is likely to have a short shelf life. This is truer for human behavior like defaulting where the factors behind its motivation can change and change quickly. As will be explained shortly, transaction data allow for continual tracking of risky behavior. Although not entirely free of non-stationarity, the monitoring of such behavior up to the point of default and even thereafter allows for credit worthiness to be updated almost in real time.

1.2.1 Transaction Behavior Data

In today's age, any licensed bank would have implemented a computerized account management system. This is true even of the most nascent Asian economies as the cost of technology is no longer insurmountable. At its most fundamental, a bank transaction system should be able to track the account balance periodically and any payments received. Such systems are known by different terms like core banking, loan origination, or loan management systems. In a borderless information technology (IT) world, these systems are increasingly developed by specialist vendors rather than the banks themselves.

The most immediate difference between transaction and PIT data is the consistency across banks and systems. Account balance is the same regardless of country, bank size, or license type. Variations like whether accrued interest is included in the balance will have negligible or no impact on any model developed using such a variable. The same could be said of delinquency. A 30-day delinquency cannot be recorded very differently across banking regimes. It is this consistency in measurement that allows Basel II to define 90-day delinquency as one of the definitions of default. Because of such uniformity, Asian banks can be considered to be on a level playing field with those in advanced economies in the area of transaction data availability.

A second advantage of transaction over PIT data is that they are system generated rather than collected. This virtually eliminates all the data adequacy and quality problems. As most banking regimes have implemented disaster recovery requirements, it is very unlikely that a bank will suffer from missing basic transaction data. Here again, Asian banks are not deficient in data quality.

The third value of transaction data is consistency across obligors and obligor types. Unlike PIT data where a variable like education level may be captured in a wide variety of values that need to be appropriately categorized, transaction data are similar if not identical throughout a system. Even if different products apply different formulas for day-count, a 30-day delinquency means that a payment has been delayed for 30 days regardless of the product concerned.

Modeling credit risk using transaction behavior data was reported by Kallberg and Udell (2003). With special access to Dun & Bradsheet's PAYDEX database which captures and stores shared corporate accounts payable (A/P) and accounts receivables (A/R) data, they were able to demonstrate that such business credit information add significant value to business failure prediction beyond the usual publicly available financial data.

The PAYDEX database tracks the promptness in both A/P and A/R accounts for a firm. Scores are assigned to different levels. For example, prompt repayment is scored 80, while slow to 90 days is scored 30. It is intuitive to conclude that a firm facing delays in its A/R is relatively more likely to encounter financial distress. Similarly, one that is financially healthy is more able to meet its A/P obligations promptly.

The approach proposed here is in the same spirit as in Kallberg and Udell with one major difference. The study using PAYDEX aimed to validate the use of business credit information as a valuable supplement to publicly available corporate data in modeling corporate credit risk. In that situation, conclusions made are applicable only to firms where trading payment behavior data are available. The additional value provided by transaction behavior only enriches a PIT model. Here, the aim is to use behavioral analysis to compensate for weak PIT models. In fact, it will be demonstrated that such analysis or scoring can significantly improve credit risk assessment even in the absence of a PIT credit scoring model.

As briefly explained earlier, Asian banks have to develop risk models for credit approval. This is both to satisfy the Basel II requirement that all obligors must be assigned a PD and the common regulatory expectation that all credit applicants are assessed on their riskiness before a facility is approved. Given these, a credit scoring model must be applicable to individuals new to the bank. But with deficient PIT data, reliable credit scoring models can seldom be successful developed. Waiting for sufficient good quality data to be collected before modeling is not a practical alternative. What this proposal involves then is a three-stage process. In the first, a rudimentary credit scoring model is developed with all available and reliable PIT data. This model is very likely to fail the necessary condition required of back-testing which will be elaborated on later. The second stage recalibrates the initial credit ratings with transaction behavior data. As in Kallberg and Udell, the focus is on payment promptness but other useful information like the level of credit facility utilization can also be investigated. Risky behavior like delinquencies results in a rating downgrade. Conversely, consistent prompt payments will lead to an upgrade. The recalibrated risk rating will replace the original one and itself be continually modified by subsequent transaction behavior. The third stage occurs a year later. By then, all remaining obligors[2] would have a credit rating. These ratings are then used to refine original PIT model. This, however, was not carried out for the consultancy project and is not reported here but it is definitely a bonus that can be extracted from the behavioral scoring efforts.

1.2.2 Back-Testing

Basel II requires that internal rating models be validated by back-testing before they can be approved for deployment. While this applies only to corporate credit rating, the same principle can guide the assessment of consumer credit scoring model reliability.

A simple yet critical requirement of model robustness for ORR is that ex-post default rates must be consistent with the order of ratings. If a rating of 1 indicates better credit worthiness than a rating of 2, the ex-post default rate among those rated 2 cannot be lower than those rated 1. This is sometimes termed the necessary condition of ranking consistency according to the Draft Supervisory Guidance on Internal Ratings-Based Systems for Corporate Credit (2003). This condition is necessary as failing it essentially means that the rating system based on the rating model is unreliable under actual use conditions.

---

[2] Some accounts may have been closed due to maturity, but defaulted ones remain in the books.

It is the aim of the proposed approach to develop a consumer credit assessment system that will produce risk ratings that can meet with the consistency test. To this end, the heuristics employed are refined continually to achieve the best results in consistency.

1.3 TRANSACTION BEHAVIOR SCORING

The bank which the author consulted for is one of the largest consumer credit institutions in a Southeast Asian country. Its main product is credit cards differentiated by target markets. For the sake of brevity, this bank will be named Bank X.

Typical of the industry, Bank X employed a consumer credit scoring system for many years. According to the bank's senior executives, the scoring model was purchased from a vendor. The basis for the rating system is not documented. A quick evaluation of the credit scores show that it will not meet with the consistency requirement if back-tested. The ex-post default rates for the 10 risk grades derived using their scoring model that the bank has used are shown in Table 1.1.

Since credit quality is declining from risk grades 1 to 10, consistency will require that the ex-post default rate is non-decreasing from the best to the worst grade. This is indeed the case for grades 1–4, but the results begin to reverse in grades 5 and 6. If validated according this standard, the bank's existing credit scoring model would not have been considered reliable.

The results are, however, not surprising. As with its peers in pre-Basel II days, Bank X has focused on legal and regulatory compliance in its consumer credit risk assessment all those years. Demographic data like gender, age, occupation, etc. were collected but the dataset was severely deficient in terms of completeness, reliability, and updatedness.

Table 1.1 Ex-post Default Rates Among 10 Risk Grades Assigned by Bank X to Consumer Clients Updated as of June 30, 2010, Using a Vendor Credit Scoring Model. Risk Grade 1 is Most Creditworthy and Risk Grade 10 is Least Creditworthy. Default is Defined as any 90-Day Delinquency within a Calendar Year from July 1, 2010, When a Risk Grade is Assigned to June 30, 2011

Risk Grade	No. of Defaulters	No. of Customers	Default Rate in Percentage
1	228	2757	8.27
2	483	4327	11.16
3	640	5307	12.06
4	932	7305	12.76
5	510	4526	11.27
6	354	3340	10.60
7	332	2814	11.80
8	155	1298	11.94
9	108	821	13.15
10	232	1367	16.97

Delinquency data like days past due were employed to upgrade or downgrade the obligor but no systematic approach was considered and developed.

A preliminary attempt was made to develop a PIT model using all available variables. Unsurprisingly, no robust model could be developed. Only two variables emerge statistically significant when either CHAID or logistic regression was applied. These are the card type and channel through which promotion is made. Both are independent of the obligor and cannot be considered relevant to ORR.

Behavioral scoring starts with the risk grades provided by the bank as of July 1, 2010. As with most banks, Bank X maps a raw credit score derived using its scoring model to its risk grades. This mapping is shown in Table 1.2. As with most credit risk scoring systems, a higher score is associated with a better credit quality.

A sample of unique obligors was provided by Bank X for the project. Some criteria were used to filter the sample for confounding factors. For example, the cardholder must be the main one, is not a bank staff and the card must not be used for corporate expense accounts. A final sample of 30,509 observations was used for the behavioral scoring.

Transaction behavior and operational data variables were evaluated for their suitability for the exercise. For each variable, the selection criterion was the percentage of reliable data available. Not unexpectedly, no demographics could be used. The final list of data fields that could be relied on are shown in Table 1.3. Of most interest are the delinquency counts and the initial raw score assigned by the bank to a customer.

The intuition underlying the behavioral scoring process is actually quite simple. Since default is defined as 90-day delinquency according to one of the Basel II prescriptions, an obligor clocking a 60-day delinquency is certainly more like to default than one having a 30-day delinquency. Similarly, a customer who stops being delinquent altogether shows signs of improved credit quality. Translating such intuition to a scoring process is, however, not straightforward. First, downgrading an obligor at the first instance of delinquency will result in a skewed default rate distribution. If a rule that

Table 1.2 Raw Behavioral Scores Mapped to Risk Grades

Behavior Score	Risk Grade
0–559	10
560–574	09
575–589	08
590–604	07
605–619	06
620–634	05
635–649	04
650–664	03
665–679	02
680–1000	01

Table 1.3 Data Fields that Could be Used to Develop Behavioral Scoring Model

No.	Variable	Description
1	CM_CARD_NMBR	Card number
2	WS-STMT-DATE	Statement date
3	CM_DELQ_HIST_1	Delinquency status at last statement
4	CM_DELQ_HIST_2, 3, ..., 12 (CM_DELQ_HIST_n)	Delinquency status at one statement before (In general, CM_DELQ_HIST_n is delinquency status at $n-1$ statements before)
5	NothingDueCount	Count of delinquency status $=0$ during last 12 statements
6	CurrentDueCount	Count of delinquency status $=1$ during last 12 statements
7	XDaysCount	Count of delinquency status $=2$ during last 12 statements
8	30DaysDelqCount	Count of delinquency status $=3$ during last 12 statements
9	60DaysDelqCount	Count of delinquency status $=4$ during last 12 statements
10	90DaysDelqCount	Count of delinquency status $=5$ during last 12 statements
11	120DaysDelqCount	Count of delinquency status $=6$ during last 12 statements
12	150DaysDelqCount	Count of delinquency status $=7$ during last 12 statements
13	180DaysDelqCount	Count of delinquency status $=8$ during last 12 statements
14	210DaysDelqCount	Count of delinquency status $=9$ during last 12 statements
15	FullPaidCount	Count of delinquency status $=B$ during last 12 statements
16	ZeroBalanceCount	Count of delinquency status $=Z$ during last 12 statements
17	DEFAULT_DATE	Default date
18	CM_BLOCK_CODE	Code for current block
19	CM_POSTING_FLAG	Posting code
20	CM_CUSTOMER_ORG	Code of customer Org
21	CM_STATUS	Code for *current status*
22	CM_DTE_OPENED	Open date of the card
23	Flag_Diff_Hist_Numb	Flagging F = Number of delinquency history and number of statements are the same T = Number of delinquency history and number of statements are different
24	No_application	Application number
25	Total_Score	Total score from credit scoring model
26	Risk_Grade	Risk grade from credit scoring
27	No_application	Application number
28	No_card	Card number

any 60-day delinquency will lead to a downgrade, there will be no defaults among grade 1. While not theoretically unsound, this severely diminishes the value of the rating system as it will be difficult to assess the risk level of those in grade 1. It will also not be consistent with the Basel II requirement that PD cannot be lower than 0.03% for the best risk grade.

Second, while it is reasonable to assess an obligor with a 60-day delinquency as being more risky than one with a 30-day delinquency, the same cannot be said when comparing one 60-day delinquency with two or more 30-day delinquencies. A habitually delinquent borrower may slip into default more easily than one who occasionally faces a liquidity problem.

Third, the issue of re-aging has to be dealt with. Here, the bank's credit policy adds its own complications.

Different banks apply different criteria to what constitutes a self-cured exposure. Some require payment of the full amount inclusive of interest accrued. Others accept a minimum sum as sufficient for the loan to be re-aged. For Bank X, it is the latter policy but with much latitude on what constitutes the minimum amount that needs to be paid.

A defaulting obligor is instantaneously assigned to the default grade which is outside of the 10 risk grades. When the exposure is re-aged, this obligor has to be assigned to one of the 10 risk grades. There is no theoretical basis for the "correct" risk grade for re-assignment.

In view of the implementation challenges, the behavioral scoring process underwent many methods of grade modification based on transaction behavior. Each method is assessed on its quality based on back-testing consistency. The eventual method selected is the one that yields the best results possible even if those are not ideal.

1.3.1 Scoring Process

The raw credit score and risk grade derived by Bank X for the obligor are used as the initial values. Since they have been shown to be unreliable, it is the premise of the project that behavioral scoring can improve on the bank's credit risk assessment.

The scoring process aims at recalibrating individual risk grades to better reflect their credit worthiness. As reasoned earlier, an obligor who has been delinquent in payment is likely to be more risky than another who has been prompt.

Scoring and recalibrations were made at the end of April and October 2011 and end of April 2012. These 6-monthly intervals correspond to the periodic compilation of transaction behavior data by the bank. It was also decided at the bank's request to strike a balance between risk updating frequency and effort expended.

To derive a consistent heuristic model, only obligors with at least 12 months of transaction history and have not defaulted in the 12-month period are included in the modeling sample. Some of these obligors may have defaulted earlier and have been re-aged according to the bank's credit policies. Whether the reinstated risk grade is appropriate is not within the project's scope.

Table 1.4 Derivation of Delta Using Delinquency Data. Negative/Positive is Impact on Obligor's Credit Quality When Delta is Added to the Raw Credit Score

Condition	Delta	Max/Min Delta	Negative/Positive
Every one time of XDays	−1	−5	Negative
Every one time of 30 DPD	−2	−10	Negative
Every one time of 90 DPD	−3	−15	Negative
Every two times of (Current Due + Nothing Due)	+1	+3	Positive
Full paid for 12 times	+5	+5	Positive

A metric termed "Delta" is created using delinquency data. Delinquencies result in negative Delta values, while consistent promptness is awarded a positive value. For instance, any occurrence of delinquency will incur a value of −1. Prompt payment over all 12 months result in a +5. A cap is placed on the maximum or minimum to constrain the impact of the model in the risk grading. This is to maintain sufficient stability in the risk rating system to allow for a meaningful rating migration matrix to be developed to meet with Basel II requirements.

In Table 1.4, there is a term "Every one time 90 DPD." DPD stands for days past due, and it will appear that a 90 DPD should be regarded as a default. It is not the case for Bank X due to its lack of daily transactions system capability. Delinquencies are collated at the end of every month. Depending on when the payment due date falls, delinquency may be recorded as XDays (where X is less than 15) or 30 DPD. If the due date falls on the 4th of the month, for example, the month-end compilation cycle will record a 30 DPD if payment has not be received even if the full 30 days delay have not been reached. On the other hand, if the due day is on the 27th of the month, the first delinquency count will be 3 or 4 days depending on whether it is a 30 or 31 day month. This means that a 90 DPD may be recorded for a less than 90-day delinquency although it could also be more than that. To satisfy the bank's preference, the 120 DPD is used to mark default.

The behavioral scoring process is applied at the end of each 12 month transaction interval but onto the raw credit score derived at the beginning of that period. How this recalibrates the risk grade of the obligor is shown in Table 1.5.

Of the sample of twenty obligors selected, only one has its risk grade downgraded from 9 to 10. This is evidence of the level of granularity that the behavioral score Delta permits. Delinquency does not automatically result in downgrading while promptness does not mean automatic upgrading. On the other hand, obligors with raw scores bordering on another risk grade are more impacted by their transaction behavior than otherwise. Besides, the ending raw score for one period becomes the beginning raw score of the next scoring iteration. Continual more or less risky behavior will eventually result in risk grade migration to reflect the more current credit worthiness.

Table 1.5 Delta Derived from Behavioral Scoring Heuristic Model Applied to Raw Scores at the Beginning of the 12-month Transaction Period to Recalibrate the Risk Grade. A Risk Grade that has been Changed by the Heuristic is Marked with an asterisk

Card No.	Beginning Raw Score	Beginning Risk Grade	Delta	Ending Raw Score	Ending Risk Grade
10001	560	9	−3	557	10*
10002	634	4	3	637	4
10003	594	7	−4	590	7
10004	500	10	0	500	10
10005	620	5	0	620	5
10006	616	6	0	616	6
10007	615	6	3	618	6
10008	645	4	2	647	4
10009	651	3	3	654	3
10010	638	4	1	639	4
10011	562	9	2	564	9
10012	515	10	2	517	10
10013	609	6	−2	607	6
10014	542	10	3	545	10
10015	598	7	3	601	7
10016	625	5	−2	623	5
10017	579	8	−1	578	8
10018	668	2	3	671	2
10019	627	5	5	632	5
10020	587	8	0	587	8

1.3.2 Validation

Following Basel II standards, validation of the resultant credit rating system is done through back-testing. Back-testing is also colloquially termed as "the taste of the pudding is in the eating." As an ORR is developed to predict default risk, its reliability must be tested against actual defaults subsequent to the ratings. While ex-post default rates matching the PD of each risk grade is perfect validation and near impossible to achieve, the necessary condition of consistency across the grades cannot be ignored. Should the default rate of a better risk grade exceed that of a poorer one, the rating system reliability is considered questionable. For many consumer credit PIT models, this consistency requirement has proven hard to meet.

Earlier analysis has shown that Bank X's internal credit scoring model would not have met with the consistency required in back-testing. This provides a suitable basis to examine if the behavioral scoring model can improve on the rating system reliability. As the behavioral scoring model is applied at six month intervals, the appropriate ex-post period for back-testing the default rates would be 12 months after each recalibration. Unfortunately, the bank's transaction data are generated up to June 2012. In essence, of

Table 1.6 Ex-post Default Rates among 10 Risk Grades Assigned by Bank X to Consumer Clients Using an Rating Recalibrated as of March 31, 2011, by the Behavioral Scoring Heuristic Model. Risk Grade 1 is Most Creditworthy, and Risk Grade 10 is Least Creditworthy. Default is Defined as any 90-day Delinquency within a Calendar Year from April 1, 2011, When a Risk Grade is Assigned to March 31, 2012

Risk Grade	No. of Defaulters	No. of Customers	Default Rate in Percentage
1	189	4634	4.08
2	393	4997	7.86
3	593	6116	9.70
4	791	7778	10.17
5	611	5796	10.54
6	452	4238	10.67
7	401	3383	11.85
8	284	2093	13.57
9	203	1275	15.92
10	332	1875	17.71

the three recalibrations, only the one performed in April 2011 could be validated with a full year's ex-post default rates. The results of this test are reported in Table 1.6.

The ex-post default rates are monotonically increasing from the best to the worst risk grade. Compared to the back-testing results of the bank's internal credit scoring model, this is strong evidence that behavioral scoring has significantly improved on the credit assessment reliability. From a regulatory compliance perspective, the recalibrated ratings are much more defendable than the original ones. For business development purposes, these ratings provide the confidence needed for better capital allocation, risk-based pricing using economic capital, cross-selling, and profitability analysis.

1.4 SIMULATION AND CONCLUSION

To further investigate the value of behavioral scoring, a simulation is performed. Four years of credit card delinquency data from a large bank in a different Southeast Asian country were used. To isolate the impact of behavioral scoring, random risk grades were assigned to all obligors in Year 1. Only obligors that remained as bank customers over all 4 years were analyzed. This substantially reduced the sample size available. To optimize the simulation, only seven risk grades were used. Results of this study are shown in Table 1.7.

In Year 1, the default rates are almost equal across the seven risk grades. This is a baseline equivalent to no credit scoring model. The default rates are rather low as it is the first year that the bank started compiling transaction data.

Table 1.7 Simulation Test of Whether Behavioral Scoring can Refine Consumer Credit Risk Ratings for Better Risk Assessment Using 4 Years of Delinquency Data

Risk Grade	Year 1 (%)	Year 2 (%)	Year 3 (%)	Year 4 (%)
1	0.15	2.34	1.05	0.00
2	0.17	0.75	1.69	1.75
3	0.17	0.75	3.47	3.51
4	0.16	1.47	3.03	4.62
5	0.00	2.92	1.59	5.13
6	0.17	2.07	2.86	0.00
7	0.16	13.33	25.00	15.38

A simple heuristic is employed. Every two 30-day delinquency count or a 60-day delinquency count results in a downgrade. Prompt payment throughout the year results in an upgrade. Unlike for the Bank X consultancy, the heuristic here is deliberately kept simple and unrefined to test if it does improve on the risk rating using the consistency test as benchmark.

As can be seen from Year 2, Year 3, and Year 4 ex-post default rates, a steady pattern of monotonic increase from the best to the worst grade emerges. In Year 4, this monotonicity becomes near perfect except for the reversal in grade 6. Over the period, the pattern is more evident each year. This simple simulation test confirms the value of behavioral scoring in enhancing consumer credit risk assessment. That the results are obtained from a different bank in a different country further supports the proposition that behavioral scoring can be applied almost universally.

Aside from contributing to better business decision-making, a rating system refined by behavioral scoring can also be leveraged to improve on any PIT credit scoring model. As reported earlier, an attempt to develop for PIT model for Bank X resulted in only two variables showing statistical significance and both are not personal attributes intrinsic to obligor risk. As is known in PIT credit scoring models, the dichotomous default/non-default outcomes is a constraint. This lack of granularity either imposes rigid thresholds on predictors or a continuum for the modeler to decide on the breaks between one risk level and another. The risk grades refined by behavioral scoring can be employed to mitigate this problem.

Rather than a binary prediction, the risk grades allow for a range of outcomes. In the case of Bank X, this can be ranged from 1 to 10 if the risk grades are used or even more granular if the raw credit scores are employed. As these outcomes have proven to be reliable indicators of default, replacing them for default/non-default can improve the quality of any PIT model. In the meantime, it also allows the bank to start collecting the needed data that can take years to be reach adequacy. Furthermore, any PIT model developed can be continually improved upon with the same risk rating system which has led to the concept of adaptive scoring.

Given its simplicity and flexibility, behavioral scoring can be easily employed by any bank to quickly develop a reliable consumer credit risk assessment system. If properly leveraged upon, this system can even be used to bootstrap and continually refine a PIT credit scoring model that is not immediately possible with existing data deficiency challenges. For Asian banks, this approach can be a significant enabler in their quest to produce internal credit ratings meeting Basel II standards.

REFERENCES

Avery, R.B., Calem, P.S., Canner, G.B., 2004. Consumer credit scoring: do situation circumstances matter? BIS Working Paper No. 146, Basle, Switzerland.

Draft Supervisory Guidance on Internal-Ratings Based Systems for Corporate Credit, 2003. Federal Deposit Insurance Corporation. Washington, DC.

Kallberg, J.K., Udell, G.F., 2003. The value of private sector business credit information sharing: the US case. Journal of Banking and Finance 27 (3), 449–469.

Ng, E.H.K., 2004. Managing Credit Data: Toward Basel II. Dren Analytics Pte Ltd., Singapore.

CHAPTER 2

Private Wealth Management in Asia

David R. Meyer
Olin Business School, Washington University in St. Louis, Campus Box 1133,
One Brookings Drive, St. Louis, MO 63130-4899, USA

2.1 INTRODUCTION

Increasing numbers of wealthy people, growing economic globalization, transformation of data telecommunications technologies, and worldwide integration of financial markets (stock exchanges, currency markets, and so on) are propelling change in the private wealth management industry and the market for its services (Maude, 2006). In the past, private bankers focused on taking deposits and providing investment advice about stocks, bonds, and real estate, as well as advising on trusts, estate planning, and the like. While these services fit those with modest wealth, perhaps under several million dollars (US) of investable wealth, such services are no longer adequate for people with wealth approaching US$5 million, as well as for those with substantially greater investable wealth. Even the family office, which formerly handled private wealth management for an individual family, is transforming, especially for extremely wealthy families. Multi-family offices are one solution to these trends, but even that approach may not suffice and a conglomerate of family offices may develop (Lowenhaupt, 2008).

The management of private wealth must deal with a global approach across many asset classes (stocks, bonds, currencies, real estate, art) and geographies (Maude, 2006). As the scale of private wealth of individuals has grown and with increasing numbers of "high net worth individuals" (HNWIs), specialization of financial service providers in sectors such as law and accounting has increased. Consequently, an entire cluster of services has emerged which includes the private wealth management units of large commercial and investment banks, private banks, and fund management firms, along with law and accounting firms. These interrelationships among service providers contribute to agglomeration of private wealth management in a few major financial centers (Beaverstock, 2012; Beaverstock et al., 2013; Lowenhaupt, 2008; World Wealth Report, 2013). Asia is the most rapidly growing market for wealth management, and if trends persist it will soon become the largest market based on numbers of wealthy and total amount of investable wealth (PWC, 2011).

The private wealth management industry employs various definitions and categories of HNWIs; the following is one widely accepted approach. The industry focuses on HNWIs who possess investable assets of US$1 million or more, excluding primary residence, collectibles, consumables, and consumer durables. This group sometimes is subdivided into those with US$1–US$5 million (millionaires next door), those with US$5–US$30 million (mid-tier millionaires), and those with US$30 million or more (ultra-HNWIs). The "millionaires next door" comprise 90% of HNWIs and 43% of HNWI wealth; the "mid-tier millionaires" comprise 7% of HNWIs and 22% of wealth; and the "ultra-HNWIs" comprise just 1% of individuals, but 35% of wealth (World Wealth Report, 2013). A brief summary of current dimensions of the wealth management industry sets the stage for examining Asia.

2.2 GLOBAL MARKET DISTRIBUTION OF PRIVATE WEALTH

The industry and its key employees—private wealth managers (or private bankers)—devote intensive effort to identifying the market distribution of HNWIs. The reason: these financial service providers typically need face-to-face access to HNWIs to initially acquire them as clients. Then, these financiers use ongoing, occasional meetings to maintain relationships and discuss investment strategies. Commercial and investment banks and fund management companies with private wealth management units or specialized firms such as private banks develop a global office structure to provide platforms for their private wealth managers to access their clients (Maude, 2006).

Before proceeding, the use of the world-region term, Asia-Pacific, needs to be clarified. It is an aggregate regional breakdown in many data sets and typically refers to mainland Asia, Southeast Asia, Japan, Australia, and New Zealand. Although the focus of this chapter is on Asia, which includes all of Asia-Pacific, minus Australia and New Zealand, the initial analysis will include the larger set of countries because the data are aggregated that way. Then the discussion will target the regional division of Asia, although the term Asia-Pacific will be used at times because it is a standard term, even when Australia and New Zealand are excluded.

The distribution of HNWIs across the world is highly uneven (Table 2.1). Most of them are concentrated in three world regions—North America, Asia-Pacific, and Europe. Latin America, the Middle East, and Africa have few HNWIs. Since 2007 the

Table 2.1 Number (Millions) of High Net Worth Individuals by Region, 2007–2012

Region	2007	2008	2009	2010	2011	2012
North America	3.3	2.7	3.1	3.4	3.4	3.7
Asia-Pacific	2.8	2.4	3.0	3.3	3.4	3.7
Europe	3.1	2.6	3.0	3.1	3.2	3.4
Latin America	0.4	0.4	0.5	0.5	0.5	0.5
Middle East	0.4	0.4	0.4	0.4	0.5	0.5
Africa	0.1	0.1	0.1	0.1	0.1	0.1
Total	10.1	8.6	10.1	10.8	11.1	11.9

Source: World Wealth Report (2013, Figure 1, p. 5).

Table 2.2 Amount of Investable Wealth (US$ Trillion) of High Net Worth Individuals by Region, 2007–2012

Region	2007	2008	2009	2010	2011	2012
North America	11.7	9.1	10.7	11.6	11.4	12.7
Asia-Pacific	9.5	7.4	9.7	10.8	10.7	12.0
Europe	10.7	8.3	9.5	10.2	10.1	10.9
Latin America	6.2	5.8	6.7	7.3	7.1	7.5
Middle East	1.7	1.4	1.5	1.7	1.7	1.8
Africa	1.0	0.8	1.0	1.2	1.1	1.3
Total	40.8	32.8	39.1	42.8	42.1	46.2

Source: World Wealth Report (2013, Figure 2, p. 5).

distribution of these wealthy individuals has been relatively stable, with one notable exception; the number in Asia-Pacific dramatically increased. The region shifted from third rank after North America and Europe to approximate equality with North America.

The amount of investable wealth of HNWIs by world region exhibits a slight difference from the distribution of number of individuals (Table 2.2). The Asia-Pacific region's total investable wealth witnessed the greatest rise, as with the number of individuals, but its total wealth ranks it as second, just behind North America. Asia-Pacific's lead over Europe by 2012 is a mirror image of Europe's lead over Asia-Pacific in 2007. The biggest discrepancy between the numbers of HNWIs and their total wealth appears in Latin America. The total wealth in that region has increased significantly and is not far behind Europe. That discrepancy suggests that HNWIs wealth in Latin America is even more concentrated in a small number of people than in the other regions.

A closer look at the 12 countries with the largest number of HNWIs in 2012 demonstrates that the wealthy are extremely concentrated in a few countries (Table 2.3). This small set accounts for just over three-fourths of all HNWIs. Within this group of 12, there is even greater clustering. The United States dominates HNWIs with 29% of the global individuals and 37% of the set of 12 countries. Japan ranks as the second largest concentration globally of HNWIs. European countries account for almost half (five) of the 12 nations, demonstrating that HNWIs are highly clustered in that region. These five comprise 20% of global HNWIs, and Germany is the undisputed leader.

2.3 ASIAN MARKET DISTRIBUTION OF PRIVATE WEALTH

The rise of the Asia-Pacific region to first or second rank, whether measured by number of HNWIs or their total wealth, needs clarification. In Asia just two countries dominate, Japan, the leader by far with 16% of the total world count of HNWIs, and China, which includes 5% of the world total (Table 2.3). The significance of Japan demands emphasis

Table 2.3 Countries with the Largest Number of High Net Worth Individuals, 2012

Region/Country	Number (1000s)	% of Selected Total	% of World Total
North America			
United States	3436	37	29
Canada	298	3	3
Europe			
Germany	1015	11	9
United Kingdom	465	5	4
France	430	5	4
Switzerland	282	3	2
Italy	176	2	1
Asia-Pacific			
Japan	1902	21	16
China	643	7	5
Australia	207	2	2
South Korea	160	2	1
Other			
Brazil	165	2	1
Selected total	9179	100	77

Source: World Wealth Report (2013, Figure 3, p. 6).

because it reveals that private wealth management firms and their private bankers must maintain a presence in that market, even while they expand in China.

In Asia-Pacific the distribution of HNWIs across the three categories of levels of wealthy follows the global distribution, with some qualification (Asia-Pacific Wealth Report, 2012; World Wealth Report, 2013). The "millionaires next door" (with US$1–US$5 million of investable wealth) comprise just over 90% of HNWIs and just over 50% of HNWI wealth, both categories somewhat larger than the world distribution of these groups. The "mid-tier millionaires" (US$5–US$30 million) comprise 8% of HNWIs and 24% of wealth, both almost identical to the global distributions. In contrast, the "ultra-HNWIs" (US$30 million or more) comprise only 0.6% of Asia-Pacific's HNWIs and 25% of wealth, compared to the world distribution of 0.9% of HNWIs and 35% of wealth. Thus, Asia-Pacific's distribution of wealth is more concentrated in the lower tier of HNWIs and less concentrated in the highest tier.

Important distinctions exist among the markets of HNWIs in Asia. The concentration of numbers of HNWIs is quite extreme (Table 2.4). Japan contains over three times as many HNWIs as China, the second largest concentration, but South Korea and India fall far below China. Relative to that country, South Korea has only one-fourth as many HNWIs and India has just over one-fifth as many. The global business centers of

Singapore and Hong Kong and highly developed Taiwan contain between 80,000 and 90,000 each, or about 5% of the number in Japan. Thailand and Indonesia are still smaller.

Since 2007, the largest aggregate gains in numbers of HNWIs have been in Japan, China, and South Korea (Table 2.4). The number of HNWIs in India has stagnated, suggesting that private wealth management firms face a challenge building their business there. Large relative gains in HNWIs in Thailand and Indonesia are from a small base; thus they still are not robust markets for private banking. Overall, the selected Asian political units which house the most HNWIs increased their numbers of these individuals by about 18% between 2007 and 2011.

The distribution of total investable wealth among HNWIs across Asia broadly follows the distribution of the number of these investors, with some notable qualifications (Table 2.5). While China's number of HNWIs is just under one-third of the count in

Table 2.4 Number of High Net Worth Individuals (Thousands) by Political Unit in Asia, 2007–2011

Political Unit	2007	2008	2009	2010	2011
Japan	1517	1366	1650	1739	1822
China	413	364	477	535	562
South Korea	118	105	127	146	144
India	123	84	127	153	126
Singapore	78	61	82	99	91
Taiwan	71	58	83	94	89
Hong Kong	96	37	76	101	84
Thailand	44	42	50	58	65
Indonesia	24	19	24	30	32
Total selected	2484	2136	2696	2955	3015

Source: Asia-Pacific Wealth Report (2012, Figure 1, p. 5).

Table 2.5 Amount of Investable Wealth (US$ Billions) of High Net Worth Individuals by Political Unit in Asia, 2007–2011

Political Unit	2007	2008	2009	2010	2011
Japan	3815	3179	3892	4135	4231
China	2109	1672	2347	2657	2706
India	437	310	477	582	477
Singapore	386	272	369	453	439
Hong Kong	523	181	379	511	408
South Korea	319	276	340	396	381
Thailand	225	190	232	272	298
Taiwan	234	176	264	302	279
Indonesia	85	61	80	100	106
Total selected	8133	6317	8380	9408	9325

Source: Asia-Pacific Wealth Report (2012 Figure 2, p. 5).

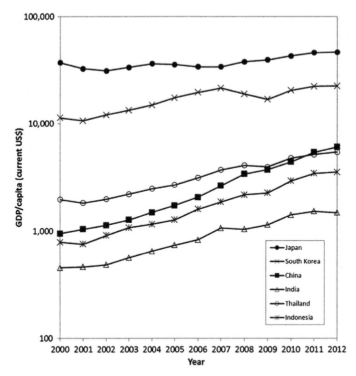

Figure 2.1 GDP/capita (current US dollars) for Asian political units, 2000–2012. *Source:* World Bank, 2013.

Japan, total investable wealth in China is almost two-thirds of the amount in Japan. This points to the growing potential of the private wealth management business in China. India reverses position with South Korea: the former's total amount of investable wealth is larger than the latter's. The most significant discrepancy consists of the global business centers of Singapore and Hong Kong, which rank close to India and South Korea as markets for private wealth managers. These cities, therefore, comprise large, concentrated markets which private bankers can readily access.

The growth potential for private wealth management in Asia can be estimated from the economic trajectory of its countries from 2000 to 2012. The rise in GDP/capita (gross domestic product per capita) provides one indicator of overall average rise in wealth. Based on this measure the various countries in Asia confront divergent paths (Figure 2.1). Japan, the largest concentration of HNWIs and of investable wealth, has experienced a stagnant GDP/capita, implying that its market for private wealth management may not grow much. South Korea has had a moderate increase in both number of HNWIs and of investable wealth since 2007, but its GDP/capita stagnated during that time, after rising significantly from 2000 to 2007. This raises warning signs about the future growth of this market for private banking.

The global centers of Hong Kong and Singapore, which are not included in Figure 2.1, possess GDP/capita which are comparable to Japan's, and their moderate per capita increases suggest that they will continue to be viable markets. Their capacity to attract HNWIs, however, is more important than their GDP/capita in determining their potential as a market for private wealth management.

China, the second largest private banking market in Asia, has experienced the fastest rise in GDP/capita of all the countries. The key to its future is whether that trajectory will continue. It remains quite poor relative to Japan and South Korea. Thailand's rise in GDP/capita has slowed noticeably since 2007, after increasing at a moderate rate from 2000 to 2007. This implies that its market for private wealth management may not be promising. Indonesia underwent a large increase in GDP/capita since 2000; nevertheless, it remains poor. Its potential as a market will depend on whether its GDP/capita continues to rise. The most problematic country for private banking is India. While its GDP/capita rose from 2000 until 2007, gains since then have been minimal, leaving India extremely poor.

The overall capacity of the economy to grow also determines the potential for private wealth management business. Asian countries have experienced volatile changes in annual% GDP from 2000 to 2012 (Figure 2.2). The cautionary point is that the severe global economic crisis of 2007–2009 resulted in large plunges in GDP growth rates across Asia. If the global economy suffers another crisis or if growth stagnates, then Asia will be negatively impacted, implying difficult times for private wealth management. Hong Kong and Singapore are not included in Figure 2.2 because their economies are directly related to the growth of Asia as a whole.

Arguably, Japan, the largest market for private wealth management in Asia, has seen the worst economic performance from 2000 to 2012; rates of GDP change cluster around zero. This bodes ill for the future of its private banking. As the second biggest market for managing HNWIs, China's growth trajectory will have the greatest impact on private banking in Asia. The rise in its growth rate to levels of 10% or more from 2000 to 2007 powered the increase in HNWIs. Nevertheless, the sharp retardation in its growth since 2007 sends a cautionary note that market extrapolations for private wealth management based on the period before 2007 may be inappropriate.

Similar to China, India experienced rapid growth in GDP from the early 2000s to 2007, and then recovered quickly from the economic crisis of 2007–2009. However, the sharp fall in its growth rate since 2010 raises a question about the future. The countries of South Korea, Thailand, and Indonesia have fluctuated within a band of about 1–5% growth rates, suggesting that potential may exist for expanding the market of private wealth management. Nonetheless, volatile growth rates of South Korea and Thailand since 2007 raises uncertainty about the impact of slower or declining growth on their HNWI market. The so-called emerging economies of Asia may not be immune to global economic difficulties.

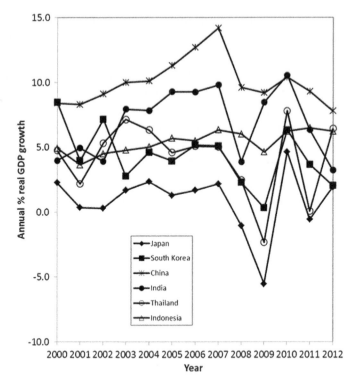

Figure 2.2 Annual % real GDP growth for Asian political units, 2000–2012. *Source:* World Bank, 2013.

2.4 ASIAN PRIVATE WEALTH MANAGEMENT

Private banking in Asia shares many characteristics with Europe and North America. Wealth managers need to focus on service, operate trustworthily with high integrity, and build strong relationships with clients (Ang, 2010). Asian HNWIs share the aims of their peers worldwide: they prefer increased control over their assets and greater options to preserve and grow capital. Consequently, they desire diversification of portfolios across many asset classes and use of hedging strategies to cope with market fluctuations and currency and country risks. Asian HNWIs desire wealth management strategies that deal with business succession and intergenerational wealth transfer. Business ownership undergirds 57% of their wealth (Asia-Pacific Wealth Report, 2012; Maude, 2006). The one area in which Asian private wealth management is most distinctive, according to the executive recruiting firm, Korn Ferry International, is that 60% of private bankers are women, whereas only 20% are women in the United States and just 10% are women in Switzerland (Vallikappen, 2013).

These goals of Asian HNWIs have implications for the structure and dynamics of private wealth management. On the one hand, the complexity of the demands suggests that private banking firms (or units of larger financial institutions) must shift to a large scale in order to cover the fixed costs of these services—financial management software, integration with global trading and investing platforms, and the like. Increasing regulatory complexity which requires large fixed investments in compliance procedures also drives this shift to larger scale (World Wealth Report, 2013).

Nonetheless, the impact of the complexity of these demands and regulatory compliance needs qualification. Surveys of emerging market HNWIs, which includes Asia, reveal that 41% view themselves as having complex needs for services, but 26% have no strong preference and 33% see themselves as having straightforward needs for services (World Wealth Report, 2013). This implies that small- and medium-size private wealth management firms have opportunities to compete with larger firms. While firms can internalize legal and accounting services to deal with regulatory compliance and develop their own financial software for clients, these can be externally purchased. Large law and accounting firms possess specialists in these areas, and they achieve economies of scale which smaller private wealth management firms can access. Furthermore, discount brokerage firms and other specialized brokerage firms offer low-cost, sophisticated trading platforms which smaller private wealth management firms can use (Pershing MD, 2012). As well, large fund management companies increasingly target private banking firms as markets for the funds' portfolio of investment products (Asset Managers Focus, 2012; Julius Baer Predicts, 2012). Therefore, small- and medium-size private banking firms do not need to internalize these products.

The implication of these trends in private wealth management suggests the following. In Asia, small- and medium-size private banking firms can coexist with the large units of commercial and investment banks and fund management companies, as well as with specialized private banking firms such as from Switzerland, which are expanding globally. The key for these smaller firms is to base themselves in major financial centers that house specialized financial and business-related services (law, accounting). Likewise, these centers are the homes of offices of the leading commercial and investment banks, fund management companies, hedge funds, private equity firms, and venture capital firms. Some of these have private wealth management units, and all of them have services that smaller private banking firms can access.

2.5 ASIAN CENTERS OF PRIVATE WEALTH MANAGEMENT

Rapid expansion of numbers of HNWIs and of their investable wealth differentiates the Asian market from other regions and has created a large demand for experienced private bankers, yet they remain in short supply (Asia-Pacific Wealth Report, 2012). This growing market has powered the rise of Hong Kong and Singapore into the top five centers of private wealth management, along with Switzerland, London, and New York. Among offshore book centers for private banking, Switzerland leads the nine top centers by a wide margin, over twice as important as London, according to a survey of wealth managers (PWC, 2011). Singapore rates almost as highly as London, and Hong Kong falls slightly lower, but higher than New York. Significantly, neither Tokyo nor Mumbai rank among these centers of private wealth management.

This raises a puzzle: why are Hong Kong and Singapore ranked so high, yet neither Tokyo and Mumbai appear in the top ranks? Singapore, a global business center, is a city-state with a small population. Hong Kong, likewise a global center, is a sovereign part of the People's Republic of China, a country not known for a sound legal system which protects private wealth. In contrast, Tokyo and Mumbai are their country's leading financial centers, and both nations have sound legal systems for the protection of private wealth management business. In Tokyo's case the puzzle is especially dramatic because Japan is the greatest center of HNWIs and of their investable wealth in Asia. Resolution of this puzzle provides clues about the character and future of private wealth management in Asia.

2.5.1 Hong Kong and Singapore

Diverse measures of financial center importance demonstrate that Hong Kong and Singapore, along with Tokyo, are the greatest financial centers in Asia. All three rank in the top five globally along with London and New York, which generally rank one and two, respectively (Taylor, 2005). The Global Financial Centre Index (GFCI) typically rates Hong Kong third and Singapore fourth after London and New York, while Tokyo ranks lower (Z/Yen, 2007–2013). This significance of Hong Kong and Singapore has deep roots that extend into the 19th century. By the latter part of that century Hong Kong was the Asia-Pacific center of finance and trade and Singapore held that regional role in Southeast Asia. These cities have never relinquished that position as the leading headquarters in Asia of the global finance and trading firms (Meyer, 2000). On the other hand, Tokyo is exhibiting signs of relative, and perhaps, absolute, decline as a financial center (Research Republic, 2008).

Thus, it is fitting that Hong Kong and Singapore are recognized as the leading centers of private wealth management in Asia (Asia-Pacific Wealth Report, 2012). They provide sound regulatory regimes under professional supervision by monetary authorities and agencies, favorable tax treatment, and legal structures for private banking to operate either as a specialized bank or as a unit of a corporate and investment bank or a fund management company (Long and Tan, 2011). Furthermore, both cities are receptive to the immigration of wealthy HNWIs from Asia and elsewhere (Pow, 2013). They contain numerous attractive residential environments, along with a full panoply of cultural, music, restaurants, clubs, and other entertainment facilities. Their international airports are among the world's largest, with superb connections across Asia and globally (Mahutga, et al., 2010). Thus HNWIs view both cities as appealing places to live.

As Asia's leading financial centers, they contain a large array of locally headquartered financial firms with private wealth management units. In Singapore, for example,

OCBC Bank, DBS, and United Overseas Bank are major locally headquartered banks with sizeable private wealth management units. OCBC formed a specialized private bank, Bank of Singapore, after purchasing the private banking assets of ING Asia (Kolesnikov-Jessop, 2012; Sen, 2011, 2013; Tan, 2011). Both cities house regional headquarters of global financial firms across the spectrum of corporate and investment banking, private equity, hedge funds, venture capital, and fund management. Among the many global corporate and investment banks are UBS, Barclays, Credit Suisse, Citigroup, Goldman Sachs, Morgan Stanley, and Deutsche Bank with large private wealth units. Consequently, each city has a vast talent pool of top financiers with expertise in Asian business. Also, they are the key centers of business services firms in Asia, both locally headquartered and regional offices of global firms. The service firms most directly relevant to private wealth management are the law and accountancy firms (Bastide, 2011; Meyer, 2000, 2009; Zhao et al., 2011).

While Hong Kong and Singapore might be viewed as merely alternative operational venues for private wealth management firms, they are often claimed to be competitors for dominance as financial centers in Asia. At the broader scale which covers all financial sectors, the Financial Secretary of the Hong Kong government talks about the city gaining a "competitive edge" and a private sector executive with Citigroup in Singapore touts the competitiveness of the city (A Hub to Bank On, 2013; Speech by FS, 2013). Others even go so far as to say the cities are fierce financial competitors (Sheng, 2012; Yiu, 2012). Not surprisingly, this competition is explicitly identified with the private banking sector and sometimes framed in battle terms as fighting for primacy or supremacy as the Asian center of private wealth management (Hooi, 2013; McQueen, 2012).

Even though Hong Kong's and Singapore's financial units of the government and their monetary authorities sometimes join in the competitive debates, both governments and monetary authorities are highly transparent about their financial administrative policies, procedures, and technical processes. These are promulgated on their websites, in research reports, and in annual reports (Hong Kong Monetary Authority, 2013; Monetary Authority of Singapore, 2012). This transparency precludes either city from gaining a substantial lead in building some advantage favorable to the private wealth management industry. Their financial departments, monetary authorities, and regulatory agencies are staffed with highly skilled professionals. As rich global business centers, they possess ample financial resources to maintain the infrastructure which supports their private banking sectors. While differentiation between Hong Kong and Singapore in terms of their attractiveness as offshore wealth centers exists, overall the disparities are relatively minor (Asia-Pacific Wealth Report, 2012).

In fact, the private wealth management sectors of Hong Kong and Singapore complement each other. Hong Kong especially draws clients from mainland China, whereas Singapore draws clients from Southeast Asia (Asia-Pacific Wealth Report, 2012). Some clients have accounts in both cities as ways to diversify their portfolios, and at the same time benefit from the sound regulatory and favorable tax treatments each city offers (Hammond, 2012). This complementarity extends to the office structures of firms. Both cities house many of the same leading global financial firms with private wealth management units and many of the same major private banking firms. HSBC, Asia's dominant bank since the late 19th century, uses Hong Kong and Singapore as its premier private banking hubs. Deutsche Bank Private Wealth Management has its largest Asian office in Singapore and its second largest in Hong Kong (Private Banks, 2012; Julius Baer to Buy, 2011; Meyer, 2000; Pictet, 2013; Sen, 2012; Wilkinson, 2013).

Although Hong Kong and Singapore rightly receive the most attention as the premier wealth management centers in Asia, many of the Asian economies have their own international financial center—Seoul in South Korea, Taipei in Taiwan, Bangkok in Thailand, Manila in the Philippines, Jakarta in Indonesia, and Kuala Lumpur in Malaysia. Domestic private banking firms and private wealth management units of domestic commercial banks in these economies are increasingly competing with global private wealth management firms (Bank of Ayudhya, 2012; Preview, 2011). Examples of these competitors include Bank Mandiri in Indonesia, CIMB in Malaysia, BDO Private Bank in the Philippines, Phatra Private Wealth in Thailand, and Samsung Securities Private Bank in South Korea. These banks leverage their business networks to develop close personal relations with clients (Private Banks, 2012). Foreign private bankers face difficulties overcoming these relations to build a client base. Taiwan is one exception. Foreign banks dominate its private wealth management market, and Hong Kong private bankers are especially active (van der Hoevel, 2012).

In these economies private wealth management firms in financial centers can access regional offices of global commercial and investment banks, as well as international and domestic business services firms in law and accountancy to provide a set of sophisticated services. Therefore, private bankers have the capacity to acquire clients in the first level of HNWIs, those with US$1–US$5 million (millionaires next door), and, perhaps, begin to serve those with US$5–US$30 million (mid-tier millionaires). Arguably, the emerging markets of China and India offer the greatest potential for private wealth management, but these markets pose significant long-term challenges for foreign firms.

2.5.2 China and India as Emerging Markets

Rapidly increasing numbers of HNWIs in China provide opportunities for domestic banks to expand their private wealth management business. The large state banks of China are briskly moving into this business. Bank of China has developed a network of private banking offices in nearly 20 cities across the country. It teams up with Julius Baer, the Swiss private bank with a worldwide set of offices, to access the Swiss bank's global product line (Private Banks, 2012). Similarly, China Construction Bank is growing its private wealth management business. As of the end of 2011, it had 245 wealth and private banking centers across China and was managing US$107 billion for affluent individuals (Haslip, 2012a). Industrial and Commercial Bank of China has its private banking headquarters in Beijing, as do the other state banks, and it has 10 branches which report to it. By 2011 it had US$65 billion of assets under management, and 60% of its wealthy clients are private entrepreneurs (Private Banks, 2011). Other large domestic banks such as China Merchants and Bank of Communications also are offering private banking services. Overall, domestic Chinese banks have a strong position in local private wealth management, and they are increasing their competitiveness in this market vis-à-vis firms based in Hong Kong which target the China market (Wright, 2012).

Leading global commercial and investment banks with Asia-Pacific headquarters in Hong Kong take divergent approaches to the China market. The private wealth management units of Barclays, Citigroup, Credit Agricole, J.P. Morgan, and Societe Generale have no offices in China. Their private bankers travel to the Mainland and/or meet their clients in Hong Kong. On the other hand, other large banks set up private banking units in China: BNP Paribas and Deutsche Bank have offices in Shanghai; HSBC has offices in Shanghai, Beijing, and Guangzhou; Standard Chartered has offices in Beijing, Shanghai, and Shenzhen, as well as units in seven other large Chinese cities; and UBS has an office in Beijing (Moiseiwitsch, 2012). Whatever their strategy toward the China market, however, these firms retain their advantage as repositories of offshore financial services under the legal system of Hong Kong and as a place where rich Chinese can hide their money from government authorities.

Although India does not rank high on the number of HNWIs and of investable wealth, the private wealth management market is substantial. Foreign firms face difficulties accessing this market because Indian financial firms have long-standing relationships with the domestic wealthy. Kotak Wealth Management, a unit of the Kotak Mahindra group of companies, is the leading private banking firm in India. It serves almost 2,000 HNWIs, and, equally important, it has a strong position as advisor and manager for 30% of the top 100 wealthy families (Private Banks, 2012). Other private wealth management firms include a unit of Ambit Holdings, IIFL Private Wealth Management, Client Associates, and Motilal Oswal Financial Services (Ashreena, 2012; de Bendern, 2013; Motilal Oswal, 2012; Nikko AM, 2011).

Competition also is emerging from banks such as Avendus Capital which started as an internet and technology advisory firm in 2000 and quickly transformed into a mid-market investment bank. Then, in 2009 it added a private wealth management unit to leverage its ties to 500 budding business families which it provides with investment banking services (Kurian, 2011). These domestic investment banks will increasingly compete with foreign investment banks that try to run private banking as a business in India.

Significant numbers of the wealthiest Indians base substantial assets in offshore financial centers, which undermines the domestic market for private bankers. In 2009 the government of India estimated that the amount of funds hidden overseas amounted to between US$0.5 trillion and US$1.4 trillion. Besides London and Zurich, Singapore is one favorite location, reflecting the longstanding business ties with India. For example,

Goldman Sachs runs its private wealth management business for India from that city (Chatterjee, 2011; Meyer, 2000). To the extent the wealthy continue this avoidance of domestic private banking, the market for ultra-HNWIs will be capped in India.

Commercial and investment banks such as Barclays, Deutsche Bank, and RBS continue to operate private banking units in India (Barclays Wealth, 2011; Haslip, 2012b; We Like, 2011). Nonetheless, other global banks are retreating from the Indian market. Nomura (Japan) reduced its head count in private banking; Credit Suisse (Switzerland) dismissed almost half of its private wealth management employees; Societe Generale (France) closed its private banking business; and Morgan Stanley (United States) sold its private banking unit to Standard Chartered. While Pictet, a major Swiss private bank, manages funds that invest in Indian equities, it does not intend to open an office in India. EFG, another leading Swiss private bank that had been among the top 10 specialized private wealth managers in India, exited the domestic market. Its key employees, along with most of the US$250 million under management, moved over to the Indian financial firm, L&T Finance Holdings (Abraham, 2012; Bhattacharya and Chakraborty, 2011; Kurian and Zachariah, 2012; StanChart, 2013).

This retreat from India does not bode well for foreign firms to capture significant shares of the country's private wealth management market, except that part based in offshore centers. Indian private bankers are increasing their penetration of the market, expanding their scale of business, and developing more sophisticated services. Foreign firms attempting to reenter the market at a later time may face formidable competition because the Indian firms will have cemented the pivotal long-term relationships with HNWIs. The combination of a strong position by Indian private bankers in managing domestic HNWIs, coupled with the offshore management of some of the wealthiest Indians' assets, explains why Mumbai does not appear as a major wealth management center.

2.5.3 Japan's Challenges

Japan remains the largest market for private banking services in Asia. Nonetheless, as with China and India, foreign firms confront formidable competitive threats from mammoth Japanese financial institutions. Domestic firms have a scale that permits them to reach much of the Japanese HNWIs through a dispersed office structure. For example, Sumitomo Mitsui Banking Corporation (SMBC) has teams of experts at 36 locations throughout Japan to advise its 20,000 customers who have financial assets of over 100 million yen, which is equivalent to about US$1 million, the standard minimum of HNWIs. Mizuho Bank charges 1500 employees with searching for HNWIs to add to its customer base (Big Banks, 2012). Japanese banks possess long-term relationships with domestic business entrepreneurs which give them considerable advantages over outsiders.

Some foreign banks have entered into joint ventures or partnerships with Japanese banks as a means to enter the private banking market. Such an approach, however, leaves the domestic bank with the network relationships that allow it to exert indirect, if not direct, control over the private wealth management business. SMBC has had an ownership stake in Barclays Bank since the financial crisis of 2008 and a working relationship with it to provide private banking services. However, SMBC recently reduced its ownership stake by half, which combined with the weakened financial condition of Barclays, hint that the private banking relationship might not last (Martin, 2013). Japanese banks have recently purchased or taken over the private banking business of foreign firms. Bank of America Merrill Lynch had a private banking joint venture with Mitsubishi UFJ Financial Group, but the American bank exited it at the end of 2012. SMBC took over the private wealth management unit of Societe Generale, the French Bank, and made the unit a wholly-owned subsidiary (SMBC, 2013).

Yet, Swiss banks with substantial private banking units are expanding in Japan. UBS aggressively enlarged its efforts since it entered the Japanese market in 2004, differentiating itself by offering what it calls "Swiss" style services—continuous relationships with the same private banker and extension of services to the clients' children. With offices in the three major metropolitan areas of Japan—Tokyo, Osaka, and Nagoya—UBS has the capacity to reach a large share of the country's wealthy (UBS Coaching, 2011).

Likewise, Credit Suisse is undergoing a major expansion in Japan, in line with its larger efforts in Asia-Pacific. Along with UBS, Credit Suisse established offices in Tokyo, Osaka, and Nagoya, and it purchased HSBC's private banking business in Japan (Credit Suisse to Acquire, 2011). It manages the regional business out of Singapore, with a large office in Hong Kong, and the Japan unit, headquartered in Tokyo, reports to Singapore (Main, 2013). Credit Suisse keeps transaction fees low for its private banking clients in Japan. It emphasizes the bank's long experience with helping business people transfer their wealth across generations and set up philanthropic foundations. This marketing ploy appeals to the large number of entrepreneurs who made their wealth beginning in the 1950s and are stepping down. Credit Suisse also has designed specialized products for wealthy with over US$13 million in financial assets, that is, for the upper end of "mid-tier millionaires" and the "ultra-HNWIs" (Honda, 2012; Kodaira, 2012).

These efforts of leading Swiss private wealth management units suggest that foreign firms with specialized expertise can compete with the large private banking units of big Japanese banks if wealth services are strategically targeted. Nevertheless, the limited success of foreign private bankers in penetrating the Japanese market probably explains why Tokyo does not rank as a major center of private banking. To be ranked high, the city needs large representation from both domestic and foreign private bankers.

2.6 SWISS PRIVATE BANKING ACROSS ASIA

China, India, and Japan, as well as other countries of Asia, are targets of Swiss private bankers. They raised their presence in Asia over the past few decades coinciding with the expansion in numbers of HNWIs and of their investable wealth (Fielding, 2013; Wilkinson, 2013). Most attention focuses on the large Swiss Banks, UBS and Credit Suisse, whose private wealth management units rank among the top in the world by

Table 2.6 Asian Offices of Swiss Private Banks with Global Presence

City	Julius Baer	Lombard Odier	Pictet
Hong Kong	X	X	X
Singapore	X	X	X
Tokyo, Japan		X	X
Osaka, Japan			X
Shanghai, China	X		
Taipei, Taiwan			X
Jakarta, Indonesia	X		

Source: Julius Baer, (2013), Lombard Odier (2013), and Pictet (2013).

market size and reputation. They expanded their private banking business across Asia, and they use Hong Kong and Singapore as management headquarters (Credit Suisse Strengthens, 2012; Li, 2013; UBS Remains, 2012).

Less recognized, but equally consequential, has been the expansion of specialized Swiss private banks in Asia. Among the leaders are Julius Baer, headquartered in Zurich, and Lombard Odier and Pictet, both headquartered in Geneva (Julius Baer, 2013; Lombard Odier, 2013; Pictet, 2013). These firms have global footprints; thus their Asian expansion is part of their larger strategy of growing their private wealth management business. They offer a full range of private banking services, access to investment funds, and sophisticated financial systems for managing accounts and investments globally. Therefore, with their promotional edge of the aura and skills of Swiss private banking they provide formidable competition to the private wealth management units of the world's largest corporate and investment banks.

All three of these private banks, like Credit Suisse and UBS, use Hong Kong and Singapore as key platforms for their private wealth management business in Asia (Table 2.6). At the same time, Lombard Odier and Pictet also use Tokyo as a major base, and Pictet also has an office in Osaka, Japan, similar to Credit Suisse and UBS. This suggests that these Swiss private bankers are seeing the same features of the Japanese private wealth management market. Although Julius Baer does not have an office in Japan, it has targeted China through Shanghai, which is the financial and industrial center of the country and home to huge numbers of HNWIs who are entrepreneurs. Pictet also has entered Taiwan, which like Shanghai, has numerous entrepreneurs, especially in manufacturing, who are HNWIs. Thus the leading Swiss banks—Credit Suisse and UBS—and the specialized top Swiss private banks are major players in Asian private banking.

2.7 CONCLUSION

Arguably, the most significant trend in global private wealth management is Asia's rise to equality with North America and Europe, with the prospect that it may become the leading center of HNWIs and of their investable wealth over the next few decades. This transformation of global wealth is propelling a restructuring of wealth management as private banking units of large global corporate and investment banks, hedge funds, and fund management firms, as well as specialized private banking firms, bulk up their activities in Asia to participate in this market expansion. At the same time, these global firms are facing increasing competition from domestic financial firms which are vigorously expanding their private wealth management business.

Generalizations about growing HNWI markets in Asia sometimes founder on an inadequate appreciation of the complexity of change in Asia. Much attention rightly focuses on China as the mostly rapidly growing, large market for private banking, yet Japan remains the biggest market. Tokyo does not rank among the centers of private wealth management globally or in Asia. That status falls to Hong Kong, as Asia-Pacific center, and Singapore, as Southeast Asia center, the leading financial metropolises of Asia. Their position as offshore business centers and regional headquarters of global corporate and investment banks, hedge funds, private equity firms, venture capital firms, and fund management companies makes them the pivots of Asian financial infrastructure and expertise. Not surprisingly, they house the greatest agglomeration of private wealth management in Asia and rank in the top-five globally.

The economic trends in Asia must be properly appreciated to understand the current structure of private wealth management and its future trajectory. China's GDP/capita has grown at rapid rates over the last few decades, yet it remains a poor country relative to Japan, North America, and Western Europe. This does not detract from its potential for a large increase in HNWIs and of their investable wealth over the next decades, but it does introduce a cautionary note. The largest, wealthiest HNWI market, Japan, faces a difficult future as its GDP/capita and economic growth stagnate, thus limiting the potential of private wealth management. India is the third largest market for private banking in Asia, but its GDP/capita has risen slowly and it remains impoverished. While other countries of Asia are growing, most of them, except for South Korea, also are poor.

As Asia's global financial centers, Hong Kong and Singapore will remain the pivots of private wealth management in the region. All leading financial firms with private banking units and major specialized private banking firms, such as the Swiss, use these cities as their management centers and bases for their most important private bankers who serve the local wealthy and reach out to the wealthy in the rest of Asia.

Private wealth management firms face challenges dealing with the HNWI markets in Asia. China's major banks are rapidly expanding private banking services to wealthy businesspeople. These services are especially targeted at the lower end of the HNWI group; thus foreign firms have difficulty reaching that market. Most of them have not set up offices in China to reach the wealth management market. They run their business from Hong Kong, and, to a lesser extent, from Singapore. The Indian HNWI market is challenging for foreign firms because domestic Indian financial firms have built long-term relations with the country's wealthy. While foreign firms benefit from the offshore private banking services they provide to the Indian wealthy, that may not be a long-term market. As the biggest market of HNWI in Asia, Japan frustrates foreign firms. Japanese financial firms have deep relations with the country's wealthy, including the business community which they have served for decades. Few foreign private wealth management firms have been successful; the notable exception seems to be Swiss private banking units of Credit Suisse and UBS and specialized private banking firms from Zurich and Geneva.

Intriguingly, Swiss private banking is making inroads in Asia and posing long-term competitive threats to global private wealth management units of commercial and investment banks. Swiss firms, including specialized banks such as Julius Baer, Lombard Odier, and Pictet, have built a global franchise which they are transferring to Asia. Thus they have the scale and infrastructure to compete with much larger global institutions. Swiss bankers explicitly sell their brand of special Swiss services, based on decades, if not hundreds of years, of experience.

Firms in the private wealth management business in Asia face increasing competitive challenges over the next few decades. Domestic competitors are emerging and expanding at rapid rates in the developing economies of China and India, as well as in small economies of the region. Japan will continue as a difficult market for foreign firms because of the grip that Japanese banks have on private banking. Looming as uncertainty in the background, and, perhaps, moving to the foreground, will be the economic growth prospects in Asia over the next few decades. Simplistic extrapolations that Asia always will grow rapidly founder on the impact of another global economic crisis. As the plunging GDP growth rates in Asian countries during 2007–2009 are a reminder, Asia will not be immune from the effects of another crisis. That will retard growth of private banking or even lead to contraction as the market declines with the plunging wealth of HNWIs.

REFERENCES

A Hub to Bank On, 2013. Business Times Singapore, 1 April.
Abraham, R., 2012. Swiss Bank converts all India funds to QFIs. Financial Chronicle, 20 November.
Ang, S.K., 2010. A qualitative study on the challenges of private banking in Asia. Journal of Wealth Management 12 (4), 68–77.
Ashreena, T., 2012. Indian reforms re-ignite investors' interest. PWM Professional Wealth Management, 1 November.
Asia-Pacific Wealth Report, 2012. Capgemini and RBC Wealth Management.
Asset Managers Focus More on Private Banks, 2012. Asian Investor, May: 6.
Bank of Ayudhya Steps up Targeting of Thai Affluent Individuals, 2012. Datamonitor, September.
Barclays Wealth Appoints Asha Mathen as Director, PCG, 2011. Indiainfoline News Service, 30 August.
Bastide, L., 2011. Singapore in the new economic geography: from geographic location to the relocation of economic dynamics. In: Gipouloux, F. (Ed.), Gateways to Globalisation: Asia's International Trading and Finance Centers. Edward Elgar, Cheltenham, UK, pp. 130–144.
Beaverstock, J.V., 2012. The privileged world city: private banking, wealth management and the bespoke servicing of the global super-rich. In: Derudder, B., Hoyler, M., Taylor, P.J., Witlox, F. (Eds.), International Handbook of Globalization and World Cities. Edward Elgar, Cheltenham, UK, pp. 378–389.

Beaverstock, J.V., Hall, S., Wainwright, T., 2013. Servicing the super-rich: new financial elites and the rise of the private wealth management retail ecology. Regional Studies 47 (6), 834–849.

Bhattacharya, N., Chakraborty, S., 2011. Global financial managers shedding staff in India. Business Standard, 13 December: 7.

Big Banks Luring Wealthy Japanese, 2012. Nikkei Weekly, 24 December.

Chatterjee, S., 2011. Profits elude bankers to the rich in booming India. Reuters News, 13 September.

Credit Suisse Strengthens Private Banking Team with New Senior Appointments, 2012. M2 Presswire, 16 April.

Credit Suisse to Acquire HSBC's Private Banking Business in Japan, 2011. Daily the Pak Banker, 29 December.

de Bendern, S., 2013. Honey, they shrunk the money. Open, 16 February.

Fielding, A., 2013. Do you need a Swiss bank? Financial Review Smart Investor, News, 15 February: 26.

Hammond, C., 2012. Asia HNWIs turn from USTs to local safe havens. Asiamoney, 1 June.

Haslip, A., 2012a. China Construction Bank: increasing its share of a developing affluent market. Datamonitor, May.

Haslip, A., 2012b. RBS the latest private bank to add philanthropy in a competitive Indian market. Datamonitor, June.

Honda, N., 2012. Banks in race for Japan's superrich. Nikkei Weekly, 11 June.

Hong Kong Monetary Authority, 2013. Annual Report, 2012. Hong Kong Special Administrative Region.

Hooi, J., 2013. HK takes on S'pore in battle for private wealth. Business Times Singapore, 16 January.

Julius Baer, 2013. <www.juliusbaer.com> (accessed 28.07.13).

Julius Baer Predicts Private Banks Will Triumph, 2012. Asian Investor, May: 6.

Julius Baer to Buy Macquarie's Asia Pvt Wealth Business, 2011. Reuters News, 13 October.

Kodaira, R., 2012. Credit Suisse, Japan and wealth. Nikkei Weekly, 16 April.

Kolesnikov-Jessop, S., 2012. Private banks of Asia seize their moment; special report: net worth. International Herald Tribune, 27 March: 20.

Kurian, B., 2011. Mid-market clients are crucial for I-banking in India. The Times of India, 30 October.

Kurian, B., Zachariah, R., 2012. L&T Fin set to scoop EFG's $250m Pvt wealth portfolio. The Times of India, 7 March.

Li, K., 2013. UBS unit follows the flow of money. South China Morning Post, 15 April.

Lombard Odier, 2013. <www.lombardodier.com> (accessed 28.07.13).

Long, J.A., Tan, D., 2011. The growth of the private wealth management industry in Singapore and Hong Kong. Capital Markets Law Journal 6 (1), 104–126.

Lowenhaupt, C.A., 2008. Freedom from wealth and the contemporary global family: a new vision for family wealth management. Journal of Wealth Management 10 (4), 21–29.

Mahutga, M.C., Ma, X., Smith, D.A., Timberlake, M., 2010. Economic globalisation and the structure of the world city system: the case of airline passenger data. Urban Studies 47 (9), 1925–1947.

Main, A., 2013. Look offshore for investment opportunities. The Australian, Finance, 9 May: 23.

Martin, B., 2013. Blue-chips slip again as Barclays investor halves its stake in £260m sale. Daily Telegraph, Business, 7 June: 7.

Maude, D., 2006. Global Private Banking and Wealth Management: The New Realities. John Wiley & Sons, Chichester, UK.

McQueen, K., 2012. High stakes: Hong Kong ranks first in Asia as a financial centre, but its private bankers are fighting for supremacy against rival Singapore. South China Morning Post, Business, 17 September: 34.

Meyer, D.R., 2000. Hong Kong as a Global Metropolis. Cambridge University Press, Cambridge, UK.

Meyer, D.R., 2009. Hong Kong's transformation as a financial center. In: Schenk, C.R. (Ed.), Hong Kong SAR's Monetary and Exchange Rate Challenges. Palgrave Macmillan, Houndmills, UK, pp. 161–188.

Moiseiwitsch, J., 2012. Blue blood banks. South China Morning Post, 30 April: 26.

Monetary Authority of Singapore, 2012. Annual Report, 2011/2012. Singapore.

Motilal Oswal Financial Services Appoints Mr. A.V. Srikanth as CEO of their Wealth Management Business, 2012. BUINPR, 21 June.

Nikko AM and Ambit Launch Joint Venture in India, 2011. Business Wire, 19 December.

Pershing MD Outlines Growth Plans for the Continent, 2012. FT Business, 24 September.

Pictet, 2013. <www.pictet.com> (accessed 28.07.13).

Pow, C.P., 2013. The world needs a second Switzerland: onshoring Singapore as the livable city for the super-rich. In: Hay, I. (Ed.), Geographies of the Super-Rich. Edward Elgar, Cheltenham, UK, pp. 61–76.

Preview for the Private Banker International 21st PBI Wealth Summit and Awards Gala Dinner 13–14 October 2011 in Singapore, 2011. ACN Newswire, 6 October.

Private Banks, 2011. FinanceAsia, 15 September.

Private Banks, 2012. FinanceAsia, September.

PWC, 2011. Anticipating a New Age in Wealth Management: Global Private Banking and Wealth Management Survey 2011. <www.pwc.com/wealth>.

Research Republic, 2008. The Future of Asian Financial Centres—Challenges and Opportunities for the City of London. Research Republic, Manchester, UK.

Sen, S.L., 2011. Asia private banking shows teflon status. Business Times Singapore, 22 December.

Sen, S.L., 2012. Deutsche Bank ramps up private bank hiring. Business Times Singapore, 21 February.

Sen, S.L., 2013. Robust growth in private wealth. Business Times Singapore, 28 February.

Sheng, L.W., 2012. Singapore has edge as Asian metals trade hub. Business Times Singapore, Top Stories, 28 May.

SMBC to Acquire Societe Generale's Private Banking Business in Japan, 2013. World Market Intelligence, 25 July.

Speech by FS at Joint Business Community Luncheon, 2013. Hong Kong Government News, 18 March.

StanChart to Acquire Morgan Stanley's Private Banking Arm, 2013. Outlook, 20 May.

Tan, M., 2011. Citi rolls out four more services for rich clients. Straits Times, 18 November.

Taylor, P.J., 2005. Leading world cities: empirical evaluations of urban nodes in multiple networks. Urban Studies 42 (9), 1593–1608.

UBS Coaching Kids of Rich Japanese, 2011. Nikkei Weekly, 24 October.

UBS Remains Asia's Wealth Advisory Leader in Asiamoney's Private Banking Poll, 2012. Asiamoney, 1 June.

Vallikappen, S., 2013. In Asia, a Financial Field That Favors Women. Bloomberg Businessweek, 22–28 April.

van der Hoevel, H., 2012. Taiwan's wealth management market is rising in affluence, making it a rewarding target. Datamonitor, May.

We Like to Pick Niches where we can Dominate, 2011. Mint, 19 August.

Wilkinson, T.L., 2013. Asia's private banks stripped bare. South China Morning Post, Business, 22 April: 6.

World Bank, 2013. World Development Indicators, Washington, DC.

World Wealth Report, 2013. Capgemini and RBC Wealth Management.

Wright, C., 2012. Private banking 2012: keeping it local in China. Euromoney, 1 February.

Yiu, E., 2012. HKEx gears up to bring bourse into the fast lane. South China Morning Post, News, 9 March: 3.

Z/Yen, 2007–2013. Z/Yen Global Financial Centre Index. <www.zyen.com>.

Zhao, S.X.B., Li, Z., Smith, C.J., 2011. China's emerging financial centers: Shanghai, Beijing and Hong Kong. In: Gipouloux, F. (Ed.), Gateways to Globalisation: Asia's International Trading and Finance Centers. Edward Elgar, Cheltenham, UK, pp. 200–216.

CHAPTER 3

The Banking Networks of Asian Financial Centers

David R. Meyer
Olin Business School, Washington University in St. Louis, Campus Box 1133,
One Brookings Drive, St. Louis, MO 63130-4899, USA

3.1 INTRODUCTION

Asian financial centers, including Tokyo, Hong Kong, Singapore, Shanghai, and Mumbai, nest within a larger set of global centers, consisting of London, New York, Frankfurt, Paris, Zurich, and others (Sassen, 1999). These centers are networked through flows of capital, inter-organizational exchanges among financial institutions, and intra-organizational management control, including movement of employees among offices of the firms (Allen, 2010; Beaverstock, 2007; Taylor, 2004).

Global financial centers have roots that reach back to at least the 18th century (Kindleberger, 1974; Meyer, 1991a,b). Whether or not firms house their global head-quarters in London, most of the major firms that aim to operate worldwide base their key financial decision makers in that city. Part of this legacy comes from the rise of the United Kingdom to trade and industrial prominence in the 18th and 19th centuries, and part has roots in the British colonial empire which reached to many parts of the world. One consequence was that London became (and remains) the hub of sophisticated information and knowledge about production and consumption in the world economy (Clark, 2002; Thrift, 1987). Financial firms that wish to tap that expertise have to locate their key decision makers there. Asia's financial centers emerged in the 19th century out of this structuring of global finance. That development frames a substantial part of contemporary banking networks in Asia.

3.2 THE ROOTS OF ASIA'S BANKING NETWORKS

The 1850s are an appropriate starting point for identifying the nascent financial centers and their networks in Asia. At that time British banks, mostly headquartered in London, began to compete with the large trading houses of Asia for financing trade and other economic activity. These banks initially moved into India with branches in Bombay (Mumbai) and Calcutta, and then moved into Southeast and East Asia with branches in Singapore, Hong Kong, and Shanghai. The banks created an intra- and inter-organizational financial network across Asia, linking the finance/trade centers of the region, and tied the region to London, as the global center of capital markets (Jones, 1993; Meyer, 2000).

As these banks entered Asia, they also came into contact with the leading international traders of the region, the Chinese merchants. The diaspora of Chinese from mainland China, which was in full bloom during the 19th century across Southeast Asia, laid the foundation for Chinese wholesalers and retailers to form a loosely integrated network of trade relations that stretched from China to Japan, and south to the Philippines to Hong Kong, and on to Vietnam, Thailand, Indonesia, Malaya, and Singapore, with tentacles from that finance/trade center to India. The rice trade constituted the pivotal business which the Chinese retailers controlled within many countries, and Chinese wholesalers handled trade across Asia. International rice merchants founded some of the earliest Chinese banks (outside China) around 1900. The Chinese merchant wholesalers of this network ran their own firms, and some of the leading merchants also served as compradors, basically in-house managers, for the foreign trading firms and banks. These bonds between the foreign finance/trade networks of capital and the Chinese networks set the defining relations among banks that persist to the present. Commercial and investment banks that participated actively in these great networks of capital had the best access to business opportunities across Asia (Coclanis, 1993; Fairbank, 1953; Hao, 1970; Meyer, 2000; Purcell, 1965).

The structuration of the banking networks of Asia is most clearly revealed through the Hongkong and Shanghai Bank (modern-day HSBC). It was founded in 1864/65 by some of the most significant British, American, German, and Indian trading firms of Asia. Because the full set of offices of these trading firms constituted a worldwide network, the bank immediately acquired a global reach which set it apart from virtually every other bank. It quickly vaulted into the ranks of the top 10 global banks, a position it retains to the present. Hong Kong housed the global headquarters of the bank, and the most significant Asian branch was in Shanghai. Simultaneously, the bank opened a London branch to participate in the global financial networks organized around that banking community (King, 1987).

Over the subsequent 50 years the Hongkong and Shanghai Bank deepened its ties to Asia and created a branch and agency network of offices across the region (Table 3.1). The core of the bank's operations, as indicated by the branch/agency network, focused on China, both internally and financing its trade with Asia and the rest of the world. At the same time, one of its most significant branches which it added a year after its founding was the Yokohama branch to handle the finance business of Japan. It quickly expanded its reach in Japan with the Kobe office and years later, the Nagasaki office. The Taipei office added in 1909 reflected Japan's imperial takeover of Taiwan from China.

Significantly, the Hongkong and Shanghai Bank almost immediately moved into India after its founding with major branches in Calcutta and Bombay (Table 3.1). These branches were integrally bound up with the British imperial reach into India, and both

Table 3.1 Branch Offices and Agency Offices of the Hongkong and Shanghai Bank in Asia as of 1918, by Year Opened

Hong Kong (1865)	*Shanghai, China (1865)*	*Yokohama, Japan (1866)*
Foochow, China (1867)	Hankow, China (1868)	Kobe/Hiogo, Japan (1869)
Saigon, Vietnam (1870)	Tientsin, China (1881)	Nagasaki, Japan (1891)
Amoy, China (1873)	Peking (Beijing), China (1885)	Taipei, Taiwan (1909)
Bangkok, Thailand (1888)	Hongkew, China (1909)	
Canton (Guangzhou), China (1909)	Tsingtao, China (1914)	*Colombo, Sri Lanka (1892)*
	Harbin, China (1915)	
Singapore (1877)	Vladivostok, Russia (1918)	*Manila, Philippines (1875)*
Penang, Malaya (1884)		Iloilo, Philippines (1883)
Malacca, Malaya (1909)	*Calcutta, India (1867)*	
Kuala Lumpur, Malaya (1910)	Rangoon, Burma (1891)	*Batavia (Jakarta), Indonesia (1884)*
Ipoh, Malaya (1910)		Surabaya, Indonesia (1896)
Johore, Malaya (1910)	*Bombay (Mumbai), India (1869)*	

Source: King, 1988, Table 2.1, p. 92.
Note: Branch offices are italicized and offices under them report to that office.

cities were the strategic finance and trade centers of the country. Because British traders and financiers had close ties reaching from London to India to Hong Kong, the bank was simply inserting itself directly into that global business network. The Southeast Asia penetration of the bank was signaled by the Saigon office (1870) which involved the bank in the trade of Vietnam, controlled by the French, and later the Bangkok (1888) office. Both of these offices reported to Hong Kong.

However, the key strategic move of the bank in Southeast Asia was the establishment of a major branch in Singapore in 1877 (Table 3.1). That city had been solidly positioned for at least three decades as the finance and trade headquarters for Chinese and foreign firms which were active across Southeast Asia. In subsequent years, the bank added branches in Malaya (Penang, Malacca, Kuala Lumpur, Ipoh, and Johor) to participate in financing imports/exports related to the resource development of that territory. Thus, by the end of the First World War, the Hongkong and Shanghai Bank had a network of branches and agency offices across Asia. Its bankers possessed the best access to knowledge about the Asian economy and business relations, and the bank was inserted into Chinese networks, as well as non-Chinese domestic networks of the region. This organizational structure of the bank, which was built between the late 1860s and the first decade of the 20th century, bares remarkable resemblance to early 21st-century financial centers and network relations of Asia. Recognizing the extraordinary resilience of these banking networks is key to understanding the contemporary networks of Asia.

During the 20th century, banking expanded in Asia as economic development transformed the economies of much of the region. A ranking of financial centers from 1900 to 1980 based primarily on commercial banks provides an overview of these changes. London and New York always ranked in the top two positions of the 10 most important centers in the world. The Asian centers in the top 10 included Hong Kong, Shanghai, Singapore, and Tokyo (Figure 3.1). Hong Kong fluctuated between third and tenth rank, suggesting that its global importance as a banking center has long roots. In contrast, Singapore only ranked in the top 10 in 1947 when it ranked sixth.

Tokyo (Yokohama before 1935) maintained a position in the top group for the entire period (Figure 3.1). With the post-World War II recovery and rapid economic growth of Japan beginning in the late 1950s, Tokyo moved solidly into the top five financial centers. Shanghai's high rank during the first half of the 20th century foreshadowed its more recent emergence as a major Asian financial center, but that ranking must be qualified. In contrast to Hong Kong, which attracted many international banks who established regional or subregional (East or Southeast Asia) headquarters, the foreign banks that came to Shanghai operated mainly in the China market. They developed collaborative, as well as, competitive relations with the Chinese banks. Shanghai has always been the leading banking center of China. It reached that status in the early 19th

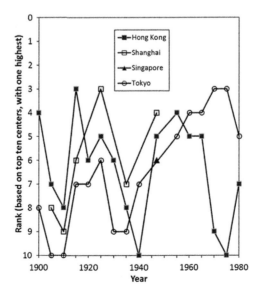

Figure 3.1 Rank of Hong Kong, Shanghai, Singapore, and Tokyo (Yokohama before 1935) as international financial centers, 1900–1980. *Source:* Reed, 1981, Table A.11, pp. 131–138.

century and retains it today. Its banks possess the most sophisticated knowledge about the Chinese economy, and they have always had close ties to the foreign banks in the city (Cheng, 2003; Ji, 2003).

3.3 ASIA'S LEADING FINANCIAL CENTERS

Since the 1980s, Asia's financial centers have increased their relative importance and their integration with global finance coinciding with the rapid economic growth of the region. Arguably, the most significant development has been the unequivocal emergence of Hong Kong as the Asia-Pacific financial center. While it is not yet on par with London and New York, it is now recognized as the third most important center in the world. Virtually all of the leading commercial and investment banks house their Asia-Pacific headquarters in Hong Kong, and a large share of them use Singapore as their Southeast Asia headquarters (Bhattacharya, 2011; Jao, 1997; Meyer, 2009).

Tokyo continues as a major global financial center, primarily on the basis of the huge Japanese commercial and investment banks headquartered there. However, global banks typically charge their Tokyo headquarters with Japan business, not East Asia or Asia-Pacific business. That decision making by global banks is consonant with the fact that Tokyo and other Japanese financial centers are outside the nexus of the foreign and Chinese networks of finance in Asia. That nexus has been Hong Kong, primarily, and Singapore, secondarily, since the late 19th century. Thus Tokyo's importance in Asia as a banking center has now slipped below Hong Kong and Singapore. These two cities are now the leading financial centers of Asia (Meyer, 2000; Research Republic, 2008).

3.3.1 The View from HSBC

The management of HSBC's Asian business provides an overall picture of the relations among financial centers as seen through the window of Asia's most important bank. The acronym, HSBC, is a reframing of the grand name of the bank, the Hongkong and Shanghai Banking Corporation, founded in 1864/65. The global headquarters was shifted to London in the 1990s in advance of the return of Hong Kong to China's sovereign control in 1997. Hong Kong remains the Asia-Pacific headquarters of the bank, and the tie to London continues that relation established in the 1860s.

A systematic chart of the organizational structure of the major Asian offices of the bank is not available, as it is for the early 20th century (Table 3.1). Nevertheless, a review of HSBC's many websites allows a simplified reconstruction of the probable reporting relations of the offices. Currently, the bank has far too many major offices to fully identify them all. The listing as reported in Table 3.2 is a partial attempt at that reconstruction. It is sufficiently detailed to provide a perspective on the bank's Asian office structure—thus the network management lines of the bank. As is evident, HSBC

Table 3.2 Leading Asian Offices of HSBC as of 2013

Hong Kong (Asia-Pacific headquarters)
  Vietnam (Ho Chi Minh City—Saigon), South Korea (Seoul), Japan (Tokyo, Osaka),
  Philippines (Manila), Taiwan (Taipei)
Singapore (Southeast Asia headquarters)
  Indonesia (Jakarta), Malaysia (Kuala Lumpur, Penang, Johor, Malacca), Thailand (Bangkok)
India headquarters (Mumbai)
  New Delhi, Calcutta, Chennai
Shanghai (China headquarters)
  Beijing, Changsha, Chengdu, Chongqing, Dalian, Dongguan, Guangzhou, Harbin,
  Hangzhou, Hefei, Jinan, Kunming, Nanjing, Nanning, Ningbo, Qingdao, Shenyang,
  Shenzhen, Suzhou, Taiyuan, Tangshan, Tianjin, Wuhan, Wuxi, Xiamen, Xi'an, Zhengzhou

Source: Various websites of HSBC.

structures itself in broad outline similar to the early 20th century. The reporting lines to the Asia-Pacific headquarters, of course, include all of the offices, but the ones explicitly listed under Hong Kong (Ho Chi Minh City—old Saigon, Seoul, and Tokyo-Osaka) most likely have direct reporting relations.

Although the exact list of countries and financial centers that report to Singapore can only be approximated, the list of cities across Southeast Asia is a partial estimate (Table 3.2). Examination of articles about HSBC's Singapore regional headquarters suggests that its CEO and the senior managers supervise Jakarta, the business centers of Malaysia (Kuala Lumpur, Penang, and others), and Bangkok (which may report to Hong Kong). This list suggests that the organization of banking relations in Southeast Asia from the headquarters of Singapore has great resilience, reflecting long-standing business ties across that subregion since the mid-19th century. Many of the other global banks, such as Goldman Sachs, Morgan Stanley, Deutsche Bank, and Credit Suisse, organize themselves similarly in Southeast Asia (see bank websites).

The organization of India by HSBC remains comparable to the 19th-century structure (Table 3.2). Mumbai (Bombay) is the country headquarters for India, and New Delhi, Calcutta, and Chennai have the most important regional offices, although other cities also have branches. Because of the close ties of India to Southeast Asia, most of the regular banking management ties of HSBC India link to Hong Kong and Singapore, as well as directly to the global headquarters in London.

In China HSBC's organization has much similarity to what emerged in the late 19th and early 20th centuries (Tables 3.1 and 3.2). Just as Shanghai was the pivotal branch office of the bank beginning in 1864/65, it is the China headquarters for HSBC today. The list of the major branches in China includes some cities which had branches over 100 years ago. Given the status of Shanghai as China's leading international financial center since the early 19th century, HSBC has simply mirrored China's banks. This replicates the long-term internal financial networks of China. The Hong Kong Asia-Pacific headquarters, as it did in the past, also has many management ties to the financial centers of South China, especially Guangzhou (Canton). Shenzhen and Dongguan are essentially "metropolitan suburbs" of Hong Kong.

As Asia's leading global bank, HSBC provides a window into the financial networks of the region. Obviously, overall financial flows within Asia are far more complex than can be indicated by the management organizational controls of HSBC. Nonetheless, the bank's overall management structure is a partial proxy for many of the long-standing economic networks of Asia. These networks have taken on new character and form, but the business networks are deeply embedded in the political economy of Asia.

3.3.2 The Ranking of Asia's Financial Centers

The Global Financial Centers Index (GFCI) provides a broad approach to evaluating the importance of Asia's financial centers; it aims to measure the competitiveness of centers (Z/Yen, 2007–2013). Since 2007 the index has been released twice a year, in March and September. The index employs a large number of statistical measures of financial centers across a wide range of indicators (96 factors as of March 2013), including what it terms instrumental factors (people, business environment, infrastructure, market access, and general competitiveness). In addition, several thousand financial professionals are asked to rate the competitiveness of the cities. As with any index, especially one with numerous components, the precise rating and ranking provide only a general indicator of the significance of a financial center. The value of the index lies in the repeated measures across time which allow broad patterns to be identified. Since 2007 over 50 centers have been ranked, and, as of 2013, the total reached 79 cities.

London and New York are always the top two and usually in the order indicated. Focusing only on the Asian financial centers, Hong Kong and Singapore always rank third and fourth globally and typically first and second, respectively, in Asia (Figure 3.2). However, sometimes the absolute difference in their ratings is small. The consistency of Tokyo's third rank, always below Hong Kong and Singapore, among Asia's financial centers provides additional support for the claim that it is not the dominant financial center of Asia.

Shanghai's rating as a financial center has risen significantly such that it is now close to Tokyo's (Figure 3.2). Perhaps, somewhat surprisingly, Seoul's rating not only has risen rapidly, but it also now achieves values comparable to Tokyo and Shanghai. Certainly, one factor elevating Seoul has been the expansion of the economy of South Korea. Its real gross domestic product (GDP) grew at an annual average rate of 5.2% from 1990 to 2012 (World Bank, 2013). Although Beijing initially experienced a rapid rise in ratings, infrastructure measures and professional evaluations now imply that it may not move into the top levels of global financial centers. India's leading financial

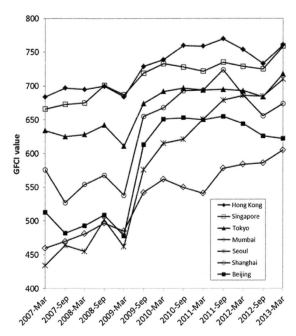

Figure 3.2 GFCI values for Asian financial centers, 2007–2013. *Source:* Z/Yen, 2007–2013.

center of Mumbai has risen in the ratings and is converging on Beijing. Nevertheless, Mumbai's ratings are far below Shanghai, as well as Hong Kong and Singapore. This suggests that Mumbai remains relatively minor in Asia. This is consistent with the fact that leading commercial and investment banks either manage their Mumbai offices from Hong Kong, and, secondarily, Singapore, or Mumbai reports directly to global headquarters in London or New York. The ranks of Asia's financial centers on the GFCI from 2007 to 2013 reveal that four of the region's centers are now in the top 10 globally (Table 3.3). Hong Kong and Singapore maintain a firm grip on the third and fourth rank. Tokyo retains a hold on ranks five to nine, indicating that it is a leading financial center. However, it often falls as many as two to four ranks below Hong Kong and Singapore. Seoul is the most important, rising financial center in Asia. Since 2009 the statistical indices and views of financial professionals have led to a major re-evaluation of Seoul such that it has joined the top 10.

Seemingly, Shanghai and Beijing were poised to move into the upper ranks of global financial centers, but over the past few years this trend has reversed (Table 3.3). While Shanghai may regain traction, evidence on Beijing appears unequivocal. The huge state-owned banks headquartered there (Agricultural Bank of China, Bank of China, China Construction Bank, and Industrial and Commercial Bank of China), whose assets rank them among the world's largest, are not the core of a sophisticated financial community

Table 3.3 World Ranks of Asian Financial Centers on Global Financial Centers Index (GFCI), 2007–2013

Date	Hong Kong	Singapore	Tokyo	Seoul	Shanghai	Beijing	Mumbai
March 2007	3	4	9	43	24	36	39
September 2007	3	4	10	42	30	39	41
March 2008	3	4	9	51	31	46	48
September 2008	4	3	7	48	34	47	49
March 2009	4	3	15	53	35	51	49
September 2009	3	4	7	35	10	22	53
March 2010	3	4	5	28	11	15	58
September 2010	3	4	5	24	6	16	57
March 2011	3	4	5	16	5	17	58
September 2011	3	4	6	11	5	19	64
March 2012	3	4	5	9	8	26	64
September 2012	3	4	7	6	19	43	63
March 2013	3	4	6	9	24	58	66

Source: Z/Yen, 2007–2013.

as measured by statistical indices or views of financial professionals. Translated into banking/financial network terms, Shanghai and, especially, Beijing are not integral participants in global networks. This is consistent with the long-standing organization of banking in China—Shanghai is the financial center for the country and foreign banks are based there to access the China market. These banks do not house their management for Asia in Shanghai (and definitely not in Beijing). Typically, Hong Kong and, secondarily, Singapore are the headquarters for Asia.

Mumbai is the pivotal point for foreign banks to access the Indian market. All of the major global banks, such as Citigroup, HSBC, Goldman Sachs, JP Morgan Chase, Morgan Stanley, Deutsche Bank, and Credit Suisse, place their India headquarters in the city. These banks are entering the Indian financial networks which radiate from Mumbai nationwide. As India's hub of finance, Mumbai houses the headquarters of all of the major domestic commercial and investment banks, along with the most significant fund management companies and private equity firms (see websites of Indian financial firms and confirmed by author's interviews). While Mumbai participates in global financial networks through the nexus of the foreign and domestic firms, the ranking of the city as a financial center—ranging between 40 and 70—suggests that it is peripheral to these networks (Table 3.3). Although India is the second largest country in the world with over 1.3 billion, it is impoverished. In 2012 the GDP/capita was just US$1,489, whereas China's was US$6,091, South Korea's was US$22,590, and Japan's was US$46,720 (World Bank, 2013). Poverty in India stands as the greatest hindrance to Mumbai's move into the top ranks of global financial centers.

3.4 ASIA'S EXCHANGES

All financial sectors have direct or indirect relations with exchanges for trading securities, but commercial and investment banks arguably are the most involved because their activities on the exchanges not only cover trading, through their trading floors and brokerage units, but also stock and bond underwriting, initial public offerings, and mergers and acquisitions. These banks and the exchanges, along with the sectors of law and accounting which provide advisory services, form a securities industry cluster (Wojcik, 2011). Most of the large global commercial and investment banks have important offices in each of the cities with major exchanges because they need to serve their clients in the country housing the exchange and in the surrounding region.

Of the six major exchanges in Asia, five are housed in the most important financial centers: the Tokyo exchange, the Hong Kong exchange, the Singapore exchange, the Mumbai (Bombay exchange), and the Shanghai exchange. The Shenzhen exchange, located in a metropolitan satellite of Hong Kong, has expanded as a direct policy action of the Beijing government (Karrenman and Van der Knaap, 2009, 2012; Lai, 2012a). The value of domestic market capitalization of these exchanges has been on an uptrend since 1990, with the exception of the Tokyo exchange (Figure 3.3). It remains the largest exchange as of 2012, but the Hong Kong exchange and the Shanghai exchange are

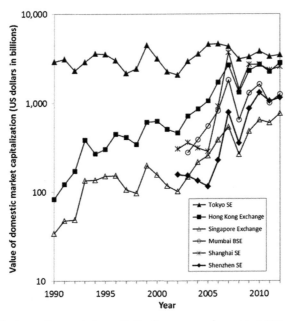

Figure 3.3 Value of domestic market capitalization on exchanges, 1990–2012. *Source:* World Federation of Exchanges.

approaching Tokyo's level. This stagnation in its domestic market capitalization provides further confirmation of the relative decline of Tokyo as a global financial center.

Hong Kong exchange's rise to second rank in Asia has been powered by the continued growth of the city as the Asia-Pacific financial center (Figure 3.3). At the same time, the growth in capitalization of Singapore's exchange has tracked Hong Kong's to a remarkable degree, albeit always smaller, additional corroboration that these cities stand as the great financial centers of Asia. Arguably, the most important transformation of stock exchanges in Asia has been the rise of the Shanghai and Shenzhen exchanges shortly after 2000. The Shanghai exchange quickly soared in market capitalization to the level of the Hong Kong exchange and almost to the level of Tokyo. Shenzhen's exchange tracked the rate of growth of Shanghai's, but has remained smaller. Likewise, the Mumbai exchange has grown significantly in market capitalization since early 2000s, but it remains much smaller than the Tokyo, Hong Kong, and Shanghai exchanges. This confirms that Mumbai is a less important financial center in Asia. Operations of the major global commercial and investment banks in Mumbai do not need the level of staffing which is required in Hong Kong and Singapore.

The value of domestic and foreign bond trading on the exchanges of Asia reveals important distinctions which partially reflect specialization of the exchanges (Figure 3.4). During the 1990s, bond trading on the Tokyo exchange dwarfed trading on the other Asian exchanges, but its trading has plummeted. This decline, coupled with

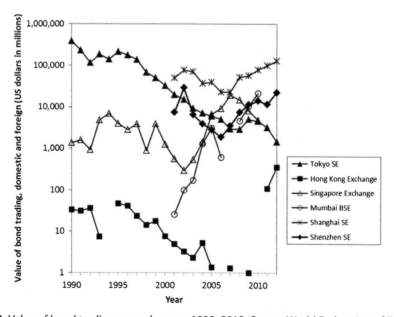

Figure 3.4 Value of bond trading on exchanges, 1990–2012. *Source:* World Federation of Exchanges.

the stagnation of domestic market capitalization on the Tokyo exchange, provides hints of the relative, if not impending absolute, decline of Tokyo as a global financial center. This implies that global commercial and investment banks may gradually shrink their operations in Tokyo.

China's Shanghai exchange has vaulted into the top position as the bond trading center of Asia, providing support for the expansion of both global commercial and investment banks in that city and domestic banks which are ramping up their exchange trading (Figure 3.4). Although significantly smaller, the Shenzhen exchange has moved into second place, along with Mumbai, as a bond trading center. While Shenzhen remains a satellite of Hong Kong, this expansion of bond trading encourages both domestic banks to expand their operations in Shenzhen and leading global banks to have some operations in that city. All of the top state-owned banks, including Bank of China, China Construction Bank, and Industrial and Commercial Bank of China, have major branches in Shenzhen (see bank websites). Nevertheless, much of the strategic decision making can remain in Hong Kong, a short distance away.

Bond trading on the Mumbai exchange has risen significantly; now, it is close to the level of the Shenzhen exchange (Figure 3.4). Nonetheless, this trading remains small and far below the Shanghai exchange. If the bond trading of China's two exchanges was combined, it would be far larger than Mumbai's. The relatively small amount of bond trading in Mumbai, India's premier financial center, underscores that it is not a major financial center in Asia. That lower level is consistent with the smaller size of the Indian economy and the much lower average income of its 1.3 billion people, compared to China which has about the same population size.

The financial centers of Asia should not be interpreted as competing with each other for exchange business, although local boosters sometimes get caught up in such rhetoric (Pauly, 2011; Sheng, 2012; Yiu, 2012). Instead, the exchanges complement each other. Both Hong Kong and Singapore draw listings from their local companies. In addition, Hong Kong's exchange attracts listings from China, whereas Singapore's exchange acquires them from firms across Southeast Asia (Indonesia, Malaysia, Thailand). Likewise, China's exchanges complement each other (Karrenman and Van der Knaap, 2009, 2012). The Hong Kong exchange captures China's large, global firms (Zhao et al., 2011). Shanghai's exchange draws firms from throughout China, from Shanghai, and from the vast industrial complex of the lower Yangtze Valley. The Shenzhen exchange attracts small- and medium-sized firms from China and especially from the Shenzhen region and elsewhere in Guangdong Province. Chinese government policies as set by its major regulatory agencies, China Securities Regulatory Commission and China Bank Regulatory Commission, heavily influence these distinctions among the exchanges. Commercial and investment banks, both domestic Chinese and foreign, also recognize this complementary character of the exchanges and organize their bank strategies to take that into account (Lai, 2012a).

3.5 CHINA'S FINANCIAL CENTERS

China's GDP of US$7.3 trillion in 2011 places it significantly beyond Japan's US$5.9 trillion, as the largest economy of Asia (World Bank, 2013). That change in status raises questions about which financial center of Asia will be the most important base for global commercial and investment banks. Japan's relative decline and stagnation of its economy will lead foreign global banks to downsize or, at most, to maintain their presence in Japan to service domestic clients. Japan's global banks will continue to use Tokyo (and Osaka) as their headquarters. The larger question is how China's financial centers fare as bases for global commercial and investment banks. While much commentary, including from Beijing officials, promotes Shanghai as China's international financial center, evidence about policies of the central government and decisions of global banks points to a more complex path for the country's leading financial centers of Beijing, Shanghai, and Hong Kong.

As the nation's capital, Beijing houses the headquarters of the major financial regulatory agencies which set policies for the banks and which monitor them. The pivotal institutions are the People's Bank of China (PBOC), the China Banking Regulatory Commission (CBRC), the State Administration of Foreign Exchange (SAFE), and the China Securities Regulatory Commission (CSRC). All of the major state-owned banks are headquartered in Beijing, along with the largest state-owned enterprises. Foreign investment banks such as Goldman Sachs, Morgan Stanley, and Credit Suisse locate their leading China offices in Beijing for lobbying these agencies, as well as other government entities that deal with various economic sectors. These same foreign offices also house top investment bankers who target the state-owned banks and enterprises as clients (Lai, 2012a,b; Zhao et al., 2011).

On the other hand, Shanghai, in accord with its role as the financial center of China since the 19th century, houses the branch offices of the regulatory agencies charged with implementing policies that directly impact the operational activities of banks in China. The foreign banks that focus on commercial banking (they also have investment banking), such as HSBC, Standard Chartered, Citibank, and Deutsche Bank, have their main China headquarters in Shanghai. This gives them access to the best information and knowledge about the Chinese economy and about private firms. Similarly, the large state-owned banks also have large Shanghai offices to target the same clients. Consequently, Shanghai comprises a cluster in which foreign and mainland China banks interact (Lai, 2012a,b; Zhao et al., 2011).

Hong Kong operates as the offshore financial center for China and as its true global center. Beijing officials have never deviated from their support of the city, and the government institutionalized this in Article 109 of the Basic Law of Hong Kong, which is its constitution. The article states that the local government is to "provide an appropriate economic and legal environment for the maintenance of the status of Hong Kong as an international financial center" (Basic Law, 1990). While the term, "international," is used, and that term is employed by Beijing officials to refer to Shanghai as China's international financial center, the policies of China's government leave no doubt that Hong Kong is its window to global capital (Jacob, 2011; Meyer, 2000; Shanghai Aims, 2012).

Foreign banks house their financial operations for China within that framework of Hong Kong as the offshore center for the country. Although commercial and investment bankers build their relationships within China, either from Shanghai or from Hong Kong, the actual implementation of financing such as currency transactions, mergers and acquisitions, loans, and private equity investments is completed in Hong Kong and subject to its legal system, which is considered highly favorable to business. The closed capital account of China—the renminbi is not fully convertible—is one reason Hong Kong serves as the offshore center for China. Nonetheless, the other factor is that the city is the Asia-Pacific headquarters of global banks and of innumerable non-financial firms. Thus corporate and investment bank financing for these firms' Asian operations is most effectively completed in Hong Kong (Lai, 2012a,b; Meyer, 2000, 2009).

3.6 CONCLUSION

The contemporary banking networks of Asia's financial centers possess deep roots in the 19th century. The insertion of European imperialism into Asia in that century established two major financial centers, Hong Kong and Singapore, both founded under British imperialism. Other colonial powers, including the Dutch involvement in Indonesia and the French in Indo-China, likewise impacted the economies, but their influence on financial centers paled next to the British. Both Hong Kong and Singapore became the meeting places of the two great social networks of capital in Asia, the Chinese and the foreign. These networks rested initially on the trading companies of Asia, and then they morphed into the banking networks.

The Hongkong and Shanghai Bank, which changed its name into modern-day HSBC, quickly became the greatest bank of Asia. Its expansion in the late 19th and early 20th centuries created a banking office structure and network across Asia which mirrored the organization of the Asian economy and its integration with Europe and North America. In many respects, that banking network remains a salient feature of Asia today. HSBC retains an organization with significant resemblance to the 19th century. The pivotal structure of Asian banking networks is that Hong Kong is the Asia-Pacific hub of the networks and Singapore is the Southeast Asia hub. They are the leading financial centers of Asia, and most of the major global commercial and investment banks use them as organizational hubs for their Asian business.

As Japan's global financial center, Tokyo remains, as it was in the late 19th century (as Yokohama), a large financial center for Japan. However, it has always been outside the nexus of the Chinese and foreign banking networks. Therefore, foreign banks, including Chinese, only use it as their Japan headquarters to access the large domestic business.

As the Japanese economy has experienced stagnation over the past several decades, Tokyo's status as a major financial center in Asia seems to have entered decline. This is indirectly indicated by the relative and absolute decline of its exchange.

The growth of India has elevated the importance of Mumbai as India's financial center, a status it has held since the 19th century and which the Hongkong and Shanghai Bank ratified when it chose Bombay for one of its major branches in 1869. Modern HSBC still houses its India headquarters in Mumbai, and other global commercial and investment banks use the city as their India headquarters. Likewise, most of the foremost Indian commercial and investment banks locate their global and domestic headquarters in Mumbai. Still, the smaller size of the Indian economy and low average income generate much less demand for banking services than arises in China; thus, Mumbai ranks below Shanghai as a financial center.

Most of the great commercial and investment banks either have their global headquarters in London or New York, or the banks place their major international banking division in these cities. Their broadly similar strategy, using Hong Kong as Asia-Pacific base and Singapore as Southeast Asia center, integrates Asian banking into global networks, especially with Europe and North America.

ACKNOWLEDGMENTS

Financial interviews were used in this chapter. They were completed from 2006 to 2008 in Hong Kong (45 interviews), Singapore (9), Beijing (6), Shanghai (13), and Mumbai (21), for a total of 94 interviews. Sectors included were corporate and investment banking, hedge funds, private equity, venture capital, fund management, and private banking. This research was supported by a grant to the author from the US National Science Foundation, No. 0451945.

REFERENCES

Allen, J., 2010. Powerful city networks: more than connections, less than domination and control. Urban Studies 47 (13), 2895–2911.

Basic Law, 1990. The Basic Law of the Hong Kong Special Administrative Region of the People's Republic of China. Hong Kong.

Beaverstock, J.V., 2007. World city networks "from below": international mobility and inter-city relations in the global investment banking industry. In: Taylor, P.J., Derudder, B., Saey, P., Witlox, F. (Eds.), Cities in Globalization: Practices, Policies and Theories. Routledge, London, pp. 52–71.

Bhattacharya, A.K., 2011. The feasibility of establishing an international financial centre in Shanghai. Journal of Asia-Pacific Business 12 (2), 123–140.

Cheng, L., 2003. Banking in Modern China: Entrepreneurs, Professional Managers, and the Development of Chinese Banks, 1897–1937. Cambridge University Press, Cambridge, UK.

Clark, G.L., 2002. London in the European financial services industry: locational advantage and product complementarities. Journal of Economic Geography 2 (4), 433–453.

Coclanis, P.A., 1993. Distant thunder: the creation of a world market in rice and the transformations it wrought. American Historical Review 98 (4), 1050–1078.

Fairbank, J.K., 1953. Trade and Diplomacy on the China Coast. Harvard University Press, Cambridge, MA.

Hao, Y., 1970. The Comprador in 19th-Century China: Bridge between East and West. Harvard University Press, Cambridge, MA.

HSBC, 2013. <www.hsbc.com> (accessed in August).

Jacob, R., 2011. Beijing expands support for Hong Kong. Ftcom, 17 August.

Jao, Y.C., 1997. Hong Kong as an International Financial Centre. City University of Hong Kong Press, Hong Kong.

Ji, Z., 2003. A History of Modern Shanghai Banking. M.E. Sharpe, Armonk, NY.

Jones, G., 1993. British Multinational Banking, 1830–1990. Oxford University Press, Oxford, UK.

Karreman, B., Van der Knaap, B., 2009. The financial centres of Shanghai and Hong Kong: competition or complementarity. Environment and Planning A 41 (3), 563–580.

Karreman, B., Van der Knaap, B., 2012. The geography of equity listing and financial centre competition in mainland China and Hong Kong. Journal of Economic Geography 12 (4), 899–922.

Kindleberger, C.P., 1974. The formation of financial centers: a study in comparative economic history, Princeton Studies in International Finance, vol. 36. Princeton University Press, Princeton, NJ.

King, F.H.H., 1987. The Hongkong Bank in late imperial China, 1864–1902: on an even keel, The History of the Hongkong and Shanghai Banking Corporation, no. 1. Cambridge University Press, Cambridge, UK.

King, F.H.H., 1988. The Hongkong Bank in the period of imperialism and war, 1895–1918, The History of the Hongkong and Shanghai Banking Corporation, no. 2. Cambridge University Press, Cambridge, UK.

Lai, K., 2012a. Differentiated markets: Shanghai, Beijing and Hong Kong in China's financial centre network. Urban Studies 49 (6), 1275–1296.

Lai, K., 2012b. Shanghai, Beijing, and Hong Kong within a financial centre network. In: Derudder, B., Hoyler, M., Taylor, P.J., Witlox, F. (Eds.), International Handbook of Globalization and World Cities. Edward Elgar, Cheltenham, UK, pp. 429–436.

Meyer, D.R., 1991a. Change in the world system of metropolises: the role of business intermediaries. Urban Geography 12 (5), 393–416.

Meyer, D.R., 1991b. The formation of a global financial center: London and its intermediaries. In: Kasaba, R. (Ed.), Cities in the World-System. Greenwood Press, NY, pp. 97–106.

Meyer, D.R., 2000. Hong Kong as a Global Metropolis. Cambridge University Press, Cambridge, UK.

Meyer, D.R., 2009. Hong Kong's transformation as a financial centre. In: Schenk, C.R. (Ed.), Hong Kong SAR's Monetary and Exchange Rate Challenges. Palgrave Macmillan, Houndmills, UK, pp. 161–188.

Pauly, L.W., 2011. Hong Kong's financial centre in a regional and global context. Hong Kong Journal 22 (July), 1–8.

Purcell, V., 1965. The Chinese in Southeast Asia. Oxford University Press, Oxford, UK.

Reed, H.C., 1981. The Preeminence of International Financial Centers. Praeger, New York.

Research Republic, 2008. The Future of Asian Financial Centres—Challenges and Opportunities for the City of London. Research Republic, Manchester, UK.

Sassen, S., 1999. Global financial centers. Foreign Affairs 78 (1), 75–87.

Shanghai Aims to be Global Financial Center, 2012. China Daily, 30 January.

Sheng, L.W., 2012. Singapore has edge as Asian metals trade hub. Business Times Singapore, Top Stories, 28 May.

Taylor, P.J., 2004. World City Network: A Global Urban Analysis. Routledge, London.

Thrift, N., 1987. The fixers: the urban geography of international commercial capital. In: Henderson, J., Castells, M. (Eds.), Global Restructuring and Territorial Development. Sage, London, pp. 203–223.

Wójcik, D., 2011. The Global Stock Market: Issuers, Investors, and Intermediaries in an Uneven World. Oxford University Press, Oxford, UK.

World Bank, 2013. World Development Indicators. Washington, DC.

Yiu, E., 2012. It's either boom or bust for Qianhai investors. South China Morning Post, Business, 14 August: 2.

Z/Yen, 2007–2013. Z/Yen Global Financial Centre Index. <www.zyen.com>.

Zhao, S.X.B., Li, Z., Smith, C.J., 2011. China's emerging financial centres: Shanghai, Beijing and Hong Kong. In: Gipouloux, F. (Ed.), Gateways to Globalisation: Asia's International Trading and Finance Centres. Edward Elgar, Cheltenham, UK, pp. 200–216.

CHAPTER 4

Dynamics of House Prices and Bank Lending in Korea

Heeho Kim[a] and Sae Woon Park[b]
[a]School of Economics and Trade, Kyungpook National University, Daegu, South Korea
[b]Department of Business Administration, Changwon National University, Changwon, South Korea

4.1 INTRODUCTION

The issues on the linkage between house prices and bank lending which are closely correlated in most countries have redrawn a special attention throughout the world since the outburst of the US subprime crisis in 2008. Financial crises resulting from excessive mortgage loans have been repeated occurrences worldwide. For example, there was a financial distress in Norway in 1987, and in Sweden and Finland in 1991. Since the crisis primarily stems from excessive bank lending with its far-reaching consequences for the world economy particularly in a housing sector, our attention is also focused on the widely discussed relationship between house prices and bank lending.

This chapter will give an account of the Korean case, where there was not such a house price retraction as seen in the US and other countries, but rather a price rise in certain areas even in an aftermath of the US subprime crisis. Kangnam area—the most expensive housing submarket in Seoul, Korea—has witnessed a sharp increase ever since especially from 2001 to early 2007. But in 2010–2011 they saw an unprecedented nose dive decline of the house price and transaction cliff in this region which is not so severe in other regions. This continuous downturn of price may lead to another financial crisis when it causes value loss to homeowners' assets and to mortgage loans of banks. In this respect, the government realizes its urgent responsibility and tries any means to stop the further devaluation of house price.

Clearly, this chapter builds on some literature on house prices and bank lending such as Hofmann (2003), Gerlach and Peng (2005), Oikarinen (2009), Birssimis and Vlassopoulos (2009), Park et al. (2010), Gimeno and Martinez-Carrascal (2010), and Kim et al. (2012). Although we use the same econometric methodology as theirs, there are some significant differences in this chapter. The previous studies on this topic are mostly based on the units of nations, but to the best of our knowledge, there have been few studies based on regional units within a nation or a metropolitan city so far. Though one can find a study of Oikarinen (2009) employing the units of cities, studies based on more specifically subdivided units like those of in-city regions are not existent except for Park et al. (2010) and Kim et al. (2012). In fact, the housing market is, by nature, a regional market rather than a national market where other asset or stock markets belong. Even if belonging to the same country or the same city, regional units of housing market may have substantial differences in household wealth, income levels, residential conditions, and government controls, which may affect house prices, and influence bank lending in turn. So it seems feasible that we may have aggregation bias in the estimation of house prices and bank lending if we examine their relationship on a national level or city basis regardless of the obvious regional differences affecting those variables.

However, there is a growing empirical literature on the regional differences of housing market depending on income, monetary policy, and the price elasticity of housing supply. For instance, Fratantoni and Schuh (2003) note that the impact of national monetary policy is different, depending on regions because monetary transmission depends on the extent and nature of regional heterogeneity of economy. Leung and Teo (2011) shows that differences in the price elasticity of housing supply can be related to stylized facts on regional differences in (1) house price levels, (2) house price volatilities, (3) monetary policy propagation mechanism, and (4) household asset portfolios by a multi-region, dynamic stochastic general equilibrium model. Allen et al. (2012) examine how house prices respond to changes in monetary policy in the nine census regions of the United States and note that regional house prices are positively correlated with money stock growth in some regions, and negatively correlated in others.

Following the insight, therefore, we first survey the growth rates of house prices for our subject areas to find out the potential number of unit categories we can possibly adopt in this chapter. The result in the study period shows that the yearly growth rates of real house prices on average are 2.87% nationwide, 5.80% in Kangnam area and 3.27% in Kangbuk area in Seoul, and 1.19% in other provincial cities. A figure of the growth rate of house prices in Kangbuk proves a little higher than that in nationwide, which means Kangbuk is a moderate and near equilibrium housing market. Thus, we determine to break down our subject areas into three categorical units (submarkets) accordingly, which comprise a premium housing submarket (Kangnam of Seoul) with a substantial price rise, a moderate market (Kangbuk of Seoul), and a stagnant market of most provincial cities (Pusan, Daegu, Incheon, Daejeon, and Ulsan), for which the growth rates of prices are far lower than nationwide.

This chapter is organized of six sections of which the remaining five are as follows. In Section 4.2, we review literature, and Section 4.3 contains the stylized facts and data in the Korean house markets. Then follow the long-run analysis in Section 4.4 and the short-run relationship in Section 4.5. Finally in Section 4.6 we put forward summary and conclusion on this research with a few suggestions added.

4.2 LITERATURE REVIEW

The relationship between bank lending and house prices has been widely tackled in literature. Among others, Hofmann (2003), Davis and Zhu (2004), Kim (2004), Oikarinen (2009), Birssimis and Vlassopoulos (2009), Gimeno and Martinez-Carrascal (2010), and La Paz and White (2012) argue that there is a significant bilateral dynamic interaction between bank lending and house prices. Aoki et al. (2004) and Iacoviello (2004, 2005) show that house prices may affect the availability of bank lending by a wealth effect. Gerlarch and Peng (2005) find a one-way causality from house prices to bank lending. These above studies suggest that house prices influence bank lending rather than the way around causality from bank lending to house prices.

On the other hand, the opposite unilateral causality can also be assumed by many studies. Bank lending may affect house prices with increased credit availability, possibly expanding the house demand against a contemporaneously fixed supply of housing stock. Kindleberger (1978) and Minsky (1982), for example, develop models that exhibit the role of credit in asset valuations particularly when it increases available liquidity. Koh et al. (2005) look into the Asian house price run-up and collapse in the 1990s and suggest that an excessive bank lending may attribute to the cause of a housing market bubble. They also argue that the financial institutions' under-pricing of the put option imbedded in non-recourse mortgage loans is a potential cause for the observed behavior of house prices. Liang and Cao (2007) find a unidirectional causality from bank lending to house prices in China. Ahearne et al. (2005) argue that a period of monetary appeasement policy is typically followed by an appreciation of house prices.

According to Park et al. (2010), house prices in Kangnam area in Seoul are not affected by bank lending in the short run, while positively affected in the long run. However, according to Kim et al. (2012), house prices in Kangnam area are not significantly affected by bank lending in the short run, while negatively affected in the long run. The reason they have different results of the analysis on the same regions may be because the two studies have different study periods—one is from 1999 to 2006 and the other is from 1999 to 2009—and because this kind of analysis is very susceptible to the study period. So it is our perception that these previous studies may not fully reflect the attributes and the long term influences of bank lending on house prices. Having the limitation in mind, we elongate the literature on the linkage between bank lending and house prices with an extended period (1999–2011) and expect to investigate more clearly the relationship between these two factors.

As seen in any other market in a free economic system, the price in housing market is also subject to a fundamental economic principle—demand and supply of houses. Typically, the demand for houses can be modeled as a function of household income, mortgage interest rates, availability of credit, and other demographic factors, while the supply of houses is expressed as a function of costs of land, construction cost, and new construction units.

4.3 APARTMENT HOUSE PRICES AND BANK LENDING: STYLIZED FACTS IN REGIONAL SUBMARKETS OF HOUSE IN KOREA

Seoul, the capital city of Korea, is divided into two areas—Kangnam (the southern part of the river) and Kangbuk (its northern part)—by the Han River running through the middle of the city. Although in the same metropolitan city (Seoul), Kangbuk is the older part showing a moderate changing behavior of house price while Kangnam area is relatively a brand new region consisting of 11 districts characterized by its well-living conditions such as decent housing interior, amenities, and favorable educational circumstances, in particular, thus rendering itself the most expensive housing area in Korea.

Of all housing types, apartment houses are considered since they are data affluent as well as one of the most popular housing types in Korea. We employ the apartment house price indexes (from January 1999 to December 2011) from the data stream of Kookmin Bank, authorized by the Korean Government. They are based not on actual transaction prices but on a survey of local real estate brokers on a regular basis. Figures 4.1 and 4.2 show the apartment house price indexes in nominal and real terms, respectively. The indexes are set to 100 in the index of January 1999, then, their natural log is taken to use for the graphs.

As in Figures 4.1 and 4.2, Kangnam area as a premium market has experienced the most dramatic appreciation of house price in 1999–2007. After this period, though, the price in this region declined more sharply than in other regions.

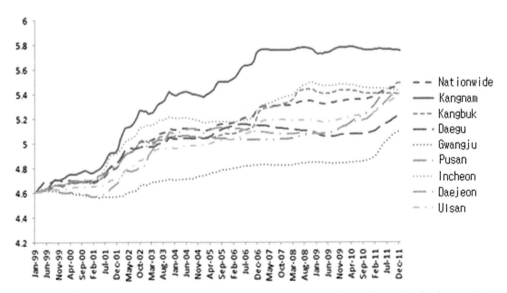

Figure 4.1 Nominal apartment house prices in Kangnam and Kangbuk of Seoul and other regional submarkets. All time series data are set to 100 in 1999:1. Their log values are shown on the graph.

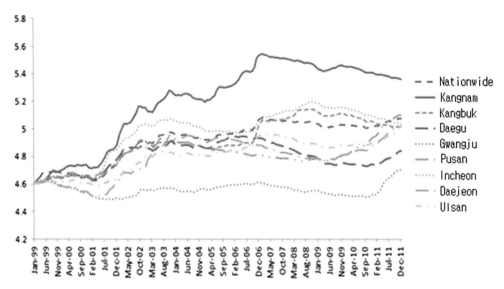

Figure 4.2 Real apartment house prices in Kangnam and Kangbuk of Seoul and other regional sub-markets. All time series data are set to 100 in 1999:1. Their log values are shown on the graph.

It was not until 1999 that the mortgage markets began to prosper in Korea.[1] Prior to the Asian financial crisis (1997), the house financing system had been underdeveloped partly because the government policies on bank lending were in favor of industrial development by concentrating the scarce resource of capital on the industry side, thus sacrificing the housing sector. After a decade of rapid economic growth in Korea, though, commercial banks have continued to emerge as the major mortgage providers. Consumer credits offered by these major commercial banks, however, were still very limited until after the Asian financial crisis, when the consumer credits accounted for only 26.4% of overall loan portfolios of the banks while the remaining 73.6% were loans to corporations. Yet, the share of the consumer credits has increased to 30.5% in 1999, 34.5% in 2000, 43.8% in 2001, and all the way to 49.5% in 2006 decreasing slightly to 45.2% in 2007, 43.7% in 2010, and 42.9% in 2011 implying that the importance of mortgage loans grew very fast in the bank's consumer loan portfolios. According to a survey by the Bank of Korea, 67.2% of consumer loans were collateralized by houses in 2011. Main reasons for the shift from the corporate sector to the households are that the corporations had to cut the demand for funds substantially to improve their previously heavily leveraged financial structure and that banks became more reluctant to

---

[1] For a brief review of the history of the Korean mortgage market, see Kim (2004) and Zhu (2006).

make loans to corporations since they suffered heavy losses from the corporate loan portfolio during the Asian financial crisis. The data are used from the Statistical Survey of the Bank of Korea.

As bank lending has become a significant factor for financing house purchases since 1999 as evidenced above, we use time series of bank lending from 1999 accordingly to investigate the dynamic of house prices and bank lending in Korea. To certify empirically that there is a real structural change in 1999, we conduct the Chow's breakpoint test for apartment house prices in Kangnam area as a function of bank lending and GDP. As a result, we find that there was a structural break around December 1998 at the 5% significance level, which is consistent with the notion that the structural relationship between bank lending and apartment house prices may have changed since 1999.

The distinctive features of the Korean mortgage market can be depicted as follows. The loan to value (LTV) in the Korean mortgage market is relatively low compared with that LTV in other countries. Furthermore, there is no put option imbedded in mortgage loans as is common in the US and other European countries. The effect of mortgage loans on house prices may vary depending on the level of LTV and the existence of put option. The feasibility of such low LTV in Korea is, for the most part, due to an informal housing financing scheme known as Chonsei. Under a Chonsei arrangement system, the tenant gives the landlord a lump-sum deposit (more than 50% of the house value) in lieu of monthly rental payments. The landlord is expected to generate a stream of income from this deposit, for instance, to buy a second house. The deposit is fully refunded at the end of the lease.

To testify our initial assumption that Kangnam area is a differentiated premium housing market, we also examined and compared the house prices under the study period, though it was not possible to get the exact standards for comparison of the house prices, namely, the height, age, location, geographic and meteorological conditions, and so on except for the size. As in Table 4.1, the average apartment house price in Kangnam area is $561,000, while $356,000 in Kangbuk, and $158,000 in other provincial cities in 2011. This suggests the house price in Kangnam area is still higher than or presumably the

Table 4.1 Apartment House Prices and its Annual Growth Rate (Unit: Thousand US Dollars)

	Nationwide	Kangnam	Kangbuk	Other Provincial Cities***
Mean*	269	561	356	158
Median*	217	586	328	148
Growth rate**	2.87%	5.80%	3.27%	1.19%***

Source: Kookmin bank.
*Apartment price at the end of 2011. **Average growth rate from 1999 to 2011. ***Average of Pusan, Daegu, Incheon, Daejeon, and Ulsan.

highest in Korea.[2] The reasons for this higher price in Kangnam house market can be put as high quality of schools, amenities, and environmental locations including an easy access to public transportation along with legal restrictions on supply and use of land and construction. For instance, the green belt (a legal restriction on the use of land to maintain the land area green colored in grasses and forests) in Seoul occupies 50% of its developable land. At the same time, controlling the growth in the Capital Region, which amounts to 11% of the nation's territory and is home to 46% of its population, remains a top priority of governmental control policy (Xiao, 2010; Xiao and Park, 2010)

Data of bank lending are obtained from the data stream of the Bank of Korea, and then measure those data of the bank lending outstanding in a given market, rather than using the total mortgage loans underwritten. The quarterly data of GDP is also used as an explanatory variable for the house prices in our analysis, which are converted into monthly data using linear interpolation. The interest rates used in this study is the composite lending rate published by the Bank of Korea. The real term instead the nominal term is used in this chapter by adjusting to the consumer price index (CPI) over the past 12 months released by Korea National Statistical Office. Data of the regional house construction permit units and the construction cost index are used to examine the effects of the supply side of houses. Data of the regional house construction permit units are from Korea Ministry of Land, Infrastructure and Transport. The construction cost index is obtained from the Construction Economy Research Institute of Korea. However, due to the lack of regionally disaggregated data on these variables, we use the house construction permit units of Seoul instead of those of Kangnam and Kangbuk areas separately. GDP and the construction cost index are also on the national basis rather than regional ones.

In Table 4.2, the descriptive statistics of all variables in each region are reported. The variables are real apartment house prices, real bank lending, and house construction permit units as well as real GDP, real interest rates, and real construction costs. Logarithms are taken in all variables except for real interest rates. They are normalized to 100 in January, 1999 before the log transformation. The mortgage loan data are set to 100 in October, 2003.

4.4 LONG-RUN ANALYSIS

In this section we turn to the econometric works to investigate the dynamics of the house prices in Korea. First of all, to examine the stationarity of time-series data, we apply the Phillip-Perron (Phillips and Perron, 1988) unit root test. The results are shown in Table 4.3. The inferred order of integration is found in the last column. The inferred order of integration of all variables is 1 except for only a variable of construction permit.

Since the data exhibits some weak seasonality, we test the seasonal unit root prior to a causality analysis between the house prices and bank lending. If the series is seasonally

---

[2] Park et al. (2010) state that the apartment price in Kangnam area is incomparably high. Xiao and Park (2010) find that the apartment price in Seoul is relatively high.

Table 4.2 Descriptive Statistics (1999:1–2011:12)

Variable	OBS	Mean	Median	Max	Min	SD
Panel A. Nationwide						
Real apartment price	156	4.91	4.96	5.08	4.61	0.15
Real bank lending	156	5.45	5.49	5.89	4.61	0.36
Construction permit	156	4.68	4.67	6.01	3.10	0.34
Panel B. Kangnam						
Real apartment price	156	5.20	5.29	5.54	4.60	0.29
Real bank lending	156	5.41	5.42	5.82	4.60	0.34
Construction permit	156	4.25	4.26	6.55	2.97	0.68
Panel C. Kangbuk						
Real apartment price	156	4.91	4.90	5.14	4.60	0.17
Real bank lending	156	5.41	5.42	5.82	4.60	0.34
Construction permit	156	4.25	4.26	6.55	2.97	0.68
Panel D. Daegu						
Real apartment price	156	4.81	4.82	4.95	4.61	0.09
Real bank lending	156	5.20	5.26	5.51	4.60	0.28
Construction permit	156	4.30	4.48	6.34	0.47	0.95
Panel E. Pusan						
Real apartment price	156	4.81	4.81	5.10	4.61	0.11
Real bank lending	156	5.44	5.52	5.86	4.61	0.36
Construction permit	156	4.43	4.51	6.22	0.18	0.95
Panel F. Incheon						
Real apartment price	156	4.98	5.03	5.20	4.61	0.18
Real bank lending	156	5.65	5.70	6.23	4.61	0.46
Construction permit	156	5.07	5.09	6.77	1.96	0.83
Panel G. Daejeon						
Real apartment price	156	4.79	4.83	5.02	4.51	0.14
Real bank lending	156	5.44	5.60	5.79	4.61	0.35
Construction permit	156	5.49	5.49	7.76	2.45	0.99
Panel H. Ulsan						
Real apartment price	156	4.80	4.83	5.01	4.59	0.12
Real bank lending	156	5.62	5.63	6.18	4.60	0.47
Construction permit	156	5.15	5.15	6.99	−0.48	1.08
Panel I. for all regions						
Real interest rates (%)	156	3.81	3.25	9.27	0.86	2.04
Real construction cost index	156	4.67	4.66	4.81	4.54	0.08
Real GDP	156	4.65	4.65	4.69	4.60	0.03
M2	156	5.06	5.02	5.58	4.61	0.31

All variables except the real interest rates are transformed by taking their natural logarithms and they have been normalized to 100 in 1999:1 prior to the log-transformation. The bank lending and the construction permit for Seoul are used instead of those for Kangnam and Kangbuk in Seoul.

Table 4.3 ADF Unit Root Test Results (1999:1–2011:12)

Variable	Levels		First Difference		Inferred Order of Integration
Panel A. Nationwide					
Real apartment price	−1.28	(T)	−6.27	(C)**	I(1)
Real bank lending	−2.32	(T)	−4.03	(C)**	I(1)
Construction permit	−8.04	(C)**			I(0)
Panel B. Kangnam					
Real apartment price	−0.79	(T)	−5.75	(C)**	I(1)
Real bank lending	−2.07	(T)	−4.49	(C)**	I(1)
Construction permit	−5.88	(C)**			I(0)
Panel C. Kangbuk					
Real apartment price	−0.89	(T)	−6.38	(C)**	I(1)
Real bank lending	−2.07	(T)	−4.49	(C)**	I(1)
Construction permit	−5.88	(C)**			I(0)
Panel D. Daegu					
Real apartment price	−1.45	(T)	−6.26	(C)**	I(1)
Real bank lending	−0.45	(T)	−4.60	(C)**	I(1)
Construction permit	−5.06	(C)**			I(0)
Panel E. Pusan					
Real apartment price	−1.58	(T)	−3.08	(C)**	I(1)
Real bank lending	−1.66	(T)	−3.98	(C)**	I(1)
Construction permit	−6.13	(C)**			I(0)
Panel F. Incheon					
Real apartment price	−0.96	(T)	−5.12	(C)**	I(1)
Real bank lending	−2.33	(T)	−3.74	(C)**	I(1)
Construction permit	−2.98	(C)**			I(0)
Panel G. Daejeon					
Real apartment price	−1.30	(T)	−6.28	(C)**	I(1)
Real bank lending	−1.32	(T)	−10.62	(C)**	I(1)
Construction permit	−8.69	(C)**			I(0)
Panel H. Ulsan					
Real apartment price	−1.33	(T)	−10.12	(C)**	I(1)
Real bank lending	−1.21	(T)	−5.62	(C)**	I(1)
Construction permit	−10.72	(C)**			I(0)
Real interest rate	−2.48	(C)	−5.22	(C)**	I(1)
Real construction cost index	−3.12	(T)	−5.55	(C)**	I(1)

(Continued)

Table 4.3 Continued

Variable	Levels		First Difference		Inferred Order of Integration
Real GDP	−2.03	(C)	−3.91	(C)*	I(1)v
M2	−2.20	(T)	−5.58	(C)**	I(1)

*Significance at the 5% level. **Significance at the 1% level.
ADF test statistics are shown in the table where the null hypothesis: The series is not stationary. T indicates the test regression includes a time trend and a constant and C indicates the test regression includes only a constant. The sample period for these series typically starts from January 1999 and ends in December 2011. The lag length is chosen using the Newey–West (1992) bandwidth selection method for kernel based estimators.

integrated, it will require the application of a higher order of seasonal differencing, rather than the use of seasonal dummy variable in a VAR model for tackling the seasonal effect. Testing for seasonal unit root in monthly time series is given in Franses (1991) such as:

$$\varphi^*(L)\, y_{8,t} = \pi_1 y_{1,t-1} + \pi_2 y_{2,t-1} + \pi_3 y_{3,t-2} + \pi_4 y_{3,t-1} + \pi_5 y_{4,t-2} + \pi_6 y_{4,t-1}$$
$$+ \pi_7 y_{5,t-2} + \pi_8 y_{5,t-1} + \pi_9 y_{6,t-2} + \pi_{10} y_{6,t-1} + \pi_{11} y_{7,t-2}$$
$$+ \pi_{12} y_{7,t-1} + \mu_t + \epsilon_t$$

where $\varphi^*(L)$ is some polynomial function of L, lag operator, for which the usual assumption applies, μ_t is the deterministic component which might include a constant, seasonal dummy variables or a trend, and

$$y_{1,t} = (1 + L)(1 + L^2)(1 + L^4 + L^8)y_t$$
$$y_{2,t} = -(1 - L)(1 + L^2)(1 + L^4 + L^8)y_t$$
$$y_{3,t} = -(1 - L^2)(1 + L^4 + L^8)y_t$$
$$y_{4,t} = -(1 - L^4)(1 - \sqrt{3}L + L^2)(1 + L^2 + L^4)y_t$$
$$y_{5,t} = -(1 - L^4)(1 + \sqrt{3}L + L^2)(1 + L^2 + L^4)y_t$$
$$y_{6,t} = -(1 - L^4)(1 - L^2 + L^4)(1 - L + L^2)y_t$$
$$y_{7,t} = -(1 - L^4)(1 - L^2 + L^4)(1 + L + L^2)y_t$$
$$y_{8,t} = (1 - L^{12})y_t$$

Applying the ordinary least squares (OLS) to the above equation gives estimates of π_i. In case there are seasonal unit roots, the corresponding parameters (p_i) in the auxiliary regression are zero (Franses, 1991). If all parameters ($p_i, i = 1,\ldots,12$) are equal to zero, it is appropriate to apply $\Delta 12$ filter (seasonal differencing at lag 12) in the model. When $p_1 = 0$, and p_2 through p_{12} are not equal to zero, seasonality can be modeled with $\Delta 1$ filter (first differencing) and seasonal dummies (monthly dummies).

House prices are believed to be slightly seasonal changing- that is, prices are slightly higher or lower at certain times of the year probably as a result of changes in the weather or season. This seasonal variation of house prices has long been notices in countries such as the UK and New Zealand, where there are four distinct seasons. The results of seasonal unit roots tests as suggested by Franses (1991) are shown in Tables 4.4 and 4.5. The results indicate very strong evidence against seasonal integration at all seasonal frequencies in each data series. As a result the seasonal effect can be appropriately modeled by using seasonal dummy variables in the regression analysis for causality for this Korean data set.

Next, we analyze the long-run relationship between apartment house prices and bank lending for each region. The analysis of the long-run relationship between regional apartment house prices, regional bank lending, real GDP, and real interest rate is

Table 4.4 Seasonal Unit Test Results of Apartment Index

	Nationwide	Kangnam	Kangbuk	Daegu	Pusan	Incheon	Daejeon	Ulsan
t-Statistics								
π_1	−2.47	−1.04	−2.65	−2.97*	−2.88	−2.94*	−3.22*	−1.87
π_2	−2.90**	−2.91**	−4.20**	−2.82**	−2.26	−2.38	−1.44	−2.35
t-Statistics								
π_3	−1.82*	−2.49**	−1.61	−2.84**	−3.34**	−2.11**	−2.28**	−4.08**
π_4	3.08**	2.60**	2.04**	−0.58	−0.74	2.89**	−0.35*	0.15**
π_5	−2.84	−3.16*	−2.52	−1.94	−3.97**	−3.49**	−4.03**	−1.00
π_6	−2.75	−3.34*	−2.15	−2.98	−3.14*	−2.20	−4.33**	−1.80
π_7	−1.90**	−1.36**	−2.62**	−2.57**	−2.21**	−2.04**	−2.09**	−2.17**
π_8	0.01**	−0.39*	1.17**	0.22**	0.75**	0.29**	0.03**	0.15**
π_9	−4.06**	−3.53**	−3.23**	−5.61**	−3.40**	−4.53**	−2.49	−4.37**
π_{10}	−3.05	−3.64**	−1.23	−1.51	−2.68	−1.96	−1.23	−1.77
π_{11}	−3.18**	−3.26**	−2.69**	−3.19**	−2.38**	−3.00**	−2.82**	−2.91**
π_{12}	1.39**	1.73**	1.26**	0.41**	−0.32*	0.70**	0.08**	−0.28*
F-statistics								
π_3, π_4	6.82**	6.96**	3.55	4.26	5.99**	6.86**	2.68	8.35**
π_5, π_6	4.25	5.77*	3.18	5.40*	7.91**	6.82**	9.65**	2.35
π_7, π_8	6.8**	6.18**	5.35*	10.5**	4.66	6.02**	8.07**	8.25**
π_9, π_{10}	9.39**	9.03**	5.28*	16.5**	6.63**	10.2**	3.12	9.60**
π_{11}, π_{12}	5.09*	5.38*	3.64	5.91**	4.46	4.86	5.15*	6.37**
$\pi_3,\ldots,\pi_{12}$	8.91**	9.26**	5.28**	14.30**	8.23**	9.25**	9.73**	8.78**

*Significance at the 10% level. **Significance at the 5% level.
Critical values are given in Franses (1991) exhibit 3.

Table 4.5 Seasonal Unit Test Results of Bank Loan

	Nationwide	Kangnam	Kangbuk	Daegu	Pusan	Incheon	Daejeon	Ulsan
t-Statistics								
π_1	−1.93	−1.73	−1.53	−2.77	−2.32	−3.84**	−1.74	−1.93
π_2	−1.86	−1.72	−2.43*	−2.50*	−2.79**	−3.46**	−2.84**	−1.86
t-Statistics								
π_3	−4.17**	−3.44**	−1.86*	−2.86**	−3.80**	−1.19	−2.70**	−4.17**
π_4	−0.71	−0.57	−3.30*	−4.46**	−1.70	−4.57**	−2.13	−0.71
π_5	−2.21	−2.73	−3.38**	−3.18*	−2.30	−3.27*	−2.84	−2.21
π_6	−3.29*	−3.59**	−3.69**	−2.81	−3.86**	−3.54**	−3.42**	−3.29*
π_7	−3.42**	−3.07**	−0.70**	−2.22**	−2.97**	−2.03**	−2.49**	−3.42**
π_8	1.43**	0.93**	−0.75	−0.27*	1.53**	−0.54	0.54**	1.43**
π_9	−1.90	−1.51	−3.40**	−6.47**	−3.73**	−3.62**	−2.42	−1.90
π_{10}	−2.29	−1.89	−2.07	−4.83**	−2.38	−4.35**	−3.66**	−2.29
π_{11}	−2.74**	−2.88**	−0.40	−2.44**	−1.12**	0.12	−1.10**	−2.74**
π_{12}	−0.83	−1.09	−2.99	0.12**	−2.33	−3.60**	−3.53**	−0.83
F-statistics								
π_3, π_4	9.18**	6.17**	7.65**	15.00**	9.19**	11.20**	6.09**	9.18**
π_5, π_6	6.42**	6.76**	6.93**	5.09*	11.1**	6.40**	5.87**	6.42**
π_7, π_8	9.08**	9.32**	4.09	11.3**	6.07**	13.20**	7.97**	9.08**
π_9, π_{10}	3.05	2.03	5.97**	23.6**	7.26**	11.1**	7.05**	3.05
π_{11}, π_{12}	7.37**	9.12**	7.57**	3.76	6.78**	9.20**	12.10**	7.37**
$\pi_3,\ldots,\pi_{12}$	9.32**	9.89**	9.60**	15.70**	11.70**	16.90**	12.80**	9.32**

*Significance at the 10% level. **Significance at the 5% level.
Critical values are given in Franses (1991) exhibit 3.

based on the multivariable approach to cointegration tests proposed by Johansen (1988, 1991, 1995). The cointegrating VAR model is given by:

$$x_t = \beta_1 x_{t-1} + \cdots + \beta_k x_{t-k} + \mu + \delta \tau_t + \varepsilon_t \tag{4.1}$$

where x is a vector of endogenous variables comprising real apartment prices, real bank lending, real interest rate, and real GDP. μ is a vector of constants, τ is a deterministic time trend, and ε is a vector of white noise error terms. We use this specification as the sequential testing procedure. Akaike information criterion (AIC), Schwarz information criterion (SIC) and Hannan-Quinn information criterion (HQ) are used for model selection such as determining the lag length of VAR.

To proceed, the VAR model can be reformulated in a vector error correction form:

$$\Delta x_t = C_1 \Delta x_{t-1} + \cdots + C_{k-1} \Delta x_{t-k+1} + C_0 x_{t-1} + \mu + \varepsilon_t \tag{4.2}$$

The Johansen methodology is based on the maximum likelihood estimation and aims at testing the rank of the matrix C_0, which indicates the number of the long-run relationships between the endogenous variables in the system. The estimation results in Table 4.6 shows that the trace statistics points toward the existence of one or two cointegration relationship except Daegu area in Korea. Thus, the case of Daegu shall be dropped out of the sample for the estimation of the house prices in this study afterward. After performing the unrestricted cointegration test (Model 1), evidence finds that the signs of coefficients of interest rate do not come out as expected for some regions. Thus, in Model 2 a zero coefficient on interest rate is imposed as a restriction of estimation, and the bank lending is a variable capturing the impact of financing costs on apartment house prices. The estimation results of Model 1 and Model 2 show that the speed of adjustment parameter of GDP of some regions is near zero, implying that GDP is weakly exogenous. So in Model 3 a restricted cointegration test is conducted again this time imposing zero on α value of GDP.

We choose to explain the relationships between the house prices and bank lending in the restricted model (Model 3) with weakly exogenous GDP. As seen in Table 4.7, an unrestricted model has less significant coefficients than the restricted models. Moreover, we note that the restricted model with weakly exogenous GDP is better than that without exogenous variables as the former has more significant variables. So, we choose to explain the relationships with this model.

In the fifth column of Table 4.7, we show the cointegration results of the apartment house prices, bank lending, and GDP. The coefficient on real bank lending for nationwide is 3.85 and significant at traditional significance level, implying that real apartment house prices and bank lending grow negatively over time nationwide. However, the coefficient in Kangnam area as a premium market of Seoul is −1.26 which means that real apartment price and bank lending grow proportionately in Kangnam area. It implies that about 1% increase in bank lending is associated with 1.26% increase in the apartment house prices of Kangnam area in the long run.

The apartment house prices and bank lending in the provincial regions other than Kangnam also tend to grow proportionately except Incheon area. The coefficients of bank lending on the house prices are statistically significant at a traditional level, and −0.71, −0.89, −2.50, and −0.01 for Kangbuk of Seoul, Pusan, Daejeon, and Ulsan, respectively. Also the estimation results of the real income effects in Table 4.7 indicate that the effects of real income on the house prices are statistically insignificant across the country, including Kangnam and other provincial markets only except Ulsan area where a huge industrial complex is located. This seems to reflect the fact that while GDP has steadily increased, the apartment house prices in these regions have remained relatively stagnant. The real income tends to positively influence the house prices only in Ulsan area.

Table 4.6 Johansen Cointegration Tests (1999:1–2011:12)

Panel A. Nationwide

		Trace test		
Real apartment price	Null hypothesis	$r=0$	$r \le 1$	$r \le 2$
Real bank lending	Trace statistics	45.30	17.75	7.45
Real GDP	p-Value	0.09*	0.58	0.53
Real interest rate				

Panel B. Kangnam

		Trace test		
Real apartment price	Null hypothesis	$r=0$	$r \le 1$	$r \le 2$
Real bank lending	Trace statistics	49.28	25.22	7.71
Real GDP	p-Value	0.04**	0.15	0.49
Real interest rate				

Panel C. Kangbuk

		Trace test		
Real apartment price	Null hypothesis	$r=0$	$r \le 1$	$r \le 2$
Real bank lending	Trace statistics	53.29	26.37	9.05
Real GDP	p-Value	0.01**	0.12	0.36
Real interest rate				

Panel D. Daegu

		Trace test		
Real apartment price	Null hypothesis	$r=0$	$r \le 1$	$r \le 2$
Real bank lending	Trace statistics	39.10	19.82	6.50
Real GDP	p-Value	0.26	0.43	0.64
Real interest rate				

Panel E. Pusan

		Trace test		
Real apartment price	Null hypothesis	$r=0$	$r \le 1$	$r \le 2$
Real bank lending	Trace statistics	74.23**	31.42**	11.82
Real GDP	p-Value	0.00	0.03	0.17
Real interest rate				

Panel F. Incheon

		Trace test		
Real apartment price	Null hypothesis	$r=0$	$r \le 1$	$r \le 2$
Real bank lending	Trace statistics	60.79**	23.25	10.09
Real GDP	p-Value	0.00	0.23	0.27
Real interest rate				

Panel G. Daejeon

		Trace test		
Real apartment price	Null hypothesis	$r=0$	$r \le 1$	$r \le 2$
Real bank lending	Trace statistics	59.18**	25.11	8.56
Real GDP	p-Value	0.00	0.16	0.41
Real interest rate				

Panel H. Ulsan

		Trace test		
Real apartment price	Null hypothesis	$r=0$	$r \le 1$	$r \le 2$
Real bank lending	Trace statistics	52.83**	19.76	6.82
Real GDP	p-Value	0.02	0.44	0.60
Real interest rate				

*Significance at 10% level.**Significance at 5% level.

Table 4.7 Unrestricted and Restricted Cointegration Tests (1999:1–2011:12)

	Model 1 Unrestricted		Model 2 Restricted		Model 3 Weak Exogenous	
	β	α	β	α	β	α
Panel A. Nationwide						
Real apartment price	1	−0.0270*	1	−0.0007	1	−0.0012*
Real bank lending	−0.20**	0.0252**	3.52**	−0.0037**	3.85**	−0.0035**
Real GDP	−2.43**	−0.0048*	−33.18**	0.0002	−32.38*	0
Real interest rate	0.04**	−0.6969**	0	0.0259	0	0.0258
Panel B. Kangnam						
Real apartment price	1	−0.0016	1	0.0019**	1	0.0146**
Real bank lending	−1.06	0.0057**	−1.32**	0.0147**	−1.26**	0.0153**
Real GDP	9.65	−0.0005*	−1.41	−0.0007	−2.57	0
Real interest rate	0.30**	−0.0700**	0	−0.0706	0	−0.0839
Panel C. Kangbuk						
Real apartment price	1	0.0032	1	0.0073	1	0.0214**
Real bank lending	−0.60**	0.0565**	−0.68**	0.0760	−0.71**	0.0833**
Real GDP	1.18	−0.0051**	1.04	−0.0051**	1.05	0
Real interest rate	0.02**	−0.2867	0	0.0519	0	−0.0105
Panel D. Pusan						
Real apartment price	1	0.0001	1	0.0001	1	−0.0038*
Real bank lending	1.05**	−0.0207**	0.86**	−0.0138**	−0.89**	−0.0145**
Real GDP	−9.68**	0.0026**	−7.83**	0.0021**	−5.34	0
Real interest rate	0.05**	−0.1265	0	0.0573	0	0.0610
Panel E. Incheon						
Real apartment price	1	0.0002	1	−0.0021	1	−0.0014
Real bank lending	0.00	0.0090**	0.45	−0.0071**	0.72	−0.0058**
Real GDP	−6.86	−0.0009	3.07	−0.0002	1.60	0
Real interest rate	0.15**	−0.1963	0	0.0449	0	0.0347
Panel F. Daejeon						
Real apartment price	1	−0.0005	1	−0.0024	1	−0.0020
Real bank lending	6.83**	−0.0099**	−2.82**	0.0107**	−2.50**	0.0121**
Real GDP	−48.08**	−0.0000	17.11	−0.0002	12.97	0
Real interest rate	0.47**	−0.0170	0	−0.0245	0	−0.0260
Panel G. Ulsan						
Real apartment price	1	−0.5185*	1	−0.4778	1	−0.0143*
Real bank lending	−0.01**	1.5232**	−0.00**	1.9783**	−0.01**	2.1707**
Real GDP	−4.62**	−0.1071*	−4.65**	−0.0976	−4.66**	0
Real interest rate	0.00	−6.3242	0	−5.2341	0	−5.7893

*Significance at the 5% level. **Significance at the 1% level.
Null hypothesis is that the number of cointegration vector is *r*. Standard errors for α are in parenthesis.

Overall, these results suggest the long-run relationship between apartment house prices and bank lending goes in the same direction during the sample period, but the movement goes insignificantly between apartment prices and real income. This finding is the same as the evidence from the existing literature on the long-run relationship between house price movements and bank lending in most of the OECD economies, as well as in Asian countries, particularly, in Hong Kong.[3] Moreover, our result is quite opposite to Park et al. (2010) and Kim et al. (2012) in the previous study on similar regions in Korea.

4.5 SHORT-RUN RELATIONSHIP

In this section, we examine the short-term dynamic relationships between real apartment house prices, bank lending, GDP, and interest rate. The above discussed cointegration test results imply that the relationship between the house prices and other explanatory variables has an error correction term—represented by the once-lagged cointegrating vector—which should enter the equation for the determination of real apartment house prices. We consider other explanatory variables as well that do not enter the cointegration relationship, but may contribute to the short-term movements in bank lending and apartment house prices. These additional variables may include changes in house construction permit unit and real construction cost index in the supply side of houses. We use the Newey–West procedures (Newey and West, 1987) to control for the heteroskedasticity and/or the autocorrelation of error terms which may frequently occur in an ordinary least square (OLS) regression. We follow a general-to-specific approach in which insignificant variables are removed step by step to obtain parsimonious equations for the change in real apartment house prices.

We estimate the apartment house price equation, where a change in real apartment house price is used as a dependent variable. The explanatory variables are four lags of the dependent variable, the current and four lags of the change in real bank lending, the change in real GDP, the change in real interest rate, the change in house construction permit unit, the change in real house construction cost index, and one lag of the cointegrating vector as an error correction term. Changes in house construction permit unit and changes in house construction cost index are intended to capture the supply-side influence on the apartment house prices. As before in the long-run analysis, the seasonal dummy is included in the estimation in order to consider the seasonality of the real house prices:

---

[3] See Gerlach and Peng (2005).

$$\Delta Y_t = \lambda_2 + \sum_{i=1}^{p} a_{2,i} \Delta X_{t-i} + \sum_{j=1}^{p} b_{2,j} \Delta Y_{t-j} + \sum_{l=1}^{p} c_{2,l} \Delta Z_{t-l} + \sum_{m=1}^{11} d_{2,m} \theta_m$$
$$+ \emptyset_2 EC_{2,t-1} + \mu_{2,t}$$

where $EC_{2,t-1} = (Y - \delta X)_{t-1}$, ΔY_t: apartment house price, ΔX_t: bank lending, ΔZ_{t-1}: other explanatory variables vector (GDP, interest rate, construction permit, construction cost), θ_m: seasonal dummy, EC: error correction cointegration vector.

Table 4.8 shows the estimation results of the final apartment house price equations obtained for nationwide as well as for Kangnam and Kangbuk in Seoul, and four other regional cities. The coefficient of real bank lending for nationwide in the second column of Table 4.8 is 0.13 and significant at traditional significance level, implying that there is a positive relationship between real apartment house prices and bank lending nationwide. This result is very in contrast to the negative long-run relationship between the real house prices and bank lending nationwide in Korea. However, the coefficient of bank lending in Kangnam area as a premium market is statistically significant, and its combined effect is −0.16 which means that real apartment price and bank lending grow inversely as shown in the third column of Table 4.8. This implies that in a premium market such as Kangnam area, a 1% increase in bank lending may bring about −0.16% fall in the apartment house prices. This result is also in a sharp contrast to the positive long-run relationship between the two variables in Kangnam area.

As expected, real income proves to have a positive influence on the apartment house prices in Kangnam area, while the interest rate does not seem to have a significant short-term influence on apartment house price in that area. The apartment house prices in Kangnam area are influenced heavily by the previous period apartment house prices. The coefficient of the lag one of the apartment house prices is 0.55 and that of the lag two is −0.16. The combined effect of the previous 3 months apartment house prices is 0.39, indicating that a 1% increase in the apartment house price in the previous 3 months leads to an increase of 0.39% in current month.

Columns 4 through 8 in Table 4.8 show the estimation results of the apartment house price equations for Kangbuk of Seoul and the four other provincial cities. The apartment house prices and bank lending in two regions, Kangbuk and Incheon, tend to grow proportionately over time. The combined coefficients of bank lending on the house prices are statistically significant at a traditional significance level and its magnitude are 0.01 and 0.23 for Kangbuk and Incheon, respectively. This indicates that there are apartment house price's positive responses of 0.01% and 0.23% for a 1% change in the bank lending in Kangbuk and Incheon, respectively, although these coefficients of the bank lending are statistically insignificant in the other regional cities. The effects of real income on the house prices are statistically significant and positive over periods across the country,

Table 4.8 The Apartment House Price Equations; Nationwide and Kangnam and Kangbuk in Seoul and Four Provincial Cities (1999:1–2011:12)

	Nationwide	Kangnam	Kangbuk	Pusan	Incheon	Daejeon	Ulsan
Bank lending (t)	0.25**		0.17**				
Bank lending ($t-1$)		−0.16**					
Bank lending ($t-2$)	−0.12**		−0.16**				
Bank lending ($t-3$)					0.23**		
GDP (t)	2.39**	3.51**	2.04**	3.00**	2.43**	1.51**	4.76**
GDP ($t-1$)				−2.80**			−2.48**
GDP ($t-2$)					−0.90*		
GDP ($t-3$)	−0.62				−1.16**		
Apartment price ($t-1$)	0.39**	0.55**	0.58**	0.83**	0.59**	0.44**	0.53**
Apartment price ($t-2$)		−0.16*					
Apartment price ($t-3$)						0.21**	
Construction permit ($t-4$)		0.00*					
Construction cost index (t)						0.32**	
Construction cost index ($t-4$)						−0.18*	
Interest rates (t)						−0.00**	
Cointegration vector ($t-1$)		0.02**			0.01**		
Adjusted R-squared	0.75	0.60	0.66	0.79	0.77	0.52	0.99

*Significance at the 5% level. **Significance at the 1% level.
The dependent variable is the change in the real apartment price in each region. The explanatory variables are four lags of the dependent variable, the current and four lags of the change in the real bank lending, the change in the real GDP, the change in the real interest rate, the change in the house construction permit unit, the change in the real house construction cost index, and one lag of the cointegrating vector. Following the general-to-specific approach, the parsimonious models are obtained by removing insignificant variables. T-statistics are shown in parentheses, using Newey–West heteroskedasticity and autocorrelation consistent standard errors.

including Kangnam and other provincial cities. A temporary change in real income seems to have positive impact on the house prices very shortly in both a premium market as well as other provincial markets. However, this is not the case of real income in the long-run analysis. It is shown that the interest rate does not have a significant short-term influence on the apartment house price in all regions except Daejeon. It seems that the apartment house prices in Kangbuk are also influenced by their past prices, while, in Pusan, they are influenced by their past and current apartment house prices.

The regression results for the real apartment house prices in Kangnam area can be compared with these results of Kangbuk and four other regional cities in order to find any difference in the determination of real house prices. It is notable to see that only the apartment house prices in Kangnam area are negatively influenced by bank lending in the short run, while the house prices in the other area and regional cities except Kangbuk and Incheon are not significantly influenced by bank lending.

As shown in evidence, bank lending does positively influence the apartment house prices in a premium market of Kangnam area in the long run, but negatively in the short-run relationship. The estimated coefficient of bank lending on house prices is much less in absolute value in the short run than in the long run, indicating that the house prices of Kangnam are less sensitive to the bank lending in the short run. Some reasons for this difference between the time span periods can be explained in the followings.

First, speculative activity may be attributable to this difference between the long- and short-run relationship in a price booming market such as Kangnam area as Xiao and Park (2010) note. Secondly, the purchasers of apartment houses in Kangnam area may not rely primarily on bank lending as is common in other regions. This can be illustrated by the lower LTV in Kangnam area than in the other regions. The average LTV in September, 2009 reported by Kookmin Bank is 39.3% in Seoul, 49.3% in Pusan, 54.1% in Daegu. By our best guess, this figure will probably be much lower in Kangnam area than other regions in Seoul as well as nationwide. At the same time, Kangnam is heavily under control of DTI restriction by government policy to subdue the speculative activities since 2003. According to Lamount and Stein (1999), house prices react more sensitively to city-specific shocks in cities where households are highly leveraged. This suggests that greater changes in LTV ratios may affect more house price dynamics, the price volatility in particular. Consequently, Kangnam area where has low LTV does not react sensitively to bank lending in the short run. Lastly, most of the purchasers of apartment houses in Kangnam area in Seoul are reportedly non-Kangnam residents. This implies that the real owners of Kangnam apartment houses are a limited number of the wealthy residing nationwide who have abundant liquidity and thus may not need to primarily rely on bank lending. According to a research by a mainstream daily newspaper (The Chosunilbo daily News, June 23, 2006) in Korea, for instance, more than 50% of the purchasers of newly constructed Kangnam apartment houses are non-Kangnam residents while in Kangbuk only 20% are non-residents in 2006. These can account for the little influence of bank lending on house prices in this Kangnam market. Gyourko et al. (2006) argue that the increasing number of high-income households is the main cause of growing spatial skewness in house prices in the US. In Korea, there has been ever widening gap in household income since the Asian financial crisis in 1997. The *Gini* coefficient for the inequality of income is increased from 0.264 in 1997 to 0.342 in 2011 in Korea according to Korean National Statistical Office.

Table 4.9 Quandt–Andrews Breakpoint Tests

	Breakpoint	Maximum LR *F*-statistic Value	Prob.
Nationwide	2004.12	1.34	0.79
Kangnam	2002.10	1.73	0.47
Kangbuk	2007.10	2.42	0.20
Pusan	2002.12	2.39	0.17
Incheon	2004.04	2.05	0.24
Daejeon	2003.10	5.76**	0.00
Ulsan	2006.06	60.58**	0.00

Apart from the demand driven factors we have addressed so far, there can also be detected supply driven factors. The housing supply in Kangnam area was limited due to the low price elasticity of housing supply as well as government restrictive policy not allowing the expansion of the Capital Region of Seoul in Korea. Leung and Teo (2011) find that both the level and volatility of the house price will be higher with lower elasticity of housing supply. Saiz (2010) also finds that highly regulated metropolitan areas typically have low estimates of the price elasticity with regard to the house supply.

To check the robustness of the test results, the break points of apartment house price equation are estimated by using Quandt–Andrew breakpoint test (Andrews, 1993; Andrews and Ploberger, 1994). The test results in Table 4.9 shows that there are no significant break points in Kangnam area and nationwide, while there is in Daejeon area in October 2003 and in Ulsan area in June 2006 as seen in Table 4.9.

Following the break point test results, we conduct the sub-period analysis of the house price changes on the two regions, Daejeon and Ulsan where break point is apparent. As reported in Tables 4.10 and 4.11, the same relationship holds qualitatively for both sub-periods, 2003 for Daejeon and 2006 for Ulsan area, as for the entire sample period.

4.6 CONCLUSION

Using VECM model, this study examines the effects of bank lending, income, interest rate on the apartment house prices both in a premium house market of Kangnam area in Seoul versus provincial markets in Korea over the period between 1999 and 2011. The previous studies indicate that the relationship between bank lending and apartment house prices is inconsistent, depending on the study periods, and causality between them. Unlikely the previous ones, this study focuses on the exact effects of bank lending on the dynamics of apartment house prices by considering the seasonal adjustment for the dependent and independent variables both. The empirical results show that the house price in a premium market is positively influenced by the bank lending in the

Table 4.10 The Apartment House Price Equations in the Sub-Period1

Region period	Daejeon	Ulsan
	1999.1–2003.10	1999.1–2006.6
GDP (t)		4.71**
Apartment price ($t-1$)	0.30**	
Apartment price ($t-3$)	0.34**	
Construction cost index ($t-1$)	0.87**	
Interest rates ($t-1$)	−0.02**	
Adjusted R-squared	0.56	0.99

**Significance at the 1% level.
The dependent variable is the change in the real apartment price in each region. The explanatory variables are four lags of the dependent variable, the current and four lags of the change in the real bank lending, the change in the real GDP, the change in the interest rate, the change in the house construction permit unit, the change in the house construction cost index, and one lag of the cointegrating vector. Following the general-to-specific approach, the parsimonious models are obtained by removing insignificant variables. T-statistics are shown in parentheses, using Newey–West heteroskedasticity and autocorrelation consistent standard errors.

Table 4.11 The Apartment House Price Equations in the Sub-Period2

Region period	Daejeon	Ulsan
	2003.11–2011.12	2006.07–2011.12
Bank lending (t)		−0.00**
Bank lending ($t-4$)		−0.00**
GDP (t)	3.06**	4.93**
GDP ($t-1$)	−2.55**	
Apartment price ($t-1$)	0.70**	
Interest rates ($t-4$)		−0.00**
Cointegration vector ($t-1$)		0.01**
Adjusted R-squared	0.66	0.99

**Significance at the 1% level.
The dependent variable is the change in the real apartment price in each region. The explanatory variables are four lags of the dependent variable, the current and four lags of the change in the real bank lending, the change in the real GDP, the change in the interest rate, the change in the house construction permit unit, the change in the house construction cost index and one lag of the cointegrating vector. Following the general-to-specific approach, the parsimonious models are obtained by removing insignificant variables. T-statistics are shown in parentheses, using Newey–West heteroskedasticity and autocorrelation consistent standard errors.
*Significance at the 5% level.

long run, as other provincial markets show positive impact of bank lending in Korea. However, in the short-run analysis, the house price in a premium market is negatively affected by bank lending, while it does not show any statistically significant impact in provincial markets generally except Kangbuk and Incheon. The house prices of Kangnam seem to respond less sensitively to the bank lending in the short run than in the long run. In general, the income growth does not cause the apartment price to rise significantly in the long run, but it has significantly positive impact on the house prices in the short-run analysis across the country.

This study has some limitations which can be improved in further studies as followings. First, the empirical results for the relationship between house prices and bank lending are varying, depending on the sample periods. From this perspective, data from much longer sample periods are needed in order to obtain more accurate and meaningful evidence than this study. Second, this study was supposed to use mortgage loans instead of bank lending because bank lending may be too broad and extensive for this house specific study. However, unfortunately, it is not a possibility to get mortgage loan data because they do not exist in Korea. Even with these limitations, this chapter may have some useful policy implications.

First, the long-term government policy such as aggregate demand changes (i.e., monetary policy or government expenditure change) may not be effective for controlling the house prices in the long run, although a temporal change in real income appears to be a factor for a house price rise in major regions and Seoul in Korea unlike expected in theory. Second, while an increase in bank lending does appear to raise the house price in the long-run relationship, it is not desirable or appropriate to increase bank lending in the government policy side, because LTV in Korea is already not so low when considering "Chonsei" house lending system though it is usually thought so compared with those in other countries. Last, the government policy to control the house prices in Kangnam as a premium market should be different from its short-run policy with its less sensitivity of house prices to change in bank lending. It should be oriented not through a change in bank lending, but through an income change in the short-run policy perspective.

APPENDIX 1. DATA DESCRIPTIONS AND SOURCES

Variables	Explanations	Sources	Adjustments
Apartment price index	Apartment price index for various region	Kookmin bank website (est.kbstar.com)	
Bank lending	Loans of all deposit-taking banks for various regions	Bank of Korea website (www.bok.or.kr)	
GDP	Gross domestic products	Korea National Statistical Office website (www.nso.go.kr)	Quarterly series converted to monthly series using interpolation
Construction permit unit	House construction permit unit for various regions	Korea Ministry of Land, Infrastructure and Transport website (www.mtlit.go.kr)	

Variables	Explanations	Sources	Adjustments
Construction cost index	House construction cost index	Construction Economy Research Institute of Korea (www.cerik.re.kr)	
Interest rate	Annual composite lending rate	Bank of Korea website (www.bok.or.kr)	

REFERENCES

Ahearne, A., Ammer, J., Doyle, B., Kole, L., Martin, R., 2005. House Prices and Monetary Policy: A Cross-Country Study. International Finance Discussion Papers 841, Board of Governors of the Federal Reserve System.

Allen, L., Kenyon, G.N., Natarajan, V.S., 2012. The regional impact of monetary policy on house prices. International Journal of Business Innovation and Research 6 (4), 391–400.

Andrews, D.W.K., 1993. Tests for parameter instability and structural change with unknown change point. Econometrica 61, 821–856.

Andrews, D.W.K., Ploberger, W., 1994. Optimal tests when a nuisance parameter is present only under the alternative. Econometrica 62, 1383–1414.

Aoki, K., Proudman, J., Vlieghe, G., 2004. House prices, consumption, and monetary policy: a financial accelerator approach. Journal of Financial Intermediation 13, 414–435.

Birssimis, S.N., Vlassopoulos, T., 2009. The interaction between mortgage financing and housing price in Greece. Journal of Real Estate Finance and Economics 39, 146–164.

Davis, E.P., Zhu, H., 2004. Bank Lending and Commercial Property Prices: Some Cross Country Evidence. BIS Working Paper, 150.

Franses, P.H., 1991. Seasonality, non-stationary and the forecasting of money time series. International Journal of Forecasting 7, 199–208.

Fratantoni, M., Schuh, S., 2003. Monetary policy, housing, and heterogeneous regional markets. Journal of Money, Credit, and Banking 35 (4), 557–589.

Gerlach, S., Peng, W., 2005. Bank lending and property price in Hong Kong. Journal of Banking & Finance 29, 461–481.

Gimeno, R., Martinez-Carrascal, C., 2010. The relationship between house prices and house purchase loans: the Spanish case. Journal of Banking and Finance 34, 1849–1855.

Gyourko, J., Mayer, C., Sinai, T., 2006. Superstar Cities. Mimeo, The Wharton School.

Hofmann, B., 2003. Bank Lending and Property Prices: Some International Evidence. The Hong Kong Institute for Monetary Research Working Paper, 22.

Iacoviello, M., 2004. Consumption, house prices and collateral constraints. Journal of Housing Economics 13, 304–320.

Iacoviello, M., 2005. House prices and borrowing constraints, monetary policy in the business cycle. American Economic Review 95, 739–764.

Johansen, S., 1988. Statistical analysis of cointegration vectors. Journal of Economic Dynamics and Control 12, 231–254.

Johansen, S., 1991. Estimation and hypothesis testing of cointegration vectors in gaussian vector autoregressive models. Econometrica 59, 1551–1581.

Johansen, S., 1995. Likelihood-based Inference in Cointegrated Vector Autoregressive Models. Oxford University Press.

Kim, K., 2004. Housing and the Korean economy. Journal of Housing Economics 13, 321–341.

Kim, H.H., Park, S.W., Lee, S.H., 2012. House price and bank lending in a premium submarket in Korea. International Real Estate Review 15 (1), 1–42.

Kindleberger, C., 1978. Manias, panics, and crashes: a history of financial crises. In: Kindleberger, C., Laffarge, J. (Eds.), Financial Crises: Theory, History and Policy. Cambridge University Press, Cambridge.

Koh, W., Mariano, R., Pavlov, A., Phang, S., Tan, A., Wacher, S., 2005. Bank lending and real estate in Asia: market optimism and asset bubbles. Journal of Asian Economics 15, 1103–1118.

Taltavull de La Paz, P., White, M., 2012. Fundamental drivers of house price change: the role of money, mortgages, and migration in Spain and the United Kingdom. Journal of Property Research 29 (4), 341–367.

Lamount, O., Stein, J.C., 1999. Leverage and house-price dynamics in US cities. RAND Journal of Economics 30, 498–514.

Leung, C.K.Y., Teo, W.L., 2011. Should the optional portfolio be regional-specific? A multi-region model with monetary policy and asset price co-movements. Regional Science and Urban Economics 41, 293–304.

Liang, Q., Cao, H., 2007. Property prices and bank lending in China. Journal of Asian Economics 18, 63–75.

Minsky, H., 1982. Can "It" Happen Again? Essays on Instability and Finance. M.E. Sharpe, New York.

Newey, W., West, K., 1987. A simple positive semi-definite, heteroskedasticity and autocorrelation consistent covariance matrix. Econometrica 55, 703–708.

Oikarinen, E., 2009. Interaction between housing prices and household borrowing: the Finnish case. Journal of Banking and Finance 33, 747–756.

Park, S.W., Bahng, D., Park, Y.W., 2010. Price run-up in housing markets, access to bank lending and house price in Korea. Journal of Real Estate Finance and Economics 40, 332–367.

Phillips, P.C.B., Perron, P., 1988. Testing for a unit root in time series regression. Biometrika 75, 335–346.

Saiz, A., 2010. The geographic determinant of housing supply. Quarterly Journal of Economics 125 (3), 1253–1296.

Xiao, Q., 2010. Crashes in real estate prices. Urban Studies 47 (8), 1725–1744.

Xiao, Q., Park, D., 2010. Seoul housing prices and the role of speculation. Empirical Economics 38 (3), 619–644.

Zhu, H., 2006. The Structure of Housing Finance Markets and House Prices in Asia. BIS Quarterly Review, December Issue, 55–69.

CHAPTER 5

The Effect of Bank Mergers on Shareholder Value and Performance in Japan

Heather Montgomery[a] and Yuki Takahashi[b]
[a]International Christian University, 3-10-2 Osawa, Mitaka-shi, Tokyo 181–8585, Japan
[b]State University of New York at Stony Brook, 100 Nicolls Road, Stony Brook, NY 11794, USA

Consolidation in the banking sector made headlines following the global financial crisis of 2008, but was already a salient feature of the global banking sector even before the crisis intensified the trend. As illustrated in Figure 5.1, which draws on data from the Federal Deposit and Insurance Corporation, European Central Bank and the Japanese Bankers Association, over the past two decades banking sector consolidation has been a global trend. Certainly, part of that decline is due to bank failures, but from the early 1990s up to 2007 the global banking industry as a whole was relatively healthy, yet the number of commercial banks continued to decline, mostly due to consolidation (Mishkin, 2012, pp. 338–339).

Japan, for example, which started with a highly concentrated banking sector from the outset,[1] has seen the number of banks fall by nearly a quarter since the late 1990s. Over the same period, total assets in Japan's banking sector have risen. Currently, more than half of the assets are held by just three large financial groups that emerged from a wave of mega-mergers around 2000–2001.

Is this trend of banking sector consolidation beneficial to the banks? The main theoretical argument behind mergers and acquisitions is the potential for creating business synergies; usually improvements in efficiency. Consolidated banks may enjoy economies of scale and scope, realizing lower costs and higher profits through benefits such as geographical diversification, product diversification and cross-selling to customers, rationalization of branch networks or the consolidation of back office operations. Research shows, however, that it can be difficult for merged banks to exploit these efficiency gains (Harada and Ito, 2011; Montgomery et al., 2013). This suggests that

---

[1] Mishkin (2012), a widely used undergraduate textbook on banking, for example, points out that while the United States has around 6500 commercial banks, Japan has only about 100, even though the economy and population of Japan are only about half the size of that of the United States (p. 341).

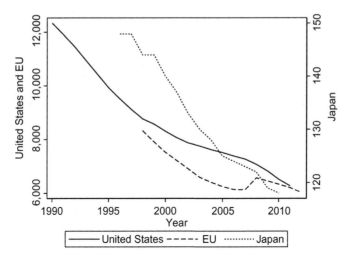

Figure 5.1 Number of banks in the united states, EU, and Japan. *Sources*: FDIC, ECB, Japanese Bankers Association. Data includes all FDIC-insured US commercial banks (US), all EU member countries' credit institutions (EU) and all members of the Japanese Bankers Association (except five banks: the Norinchukin Bank, Citibank Japan, Orix Trust & Banking, Nomura Trust & Banking and Seven Bank).

mergers may be motivated by other potential benefits, perhaps the promise of monopoly profits thanks to increased market power,[2] or simply survival as they become "too big to fail."

In this chapter, we examine the impact of bank mergers on shareholder value and other measures of performance. Do bank mergers and acquisitions create value? Or are the difficulties banks seem to have in exploiting efficiency gains reflected in their stock market value? What about the longer-term impact of bank mergers on other indicators of performance? To explore these questions, we analyze the performance of bank mergers in Japan since the end of the so-called "Financial Big Bang" in the late 1990s: a deregulation of the sector that intended to promote competition.

The rest of this chapter is organized as follows. In section 5.1, we briefly review the existing literature on bank mergers and shareholder wealth and performance. Section 5.2 gives an overview of Japan's financial sector and the merger events analyzed. Section 5.3 explains the details of our methodological approach and section 5.4 the data used in our analysis. In section 5.5, we discuss our findings on both shareholder value and performance ratios. Section 5.6 concludes.

---

[2] Hankir et al. (2011) find that investors believe that shareholder gains from M&A events in the banking industry come overwhelmingly from exploitation of market power rather than alternative explanations such as efficiency enhancements.

5.1 LITERATURE REVIEW

DeYoung et al. (2009) provide a comprehensive review of the abundant literature on the effect of bank mergers on shareholder wealth and bank performance in the United States and Europe. Their review suggests that European bank mergers in general result in both performance improvement and shareholder wealth creation. North American bank mergers also seem to improve performance in general, but the evidence on the impact of bank mergers on shareholder wealth is mixed. One clear finding that emerges, however, is that mergers in which post-merged entity is deemed to become "too big to fail" positively affect shareholder wealth.

Our own review of the comparatively sparse literature on bank mergers and performance in Japan is less optimistic. In an analysis of five mergers during the crisis period of the late 1990s to the early 2000s, Harada and Ito (2011) find that Japanese bank mergers did not result in financially healthier institutions.[3] Hosono et al. (2009) find that bank mergers in Japan 1990–2004 were motivated by both too-big-to-fail policies and efficiency-improving motives, though neither of the objectives were actually met. In an analysis of the formation of bank holding companies by Japan's smaller regional banks, Yamori et al. (2003) conclude that those mergers had not achieved efficiency gains.[4]

The literature on the effects of bank mergers on shareholder wealth in Japan is even more limited. The only study that directly addresses our research question is an event study analysis of the formation of five Japanese regional bank holding companies on shareholder wealth included in the broader study cited above by Yamori et al. (2003). However, the results of that study are inconclusive: the authors find that the market did not regard announcements of the formation of regional bank holding companies as significant events.

Uchino and Uesugi (2012) analyze a somewhat different, but related question. In an analysis of the merger of Bank of Tokyo-Mitsubishi and UFJ Bank in 2005 they find that the borrowing costs of client firms rose, but do not find any significant difference between the increase in borrowing costs of clients of the acquiring bank (in this case, the Bank of Tokyo-Mitsubishi) and clients of the target bank (UFJ Bank). Their finding suggests that, in contrast with evidence from the United States or Europe, the effects of bank mergers in Japan may not have heterogeneous effects on acquirer and target banks.

---

[3] They also point out that it is difficult to identify merger acquirer and target under Japanese accounting rule. As discussed later, we also analyze acquirer vs. target, and define target as the bank whose financial institution code is not inherited to new entity.

[4] There is, however, evidence that Japanese small mutual banks achieved efficiency improvement after merger (Yamori and Harimaya, 2009, 2010).

Although work directly related to our research question are limited, there are several other studies that examine the impact of bank *failures* on shareholder wealth or performance in Japan and the implications from this body of research may be relevant here. Yamori and Murakami (1999) analyze Hokkaido Takushoku Bank's failure on its client firm shareholder wealth and find that the closer the relation with the Hokkaido Takushoku Bank, the higher the negative abnormal return of its client firms. Brewer et al. (2003) also find that shareholders of client firms are adversely affected by bank failures, but they find that these negative effects are also experienced by non-client firms. Taking a different approach, Hori (2005) analyzes Hokkaido Takushoku Bank's failure on its client firms' post-event profitability and finds that the client firms do not necessarily report lower profits relative to non-client firms. Taken together, this literature suggests that the effects of bank failures on shareholder wealth and certain measures of performance do not necessarily coincide. Research by Miyajima and Yafeh (2007) sheds some light on the seemingly contradictory findings of Yamori and Murakami (1999) and Hori (2005). Analyzing the effect of the formation of Mizuho Holdings, Sumitomo Mitsui Banking Corporation, and UFJ Holdings on non-financial firms' shareholder wealth, they find that although the announcements did not affect client firms' returns in aggregate, the announcements positively affected the abnormal returns of bank finance-dependent firms.

There is clearly room in the existing literature for more analysis of this important question. Our study contributes to the existing literature as the only comprehensive study of the large number of bank mergers that emerged in Japan after deregulation of the industry in the late 1990s. We examine the effects of these mergers on both shareholder wealth and indicators of bank performance and explore the possibility of heterogeneous effects of bank mergers on different kinds of banks and different kinds of mergers that go beyond the standard acquirer vs. target analysis.

5.2 M&A IN JAPAN'S FINANCIAL SECTOR

Over our sample period of 1994–2010, there were 38 merger and acquisition (M&A) events in Japan's banking sector, nearly all of them domestic deals. Table 5.1 presents some summary statistics of the M&A events included in our analysis and Appendix Table A1 gives specific details on each deal. The summary statistics show that most of the acquirers and targets were medium to large-sized banks and the most common pattern seems to be city bank taking over a different kind of bank, presumably with a slightly different line of business, or a regional bank taking over another regional bank. The number of mergers peaked in 1999 and 2000: those 2 years witnessed about a third of the total M&A deals in our entire sample. 1999–2000 also saw the emergence of what we call the "mega-banks": the three huge financial groups—Mizuho, Tokyo-Mitsubishi-UFJ and The Sumitomo-Mitsui Banking Corporation—all with total assets of more than 80 trillion yen.

Table 5.1 Summary Statistics: Description of Merger Announcements

	Acquirer		Target	
By size		of which highly capitalized		of which highly capitalized
Mega	1	1	1	0
Large	12	7	9	3
Medium	20	1	16	2
Small	2	0	1	0
By type		of which cross-type merger		of which cross-type merger
Bank Holding Company	1	0	4	0
City	12	8	6	2
Trust	3	0	6	5
Long-term credit	0	0	1	1
Regional	13	0	4	2
Regional II	8	0	8	1
By year		of which mega-merger		of which mega-merger
1994	2	0	2	0
1995	0	0	0	0
1996	0	0	0	0
1997	1	0	0	0
1998	3	0	2	0
1999	5	3	5	4
2000	7	2	7	4
2001	5	0	2	0
2002	1	0	1	0
2003	2	0	1	0
2004	3	1	2	1
2005	0	0	0	0
2006	1	0	1	0
2007	1	0	2	0
2008	3	0	2	0
2009	2	0	1	0
2010	1	0	1	0
Total	37		29	
Total (pre-cleaned)	39		31	
Total number of events	37			
Total number of events (pre-cleaned)	38			

Notes: Bank type follows categorization by Japanese Bankers Association.

5.3 METHODOLOGY

5.3.1 Obtaining Excess Returns

Our first analysis uses event study methodology. We estimate banks' excess returns around merger announcement dates using what MacKinlay (1997) refers to as a "market model":

$$r_{i,t}^{Stock} = \alpha_i + \beta_i r_t^{Market} + \varepsilon_{i,t} \tag{5.1}$$

where $r_{i,t}^{Stock}$ and r_t^{Market} are return on stock i at time t (return on stock i over a holding period from $t-1$ to t) and return on market index at time t, respectively. We use a market capitalization-weighted index, TOPIX (Tokyo Stock Price Index), for the market index. α_i and β_i are coefficients to be estimated for stock i. $\varepsilon_{i,t}$ is the error term of stock i at time t, which is orthogonal to the information available at time $t-1$, I_{t-1}, $E[\varepsilon_t | I_{t-1}] = 0$. This suggests that ordinary least squares (OLS) gives unbiased and efficient estimates and is thus the preferred specification for equation (5.1). Time frequency is daily, excluding non-business days.

We first estimate equation (5.1) over the estimation window and obtain coefficient estimates $\hat{\alpha}_i$ and $\hat{\beta}_i$. Those estimates are then used in equation (5.2) and calculate a normal return, $r_{i,t}^{Stock-Normal}$, over the event window:

$$r_{i,t}^{Stock-Normal} = \hat{\alpha}_i + \hat{\beta}_i r_t^{Market} \tag{5.2}$$

Because these coefficients are estimated before the effect of the event takes place, equation (5.2) gives a return in the absence of merger announcements.

The abnormal return, $AR_{i,t}$, is calculated by subtracting this predicted normal return from the actual realized return:

$$AR_{i,t} = r_{i,t}^{Stock} - r_{i,t}^{Stock-Normal} \tag{5.3}$$

As seen from equation (5.3), the abnormal return is the deviation of the actual realized return from the normal return and thus represents excess returns triggered by the merger announcement.

Since the abnormal return only shows the excess return on a certain day and not over the entire event window, the period over which the merger announcement may have affected stock returns, we aggregate abnormal returns over the event window and calculate the cumulative abnormal return, CAR_i, for each bank:

$$CAR_i = \Sigma_t AR_{i,t} \tag{5.4}$$

Under the null hypothesis, the abnormal returns follow a normal distribution:

$$AR_{i,t} \sim N\left(0, \sigma_i^2\right) \tag{5.5}$$

where σ_i^2 is the variance of $AR_{i,t}$, which consists of the variance of the error term in equation (5.1), σ_ε^2, and the variance due to the sampling error, which approaches zero with a large estimation window.

Under the null hypothesis, cumulative abnormal returns asymptotically follow a normal distribution:

$$CAR_i \sim N\left(0, L\sigma_i^2\right) \tag{5.6}$$

where L is number of days in the event window. The test statistic z_i is calculated as:

$$z_i = \frac{CAR_i}{\hat{\sigma}_i \sqrt{L}} \tag{5.7}$$

where $\hat{\sigma}_i$ is the sample standard deviation of abnormal return in the event window of bank i.

Finally, as our stock price data already account for stock splits and dividend payments, return on stock i at time t is simply defined as the price change over a day:

$$r_{i,t}^{Stock} = \frac{p_{i,t} - p_{i,t-1}}{p_{i,t-1}} \tag{5.8}$$

where $p_{i,t}$ and $p_{i,t-1}$ are price of stock i at time t and $t-1$, respectively.

We estimate abnormal returns over 4 different event windows (in the following, t represents the announcement date): pre-announcement $(t-30, t+1)$, or 1 month prior to the merger announcement, announcement $(t-1, t+1)$, the days just before and after announcement, post-announcement $(t-1, t+30)$, 1 month after the merger announcement, and long-run post-announcement $(t-1, t+360)$, nearly 1 year after the merger announcement. The estimation window consists of 120 days, starting from 120 days before the first day of each event window.

5.3.2 Shareholder Value Creation Analysis

To examine the determinants of shareholder value around merger events, we compare cumulative abnormal returns between banks and mergers with different characteristics, including acquirer vs. target banks and huge "mega-mergers" vs. regular mergers. In the tables below we compare the differences in mean and median and report test statistics indicating whether the differences are statistically significant at conventional levels.

We then regress those cumulative abnormal returns on those as well as other characteristics to obtain a more complete picture of what would determine whether merger events are value creating. Since the cumulative abnormal return is a point estimate, we account for standard errors in the regression using weighted least squares with the inverse of the square of the standard error of the cumulative abnormal return as a weight, following the methodology of Campa and Hernando (2006) in their analysis of European financial industry mergers.[5] The resulting model is:

$$\frac{CAR_i}{w_i} = \beta_0 \frac{1}{w_i} + \beta_1 \frac{Target_i}{w_i} + \beta_2 \frac{Mega_i}{w_i} + \beta_3 \frac{HighCapitalized_i}{w_i}$$
$$+ \beta_4 \frac{LowCapitalized_i}{w_i} + \beta_5 \frac{CrossTypeMerger_i}{w_i} + \frac{\varepsilon_i}{w_i} \qquad (5.9)$$

where $w_i = \hat{\sigma}_i \sqrt{L}$ is the standard error of the cumulative abnormal return of bank i. The idea is that the larger the weight (i.e. the smaller the standard error), the more accurate the cumulative abnormal return point estimate.

$Target_i$ is a dummy variable indicating a target bank, defined as the bank whose financial institution code is not inherited to new entity. $Mega_i$ is a dummy variable identifying mergers in which the anticipated post-merger asset size exceeds 80 trillion yen. $HighCapitalized_i$ and $LowCapitalized_i$ are 0–1 dummies identifying banks with particularly high or low capitalization ratios as defined as a ratio of market capitalization to total book assets in the top or bottom 25%, respectively, 30 days before the event. $CrossTypeMerger_i$ identifies mergers in which acquirer and target belong to different bank types (regional, city, long-term credit and trust banks), and therefore are presumably focused on different business lines. ε_i is the error term.

5.3.3 Performance Ratio Analysis

To get insight into longer-term post-merger bank performance, we also analyze balance sheet and income statement-based performance ratios. Since we do not have post-merger targets in most cases, we focus on acquirer banks and examine the effect of merger on acquirer banks.

Our objective is to measure the effect of bank mergers on bank performance, comparing the "treatment" group of merged banks to a "control" group of similar banks that did *not* merge, before and after the merger completions. This question really calls for difference-in-difference analysis. However, finding an appropriate control group is difficult: a simple comparison of the post-merger period performance of acquirers and other banks that did not merge may reflect not only the impact of the merger on bank performance, but also other pre-merger differences between acquirer banks and non-merging banks that affected performance. As we show below in Table 5.5, those differences can be significant.

We address this issue by comparing the post-merger performance of acquirer banks with a weighted combination of non-merging banks that are chosen to resemble the characteristics of acquirers in the pre-merger period. This methodology, conceptualized

---

[5] See Greene (2011) for the technique.

by Abadie and Gardeazabal (2003) as a "synthetic" control method, creates "synthetic" acquirer banks in the absence of a merger event, thus giving us a control group against which to compare the actual acquirer banks which experienced a merger event.

The synthetic control method implements the following algorithm for each bank and each performance ratio to construct the synthetic acquirer control group:

$$W^* = \arg\min_{W \in \varpi} \sqrt{(\overline{X}_1 - \overline{X}_0 W)' V (\overline{X}_1 - \overline{X}_0 W)} \qquad (5.10)$$

where W is a $J \times 1$ vector of weights whose elements are non-negative and sum to one, with J representing the number of non-merging banks: $\varpi = \left\{ (w_1, \ldots, w_j)' \mid w_1 + \cdots + w_j = 1, w_i \geqslant 0 \ i = 1, \ldots, j \right\}$. W^* is the vector of optimal weights. $\overline{X}_1$ is a scalar of pre-merger performance ratio of a merging bank, averaged over the pre-merger period. $\overline{X}_0$ is a $1 \times J$ vector whose elements are pre-merger performance ratio of non-merging bank j, averaged over the pre-merger period for each non-merging bank. The synthetic acquirer bank's performance ratio at time t, for both pre- and post-merger period, is defined as $X_{1t}^* = X_{0t} W^*$. V above is a scalar that minimizes mean squared error of X_{1t}^* against the actual acquirer bank's performance ratio in the pre-merger period.

With acquirer and synthetic acquirer banks as a treatment and control group, respectively, we estimate the following difference-in-difference pooled cross section model:

$$y_{i,t} = \beta_0 + \beta_1 Merger_i + \beta_2 Mega_i + \sum_{k=1}^{5} \gamma_k PostMerger \ k \ year_{i,t}$$

$$+ \sum_{k=1}^{5} \delta_k Merger_i \times PostMerger \ k \ year_{i,t} + \beta_3 HighCapitalized_i + \beta_4 LowCapitalized_i$$

$$+ \beta_5 CrossTypeMerger_i + \theta_t T_t + \rho_i I_i + \varepsilon_{i,t} \qquad (5.11)$$

where $y_{i,t}$ is the performance ratio of bank i at time t. $Mega_i$, $HighCapitalized_i$, $LowCapitalized_i$, and $CrossTypeMerger_i$ are as defined in equation (5.9), but now book value is used for high and low capitalization. These variables are defined a year prior to the merger event and thus time invariant. T_t represents time-fixed effects and I_i bank-type dummies. $\varepsilon_{i,t}$ is the error term.

$PostMerger \ k \ year_{i,t}$ is a dummy variable for bank i (more precisely bank-event i) that takes a value of 1 in the kth year after merger and 0 otherwise. This variable captures the change of performance ratios in the 5 years following a merger. The time subscript shows that the merger year is different for each bank. $Merger_i$ is a 0–1 dummy that equals 1 for acquirers and 0 for the group of synthetic acquirers. This variable captures the difference between the treatment group, that experienced a merger event, and the control group.

The main variables of interest are the difference-in-difference terms $Merger_i \times PostMerger\ k\ year_{i,t}$, which are the interaction of the terms $Merger_i$ and $PostMerger\ k\ year_{i,t}$ and thus capture the effect of merger events on acquirer banks relative to our control group of synthetic acquirer banks for the kth year after the merger.

5.4 DATA DESCRIPTION

Bank stock data is from the Nikkei NEEDS database; covering the period from 1990 to 2011. The data contains each bank's stock price, already accounting for stock splits and dividend payments, as well as market capitalization of each bank and stock price index TOPIX.

Bank balance sheet and income statement data is from the Japanese Bankers Association's (JBA) "Financial Statement of All Banks," which contains individual bank's detailed balance sheet and income statement items and is available from JBA's website. We use unconsolidated data from 1996 to 2010.

Merger announcement and completion dates are obtained from Nikkei Telecom 21, a Nikkei newspaper article archive. First referencing the JBA's list of transitions of Japanese banks, we checked the *Nihon Keizai Shimbun* and *Nikkei Kinyu Shimbun* (Japan's leading economic and financial newspapers) for all periods for which we have sufficient stock data to estimate the market model explained above, and define the date on which the merger was first announced in the press as the announcement date. This yields 38 announcement dates between October 1994 and July 2010. The corresponding completion dates, which we use in the performance ratio analysis, are determined in a similar way and then double-checked by referring to the JBA's "Transition of Japanese Banks" database. For both merger announcement and completion, event dates are set to these dates, or to the following business day if these dates are on non-business days.

We examine the formation of new bank holding companies and mergers and acquisitions between banks in different bank holding companies, including "subsidiarization," an acquisition of the target's majority ownership while maintaining the target as a separate entity. However, we do not examine mergers and acquisitions in which both the acquirer and target are already in the same bank holding company or the acquirer already owns a majority of the target's shares.[6] We also do not examine "rescue" mergers in which the target bank is already insolvent and under governmental control.

For analysis of excess returns we exclude banks that have returns of zero for more than 1/2 of the days in the estimation window or event window to have reliable abnormal return estimates. This step drops 1 event and 4 banks and leaves us a sample of 37 events among 66 listed banks between 1994 and 2010.

---

[6] However, as a special case, we do include the so-called "reverse" merger between SMBC and Wakashio Bank.

For analysis of performance ratios we use banks with balance sheet and income statements available at least a year before the merger completion. Unlike for excess return analysis, we instead use subsidiary bank data to analyze merger events involving bank holding companies, since the JBA does not provide bank holding company data. This yields a sample of 33 events with 37 pre-merger acquirer banks, 37 pre-merger target banks, and 35 post-merger acquirer banks between 1996 and 2010.

5.5 RESULTS

5.5.1 Shareholder Value Creation

Cumulative abnormal returns—acquirer vs. target

Table 5.2 summarizes the calculated cumulative abnormal returns for our sample of banks, analyzing the results for acquirer and target banks in four distinct periods. Since the cumulative abnormal return, as explained above, is an estimate, we include both the mean and median observation for each group of banks in each window, and look for statistically significant differences between the two groups using a t-test (for the means) and a Wilcoxon rank-sum test (for the medians).

Looking at the first column of Table 5.2, we see a little bit of activity in returns prior to the announcement of a merger event. Cumulative abnormal returns are

Table 5.2 Analysis of Excess Returns: Acquirer vs. Target

	(1)	(2)	(3)	(4)
	Pre-Announcement	Announcement	Post-Announcement	Post-Announcement Long-Run
	CAR on $(t-30, t+1)$	CAR on $(t-1, t+1)$	CAR on $(t-1, t+30)$	CAR on $(t-1, t+360)$
Acquirer				
Mean	0.049**	0.038**	0.014	−0.114
Median	0.022	0.011	0.004	−0.039
Obs.	37	36	37	28
Target				
Mean	0.062*	0.064**	−0.002	−0.010
Median	0.060*	0.046***	0.028	−0.021
Obs.	28	27	28	20
Difference				
Mean	−0.013	−0.026	0.016	−0.104
Median	−0.038	−0.036*	−0.024	−0.018

*Statistical significance at the 10% level.**Statistical significance at the 5% level.***Statistical significance at the 1% level.

positive for both acquirer and target banks in the month prior to announcement. Those returns are larger in the case of target banks, although the difference is not statistically significant.

In column 2 we note that right at announcement, there is a jump up in cumulative abnormal returns. Those returns are again a bit larger for target banks, posting 4.6% or 6.4% of returns, and highly statistically significant.

In the month after announcement, as reported in column 3, cumulative abnormal returns fall back. The long-term perspective 1 year out bears out this finding: column 4 reports that on average cumulative abnormal returns even turn negative for both acquirer and target banks, although post-announcement returns are not statistically significantly different from zero for either group.

Cumulative abnormal returns—mega-mergers

One of the distinctive characteristics of M&As in Japan's financial sector is the sheer size of the deals. Especially around the peak of 1999–2000, a new class of what we term "mega-banks" emerged. These are the three financial groups of Mizuho, Tokyo-Mitsubishi UFJ, and Sumitomo-Mitsui. The debate around whether mergers create business synergies or simply make banks that are "too big to fail" is especially centered around these largest deals. For that reason, we also analyze the influence of size on the cumulative abnormal returns of the banks in our sample in Table 5.3.

Looking at the first column of Table 5.3, we see that for banks entered into a non-mega merger there is no large run-up in cumulative abnormal returns in the month prior to announcement of a merger event. However, for banks entering into a mega-merger, there is a large and statistically significant run-up in cumulative abnormal returns prior to the merger announcement. On average, banks involved in a mega-merger saw returns of 16.5% or 17.5% in the month before the announcement. Those returns were statistically significantly higher than the returns for banks entering into "non-mega" mergers.

On announcement, in column 2, we see a similar trend. Banks involved in mega-mergers post returns about 7.9% (the median) or 12.9% (the mean) higher than normal in the two days surrounding the merger announcement and those excess returns are highly statistically significant. Banks involved in other mergers also posted statistically significantly positive returns on announcement, but those returns were more modest, in the range of 1–2%. The difference between cumulative abnormal returns for banks entering into mega-mergers and banks entering into other mergers is positive and highly statistically significant. Shareholders of banks entering into mega-mergers earned abnormal returns of around 11% on average.

As reported in column 3, 1 month after announcement abnormal returns tend to fall back to normal. In the long-run, a year after the merger announcement (column 4), neither bank group demonstrates any significant positive returns and mean and median cumulative abnormal returns even turn negative for banks entering into non-mega mergers.

Table 5.3 Analysis of Excess Returns: Mega vs. Non-Mega Merger

	(1)	(2)	(3)	(4)
	Pre-Announcement	Announcement	Post-Announcement	Post-Announcement Long-Run
	CAR on $(t-30, t+1)$	CAR on $(t-1, t+1)$	CAR on $(t-1, t+30)$	CAR on $(t-1, t+360)$
Mega-merger				
Mean	0.165***	0.129***	0.116*	0.161
Median	0.175***	0.079***	0.087*	0.291
Obs.	15	15	15	12
Non-mega merger				
Mean	0.021	0.024*	−0.026	−0.148
Median	0.026	0.012**	0.005	−0.093
Obs.	50	48	50	36
Difference				
Mean	0.145***	0.105***	0.142**	0.308
Median	0.150***	0.068***	0.082**	0.385

*Statistical significance at the 10% level.**Statistical significance at the 5% level.***Statistical significance at the 1% level.
Note: Mega-merger is a merger in which the anticipated post-merger asset size exceeds 80 trillion yen.

In summary, for those banks involved in a "mega-merger"—creating one of the largest institutions in the country (or, indeed, the world) with total assets of over 80 trillion yen—we do see evidence of a run-up in cumulative abnormal returns in the month prior to M&A announcements, as well as the 2 days right around the announcement date. Those returns are large, in the range of 17% on average, statistically significant, and statistically significantly higher than the cumulative abnormal returns of banks involved in other, "non-mega," mergers. However, we do not find strong evidence that those abnormal returns are sustained in the long-run.

Cumulative abnormal returns—regression analysis

To further investigate the impact of these and other characteristics on shareholder value, we next turn to regression analysis. The results of estimation of equation (5.9), above, are reported in Table 5.4.

Looking at Table 5.4, we see the results reported above are mostly confirmed. The main predictor of excess returns surrounding announcement of an M&A is whether the deal is a mega-merger or not. In the 1 month pre-announcement window, banks involved in mega-merger deals post large, positive, and highly statistically significant excess returns of around 10%. Column 2 indicates that those excess returns mostly come in the 2 days surrounding announcement of the merger. Readers will also note

Table 5.4 Analysis of Excess Returns: Weighted Least Squares Regression

	(1)	(2)	(3)	(4)
Sample	Announcement Date			
Specification	Weighted Least Squares			
Dependent Variable	Pre-Announcement	Announcement	Post-Announcement	Post-Announcement Long-Run
	CAR on $(t-30, t+1)$	CAR on $(t-1, t+1)$	CAR on $(t-1, t+30)$	CAR on $(t-1, t+360)$
Target	0.014	0.050**	−0.002	0.223
	[0.033]	[0.023]	[0.039]	[0.263]
Mega-merger	0.104**	0.108***	0.075	0.192
	[0.046]	[0.041]	[0.059]	[0.312]
High capitalized	0.041	0.129***	0.013	0.296
	[0.038]	[0.021]	[0.054]	[0.303]
Low capitalized	0.030	0.063***	0.041	−0.051
	[0.029]	[0.018]	[0.037]	[0.277]
Cross-type merger	−0.020	−0.060**	0.043	−0.159
	[0.038]	[0.029]	[0.051]	[0.327]
Constant	−0.007	−0.063***	−0.037	−0.212
	[0.022]	[0.006]	[0.026]	[0.184]
Observations	61	59	61	44
R-squared	0.14	0.57	0.11	0.08
Weight	$\frac{1}{\hat{\sigma}_i \sqrt{L}}$	$\frac{1}{\hat{\sigma}_i \sqrt{L}}$	$\frac{1}{\hat{\sigma}_i \sqrt{L}}$	$\frac{1}{\hat{\sigma}_i \sqrt{L}}$

Statistical significance at the 5% level.*Statistical significance at the 1% level.
Notes: Standard errors in brackets below each coefficient estimate.

in column 2 that banks that are particularly poorly or well capitalized also post highly statistically significant excess returns right at announcement. Target banks, whether entering a mega-merger or not, accumulate positive excess returns of around 5% in the 2 days surrounding announcement of an M&A deal. For all banks, though, these gains dissipate in the long-run post-announcement window 1 year after the M&A deal announcement. This motivates us to explore our next question, about the effect of M&A events on longer-term measures of performance.

5.5.2 Performance Ratios

To explore the longer-term impact of mergers and acquisitions on performance, we turn next to regression analysis of various longer-term measures of performance such as profitability, solvency, inefficiency, lending intensity, provisioning, risk profile, and liquidity. Profitability is measured by the return on equity (net income to total equity), solvency by the capitalization ratio (the ratio of equity to assets), inefficiency by the cost to income ratio (the ratio of ordinary expenses to ordinary revenue), lending intensity by the loan to asset ratio, provisioning by the ratio of loan loss provisions to total loans, risk profile by the non-performing loan ratio, and liquidity by the ratio of liquid assets to total assets.

Performance ratios—pre-merger acquirer vs. all banks

Table 5.5 compares mean and median values of the various performance ratios for acquirer banks, the entire sample of all banks, and the synthetic control group ("synthetic acquirers") prior to an M&A event.

Looking at Table 5.5, readers may note that prior to a merger event, acquirer banks tend to be statistically significantly less profitable, less solvent and less well-provisioned, despite having a slightly higher ratio of non-performing loans, than the sample as a whole. However, mean and median values for the "synthetic acquirers" reported in Table 5.5 appear much more similar to the pre-merger acquirer group, as we would hope for an appropriate control group.

Performance ratios—regression analysis

We next analyze a "difference-in-difference" specification which compares the difference in "treatment" banks, which experienced a merger event, before and after the event, to the difference in a group of synthetically constructed "control" banks, which never experienced a merger during the sample period, before and after those same events. The main results[7] based upon equation (5.11) are reported in Table 5.6.

Looking at the first row of Table 5.6, we note that banks that experienced mergers tend on average to be less solvent (have lower capital ratios) and more lending intensive than the control group of banks that did not experience a merger event. Banks involved in mega-mergers, however, reverse that tendency, and are statistically significantly *more* solvent and *less* lending intensive than the control group. Acquirers entering into a mega-merger are also statistically significantly more liquid than the control group.

The treatment group of merged banks demonstrates a tendency to become statistically significantly less profitable, less solvent, and more inefficient in the first 2–4 years after experiencing a merger event. Note that this trend remains even after controlling for time fixed effects and other bank characteristics such as type, capitalization ratio, and whether the bank merger was between banks of different types.

The results reported in Table 5.6 are illustrated graphically in Figure 5.2, which plots the evolution of some of the key performance ratios around merger events for all the banks in the sample, as well as the treatment group of acquirer banks and control group of synthetic acquirer banks.

---

[7] In the interest of brevity, we do not report all coefficient estimates, but only those of most interest. Post-merger-year dummies in general, for example, are estimated as a control but not statistically significant in general, so are not reported below.

Table 5.5 Analysis of Performance Ratios: Pre-Merger Acquirer vs. All Banks and Synthetic Acquirer

	(1)	(2)	(3)	(4)	(5)	(6)	(7)
	Profitability	Solvency	Inefficiency	Lending Intensity	Provisioning	Risk Profile	Liquidity
	Return on Equity (%)	Capitalization Ratio (%)	Cost to Income Ratio (%)	Loan to Asset Ratio (%)	Loan Loss Provisions to Total Loans (%)	Non-Performing Loan Ratio (%)	Liquidity Ratio (%)
Pre-merger acquirer							
Mean	−12.83	3.76	108.05	68.15	0.95	3.38	6.46
Median	1.63	3.58	97.82	70.43	0.58	2.84	5.87
Obs.	255	255	255	255	244	255	231
Pre-merger all banks							
Mean	−7.85	4.06	108.67	68.91	1.10	3.24	6.88
Median	−9.18	3.71	110.96	69.40	0.79	3.26	7.04
Obs.	255	255	255	255	255	255	255
Pre-merger synthetic acquirer							
Mean	−12.20	3.79	107.47	68.27	0.87	3.30	6.44
Median	−0.98	3.74	99.83	71.15	0.64	2.95	5.85
Obs.	249	249	249	249	198	249	185

Table 5.6 Analysis of Performance Ratios: Pooled OLS

	(1)	(2)	(3)	(4)	(5)	(6)	(7)
Sample	Acquirer and Synthetic Acquirer						
Specification	Pooled OLS with Time-Fixed Effects & Bank-Type Dummies						
Dependent Variable	Profitability	Solvency	Inefficiency	Lending Intensity	Provisioning	Risk Profile	Liquidity
	Return on Equity (%)	Capitalization Ratio (%)	Cost to Income Ratio (%)	Loan to Asset Ratio (%)	Loan Loss Provisions to Total Loans (%)	Non-Performing Loan Ratio (%)	Liquidity Ratio (%)
Merger	0.64	−0.25***	0.11	−0.68*	0.05	−0.14	0.47**
	[3.547]	[0.071]	[1.957]	[0.373]	[0.066]	[0.130]	[0.196]
Mega-merger	6.93	0.23**	−4.56	−5.69***	−0.02	−0.22	2.45***
	[5.725]	[0.114]	[3.158]	[0.602]	[0.124]	[0.210]	[0.304]
Merger × Post-merger 1 year	−39.08***	−0.88***	18.28***	1.48	0.35*	−0.26	0.29
	[11.199]	[0.224]	[6.179]	[1.179]	[0.202]	[0.410]	[0.666]
Merger × Post-merger 2 year	−28.86**	−0.93***	21.67***	0.05	0.47**	−0.54	0.37
	[11.831]	[0.236]	[6.528]	[1.245]	[0.227]	[0.433]	[0.666]
Merger × Post-merger 3 year	−7.07	−0.70***	3.55	−1.14	0.24	−0.56	0.72
	[12.009]	[0.240]	[6.626]	[1.264]	[0.260]	[0.440]	[0.659]
Merger × Post-merger 4 year	2.30	−0.55**	−1.03	−2.03	0.15	−0.32	0.55
	[13.309]	[0.266]	[7.343]	[1.401]	[0.282]	[0.488]	[0.735]
Merger × Post-merger 5 year	−3.57	−0.34	8.24	−1.46	0.59**	−0.43	0.52
	[13.860]	[0.277]	[7.647]	[1.459]	[0.289]	[0.508]	[0.753]
Trust	14.16*	0.16	−4.16	−6.54***	0.41**	0.72**	−2.12***
	[7.765]	[0.155]	[4.284]	[0.817]	[0.162]	[0.284]	[0.447]

(Continued)

Table 5.6 Continued

	(1)	(2)	(3)	(4)	(5)	(6)	(7)
Sample	Acquirer and Synthetic Acquirer						
Specification	Pooled OLS with Time-Fixed Effects & Bank-Type Dummies						
Dependent Variable	Profitability	Solvency	Inefficiency	Lending Intensity	Provisioning	Risk Profile	Liquidity
	Return on Equity (%)	Capitalization Ratio (%)	Cost to Income Ratio (%)	Loan to Asset Ratio (%)	Loan Loss Provisions to Total Loans (%)	Non-Performing Loan Ratio (%)	Liquidity Ratio (%)
Regional	4.42	0.43***	0.10	8.62***	0.06	0.39	0.41
	[7.179]	[0.143]	[3.961]	[0.755]	[0.154]	[0.263]	[0.368]
Regional II	0.55	0.36**	0.69	13.15***	0.13	0.41	0.05
	[7.603]	[0.152]	[4.195]	[0.800]	[0.160]	[0.279]	[0.393]
High capitalized	−6.39	1.16***	−2.15	0.23	−0.13	−0.48**	1.50***
	[6.547]	[0.131]	[3.612]	[0.689]	[0.141]	[0.240]	[0.331]
Low capitalized	−5.05	−0.45***	1.83	0.47	−0.10	0.05	−0.46**
	[3.580]	[0.071]	[1.975]	[0.377]	[0.067]	[0.131]	[0.188]
Cross-type merger	2.93	0.21	0.39	0.63	−0.04	−0.05	0.27
	[6.294]	[0.126]	[3.472]	[0.662]	[0.128]	[0.231]	[0.314]
Constant	−10.94	3.79***	113.56***	61.52***	0.82***	5.08***	6.67***
	[9.893]	[0.198]	[5.458]	[1.041]	[0.200]	[0.362]	[0.530]
Year dummies	Yes	Yes	Yes	Yes	Yes	Yes	Yes
Observations	912	912	912	912	705	912	741

*Statistical significance at the 10% level.**Statistical significance at the 5% level.***Statistical significance at the 1% level.
Notes: Standard errors in brackets below each coefficient estimate.
The sample consists of acquirer banks and synthetic acquirer banks both before and after the event.

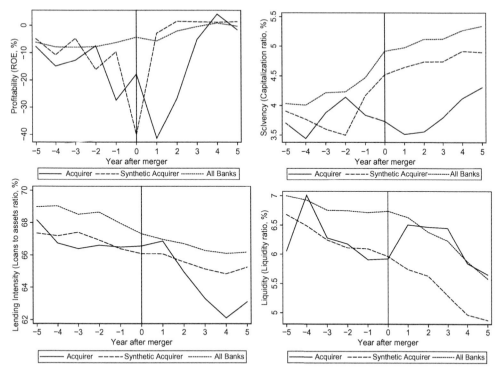

Figure 5.2 Acquirer, synthetic acquirer, and all banks around the merger events.

Given the findings above on the significance of the size of the merger event on shareholder value, we further explore the post-merger performance of the mega-banks. In Table 5.7 we report the main estimation results[8] with a version of equation (5.11), interacting the post-merger year dummies with the dummy variables for mega-mergers and merger banks to see whether banks that experience mega-mergers behave differently from other banks in the first 5 years after merger. In most cases, the mega, merger banks, and post-merger year interaction terms are not statistically significantly different from zero, suggesting that mega-banks do not behave significantly different in the post-merger period than other merged banks.

5.6 CONCLUSIONS

Consolidation, a global trend in the banking sector, intensified in the wake of the global financial crisis of 2008 but was already in motion in the decades leading up to the crisis. This trend was particularly evident in Japan, where a wave of mergers starting in the late

---

[8] Again, some coefficient estimates are not reported to save space.

Table 5.7 Analysis of Performance Ratios: Pooled OLS with Mega-Merger Interactions

	(1)	(2)	(3)	(4)	(5)	(6)	(7)
Sample	Acquirer and Synthetic Acquirer						
Specification	Pooled OLS with Time-Fixed Effects & Bank-Type Dummies						
	Profitability	Solvency	Inefficiency	Lending Intensity	Provisioning	Risk Profile	Liquidity
Dependent Variable	Return on Equity (%)	Capitalization Ratio (%)	Cost to Income Ratio (%)	Loan to Asset Ratio (%)	Loan Loss Provisions to Total Loans (%)	Non-Performing Loan Ratio (%)	Liquidity Ratio (%)
Merger	0.63 [3.877]	−0.23*** [0.077]	0.34 [2.141]	−0.13 [0.399]	0.06 [0.071]	−0.08 [0.141]	0.34 [0.218]
Merger × Mega	0.06 [9.715]	−0.15 [0.194]	−1.43 [5.365]	−3.45*** [1.001]	−0.08 [0.193]	−0.37 [0.353]	0.75 [0.489]
Merger × Post-merger 1 year	42.81 [29.874]	0.89 [0.596]	−17.25 [16.499]	−0.93 [3.077]	−0.35 [0.629]	−1.26 [1.084]	−1.22 [1.541]
Merger × Mega × Post-merger 2 year	28.86 [30.238]	0.48 [0.604]	−14.47 [16.700]	−4.29 [3.114]	0.70 [0.794]	−1.42 [1.098]	1.87 [1.541]
Merger × Post-merger 3 year	1.10 [30.348]	−0.09 [0.606]	1.68 [16.760]	−4.80 [3.126]	−0.51 [0.962]	−1.40 [1.101]	−0.56 [1.536]
Merger × Mega × Post-merger 4 year	2.12 [33.117]	0.49 [0.661]	−4.75 [18.289]	−5.17 [3.411]	−0.38 [0.736]	−1.77 [1.202]	−0.24 [1.683]
Merger × Mega ×	10.94 [33.486]	0.22 [0.668]	−17.00 [18.493]	−6.52* [3.449]	−0.91 [0.930]	−1.72 [1.215]	−0.76 [1.698]

Post-merger
5 year

Trust	14.17*	0.16	−4.18	−6.54***	0.40**	0.72**	−2.08***
	[7.783]	[0.155]	[4.298]	[0.802]	[0.165]	[0.283]	[0.446]
Regional	4.24	0.42***	0.15	8.60***	0.03	0.41	0.45
	[7.198]	[0.144]	[3.975]	[0.741]	[0.158]	[0.261]	[0.367]
Regional II	0.41	0.36**	0.72	13.14***	0.10	0.43	0.06
	[7.622]	[0.152]	[4.209]	[0.785]	[0.165]	[0.277]	[0.391]
High capitalized	−6.58	1.15***	−2.11	0.22	−0.14	−0.47**	1.50***
	[6.564]	[0.131]	[3.625]	[0.676]	[0.142]	[0.238]	[0.329]
Low capitalized	−5.14	−0.45***	1.83	0.46	−0.10	0.05	−0.44**
	[3.591]	[0.072]	[1.983]	[0.370]	[0.067]	[0.130]	[0.187]
Cross-type merger	2.72	0.20	0.44	0.62	−0.10	−0.05	0.26
	[6.311]	[0.126]	[3.485]	[0.650]	[0.136]	[0.229]	[0.312]
Constant	−10.84	3.79***	113.42***	61.29***	0.85***	5.00***	6.66***
	[9.967]	[0.199]	[5.504]	[1.026]	[0.203]	[0.362]	[0.531]
Year dummies	Yes	Yes	Yes	Yes	Yes	Yes	Yes
Observations	912	912	912	912	705	912	741

*Statistical significance at the 10% level.**Statistical significance at the 5% level.***Statistical significance at the 1% level.
Notes: Standard errors in brackets below each coefficient estimate.
The sample consists of acquirer banks and synthetic acquirer banks both before and after the event.

1990s resulted in more than half of the industry's total assets being comprised of just three large financial groups. This chapter sets out to contribute to the existing literature on bank mergers by exploring the impact of these merger events on the shareholder value and performance of the banks involved.

In the analysis of shareholder value, consistent with studies in the United States and Europe, we find some evidence of excess returns just around the announcement of an M&A deal, particularly for target banks. But much larger and highly significant differences are revealed across banks depending on the expected size of the newly-merged entity. Banks entering into a mega-bank enjoy large and highly statistically significant excess returns, which are in turn significantly higher than those of the other banks in the sample, particularly in the few days surrounding the merger announcement.

Regression analysis confirms that although targets exhibit positive excess returns right at announcement of a merger, the main variable determining whether an M&A event announcement generates excess returns is the expected size of the merged entity. Banks merging into mega-banks with total assets of over 80 trillion yen post large, highly statistically significant excess returns in the month before and just around announcement, on the order of about 10%. Those excess returns are not sustained in the long-run, one year after announcement.

Interestingly in light of the above, analysis of performance ratios indicates that the size of the merger event is *not* a significant factor. Although banks entering into mega-mergers are different by some criteria, there is no statistically significant difference in the performance of mega-banks as compared to the rest of the treatment group in the first 5 years of the post-merger period. Merged banks on the whole seem to perform poorly. They demonstrate statistically significantly worse performance in terms of profitability, solvency, and inefficiency 2–4 years after merger, regardless of whether they are mega-banks or not.

This leaves us with some unanswered questions. If performance is not statistically significantly different for mega-mergers, and if the performance for mergers as a whole is *worse* than our control group after merger, then why do banks entering into mega-mergers exhibit such large and highly statistically significant positive run-ups in returns before merger announcement dates? The findings of this study suggest it is unlikely that market participants see the mega-mergers as strategic business mergers that will improve bank performance in the long-run. Taken together, the findings here on shareholder value and longer-term performance suggest that market participants are simply making a "flight-to-safety" as shareholders focus on banks that will become "too big to fail" and thus presumably benefit from regulatory forbearance.

APPENDIX

Table A1 Bank Merger Dates

Post-Merger Bank Name	Announcement Date	Completion Date*	Acquirer Bank	Target Bank	Mega-Merger	Cross-Type Merger	Type of Merger
Mitsubishi Bank	October 12, 1994	November 10, 1994 (none)	Mitsubishi Bank[a]	Nippon Trust Bank[a]	No	Yes	Subsidiarization
Bank of Tokyo Mitsubishi	March 29, 1995	April 1, 1996 (April 1996)	Mitsubishi Bank[a]	Bank of Tokyo[a]	No	No	Merger
Namihaya Bank	October 9, 1997	October 1, 1998 (October 1998)	Fukutoku Bank[a]	Bank of Naniwa	No	No	Merger
Minato Bank	May 15, 1998	April 1, 1999 (April 1999)	Hanshin Bank[a]	Midori Bank	No	No	Merger
Chuo Mitsui Trust & Banking	January 20, 1999	*April 1, 2000* (April 2000)	Chuo Trust & Banking[a]	Mitsui Trust & Banking[a]	No	No	Merger
Fuji Bank	*January 23, 1999*	March 31, 1999 (none)	Fuji Bank[a]	Yasuda Trust & Banking[a]	No	Yes	Subsidiarization
Kinki Osaka Bank	May 18, 1999	*April 1, 2000* (April 2000)	Bank of Osaka[a]	Bank of Kinki[a]	No	No	Merger
Mizuho Holdings (later Mizuho FG)	August 20, 1999	September 29, 2000 (April 2002)	Dai-Ichi Kangyo Bank[a]	(i)Fuji Bank[a] (ii)Industrial Bank of Japan[a]	Yes	Yes	Merger
Sumitomo Mitsui BC	October 14, 1999	*April 1, 2001* (April 2001)	Sumitomo Bank[a]	Sakura Bank[a]	Yes	No	Merger
Sapporo Hokuyo Holdings	February 10, 2000	April 2, 2001 (October 2008)	North Pacific Bank[a]	Sapporo Bank[a]	No	No	Merger
UFJ Holdings	March 14, 2000	April 2, 2001 (January 2002)	Sanwa Bank[a]	Tokai Bank[a]	Yes	No	Merger

(Continued)

Table A1 Continued

Post-Merger Bank Name	Announcement Date	Completion Date*	Acquirer Bank	Target Bank	Mega-Merger	Cross-Type Merger	Type of Merger
Mitsubishi Tokyo FG	April 19, 2000	April 2, 2001 (October 2001)	Bank of Tokyo Mitsubishi[a]	(i)Mitsubishi Trust & Banking[a] (ii)Nippon Trust Bank[a] (iii)Tokyo Trust Bank	Yes	Yes	Merger
Sakura Bank	June 9, 2000	July 25, 2000 (none)	Sakura Bank[a]	Minato Bank[a]	No	Yes	Subsidiarization
UFJ Holdings	July 6, 2000	April 2, 2001 (January 2002)	Sanwa Bank[a]	(i)Tokai Bank[a] (ii)Toyo Trust & Banking[a] (iii)Tokai Trust Bank	Yes	Yes	Merger
Sanwa Bank	September 29, 2000	January 17, 2001 (none)	Sanwa Bank[a]	Senshu Bank[a]	No	Yes	Subsidiarization
Momiji Holdings	November 1, 2000	September 28, 2001 (May 2004)	Hiroshima Sogo Bank[a]	Setouchi Bank[a]	No	No	Merger
Fukuoka City Bank	March 14, 2001	December 21, 2001 (none)	Fukuoka City Bank[a]	Bank of Nagasaki	No	No	Subsidiarization
Kyushu Shinwa Holdings	March 14, 2001	April 1, 2002 (April 2003)	Shinwa Bank[a]	Kyushu Bank[a]	No	No	Merger
Chuo Mitsui Trust & Banking	May 23, 2001	June 29, 2001 (April 2012)	Chuo Mitsui Trust & Banking[a]	Sakura Trust & Banking	No	No	Subsidiarization
Daiwa Bank Holdings	August 1, 2001	December 12, 2001 (March 2003)	Daiwa Bank[a]	(i)Kinki Osaka Bank[a] (ii)Nara Bank	No	Yes	Merger

Daiwa Bank Holdings (later Resona Holdings)	*September 8, 2001*	March 1, 2002 (March 2003)	Asahi Bank[a]	(i)Daiwa Bank[a] (ii)Kinki Osaka Bank[a] (iii)Nara Bank[a]	No	No	Merger
Kanto Tsukuba Bank	March 13, 2002	April 1, 2003 (April 2003)	Tsukuba Bank	Kanto Bank[a]	No	No	Merger
Nishi-Nippon City Bank	April 19, 2002	October 1, 2004 (October 2004)	Fukuoka City Bank[a]	Nishi-Nippon Bank[a]	No	No	Merger
Sumitomo Mitsui BC	December 26, 2002	March 17, 2003 (March 2003)	Sumitomo Mitsui Banking Corporation	Wakashio Bank	No	Yes	Merger
Kansai Urban Banking Corporation	April 1, 2003	*February 1, 2004* (February 2004)	Bank of Kansai[a]	Kansai Sawayaka Bank	No	No	Merger
Hokuhoku FG	May 23, 2003	September 1, 2004 (none)	Hokuriku Bank[a]	Hokkaido Bank[a]	No	No	Merger
Mitsubishi UFJ FG	July 14, 2004	*October 1, 2005* (January 2006)	Mitsubishi Tokyo Financial Group[a]	UFJ Holdings[a]	Yes	No	Merger
Kirayaka Holdings	October 29, 2004	October 3, 2005 (May 2007)	Shokusan Bank[a]	Yamagata Shiawase Bank	No	No	Merger
Kiyo Holdings	*November 20, 2004*	February 1, 2006 (October 2006)	Kiyo Bank[a]	Wakayama Bank	No	No	Merger
Yamaguchi FG	*March 19, 2005*	October 2, 2006 (none)	Yamaguchi Bank[a]	Momiji Holdings[a]	No	No	Merger
Fukuoka FG	*May 13, 2006*	April 2, 2007 (none)	Bank of Fukuoka[a]	Kumamoto Family Bank[a]	No	No	Merger

(Continued)

Table A1 Continued

Post-Merger Bank Name	Announcement Date	Completion Date*	Acquirer Bank	Target Bank	Mega-Merger	Cross-Type Merger	Type of Merger
Fukuoka FG	*May 3, 2007*	October 1, 2007 (none)	Fukuoka Financial Group[a]	Kyushu Shinwa Holdings[a]	No	No	Merger
Senshu Ikeda Holdings	February 21, 2008	October 1, 2009 (May 2010)	Bank of Ikeda[a]	Senshu Bank[a]	No	No	Merger
Fidea Holdings	May 13, 2008	October 1, 2009 (none)	Shonai Bank[a]	Hokuto Bank	No	No	Merger
Tomony Holdings	January 27, 2009	April 1, 2010 (none)	Kagawa Bank[a]	Tokushima Bank[a]	No	No	Merger
Kansai Urban Banking Corporation	February 26, 2009	March 1, 2010 (March 2010)	Kansai Urban Banking Corporation[a]	Biwako Bank[a]	No	No	Merger
Tsukuba Bank	*April 29, 2009*	March 1, 2010 (March 2010)	Kanto Tsukuba Bank[a]	Ibaraki Bank	No	No	Merger
Sumitomo Mitsui Trust Holdings	October 28, 2009	April 1, 2011 (April 2012)	Sumitomo Trust & Banking[a]	Chuo Mitsui Trust Holdings[a]	No	No	Merger
Juroku Bank	July 30, 2010	December 22, 2010 (September 2012)	Juroku Bank[a]	Gifu Bank[a]	No	No	Merger

[a]The bank was listed on the announcement day.
*Under completion date, actual book merger.
Notes: Italic dates were non-business days and thus shifted to the next business days in the analysis.

ACKNOWLEDGMENTS

The authors thank discussants and participants at the 2013 Japan Economics Association Meetings, Nippon Finance Association Meetings, Asia-Pacific Economic Association Meetings, and Institute for Developing Economies seminar. We would particularly like to thank, without implicating, Kaoru Hosono, Masahiro Hori, and Seiro Ito for comments on earlier drafts.

REFERENCES

Abadie, A., Gardeazabal, J., 2003. The economic costs of conflict: a case study of the Basque country. American Economic Review 93 (1), 113–132.

Brewer III, E., Genay, H., Hunter, W.C., Kaufman, G.G., 2003. The value of banking relationships during a financial crisis: evidence from failures of Japanese banks. Journal of Japanese and International Economies 17 (3), 233–262.

Campa, J.M., Hernando, I., 2006. M&As performance in the European financial industry. Journal of Banking and Finance 30 (12), 3367–3392.

DeYoung, R., Evanoff, D.D., Molyneux, P., 2009. Mergers and acquisitions of financial institutions: a review of the post-2000 literature. Journal of Financial Services Research 36 (2–3), 87–110.

Greene, W.H., 2011. Econometric Analysis, seventh ed. Prentice Hall, Upper Saddle River, NJ.

Hankir, Y., Rauch, C., Umber, M.P., 2011. Bank M&A: a market power story? Journal of Banking and Finance 35, 2341–2354.

Harada, K., Ito, T., 2011. Did mergers help Japanese mega-banks avoid failure? Analysis of the distance to default of banks. Journal of the Japanese and International Economies 25 (1), 1–22.

Hori, M., 2005. Does bank liquidation affect client firm performance? Evidence from a bank failure in Japan. Economicss Letters 88 (3), 415–420.

Hosono, K., Sakai, K., Tsuru, K., 2009. Consolidation of banks in Japan: causes and consequences. In: Financial Sector Development in the Pacific Rim, East Asia Seminar on Economics, vol. 18. University of Chicago Press, Chicago, IL, pp. 265–309.

MacKinlay, A.C., 1997. Event studies in economics and finance. Journal of economic literature 35 (1), 13–39.

Mishkin, F.S., 2012. Economics of Money, Banking, and Financial Markets, 10th ed. Prentice Hall.

Miyajima, H., Yafeh, Y., 2007. Japan's banking crisis: an event-study perspective. Journal of Banking and Finance 31, 2866–2885.

Montgomery, H., Harimaya, K., Takahashi, Y., 2013. Too Big to Succeed? Banking Sector Consolidation and Efficiency. Mimeograph. <https://dl.dropboxusercontent.com/u/47122510/Efficiency.pdf>.

Uchino, T., Uesugi, I., 2012. The effects of a megabank merger on firm-bank relationships and borrowing costs. Discussion Paper No. 12022, Research Institute of Economy, Trade and Industry (RIETI). <http://ideas.repec.org/p/eti/dpaper/12022.html>.

Yamori, N., Harimaya, K., 2009. Mergers decision in Japanese small mutual banks: Efficiency improvement or empire buildings? Corporate Ownership and Control 7 (2), 117–125.

Yamori, N., Harimaya, K., 2010. Do managers of mutual institutions choose efficiency-improving mergers? The recent experience of Japanese credit associations. IUP Journal of Bank Management IX (1 and 2), 7–11.

Yamori, N., Murakami, A., 1999. Does bank relationship have an economic value? The effect of main bank failure on client firms. Economics Letters 65 (1), 115–120.

Yamori, N., Harimaya, K., Kondo, K., 2003. Are banks affiliated with bank holding companies more efficient than independent banks? The recent experience regarding Japanese regional BHCs. Asia-Pacific Financial Markets 10 (4), 359–376.

CHAPTER 6

A Regime-Switching Analysis of Asian Bank Stocks

Kin-Yip Ho[a], Yanlin Shi[a], and Zhaoyong Zhang[b]
[a]The Australian National University, Research School of Finance, Actuarial Studies and
Applied Statistics ANU College of Business and Economics, Canberra, ACT 0200, Australia
[b]Edith Cowan University, School of Business Faculty of Business and Law,
270 Joondalup Drive, Joondalup, WA 6027, Australia

6.1 INTRODUCTION

The Asian banking systems have been hit by several large shocks ever since the 1997–1998 Asian financial crisis (Mohanty and Turner, 2010). In particular, the East Asian financial crisis of 1997–1998 generated considerable turbulence to the stability of the financial systems in the region. One important lesson learnt by these economies from the financial crisis is that it is important to establish both a more resilient domestic economic and financial system and a better functioning global financial system as keys to crisis prevention, management, and resolution (Kawai, 2009). The crisis has led to the structural changes in the banking industry and the corporate governance in Asia (Soedarmono et al., 2011). For example, from 1997 to 2003, most of the Asian countries launched reforms in their financial supervisory systems (Hsu and Liao, 2010). A result from such reforms has been the rapid growth of bank consolidations or mergers and acquisitions (M&As) in these countries, which peaked at 25% per year as of 2003. Foreign Direct Investment (FDI), notably cross-border M&As involving banks in emerging countries, increased rapidly from US$2.5 billion during 1991–1995 to US$67.5 billion during 2001–2005 (Domanski, 2005; Moshirian, 2008). On the other hand, the recent global financial crisis (GFC) has shaken the consensus on how to run macroeconomic policy and forced the governments to consider the use of macroprudential instruments, such as cyclical capital requirements, leverage ratios, or dynamic provisioning etc., which can help decrease financial risks (Blanchard et al., 2013). With the proactive government intervention, the bank performance in terms of solvency, credit risk, and profitability has improved substantially in Asia (Ding et al., 2013). Overall the Asian banks have become better capitalized, their external exposures have been reduced, and credit risks have been managed more effectively (Mohanty and Turner, 2010).

The banking industry plays an important role in the model financial system. Since business firms significantly depend on banks for their external funding (Adams, 2008), the health of the economy is closely related to the soundness of its banking system, and both are inseparable. Thus, the top priority of the bank supervision and regulation is to ensure a safe and sound banking system and to prevent financial system instability. Moreover, corporate sector vulnerability is more likely to affect bank soundness through risk-shifting mechanisms in bank-based financial systems (Stiglitz and Weiss, 1981). Therefore, the market prices or returns of bank stocks, which contain important information like banking stability, have become an important research topic in finance.

What drives stock returns is an extensively debated question. Among the many studies, Veronesi (1999) suggests that return changes according to the arrival of public information in the market will cause investors to behave differently depending on the contents of the information. Therefore, returns could be affected by the sentiment of information a finding which is supported by numerous studies (Hafez, 2009; Leinweber and Sisk, 2011; Moinz et al., 2011). As to the source of public information arrival, Ho et al. (2013) argue that both firm-specific and macroeconomic news can significantly affect the volatility of stock returns. Do Asian banks perform differently toward the arrival of public information? How do firm-specific and macroeconomic news affect stock returns of Asian banks? We conduct a preliminary assessment of news impacts on the daily stock returns of 20 selected Asian banks from Japan, China, Singapore, and Korea from January 1, 2000, to December 31, 2012. The results are reported in Table 6.1. Results indicate that stock returns of these banks are affected significantly by the arrival of public information. The negative news is found to affect stock returns negatively in most cases, while positive news affects the stock returns positively. Both negative and positive news effects, in general, are very symmetric. In addition, firm-specific news tends to have a profound impact on stock returns in comparison with the impact of macroeconomic news. These findings motivate us to further investigate the dynamic impact of firm-specific and macroeconomic news announcements on Asian bank stock returns by applying a regime-switching framework.

Due to the asymmetric information about the state of the economy, investors overreact to bad news in good times and underreact to good news in bad times (see, for instance, Veronesi, 1999). News effects should be studied separately in different states since stock volatility is not time invariant. This can be observed in Figure 6.1 where the stock returns of four selected banks are plotted. The volatility of returns varies substantially over time and become more volatile during the global financial crisis (GFC) period in all cases. Therefore, a key question is the following: What are the impacts of daily firm-specific and macroeconomic news on the stock returns of Asian banks surrounding the proximity of their first release of information. Do news effects depend on the state of stock returns? Are there any differences between the impacts of negative news sentiment and positive news sentiment on returns? Does firm-specific news have a greater impact on returns than macroeconomic news? The purpose of this chapter is to examine the relationship between news sentiment and stock returns of Asian banks at different states by employing the Markov Regime-Switching (MRS) model proposed by Hamilton (1988, 1989, 1994). In this regime-switching framework, two states are classified, namely the "calm" (low-volatility) state and the "turbulent" (high-volatility)

Table 6.1 Preliminary Estimates of News Impact on Return

Ticker	λ_1	λ_2	λ_3	λ_4
053000:KS	−0.4374	0.4658	−0.0426	0.0212
055550:KS	−0.4704	0.4923	−0.2373	0.0977
0939:HK	−0.5080	0.6170	−0.0514	0.1490
1398:HK	−0.2855	0.8628	−0.1328	0.1080
3328:HK	−0.6932	0.2916	−0.1537	0.2151
3968:HK	−1.1334	0.2536	−0.3584	0.1523
3988:HK	−0.3209	0.5957	−0.1667	0.0283
8303:JP	0.0186	0.6828	0.3425	0.0390
8304:JP	−0.9410	0.8622	0.5127	−0.0820
8306:JP	−0.3463	0.4981	0.0029	−0.0142
8308:JP	−0.1591	0.5986	0.1431	0.1439
8316:JP	−0.5499	0.8291	−0.0456	0.0817
8331:JP	−0.0955	0.1068	−0.0714	0.2357
8332:JP	−0.2263	0.2475	−0.0609	0.2766
8355:JP	−0.3785	0.3109	0.1151	0.0828
8403:JP	0.0374	0.3400	0.0404	0.0554
8411:JP	−1.3408	−0.2643	−0.1259	0.0820
DBSM:SI	0.0680	0.9453	−0.2468	0.0115
OCBC:SI	−0.2049	0.4249	−0.1162	0.1239
UOBH:SI	−0.5809	0.2443	−0.0923	0.1563

Summarized Estimates

	Mean	Std Dev.	Median	Q_1	Q_3	Skew
λ_1	−0.4274	0.3761	−0.3624	−0.5577	−0.1934	−0.8309
λ_2	0.4702	0.2954	0.4790	0.2821	0.6334	−0.3844
λ_3	−0.0373	0.1994	−0.0662	−0.1380	0.0122	1.1013
λ_4	0.0982	0.0876	0.0903	0.0364	0.1498	0.1077

Note: RavenPack News Analytics—Dow Jones Edition—is used to construct the news sentiment variables. There are four news dummy variables constructed to indicate the occurrence of negative and positive firm-specific and macroeconomic news. The estimates of news impact on stock returns are obtained by estimating the following model: $r_t = \mu + \lambda_1 I(WCSS_{f,t}^N > 0) + \lambda_2 I(WCSS_{f,t}^P > 0) + \lambda_3 I(WESS_{m,t}^N > 0) + \lambda_4 I(WESS_{m,t}^P > 0) + \varepsilon_t$ where r_t is the daily return in percentage at day t, $WCSS_{f,t}$ is the weighted average composite sentiment score as the proxy for the firm-specific news, and $WESS_{m,t}$ is the weighted average event sentiment score as the proxy for macroeconomic news. Superscripts N and P indicate that the average sentiment score is constructed with only negative or positive news. $I(\cdot)$ is the indicator function that gives 1 when the condition inside the brackets is true and gives 0 otherwise. Also, the descriptive statistics are summarized for coefficients of news variables, including mean value (*Mean*), standard deviation (*Std Dev.*), median value (*Median*), 25 percentile (Q_1), 75 percentile (Q_3), and skewness (*Skew*).

state, and the intercept of returns is allowed to switch between the states. The results show that both the occurrence and sentiment of the news announcements have predictive power for future stock returns, and positive news is found to have different impact on stock returns at different states in comparison with negative news. We find that the magnitude of news effects is different, depending on the types of news and regimes of stock returns. These findings have important implications for policy makers seeking

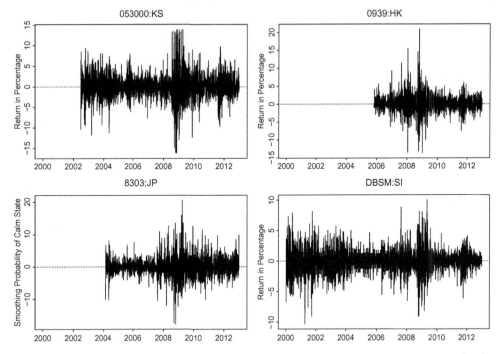

Figure 6.1 Return series in percentage. This figure presents the return series in percentage for the four selected banks. The title for each graph is the corresponding ticker for the stock.

stability of a financial system and for investors in predicting the potential effects of news releases on the returns of banks they are monitoring.

The rest of this chapter is structured as follows. Section 6.2 briefly describes the RavenPack news database, followed by data description in Section 6.3. In Section 6.4, we discuss the model and methodology used in this study, and Section 6.5 analyzes the estimation results. Section 6.6 concludes.

6.2 RAVENPACK NEWS DATABASE

RavenPack News Analytics—Dow Jones Edition—is a comprehensive database covering more than 1200 types of firm-specific and macroeconomic news events. RavenPack automatically tracks and monitors relevant information on tens of thousands of companies, government organizations, influential people, key geographical locations, and all major currencies and traded commodities. The service includes analytics on more than 170,000 entities in over 100 countries and covers over 98% of the investable global market. Among the many benefits, RavenPack delivers sentiment analysis and event data most likely to impact financial markets and trading around the world, in a matter of milliseconds. RavenPack continuously analyzes relevant information from major real-time newswires and trustworthy sources, such as Dow Jones Newswires, regional editions of the Wall Street Journal and Barron's, and Internet sources including financial sites, blogs, local and regional newspapers, to produce real-time news sentiment scores. All relevant news items about entities are classified and quantified according to their sentiment, relevance, topic, novelty, and market impact. In terms of sentiment, RavenPack uses a proprietary computational linguistic analysis algorithm to quantify positive and negative perceptions on facts and opinions reported in the news. The core of the algorithm can be divided into two steps. First, RavenPack builds up a historical database of words, phrases, combinations, and other word-level definitions which affect the target company, market, or asset class. Subsequently, the text in the specific news story is compared with the historical database and the sentiment score is generated accordingly.[1]

In this study, we use only the news relevance score (*REL*), composite sentiment score (*CSS*), event sentiment score (*ESS*), and event novelty score (*ENS*) from the RavenPack database to construct our news variables. The algorithms to generate these scores are described in Appendix B. *REL* is a score that indicates how strongly the news story is related to a particular company and it ranges from 0 to 100. A high *REL* suggests that the news story is highly relevant to the corresponding stock. *CSS* is a sentiment score that ranges from 0 to 100 and represents the news sentiment of a given story by combining various sentiment analysis techniques. The direction of the score is determined by emotionally charged words and phrases embedded in the news story, which is typically rated by experts as having short-term positive or negative share price impact. A high score (above 50) indicates a positive intraday stock price impact, while a low score (below 50) indicates a negative impact. *ESS* is a granular score that ranges from 0 to 100 and specifies whether the news story conveys positive or negative sentiment about the macroeconomy.[2] The score is constructed in two steps. First, a set of news (training set) is categorized by a group of financial experts based on the degree to which they have short-term positive or negative macroeconomic impact. Second, their lassification is encapsulated in an algorithm that generates a score range from 0 to 100. A high score (above 50) indicates positive sentiment, while a low score (below 50) indicates negative sentiment. *ENS* is a score that ranges from 0 to 100. The score measures

---

[1] RavenPack's unique and innovative dataset is backed up by rigorous research. To acknowledge its importance of incorporating news analytics into systematic and discretionary trading and investment, RavenPack has won the "Best Specialist Research" category at the 2012 Technical Analyst Awards and the "Best Specialist Data Provider" at the 2013 Technical Analyst Awards.

[2] Four major groups of macroeconomic news are used: (1) National Income and Gross Domestic Product (GDP); (2) employment; (3) interest rates; and (4) public finance announcement, including money supply. Also, the macroeconomic news is collected individually for Japan, China, Singapore, and Korea. The corresponding news variables are then constructed based on the macroeconomic news of the country of the bank only.

how "new" or "novel" a news story is in the past 24–hour period. The first story reporting a categorized event about the macroeconomy is considered to be the most novel and receives a score of 100.

6.3 DATA AND SAMPLE

6.3.1 Return Series

Our stock price samples comprise of daily data of 20 selected Asian banks (based on their market cap and data availability), including ten from Japan, five from China traded on the Hong Kong stock exchange, three from Singapore, and two from Korea. The sample period ranges from January 1, 2000, to December 31, 2012. The complete list of names and tickers of the 20 banks can be found in Appendix A. Our data are sourced from Thomson Reuters Tick History (TRTH) database, which contains microsecond-time-stamped tick data going back to January 1996. The database covers 35 million OTC and exchange-traded instruments worldwide, provided by the Securities Industry Research Centre of Australasia (SIRCA). Define $\{S_0, S_1, \ldots, S_{T-1}, S_T\}$ as the sequence of daily closing price for one firm at times $\{0, 1, \ldots, T-1, T\}$. The corresponding daily return at time t is

$$r_t = 100 \times \log(S_t/S_{t-1}). \tag{6.1}$$

6.3.2 News Variables

We use a news database provided by RavenPack News Analytics to proxy for public information arrivals. There are six news variables to be constructed using score data from the RavenPack database. In particular, we use *REL* and *CSS* to construct the firm-specific news variables, and *ESS* and *ENS* to construct the macroeconomic news variables.

To control for the effect of news sentiment, two weighted average sentiment scores of news variables are constructed as follows. For firm-specific news, the weighted average composite sentiment score is:

$$WCSS_{f,t} = \frac{1}{T} \sum_{all\ \tau} \frac{(CSS_\tau - 50)REL_\tau}{100}, \tag{6.2}$$

where T is the total number of news stories in the daily interval $[t-1, t]$ and $\tau \in [t-1, t]$. Similarly, for macroeconomic news, the weighted average event sentiment score at time t is:

$$WESS_{m,t} = \frac{1}{T} \sum_{all\ \tau} \frac{(ESS_\tau - 50)ENS_\tau}{100}. \tag{6.3}$$

Furthermore, to test for the possible asymmetric effects of negative and positive news, we construct the following four weighted average sentiment score for both negative and positive firm-specific and macroeconomic news.

$$WCSS_{f,t}^{N} = \frac{1}{\sum_{all\,\tau} I(CSS_\tau < 50)} \sum_{all\,\tau} \frac{I(CSS_\tau < 50)|CSS_\tau - 50|REL_\tau}{100}, \quad (6.4)$$

$$WCSS_{f,t}^{P} = \frac{1}{\sum_{all\,\tau} I(CSS_\tau > 50)} \sum_{all\,\tau} \frac{I(CSS_\tau > 50)|CSS_\tau - 50|REL_\tau}{100}, \quad (6.5)$$

$$WESS_{f,t}^{N} = \frac{1}{\sum_{all\,\tau} I(ESS_\tau < 50)} \sum_{all\,\tau} \frac{I(ESS_\tau < 50)|ESS_\tau - 50|ENS_\tau}{100}, \quad (6.6)$$

$$WESS_{f,t}^{P} = \frac{1}{\sum_{all\,\tau} I(ESS_\tau > 50)} \sum_{all\,\tau} \frac{I(ESS_\tau > 50)|ESS_\tau - 50|ENS_\tau}{100}, \quad (6.7)$$

where $I(\cdot)$ is the indicator function that gives 1 when the condition inside the brackets is true and gives 0 otherwise. Superscripts N and P stand for the negative and positive news, and subscripts f and m stand for the firm-specific and macroeconomic news, respectively.

6.4 MARKOV REGIME-SWITCHING (MRS) MODEL

The MRS model is proposed by Hamilton (1988, 1989, 1994). Let $\{s_t\}$ be a stationary, irreducible Markov process with discrete state space $\{1,2\}$ and transition matrix $P = [p_{jk}]$ where $p_{jk} = P(s_{t+1} = k \mid s_t = j)$ is the transition probability of moving from state j to state k ($j, k \in \{1,2\}$) and its transition probabilities determine the persistence of each regime or state. Then, we have a standard MRS model specified as follows:

$$r_t = \mu_{s_t} + \varepsilon_{s_t,t} \text{ and } \varepsilon_{s_t,t} = \sigma_{s_t}\eta_t \text{ where } \eta_t \overset{iid}{\sim} N(0,1), \quad (6.8)$$

where $\varepsilon_{s_t,t}$ is the error term at time t in state s_t, η_t is an identical and independent sequence following Gaussian distribution with 0 mean and unit standard deviation, and σ_{s_t} is the standard deviation of $\varepsilon_{s_t,t}$ at time t in state s_t. In this chapter, we set $\sigma_1 < \sigma_2$, so that states 1 and 2 will indicate the "calm" (low-volatility) and "turbulent" (high-volatility) states, respectively, for the return series.

We notice that in Eq. (6.8), the distribution of innovation is assumed to be Gaussian. However, enormous evidence suggests that financial series is rarely Gaussian but typically leptokurtic and exhibits heavy-tail behavior (Bollerslev, 1987; Susmel and Engel, 1994). In addition, Student's t-distribution is a widely used alternative, which can accommodate the excess kurtosis of the innovations (Bollerslev, 1987). On the other hand, as noted by Klaassen (2002), Ardia (2009), and Haas (2009), if regimes are not Gaussian but leptokurtic, the use of within-regime normality can seriously affect the identification of the regime process. The reason can be found in Haas and Paolella (2012), who further argue that Quasi Maximum Likelihood Estimation (QMLE) based on Gaussian components does not provide a consistent estimator of the MRS model. Therefore, we modify the standard MRS model by assuming that the innovations in Eq. (6.8) follow a Student's t-distribution with degree of freedom v (MRS-t model) as follows:

$$r_t = \mu_{s_t} + \varepsilon_{s_t,t} \text{ and } \varepsilon_{s_t,t} = \sigma_{s_t}\eta_t \text{ where } \eta_t \overset{iid}{\sim} t(0,1,v). \tag{6.9}$$

We estimate parameters of the MRS-t model using maximum likelihood estimation (MLE). The conditional density of $\varepsilon_{s_t,t}$ is given as follows:

$$\Omega_{t-1} = \left\{ \varepsilon_{s_{t-1},t-1}, \varepsilon_{s_{t-2},t-2}, \ldots, \varepsilon_{s_1,1} \right\}, \tag{6.10}$$

$$\theta = \left(\mu_1, \mu_2, p_{11}, p_{22}, v, \sigma_1, \sigma_2 \right)',$$

$$f(\varepsilon_{s_t,t}|s_t = j, \theta, \Omega_{t-1}) = \frac{\Gamma[(v+1)/2]}{\Gamma(v/2)\sqrt{\pi(v-2)}\sigma_j} \left[1 + \frac{\varepsilon_{j,t}^2}{(v-2)\sigma_j} \right]^{\frac{v+1}{2}},$$

where Ω_{t-1} is the information set at time $t-1$, θ is the vector of parameters, $\Gamma(\cdot)$ is the Gamma function, and $f(\varepsilon_{s_t,t}|\theta, \Omega_{t-1})$ is the conditional density of $\varepsilon_{s_t,t}$. This stems from the fact that at time t, $\varepsilon_{s_t,t}$ follows a Student's t-distribution with mean 0, variance σ_{s_t}, and degrees of freedom v given time $t-1$.

By inserting the filtered probability in state j at time $t-1$, $\omega_{j,t-1} = P(s_{t-1}=j \mid \theta, \Omega_{t-1})$, into Eq. (6.10) and integrating out the state variable s_{t-1}, we have the following density function

$$f(\varepsilon_{s_t,t}|\theta, \Omega_{t-1}) = \sum_{j=1}^{2}\sum_{k=1}^{2} p_{jk}\omega_{j,t-1}f(\varepsilon_{s_t,t}|s_t = j, \theta, \Omega_{t-1}), \tag{6.11}$$

where $\omega_{j,t-1}$ can be obtained by an integrative algorithm given in Hamilton (1989). The log–likelihood function corresponds to Eq. (6.11) is as follows:

$$L(\theta|\varepsilon) = \sum_{t=2}^{T} \ln f(\varepsilon_{s_t,t}|\theta, \Omega_{t-1}) \text{ where } \varepsilon = \left(\varepsilon_{s_t,1}, \varepsilon_{s_t,2}, \ldots, \varepsilon_{s_t,T} \right)', \tag{6.12}$$

and the MLE estimator $\hat{\theta}$ is obtained by maximizing Eq. (6.12).

In order to identify which state the return series lies in at time t, we extract the smoothing probability of the "calm" state as follows (Hamilton, 1988, 1989, 1994),

$$P(s_t = 1|\theta, \Omega_T) = \omega_{1,t} \left[\frac{p_{11}P(s_{t+1} = 1|\theta, \Omega_T)}{P(s_{t+1} = 1|\theta, \Omega_t)} + \frac{p_{12}P(s_{t+1} = 2|\theta, \Omega_T)}{P(s_{t+1} = 2|\theta, \Omega_t)} \right]. \quad (6.13)$$

Using the fact that $P(s_T = 1 | \theta, \Omega_T) = \omega_{1,T}$, the smoothing probability series $P(s_t = 1 | \theta, \Omega_T)$ can be generated by iterating Eq. (6.13) backward from T to 1.

To test the effects of the news variables on stock returns, we extend Eq. (6.8) by including the news variables,

$$r_t = \mu_{s_t} + \lambda_{s,t} News_t + \varepsilon_{s_t,t}, \quad (6.14)$$

where $News_t$ is a vector of news variables and $\lambda_{s,t}$ is a vector of corresponding coefficients.

6.5 EMPIRICAL RESULTS

In this section, we describe some summary statistics of our dataset first. We then fit the MRS-t models without news variables to produce the smoothing probability series and discuss results relating to the sign and dummy of the news sentiment variables. Finally, we estimate the MRS-t models refitted with the news sentiment variables.

6.5.1 Descriptive Statistics of the Dataset

The descriptive statistics of the four sentiment scores, CSS_τ, REL_τ, ESS_τ, and ENS_τ, used to construct our news variables are summarized in Panel A of Table 6.2. It is noted that the mean of CSS_τ is very close to 50, indicating that on average the news stories are neutral. The mean of ESS_τ is 58.2844 and greater than 50, suggesting that, from the experts' point of view, the macroeconomic news of Japan, China, Singapore, and Korea received during the entire period is overall positive.

The descriptive statistics of the stock return and news variables are summarized in Panel B of Table 6.2. As it can be seen in Panel B, the mean of the return in percentage is around 0, while the mean of the absolute return in percentage is 1.7151. For the weighted average sentiment of news variables, the mean of $WCSS_{f,t}$ is slightly less than 0, with a value of -0.1679. This suggests that on average the firm-specific news sentiment is negative during the sample period and is consistent with the fact that $WCSS_{f,t}^N$ has a greater mean than $WCSS_{f,t}^P$. As for the macroeconomic news, the mean of $WESS_{m,t}$ is 2.4232 and greater than 0. However, the variation of macroeconomic news sentiment is much greater than that of the firm-specific news sentiment, with a standard deviation of 12.0093 (compared with 1.3233 for $WCSS_{f,t}$). Also, $WESS_{m,t}$ is only slightly positively skewed (the skewness is equal to 0.7363), while $WCSS_{f,t}$ is negatively skewed with a value of -5.0245.

Table 6.2 Datasets Descriptive Statistics

	Mean	Std Dev.	Median	Q_1	Q_3	Skew
Panel A: Descriptive Statistics of News Database						
CSS_τ	49.3589	7.6356	50.0000	47.0000	52.0000	−0.9636
REL_τ	26.4233	28.5825	15.0000	3.0000	39.0000	1.1914
ESS_τ	58.2844	27.3921	50.0000	50.0000	95.0000	−0.1111
ENS_τ	75.2370	24.2622	75.0000	56.0000	100.0000	−0.7438
Panel B: Descriptive Statistics of Variables						
r_t	−0.0018	2.5035	0.0000	−1.2215	1.1889	0.1568
$|r_t|$	1.7151	1.8237	1.2048	0.5552	2.2918	2.9566
$WCSS_{f,t}$	−0.1679	1.3233	0.0000	−0.3165	0.1450	−5.0245
$WCSS_{f,t}^N$	0.5133	1.1601	0.0988	0.0000	0.5770	7.9749
$WCSS_{f,t}^P$	0.3453	0.6434	0.0775	0.0000	0.4552	5.0598
$WESS_{m,t}$	2.4232	12.0093	0.0000	0.0000	0.0000	0.7363
$WESS_{m,t}^N$	1.7156	6.5618	0.0000	0.0000	0.0000	4.5490
$WESS_{m,t}^P$	4.1388	9.8823	0.0000	0.0000	0.0000	2.6701

Note: This table presents the summary descriptive statistics of all the variables employed in this study (observations of each variable are compounded for all the 20 stocks). CSS_τ and REL_τ are the composite sentiment score and relevance score of each firm-specific news story, respectively. ESS_τ and ENS_τ are the event sentiment score and event novelty score of each macroeconomic news story, respectively. $|r_t|$ is the absolute percentage return. The sample period is from January 1, 2000, to December 31, 2012. For explanation of other variables, please see the note for Table 6.1.

6.5.2 MRS-t Model Without News Variables

Before fitting the return series into MRS-t models, we have conducted a few tests for normality and the Gaussian distribution, and Table 6.3 reports the results. As can be seen from Table 6.3, none of the daily returns of the Asian banks show a value of kurtosis

Table 6.3 Test for Normality

Ticker	Kurt.	J.B.	K.S.	Ticker	Kurt.	J.B.	K.S.
053000:KS	4.7070	0.0000	0.0000	8308:JP	9.0692	0.0000	0.0000
055550:KS	3.6554	0.0000	0.0000	8316:JP	4.4490	0.0000	0.0000
0939:HK	7.8517	0.0000	0.0000	8331:JP	5.5016	0.0000	0.0000
1398:HK	5.0578	0.0000	0.0000	8332:JP	6.6395	0.0000	0.0000
3328:HK	5.3727	0.0000	0.0000	8355:JP	5.3647	0.0000	0.0000
3968:HK	5.3884	0.0000	0.0000	8403:JP	3.5801	0.0000	0.0000
3988:HK	8.6492	0.0000	0.0000	8411:JP	5.3094	0.0000	0.0000
8303:JP	4.5658	0.0000	0,0000	DBSM:SI	2.7628	0.0000	0.0000
8304:JP	21.1855	0.0000	0.0000	OCBC:SI	6.6900	0.0000	0.0000
8306:JP	3.4929	0.0000	0.0000	UOBH:SI	4.1595	0.0000	0.0000

Note: This table presents the kurtosis and normality tests for daily return of Asian banks. *Kurt.* is the kurtosis, *K.S.* is the *p*-value of Kolmogorov–Smirnov normality test, and *J.B.* is the *p*-value of Jarque-Bera normality test.

close to 0, and even the smallest one is equal to 3.4929. Recall that for Gaussian distribution, the kurtosis should be equal to 0. Therefore, this result suggests that it is very possible that none of the return is Gaussian. However, the results of the Jarque-Bera and Kolmogorov–Smirnov tests confirm that the null hypothesizes of normal (Gaussian) distribution should be rejected in all cases given that the p-values are close to 0.

Since none of the distribution of return series is Gaussian, we fit the daily returns data into the MRS-t models as specified in Eq. (6.9) and report the results in Table 6.4. We note that all the estimates of the transition probability are very close to 1 with the

Table 6.4 Estimates of MRS Model without News

Ticker	p_{11}	p_{22}	μ_1	μ_2	σ_1^2	σ_2^2
053000:KS	0.9917	0.9810	0.0377	−0.1189	1.3872	2.9927
055550:KS	0.9952	0.9947	0.0348	0.0244	1.1501	2.3602
0939:HK	0.9933	0.9832	0.0532	0.0027	0.9279	2.6647
1398:HK	0.9921	0.9815	0.0292	−0.0825	0.9683	2.6412
3328:HK	0.9928	0.9780	0.0231	0.0295	1.0496	2.9057
3968:HK	0.9971	0.9886	0.0677	−0.1401	1.4493	3.2231
3988:HK	0.9882	0.9849	0.0226	−0.0202	0.5271	2.2271
8303:JP	0.9922	0.9938	−0.1145	−0.1515	1.0238	2.6125
8304:JP	0.9824	0.9824	0.0438	−0.2290	1.3543	2.6563
8306:JP	0.9927	0.9917	−0.0266	−0.1362	0.8995	2.3758
8308:JP	0.9847	0.9795	−0.1513	−0.0646	1.0775	2.7966
8316:JP	0.9955	0.9926	−0.0172	−0.0864	0.9578	2.7537
8331:JP	0.9894	0.9832	−0.0478	0.0334	0.7312	2.1600
8332:JP	0.9937	0.9900	−0.0376	−0.0293	0.7556	2.2093
8355:JP	0.9933	0.9923	−0.0052	−0.0451	0.4548	1.7265
8403:JP	0.9907	0.9946	0.0020	−0.0797	1.0782	2.6115
8411:JP	0.9942	0.9889	−0.0087	−0.0670	0.9663	2.9337
DBSM:SI	0.9934	0.9930	0.0319	−0.0716	0.2262	1.7738
OCBC:SI	0.9939	0.9896	0.0446	−0.0489	0.2645	1.7248
UOBH:SI	0.9904	0.9896	0.0518	−0.0499	0.1331	1.6959

Summarized Estimates

	Mean	Std Dev.	Median	Q_1	Q_3	Skew
p_{11}	0.9919	0.0035	0.9928	0.9907	0.9938	−1.1552
p_{22}	0.9877	0.0054	0.9892	0.9830	0.9924	−0.2913
μ_1	0.0017	0.0563	0.0228	−0.0196	0.0392	−1.2600
μ_2	−0.0665	0.0666	−0.0658	−0.0945	−0.0270	−0.4488
σ_1^2	2.5422	0.8866	2.6171	1.9816	2.9380	0.1786
σ_2^2	12.7542	5.4004	13.6258	9.0000	15.8725	0.3533

Note: This table presents the estimates of MRS model without news for the Asian Banks. p_{11} and p_{22} are the transition probabilities of the "calm" and "turbulent" states, respectively. For explanation of other variables, please see the note in Table 6.1.

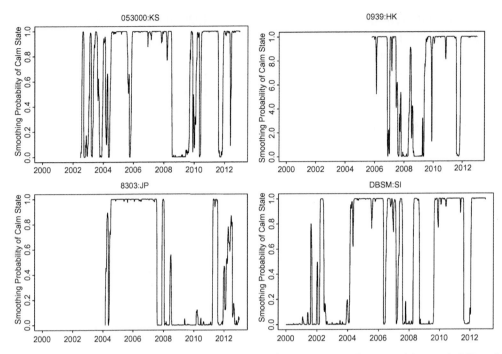

Figure 6.2 Smoothing probability of calm state. This figure presents the smoothing probability of the calm state for the four selected stocks. The title for each graph is the corresponding ticker for the stock.

mean estimate close to 0.99, implying that the regimes are persistent, and each state (no matter the "calm" or "turbulent" state) has a constant expected duration. Furthermore, we note that the mean value of the expected return (μ) is 0.0017 in the "calm" state and −0.0665 in the "turbulent" state. This finding suggests that when it is in the "turbulent" state or the volatility becomes greater, the expected return tends to be smaller.

To identify which state the return series tends to stay at a particular day, we estimate the smoothing probability of the "calm" state as specified in Eq. (6.13). We report in Figure 6.2 only the estimation results for the four banks' smoothing probability series. As a rule of thumb, if the smoothing probability is close to 1, the return tends to stay in the "calm" state and otherwise in the "turbulent" state. As displayed in Figure 6.2, all of the four returns fall in the "turbulent" state during the 2008 GFC. In particular, the Japanese bank appears to suffer longer in the "turbulent" state as the probability remains a value close to 0 from late 2007 up to early 2011. On the other hand, during the pre-GFC period in 2004–2008 and the post-GFC period in 2000–2012, almost all the stocks returns are in the "calm" state. The empirical results show that the status of the regime persistence for the Asian banks is consistent with the performance of the global economy during the sample period.

6.5.3 Effects of News Sentiment Sign

As we discussed early, the effects of negative and positive news tend to be symmetric in the uni-regime framework. To empirically investigate the news effects, we assume in the first instance that both negative news and positive news have a symmetric effect on stock returns, defined as signs of the news sentiment variables, namely $sign(WCSS_{f,t})$ and $sign(WESS_{m,t})$. $sign(\cdot)$ is a function of the news variables which has a value of -1, 0, and 1 when the value of the news variables (either $WCSS$ or $WESS$) in the function is negative, exactly 0, and positive, respectively. In other words, when the value of the news variables is equal to -1, 0, or 1, it implies that the news is defined as negative, neutral, or positive news. We then substitute the news variable in Eq. (6.14) by both $sign(WCSS_{f,t})$ and $sign(WESS_{m,t})$ and estimate the new MRS model with both firm-specific and macroeconomic news. We report the estimation results in Table 6.5 and

Table 6.5 Estimates of MRS Model with Firm-specific and Macroeconomic News

Ticker	p_{11}	p_{22}	λ_{11}	λ_{12}	λ_{21}	λ_{22}
053000:KS	0.9917	0.9803	0.2396	−0.0537	0.6858	0.2483
055550:KS	0.9956	0.9951	0.3150	0.0989	0.5313	0.1263
0939:HK	0.9939	0.9864	0.3658	−0.0504	0.8541	0.6501
1398:HK	0.9915	0.9800	0.3485	0.0240	0.9557	0.5257
3328:HK	0.9922	0.9767	0.2517	0.0293	0.8767	0.8135
3968:HK	0.9969	0.9881	0.3929	0.0858	1.5881	0.7081
3988:HK	0.9881	0.9846	0.2163	0.0250	0.6311	0.2922
8303:JP	0.9936	0.9958	0.1357	0.0817	0.3070	−0.1405
8304:JP	0.9808	0.9808	0.3641	−0.1306	0.9022	−0.3301
8306:JP	0.9929	0.9919	0.2365	0.0571	0.5463	−0.1321
8308:JP	0.9849	0.9789	0.0065	0.0382	0.6415	0.1105
8316:JP	0.9953	0.9922	0.3122	0.0345	1.2239	0.1204
8331:JP	0.9891	0.9826	0.0464	0.0269	0.1021	0.2427
8332:JP	0.9936	0.9898	0.1032	0.0032	0.5005	0.3030
8355:JP	0.9932	0.9914	0.0250	−0.0271	0.6506	0.0126
8403:JP	0.9908	0.9947	0.0613	0.0460	0.1615	0.0089
8411:JP	0.9937	0.9876	0.1667	0.0157	1.1906	0.1946
DBSM:SI	0.9927	0.9921	0.2257	0.0603	0.6756	0.0042
OCBC:SI	0.9948	0.9906	0.2236	0.1420	0.5242	0.1217
UOBH:SI	0.9909	0.9898	0.2724	0.1518	0.5388	0.1209

Note: This table presents the estimation results of the MRS model with sign of firm-specific and macroeconomic news variables for the Asian Banks, specified as follows:

$$\text{when } s_t = 1, r_t = \mu_1 + \lambda_{11} Sign(WCSS_{f,t}) + \lambda_{12} Sign(WESS_{m,t}) + \varepsilon_{1,t} \text{ and } \varepsilon_{1,t} = \sigma_1 \eta_t \text{ where } \eta_t \overset{iid}{\sim} t(0,1,v),$$

$$\text{when } s_t = 2, r_t = \mu_2 + \lambda_{21} Sign(WCSS_{f,t}) + \lambda_{22} Sign(WESS_{m,t}) + \varepsilon_{2,t} \text{ and } \varepsilon_{2,t} = \sigma_2 \eta_t \text{ where } \eta_t \overset{iid}{\sim} t(0,1,v),$$

where $Sign(\cdot)$ is a function gives $-1, 0$, and 1 when values inside the bracket is negative, exactly 0, and positive, respectively. For the explanation of other variables, please see the note in Table 6.4.

the summary descriptive statistics of the estimates in Panel A of Table 6.8. As it can be seen from Tables 6.5 and 6.8, the estimates of the transition probability from the new model are found quite similar to those in the model without news. This finding suggests that news sentiments do not affect the states of the returns. Moreover, most of the coefficients of the news sentiments are found positive, and all the average estimates of the news variables are greater than 0. This finding is consistent with our expectation that positive news can increase returns and negative news can reduce returns. Furthermore, it is interesting to note that the effects of the news variables on stock returns are different in the different states. Overall, the news effects in the "calm" state are found to be weaker than those in the "turbulent" states, and the effect of firm-specific news is found much greater than that of the macroeconomic news in both states. As displayed in Panel A, the estimated coefficients of λ_{11} and λ_{21} are, respectively, equal to 0.2154 in the "calm" state and 0.7044 in the "turbulent" state, while the estimates of λ_{12} and λ_{22} are 0.0329 in the "calm" state and 0.2001 in the "turbulent" state, respectively. Finally, the results show that the effects of both firm-specific news and macroeconomic news are asymmetric across states and become much larger during the "turbulent" state than those in the "calm" state. This finding seems to be consistent with our casual observation that market participants tend to become more news sensitive and often overreact to the news release during the crisis period.

6.5.4 Effects of News Sentiment Dummy

We continue examining the news effects on returns by differentiating the news effects in our model estimation, rather than assuming a symmetric effect of both negative and positive news as in the previous section. We set two dummy variables, respectively, for negative and positive firm-specific news as $I(WCSS_{f,t} < 0)$ and $I(WCSS_{f,t} > 0)$, and two dummy variables for negative and positive macroeconomic news as $I(WESS_{m,t} < 0)$ and $I(WESS_{m,t} > 0)$. We then estimate the MRS-t model with these news dummy variables and report the results with the firm-specific dummy variables in Table 6.6 and the results with the macroeconomic dummy variables in Table 6.7. The summary descriptive statistics of the estimates are reported in Panels B and C of Table 6.8.

The results show in Table 6.6 that positive firm-specific news tends to affect stock returns positively, while negative firm-specific news affects returns negatively in both states. The mean estimates of firm-specific news reported in Panel B of Table 6.8 confirm this finding, where the mean estimates of λ_{11} and λ_{22} are negative in both states and for λ_{12} and λ_{22} they are positive. It is also interesting to note that the mean estimates of λ_{21} and λ_{22} are, respectively, greater than those of λ_{11} and λ_{12}, indicating that the effects of firm-specific news are larger in the "turbulent" state than in the "calm" state. Finally, the results in Panel B show that both the mean and median of the estimate have similar values and the mean estimates of the news variables in the same state are also very close. This finding lends support to our early argument that the effect

Table 6.6 Estimates of MRS Model with Firm-specific News Dummies

Ticker	p_{11}	p_{22}	λ_{11}	λ_{12}	λ_{21}	λ_{22}
053000:KS	0.9916	0.9803	−0.2195	0.2566	−0.6864	0.6794
055550:KS	0.9954	0.9949	−0.4684	0.1769	−0.3863	0.6729
0939:HK	0.9941	0.9866	−0.3019	0.4267	−1.0724	0.6486
1398:HK	0.9919	0.9807	−0.2236	0.4750	−0.0078	1.9177
3328:HK	0.9925	0.9783	−0.5640	0.0250	−1.0069	0.7445
3968:HK	0.9970	0.9882	−0.6884	0.1562	−2.4987	0.6744
3988:HK	0.9880	0.9844	0.1999	0.6296	−1.0104	0.2752
8303:JP	0.9921	0.9940	0.1307	0.3967	0.0464	0.9191
8304:JP	0.9823	0.9698	−0.1235	0.9146	−1.5969	0.1252
8306:JP	0.9928	0.9918	−0.1857	0.2850	−0.3928	0.7021
8308:JP	0.9852	0.9794	0.1151	0.1831	−0.5157	0.7848
8316:JP	0.9953	0.9922	−0.2750	0.3507	−0.9829	1.4785
8331:JP	0.9893	0.9830	−0.1154	0.0028	−0.0109	0.1731
8332:JP	0.9938	0.9900	−0.1481	0.0646	−0.5163	0.5162
8355:JP	0.9932	0.9912	0.1445	0.1064	−0.7236	0.6319
8403:JP	0.9909	0.9947	0.0029	0.1139	0.1364	0.5771
8411:JP	0.9937	0.9878	−0.7076	−0.3742	−1.8773	0.4941
DBSM:SI	0.9927	0.9922	−0.4635	−0.0139	−0.1487	1.2053
OCBC:SI	0.9948	0.9904	−0.1921	0.2581	−0.1823	0.8732
UOBH:SI	0.9913	0.9902	0.4570	1.0010	−1.1970	−0.1230

Note: This table presents the estimation results of the MRS model with dummy variables of firm-specific news for the Asian Banks with the following specification:

$$\text{when } s_t = 1, r_t = \mu_1 + \lambda_{11}I(WCSS_{f,t} < 0) + \lambda_{12}I(WCSS_{f,t} > 0) + \varepsilon_{1,t} \text{ and } \varepsilon_{1,t} = \sigma_1\eta_t \text{ where } \eta_t \overset{iid}{\sim} t(0,1,v),$$

$$\text{when } s_t = 2, r_t = \mu_2 + \lambda_{21}I(WCSS_{f,t} < 0) + \lambda_{22}I(WCSS_{f,t} > 0) + \varepsilon_{2,t} \text{ and } \varepsilon_{2,t} = \sigma_2\eta_t \text{ where } \eta_t \overset{iid}{\sim} t(0,1,v).$$

For the explanation of other variables, please see the note in Table 6.4.

of firm-specific news within a state is stable and evenly distributed, and the effects of negative and positive firm-specific news within the same state are roughly symmetric.

When the macroeconomic news dummy variables are included, the results are different. As displayed in Table 6.7, although most of the estimates of λ_{11} and λ_{21} are still negative, a number of estimates of λ_{12} turn negative as well. The values of the mean and median in Panel C of Table 6.8 also show that, though positive macroeconomic news can affect the returns positively in the "calm" state, both the mean and median of λ_{12} have similar values close to 0. As a result, this finding seems to suggest that in general the positive macroeconomic news can positively affect returns in the "calm" state, but the effect is very limited. However, the effects of the macroeconomic news during the "turbulent" state are much stronger than those in the "calm" state, and the effects of both negative and positive macroeconomic news are also found to be nearly symmetric in the "turbulent" state. This finding is consistent with that from our previous model

Table 6.7 Estimates of MRS Model with Macroeconomic News Dummies

Ticker	p_{11}	p_{22}	λ_{11}	λ_{12}	λ_{21}	λ_{22}
053000:KS	0.9918	0.9809	0.1275	−0.0026	−0.3504	0.1903
055550:KS	0.9956	0.9951	0.1323	0.2753	−0.7717	−0.1086
0939:HK	0.9929	0.9824	−0.0694	−0.0770	−0.9080	0.6087
1398:HK	0.9917	0.9808	−0.2480	−0.1107	−0.5655	0.5803
3328:HK	0.9928	0.9782	−0.1484	−0.0019	−1.0771	0.7363
3968:HK	0.9970	0.9884	−0.3374	−0.0349	−0.7369	0.8941
3988:HK	0.9884	0.9855	−0.1266	−0.0811	−0.8671	0.1066
8303:JP	0.9936	0.9958	−0.0056	0.1345	0.1410	−0.1341
8304:JP	0.9865	0.9684	−0.1723	−0.2597	1.4074	0.0335
8306:JP	0.9929	0.9919	−0.1931	−0.0058	0.1492	−0.0590
8308:JP	0.9848	0.9793	−0.0210	0.0452	0.2319	0.2668
8316:JP	0.9955	0.9926	−0.1801	−0.0213	−0.2069	0.1801
8331:JP	0.9890	0.9826	−0.0041	0.0356	−0.0870	0.3412
8332:JP	0.9936	0.9896	0.0396	0.0171	−0.2331	0.3713
8355:JP	0.9932	0.9916	0.1799	0.0275	0.0835	0.0813
8403:JP	0.9907	0.9946	0.1127	0.0987	0.0197	0.0283
8411:JP	0.9942	0.9888	−0.1098	−0.0166	−0.2633	0.1839
DBSM:SI	0.9935	0.9930	−0.3240	−0.0321	−0.2466	0.0765
OCBC:SI	0.9939	0.9897	−0.3158	0.1164	0.0196	0.2782
UOBH:SI	0.9901	0.9892	−0.3888	0.0559	0.1412	0.3365

Note: This table presents the estimation results of the MRS model with dummy variables of macroeconomic news for the Asian Banks with the following specification:

$$\text{when } s_t = 1, r_t = \mu_1 + \lambda_{11}I(WESS_{m,t} < 0) + \lambda_{12}I(WESS_{m,t} > 0) + \varepsilon_{1,t} \text{ and } \varepsilon_{1,t} = \sigma_1 \eta_t \text{ where } \eta_t \overset{iid}{\sim} t(0, 1, \nu),$$

$$\text{when } s_t = 2, r_t = \mu_2 + \lambda_{21}I(WESS_{m,t} < 0) + \lambda_{22}I(WESS_{m,t} > 0) + \varepsilon_{2,t} \text{ and } \varepsilon_{2,t} = \sigma_2 \eta_t \text{ where } \eta_t \overset{iid}{\sim} t(0, 1, \nu).$$

For the explanation of other variables, please see the note in Table 6.4.

estimation when both negative and positive news are assumed to have a symmetric effect on returns.

6.5.5 Effects of News Sentiment

In the previous sections, we have empirically examined the news effects in different states and with different news sentiments (negative or positive) and sources (firm-specific or macroeconomic). In this section, we investigate whether the sentiment score can also significantly affect returns. We first assume that both negative and positive sentiment scores have symmetric effects on the returns in our model estimation and then remove this assumption to estimate the effects of different news sentiments on returns.

With the assumption of the symmetric effects of both the negative and positive sentiment scores, we extend and estimate the MRS-t model specified in Eq. (6.14) by including both $WCSS_{f,t}$ and $WESS_{m,t}$ in the specification. Table 6.9 presents the

Table 6.8 Summary Outputs of MRS Models with News

	Mean	Std Dev.	Median	Q_1	Q_3	Skew
Panel A: Firm-specific and Macroeconomic News Sign						
p_{11}	0.9918	0.0038	0.9928	0.9909	0.9937	−1.3303
p_{22}	0.9875	0.0059	0.9889	0.9821	0.9920	−0.3201
λ_{11}	0.2154	0.1198	0.2311	0.1275	0.3129	−0.2847
λ_{12}	0.0329	0.0662	0.0319	0.0125	0.0656	−0.3941
λ_{21}	0.7044	0.3574	0.6461	0.5295	0.8831	0.5558
λ_{22}	0.2001	0.2916	0.1240	0.0117	0.2949	0.4858
Panel B: Firm-specific News Dummy Only						
λ_{11}	0.9919	0.0035	0.9926	0.9912	0.9939	−1.1543
λ_{22}	0.9870	0.0066	0.9891	0.9824	0.9919	−0.8497
λ_{11}	−0.1813	0.3040	−0.1889	−0.3423	0.0310	0.0574
λ_{12}	0.2717	0.3178	0.2198	0.0959	0.4042	0.5707
λ_{21}	−0.7315	0.6923	−0.6014	−1.0259	−0.1739	−0.8331
λ_{22}	0.6985	0.4587	0.6736	0.5107	0.8069	0.7528
Panel C: Macroeconomic News Dummy Only						
p_{11}	0.9921	0.0031	0.9929	0.9905	0.9937	−0.7331
p_{22}	0.9869	0.0070	0.9890	0.9820	0.9921	−0.8182
λ_{11}	−0.1026	0.1710	−0.1182	−0.2068	0.0068	0.0137
λ_{12}	0.0081	0.1073	−0.0023	−0.0328	0.0479	0.0359
λ_{21}	−0.2060	0.5529	−0.2200	−0.6083	0.0979	0.8239
λ_{22}	0.2496	0.2791	0.1871	0.0658	0.3488	0.6949

Note: This table presents the summary descriptive statistics of the estimates from MRS models with news variables in this study. For the explanation of other variables, please see the note in Table 6.1.

estimation results for all the bank stocks, and the summary descriptive statistics of the estimates are in Panel A of Table 6.12. It can be seen in Table 6.9 that the estimates of the transition probability are very similar to those reported in Table 6.4, implying that the news sentiment scores do not affect the states of the returns. When the effects of both negative and positive sentiment scores are assumed to be symmetric, the results show that most of the coefficients of the firm-specific news are positive in both states, while the estimates of the macroeconomic news are found mostly negative during the "calm" state and positive in the "turbulent" state. This finding suggests that negative (positive) firm-specific news sentiment may reduce (increase) returns in both states. The values of the mean and median reported in Panel A of Table 6.12 further confirm such effects on stock returns. However, the effects of the macroeconomic news on stock returns are different at various states. The mean and median of λ_{12} have similar negative values quite close to 0 in the "calm" state, and the values for λ_{22} are positive and slightly greater than 0. The results suggest that macroeconomic news sentiment scores are either

Table 6.9 Estimates of MRS Model with Firm-specific and Macroeconomic News Sentiment

Ticker	p_{11}	p_{22}	λ_{11}	λ_{12}	λ_{21}	λ_{22}
053000:KS	0.9917	0.9811	0.0239	0.0001	0.2074	−0.0088
055550:KS	0.9954	0.9950	0.1980	0.0034	0.1871	0.0004
0939:HK	0.9939	0.9857	0.1925	−0.0026	0.4586	0.0174
1398:HK	0.9916	0.9802	0.2973	−0.0039	0.5212	0.0255
3328:HK	0.9925	0.9776	0.2329	0.0013	0.0214	0.0268
3968:HK	0.9969	0.9881	0.3835	−0.0012	0.5061	0.0321
3988:HK	0.9881	0.9853	0.4492	−0.0023	0.9506	0.0051
8303:JP	0.9928	0.9950	−0.0316	0.0000	0.1974	−0.0071
8304:JP	0.9809	0.9785	−0.0012	−0.0095	0.2819	−0.0091
8306:JP	0.9929	0.9920	0.2151	−0.0020	0.9473	0.0001
8308:JP	0.9842	0.9790	0.0737	−0.0002	0.4634	0.0078
8316:JP	0.9953	0.9922	0.2276	−0.0032	0.5325	0.0222
8331:JP	0.9892	0.9828	−0.0013	0.0007	0.0546	0.0121
8332:JP	0.9937	0.9898	0.0226	−0.0017	0.1172	0.0145
8355:JP	0.9931	0.9906	−0.0116	−0.0026	0.1917	−0.0059
8403:JP	0.9905	0.9942	−0.0302	−0.0013	0.2082	0.0039
8411:JP	0.9939	0.9881	0.2144	−0.0021	1.5023	0.0160
DBSM:SI	0.9930	0.9926	0.1613	0.0012	0.4396	0.0044
OCBC:SI	0.9941	0.9898	0.0851	0.0057	0.2528	0.0042
UOBH:SI	0.9903	0.9895	0.0447	0.0023	0.1887	0.0074

Note: This table presents the estimates of MRS model with firm-specific and macroeconomic news sentiment variables for the Asian Banks with the following specification:

$$\text{when } s_t = 1, r_t = \mu_1 + \lambda_{11} WCSS_{f,t} + \lambda_{12} WESS_{m,t} + \varepsilon_{1,t} \text{ and } \varepsilon_{1,t} = \sigma_1 \eta_t \text{ where } \eta_t \overset{iid}{\sim} t(0, 1, \nu),$$

$$\text{when } s_t = 2, r_t = \mu_2 + \lambda_{21} WCSS_{f,t} + \lambda_{22} WESS_{m,t} + \varepsilon_{2,t} \text{ and } \varepsilon_{2,t} = \sigma_2 \eta_t \text{ where } \eta_t \overset{iid}{\sim} t(0, 1, \nu).$$

For the explanation of other variables, please see the note in Table 6.4.

ignored by the market during the "calm" state or have very limited effects on the returns in the "turbulent" state. In general, with the symmetric assumption, firm-specific news sentiment scores have much profound effects on returns in comparison with macroeconomic news sentiment. Finally, it is also interesting to note that firm-specific news sentiment has greater effects on returns in the "turbulent" state than in the "calm" state.

We continue assessing the effects of news sentiment on returns by differentiating the news sentiment scores into positive and negative news, denoted as $WCSS_{f,t}^{N}$ and $WCSS_{f,t}^{P}$ for firm-specific news and $WESS_{m,t}^{N}$ and $WESS_{m,t}^{P}$ for macroeconomic news, respectively. We then estimate Eq. (6.14) by including these news terms and report the results with the inclusion of the firm-specific news sentiment in Table 6.10 and those with the macroeconomic news sentiment in Table 6.11. Panels B and C of Table 6.12 present the summary descriptive statistics of the estimates with respect to the firm-specific news sentiment and macroeconomic news sentiment.

Table 6.10 Estimates of MRS Model with Firm-specific News Sentiment

Ticker	p_{11}	p_{22}	λ_{11}	λ_{12}	λ_{21}	λ_{22}
053000:KS	0.9913	0.9813	0.0751	0.1995	−0.2189	0.1001
055550:KS	0.9950	0.9946	0.0772	0.2431	−0.2000	0.1431
0939:HK	0.9936	0.9845	−0.2595	0.1314	−0.3813	0.5648
1398:HK	0.9919	0.9804	−0.3269	0.2606	−0.4408	0.6095
3328:HK	0.9926	0.9780	−0.2869	0.1652	−0.4889	−0.2274
3968:HK	0.9969	0.9878	−0.4873	0.2226	−0.8965	0.1418
3988:HK	0.9885	0.9858	−0.7023	0.2243	−0.9967	0.9292
8303:JP	0.9933	0.9956	0.0469	0.2461	−0.1733	0.3710
8304:JP	0.9808	0.9747	0.0246	0.3487	−0.2767	0.3591
8306:JP	0.9928	0.9919	−0.1844	0.2961	−0.8162	1.8730
8308:JP	0.9844	0.9792	−0.0835	0.0131	−0.3362	1.1451
8316:JP	0.9954	0.9921	−0.2424	0.1949	−0.5277	0.6078
8331:JP	0.9895	0.9831	0.0097	0.0965	−0.0401	0.1432
8332:JP	0.9937	0.9901	−0.0268	−0.0483	−0.1050	0.1645
8355:JP	0.9930	0.9912	0.0182	0.2235	−0.1836	0.0566
8403:JP	0.9903	0.9942	0.0716	0.1223	−0.2253	−0.0276
8411:JP	0.9939	0.9881	−0.2650	0.1228	−1.2676	3.1967
DBSM:SI	0.9929	0.9925	−0.1412	0.1897	−0.3525	0.6966
OCBC:SI	0.9940	0.9897	−0.0685	0.1152	−0.2058	0.4337
UOBH:SI	0.9905	0.9896	−0.0311	0.1349	−0.1424	0.4115

Note: This table presents the estimates of MRS model with firm-specific news sentiment variable for the Asian Banks with the following specification:

$$\text{when } s_t = 1, r_t = \mu_1 + \lambda_{11} WCSS_{f,t}^N + \lambda_{12} WCSS_{f,t}^P + \varepsilon_{1,t} \text{ and } \varepsilon_{1,t} = \sigma_1 \eta_t \text{ where } \eta_t \overset{iid}{\sim} t(0, 1, v),$$

$$\text{when } s_t = 2, r_t = \mu_2 + \lambda_{21} WCSS_{f,t}^N + \lambda_{22} WCSS_{f,t}^P + \varepsilon_{2,t} \text{ and } \varepsilon_{2,t} = \sigma_2 \eta_t \text{ where } \eta_t \overset{iid}{\sim} t(0, 1, v).$$

For the explanation of other variables, please see the note in Table 6.4.

As displayed in Table 6.10 and Panel B of Table 6.12, negative firm-specific news sentiment tends to affect stock returns negatively, especially during the "turbulent" state, while positive firm-specific news sentiment always promotes stock returns in both states. In addition, the effects of firm-specific news sentiment scores are larger in the "turbulent" state than in the "calm" state and the effects of positive firm-specific news sentiment are greater than those of the negative firm-specific news sentiment in both states. This is further confirmed by the values of the mean and median of the estimates of these news sentiment scores reported in Panel B of Table 6.12. Thus, when news sentiment is considered, the results show that the effects of negative and positive firm-specific news on returns are not symmetric. Without the symmetric effects assumption, the effects of firm-specific news sentiment on returns are still greater in the "turbulent" state than in the "calm" state.

Table 6.11 Estimates of MRS Model with Macroeconomic News Sentiment

Ticker	p_{11}	p_{22}	λ_{11}	λ_{12}	λ_{21}	λ_{22}
053000:KS	0.9917	0.9810	0.0046	−0.0014	−0.0002	−0.0017
055550:KS	0.9956	0.9952	0.0041	0.0047	−0.0183	−0.0071
0939:HK	0.9930	0.9831	−0.0001	−0.0010	−0.0308	0.0176
1398:HK	0.9916	0.9808	−0.0034	−0.0025	−0.0294	0.0191
3328:HK	0.9929	0.9786	−0.0049	0.0016	−0.0332	0.0233
3968:HK	0.9970	0.9884	−0.0107	0.0002	−0.0414	0.0287
3988:HK	0.9884	0.9859	−0.0010	−0.0022	−0.0303	0.0014
8303:JP	0.9929	0.9950	−0.0014	0.0063	−0.0098	−0.0136
8304:JP	0.9861	0.9682	−0.0191	−0.0157	0.0891	−0.0094
8306:JP	0.9928	0.9918	−0.0072	0.0007	0.0066	−0.0004
8308:JP	0.9847	0.9794	−0.0091	0.0006	0.0182	0.0168
8316:JP	0.9954	0.9926	−0.0146	−0.0042	−0.0204	0.0225
8331:JP	0.9892	0.9830	−0.0014	0.0017	0.0043	0.0181
8332:JP	0.9936	0.9897	0.0025	0.0002	−0.0051	0.0179
8355:JP	0.9933	0.9924	0.0034	−0.0007	0.0091	−0.0006
8403:JP	0.9905	0.9943	0.0073	−0.0037	0.0081	0.0067
8411:JP	0.9941	0.9887	−0.0072	−0.0043	−0.0123	0.0288
DBSM:SI	0.9933	0.9928	−0.0099	−0.0009	−0.0063	0.0049
OCBC:SI	0.9936	0.9895	−0.0141	0.0040	−0.0026	0.0061
UOBH:SI	0.9902	0.9892	−0.0146	0.0019	−0.0009	0.0128

Note: This table presents the estimates of MRS model with macroeconomic news sentiment variable for the Asian Banks with the following specification:

$$\text{when } s_t = 1, r_t = \mu_1 + \lambda_{11} WESS_{m,t}^N + \lambda_{12} WESS_{m,t}^P + \varepsilon_{1,t} \text{ and } \varepsilon_{1,t} = \sigma_1 \eta_t \text{ where } \eta_t \overset{iid}{\sim} t(0,1,v),$$

$$\text{when } s_t = 2, r_t = \mu_2 + \lambda_{21} WESS_{m,t}^N + \lambda_{22} WESS_{m,t}^P + \varepsilon_{2,t} \text{ and } \varepsilon_{2,t} = \sigma_2 \eta_t \text{ where } \eta_t \overset{iid}{\sim} t(0,1,v).$$

For the explanation of other variables, please see the note in Table 6.4.

With the inclusion of the macroeconomic news sentiment, the results in Table 6.11 show that the estimates of the negative macroeconomics news sentiment, λ_{11} and λ_{21}, are mostly negative in both states, while those for the positive news sentiment, λ_{12} and λ_{22}, are mostly positive. The finding is similar to the one reported in Table 6.7 when the news sentiment dummy variables were included in the model estimation. The values of the mean and median reported in Panel C of Table 6.12 show similar values with the same sign and all are small and close to 0, indicating that both negative and positive macroeconomic news sentiment scores have limited impacts on returns in both states. In comparison, we find that positive macroeconomic news sentiment tends to promote the market and has slightly larger impacts than negative news sentiment on stock returns during the "turbulent" state. This appears to suggest that, during the "turbulent" state, any positive news sentiment is welcomed by the market and tends to boost investor confidence and market expectations in the future. This finding is also different from the

Table 6.12 Summary Outputs of MRS Models with News Sentiment

	Mean	Std Dev.	Median	Q_1	Q_3	Skew
Panel A: Firm-specific and Macroeconomic News Sentiments						
p_{11}	0.9917	0.0038	0.9928	0.9905	0.9939	−1.3243
p_{22}	0.9874	0.0057	0.9888	0.9824	0.9920	−0.3423
λ_{11}	0.1373	0.1412	0.1232	0.0166	0.2182	0.5334
λ_{12}	−0.0009	0.0031	−0.0013	−0.0024	0.0008	−0.4266
λ_{21}	0.4115	0.3623	0.2674	0.1910	0.5099	1.4890
λ_{22}	0.0084	0.0122	0.0062	0.0004	0.0163	0.2719
Panel B: Firm-specific News Sentiment Only						
p_{11}	0.9917	0.0037	0.9929	0.9905	0.9938	−1.3922
p_{22}	0.9872	0.0061	0.9888	0.9827	0.9920	−0.4611
λ_{11}	−0.1391	0.2073	−0.0760	−0.2609	0.0198	−1.0391
λ_{12}	0.1751	0.0932	0.1923	0.1227	0.2290	−0.4865
λ_{21}	−0.4138	0.3320	−0.3064	−0.4986	−0.1959	−1.1423
λ_{22}	0.5846	0.7742	0.3913	0.1428	0.6313	2.0244
Panel C: Macroeconomic News Sentiment Only						
p_{11}	0.9920	0.0031	0.9929	0.9904	0.9936	−0.7414
p_{22}	0.9870	0.0069	0.9890	0.9825	0.9924	−0.9050
λ_{11}	−0.0048	0.0075	−0.0042	−0.0101	0.0006	−0.1680
λ_{12}	−0.0007	0.0045	−0.0002	−0.0023	0.0016	−1.5134
λ_{21}	−0.0053	0.0277	−0.0057	−0.0227	0.0048	1.7499
λ_{22}	0.0096	0.0127	0.0097	−0.0005	0.0183	−0.1577

This table presents the summary descriptive statistics of the estimates from MRS models with news sentiment in this study. For the explanation of other variables, please see the note in Table 6.1.

previous one when the effects of both negative and positive macroeconomic news are assumed to be symmetric.

6.6 CONCLUSION

In this chapter we have examined the impacts of firm-specific and macroeconomic news announcements on major Asian bank stock returns by applying a regime-switching framework. In particular, we have studied the daily return dynamics and its relation with firm-specific and macroeconomic news sentiment for banks selected from Japan, China, Singapore, and Korea, during the January 1, 2000–December 31, 2012 period. By modeling stock returns via a regime-switching framework, we have systematically analyzed the state structure of the returns over the sample period and examined the effects of both negative and positive news on returns under different scenarios. The results suggest that both the occurrence and sentiment of news announcements have predictive power for future stock returns and positive news is found to have a different impact on stock returns at different states in comparison with negative news. In addition, we find that the magnitudes of news effects are different, depending on the type of news and regimes of stock returns. News effects are larger in the "turbulent" state than in the "calm" state. These findings are consistent with those in Veronesi (1999) who argues that news effects are different depending on the states. Firm-specific news in general has a greater effect on returns than macroeconomic news. The effects of negative and positive news are found roughly symmetric in both states and positive macroeconomic news has limited effects on the returns in the "calm" state. Finally, the results show that the positive firm-specific news sentiment has a larger effect on returns than the negative news sentiment in both states and the positive macroeconomic news sentiment has a greater effect than the negative macroeconomic news sentiment in the "turbulent" state.

These findings have important implications for policy makers in seeking stability of financial system and for investors in predicting the potential effects of news release on the returns of banks that they are monitoring. Since the change in stock returns of banks contains important information about the stability of the banking industry, our results can provide useful information for supervisory bodies to assess news effects on the performance of the banking industry. The daily impact of newswire messages will assist traders to anticipate the potential effects of news on bank returns and adjust their strategies proactively in response to the changes in news sentiment.

6.7 APPENDIX A: SELECTED 20 ASIAN BANKS LIST

Company Name	Ticker
Woori Financial Group	053000:KS
Shinhan Financial Group	055550:KS
China Construction	0939:HK
Industrial & Commercial Bank of China	1398:HK
Bank of Communications	3328:HK
China Merchants Bank	3968:HK
Bank of China	3988:HK
Mitsubishi UFJ Financial Group	8303:JP
Mizuho Financial Group	8304:JP
Sumitomo Mitsui Financial	8306:JP
Resona Holdings	8308:JP
Sumitomo Mitsui Trust	8316:JP
Hokuhoku Financial Group	8331:JP
Shizuoka Bank	8332:JP
Sapporo Hokuyo	8355:JP
Daishi Bank	8403:JP
Shiga Bank	8411:JP
DBS Group	DBSM:SI
Overseas-Chinese Banking Corporation	OCBC:SI
United Overseas Bank	UOBH:SI

6.8 APPENDIX B: RAVENPACK ALGORITHMS

6.8.1 Market Response Methodology

RavenPack's Market Response methodology underpins the composite sentiment score (CSS) and is based on a Rule Base that identifies and maps individual words or word combinations in the story headline to the price impact on stocks of companies mentioned in the headline. The price impact is measured in the hours ahead of the arrival of the news item and is transformed into an impact score using advanced machine learning techniques.

Step One: A Classification Base is defined: Develop a Classification Base, or define the types of stories that contain the content relevant for tagging.

Step Two: A large sample is analyzed to create a Rule Base: A sample set of stories in the Classification Base developed in step one is drawn from RavenPack's news database for a fixed date range. The headlines of these stories are extracted and parsed into words to form a list of candidates of individual words and word combinations that are typical for such headline stories.

Step Three: Create an Impact Score using the Rule Base: Different advanced machine learning techniques are applied with the objective of creating an Impact Score that identifies the probability of the volatility of a particular stock to be either higher or lower than the volatility of the market.

Step Four: Generate historical analysis and enable real-time tagging: This process involves several consistency checks of historical data and generation of volume statistics. When this process is complete, the series is published.

Step Five: Quarterly re-evaluation: Classifiers are re-evaluated on a quarterly basis. This process involves completing step two for stories sampled outside of the date range of the original sample or most recent quarterly re-evaluation. If the accuracy level is 10% lower than the level when the series was originally released, a new series is developed.

6.8.2 Expert Consensus Tagging Methodology

RavenPack's Expert Consensus Methodology underpins the event sentiment score (ESS) and entails a group of financial experts manually tagging a set of stories that is later used as a basis for automated computer classification using a Bayes Classifier.

Step One: A Classification Base is defined: Develop a Classification Base, or define the types of stories that contain the content relevant for tagging.

Step Two: Experts build an internal Tagging Guide: A team of in-house experts with extensive backgrounds in linguistics, finance, and economics first develop and agree upon a set of parameters and basic assumptions that will guide sentiment tagging.

Step Three: A large sample is tagged: A sample set of stories in the Classification Base developed in step one is drawn from RavenPack's news database for a fixed date range. Stories are randomly selected for tagging. A group of experts read and classify the sample using the Tagging Guide developed in step two.

Step Four: Software is trained from sample to automate tagging: A Bayes Classifier uses supervised learning to discern patterns in expert tagging and establish rules for future automation. This automated tagging process must meet exceptional levels of accuracy in order to be made available to clients. In cases when accuracy is not sufficiently high, step three is repeated with a larger sample set.

Step Five: Generate historical analysis and enable real-time tagging: Historical analysis is generated and real-time tagging is enabled. This process involves several consistency checks of historical data and generation of volume statistics. When this process is complete, the series is published.

Step Six: Quarterly re-evaluation: Classifiers are re-evaluated on a quarterly basis. This process involves completing step three for stories sampled outside of the date range of the original sample or most recent quarterly re-evaluation. The results of this expert classification are compared to the results of automated classification. If the accuracy level is 10% lower than the level when the series was originally released, a new series is developed.

6.8.3 Factors in the Event Sentiment Score

In addition to the expert consensus survey data, the ESS has a strength component that is influenced by a variety of factors, depending on the type of event. RavenPack systematically extracts information from every news story to model these factors and determine how positive or negative each event should be. Here is a list of some of these factors:

Emotional Factor: There are 5 scales containing groups of words and phrases in the RavenPack emotional magnitude component of ESS: Low, Moderate, Substantial, Severe, and Critical Magnitude. Each component contains words that signify the magnitude of an event as described by the author of the story.

Weather and Climate Factor: Tracks official scales to measure extreme weather such as the Richter scale or the Volcanic Eruption Index.

Analyst Rating Factor: Covers over 150 different broker and analyst rating scales for stocks (e.g., strong buy, buy, hold, sell, strong sell).

Credit Rating Factor: Consolidates the three main credit rating scales by Moody's, Fitch, and S&P (e.g., AAA, AA, BB, C, etc.) into one normalized scale.

Fundamental Comparison Factor: Extracts and calculates numerical differences between actual and estimated values in earnings, revenues, dividends, macroeconomic indicators, and any other financial or economic announcement. Performs arithmetic and translates fundamental percentage changes into a normalized score within the ESS ranges.

Casualties Factor: Identifies how many people are dead or injured as a result of an event and uses this as sentiment strength factor, particularly for natural disasters and industrial accidents.

REFERENCES

Adams, C., 2008. Emerging East Asian banking systems 10 years after the 1997/98 crisis. Working Paper, Asian Development Bank Regional Economic Integration.

Ardia, D., 2009. Bayesian estimation of a Markov-switching threshold asymmetric GARCH model with student-t innovations. The Econometrics Journal 12 (1), 105–126.

Blanchard, O., Dell'Ariccia, G., Mauro, P., 2013. Rethinking macroeconomic policy II: getting granular, IMF Staff Discussion Note 13/03.

Bollerslev, T., 1987. A conditional heteroskedastic time series model for speculative prices and rates of return. The Review of Economics and Statistics 69 (3), 542–547.

Ding, C.G., Wu, C.H., Chang, P.L., 2013. The influence of government intervention on the trajectory of bank performance during the global financial crisis: a comparative study among Asian economies. Journal of Financial Stability 9 (4), 556–564.

Domanski, D., 2005. Foreign banks in emerging economies: changing players changing issues. BIS Quarterly Review, 69–81.

Haas, M., 2009. Value-at-risk via mixture distributions reconsidered. Applied Mathematics and Computation 215 (6), 2103–2119.

Haas, M., Paolella, M.S., 2012. Mixture and regime-switching GARCH models. In: Bauwens, L., Hafner, C., Laurent, S. (Eds.), Handbook of volatility models and their applications. Willey, United Kingdom.

Hafez, P.A., 2009. Impact of news sentiment on abnormal stock returns. RavenPack White Paper.

Hamilton, J.D., 1988. Rational-expectations econometric analysis of changes in regime: an investigation of the term structure of interest rates. Journal of Economic Dynamics and Control 12 (2–3), 385–423.

Hamilton, J.D., 1989. A new approach to the economic analysis of nonstationary time series and the business cycle. Econometrica 57 (2), 357–384.

Hamilton, J.D., 1994. Time Series Analysis. Princeton University Press, Princeton.

Ho, K.Y., Shi, Y., Zhang, Z., 2013. How does news sentiment impact asset volatility? Evidence from long memory and regime-switching approaches. The North American Journal of Economics and Finance 26, 436–456.

Hsu, C.M., Liao, C.F., 2010. Financial turmoil in the banking sector and the Asian Lamfalussy process: the case of four economies. Working Paper (ADBI No. 221).

Kawai, K., 2009. Reform of the international financial architecture: an Asian perspective. ADBI Working Paper Series, No. 167.

Klaassen, F., 2002. Improving GARCH volatility forecasts with regime-switching GARCH. Empirical Economics 27 (2), 363–394.

Leinweber, D., Sisk, J., 2011. Relating news analytics to stock returns. In: Mitra, G., Mitra, L. (Eds.), The Handbook of News Analytics in Finance. Willey, United Kingdom.

Mohanty, M., Turner, P., 2010. Banks and financial intermediation in emerging Asia: reforms and new risks. Working Paper (BIS No. 313).

Moniz, A., Brar, G., Davies, C., Strudwick, A., 2011. The impact of news flow on asset returns: an empirical study. In: Mitra, G., Mitra, L. (Eds.), The Handbook of News Analytics in Finance. Willey, United Kingdom.

Moshirian, F., 2008. Financial services in an increasingly integrated global financial market. Journal of Banking and Finance 32 (11), 2288–2292.

Soedarmono, W., Machrouh, F., Tarazi, A., 2011. Bank market power, economic growth and financial stability: evidence from Asian banks. Journal of Asian Economics 22 (6), 460–470.

Stiglitz, J., Weiss, A., 1981. Credit rationing with imperfect information. American Economic Review 71 (3), 393–410.

Susmel, R., Engel, R., 1994. Hourly volatility spillovers between international equity markets. Journal of International Money and Finance 13 (1), 3–25.

Veronesi, P., 1999. Stock market overreaction to bad news in good time: a rational expectations equilibrium model. Review of Financial Studies 12 (5), 975–1007.

CHAPTER 7

Embedded Predictor Selection for Default Risk Calculation: A Southeast Asian Industry Study

Wolfgang Karl Härdle[a,c] and Dedy Dwi Prastyo[a,b]

[a]Humboldt-Universität zu Berlin, Ladislaus von Bortkiewicz Chair of Statistics, Center for Applied Statistics and Economics (C.A.S.E.), Unter den Linden 6, 10099 Berlin, Germany
[b]Department of Statistics, Institut Teknologi Sepuluh Nopember (ITS), Jl. Arief Rahman Hakim, Sukolilo, Surabaya 60111, Indonesia
[c]Lee Kong Chian School of Business, Singapore Management University, 50 Stamford Road, Singapore 178899

7.1 INTRODUCTION

The event of default can place stakeholders in to financial trouble. Moreover, the default effect to economy depends on the size of company and the systemic implication of the defaulting company. Probability of default (PD) analysis is one of the main tasks of rating agencies in credit risk assessment as well as of banks and other financial companies. Credit scoring analysis is used to obtain the PD of companies as well as of individual clients. Altman and Hotchkiss (2006) identified at least two important factors stimulating the development of credit scoring models: first, the implications of Basel's proposed capital requirements on credit assets, second the enormous amounts and rates of defaults. As a consequence, banks and other financial institutions either developed or modified their existing internal credit risk systems. Key element for the internal rating based (IRB) approach are PD and loss given default (LGD). Hence, financial industry and researchers continuously develop the methods to assess PD and LGD on credit risk analysis.

The majority of studies on default analysis is based on comparison of financial ratios of default and non–default companies. Beaver (1966) introduced univariate discriminant analysis (DA) by using different threshold points for different single financial ratios. In the single financial ratio sense, it was found that cash-flow to total debt provided the most accurate default prediction, followed by net income to total asset ratio. However, default events are too complex to be explained by a single predictor. Therefore, Altman (1968) introduced multivariate DA to incorporate multifinancial ratios. He used five financial ratios as discriminating predictors: working capital to total assets, retained earnings to total assets, earnings before interest and taxes (EBIT) to total assets, market value of equity to book value of the total debt, and sales to total assets. The accounting data for the defaulted company are obtained from annual financial report available prior to the default date. The multivariate DA approach is also known as Altman's Z-score analysis since it yields a Z score representing ordinal ranking of credit score. The coefficients in DA are difficult to interpret and the Z-score does not have an interpretation as PD.

Logit and probit regression are mostly employed in the next development of default risk analysis, see Martin (1977), Ohlson (1980), Lo (1986), Lau (1987), and Platt et al. (1994). The logit model lends itself to a direct statistical inference of significance test. The logit function is bounded between zero and one therefore it suitable to represent PD. The PD obtained from the logit model, also known as Ohlson's O-score, can be used to rank-order companies. In addition, the coefficients of logit model have natural interpretations, i.e., a positive coefficient implies that an increase in the value of a single financial ratio will increase the PD.

A company's financial ratio may relate to PD in nonlinear way and too complex for linier parametric approaches. For this purpose non-parametric classification techniques are proposed such as Classification and Regression Tree, Bayesian Additive Classification Tree (Zhang and Härdle, 2010), k-Nearest Neighbors (Henley and Hand, 1996), Artificial Neural Network (Tam and Kiang, 1992; Wilson and Sharda, 1994; and Altman et al. 1994). The application of Support Vector Machines (SVM) in credit scoring analysis, Härdle et al. (2009), Chen et al. (2011), and Härdle et al. (2014), typically outperformed competing models since SVM has a unique global solution, see Vapnik (1998) and Steinwart and Christmann (2008). The nonparametric approaches are chosen because they provide a more flexible approach, i.e. they are able to accommodate possible non-monotone relations between univariate financial ratio and the PD in various forms. Regulatory institutions and credit officers may not accept though these sophisticated approaches although they exhibit superior performance. In order to strike a balance between interpretability and model flexibility we propose to calibrate a logistic regression with embedded variable selection. This approach is pursued using regularization in the underlying parametric model.

The embedded variable selection yields a sparse representation which is required to discard irrelevant default predictors. Most of the estimation techniques that employ supervised classification methods typically using a large dimension of predictors, although only a lower dimension of subset is relevant. Furthermore, the financial ratios typically exhibit high correlation so any regression model is not functionable. In addition, over fitting, instability, and large standard error of the estimates may occur. Hence, variable selection by regularization comes to the rescuing since it discards irrelevant default predictors yielding a parsimonious model.

A least absolute shrinkage and selection operator (Lasso) and an elastic-net penalty serve as a regularization term. The analysis is applied to financial report data of individual companies from Southeast Asia. The data are collected and prepared by the Risk Management Institute (RMI) at the National University of Singapore (NUS). The next section describes the dataset in more detail and defines the financial ratios. The third section presents the regularization technique as an embedded predictor selection. The last two sections cover the empirical result as well as the conclusion.

7.2 DATA AND DEFAULT PREDICTORS

The data has been kindly provided by the Risk Management Institute (RMI) at the National University of Singapore (NUS). The data consist of financial report of companies in the Southeast Asian region span from 1998 to 2012. We index the financial report in such a way to obtain the financial information on regular monthly basis in order to match the default event database.

The event that are used to define default observation include bankruptcy filings under Chapters 7, 11, and 15, administration, arrangement, liquidation, protection, receivership, rehabilitation, reorganization, restructuring, supreme court declaration, winding up, and work out. Moreover, default corporation action also used to define default observation: coupon and principal payment, coupon payment only, debt restructuring, interest payment, loan payment, and principal payment. The ith company is assigned as default if it files a credit event report within 1 year period from the date of the financial report; otherwise it is assigned as non-default.

The sample used on our study are companies from industry sector based on Bloomberg industry classification system: aerospace/defense, building materials, electrical component and equipments, electronics, engineering and construction, environmental control, hand/machine tools, machinery-construction and mining, machinery-diversified, metal fabricate/hardware, miscellaneous manufacture, packaging and container, shipbuilding, transportation as well as trucking and leasing.

Tables 7.1 and 7.2 describe the distributions of non-default and default companies across countries before and after, respectively, filtering process. We remove observations containing missing values as a consequence there is no default observation in Philippines remaining in the data set. Hence, we exclude Philippines from the analysis.

The country names represent in which country the companies operate to ensure that they are within the same country are subject to the same disclosure and accounting rules. We apply our method for each country separately such that the different number of the companies does not affect our analysis. One aim it to check whether the relevant default predictors across countries are identical or not.

Table 7.1 Distribution of Companies Across Countries before Filtering Process

Country	Non-Default	Default (%)	Total
Indonesia	929	6 (0.64)	935
Malaysia	7482	111 (1.46)	7593
Philippines	559	19 (3.29)	578
Singapore	1649	10 (0.60)	1659
Thailand	2791	31 (1.10)	2822
Total	13410	177 (1.30)	13587

Table 7.2 Distribution of Companies Across Countries after Filtering Process

Country	Non-Default	Default (%)	Total
Indonesia	370	6 (1.60)	376
Malaysia	2153	45 (2.05)	2198
Singapore	631	9 (1.41)	640
Thailand	1390	16 (1.14)	1406
Total	4544	76 (1.65)	4620

The financial ratios as default predictors are grouped into seven categories as described in Table 7.3: profitability, leverage, cost structure, liquidity, activity as well as dynamics and company size. We used these financial ratios as attributes potentially affecting the default. Based on information from the RMI database, notice that the operating income (OI) variable used in our study are similar to EBIT. Therefore, all financial ratio computed from EBIT are already represented by OI and vice versa. We transform the company size attributes in log value in order to make them comparable to the other attributes.

7.3 EMBEDDED PREDICTOR SELECTION

We are given a training data set with sample size n, predictors $x_i \in \mathbb{R}^p, i = 1, \ldots, n$ and p is number of default predictors, associates with response variable y_i that denote default ($y_i = 1$) and non-default ($y_i = 0$) event. In the context of credit scoring, default prediction is the classification problem that can be formulated as a regularization (or penalization) of a loss function $L\{y, f(x)\}$ as:

$$\min_{\beta_0, \beta} \sum_{i=1}^{n} L\{y_i, f(x_i)\} + \lambda R(\beta), \tag{7.1}$$

where $f(x)$ is a classifier with parameters β_0 and $\beta = (\beta_1, \ldots, \beta_p)^{\mathrm{T}}$. The regularization term $R(\beta)$ is a function of parameters with tuning parameter λ. In this chapter we employ the Lasso and elastic-net as regularization term.

7.3.1 Lasso and Elastic-Net Penalties

Tibshirani (1996) introduced Lasso regularization by employing the L_1-norm penalty to yield a sparse solution, i.e. many estimates shrink to zero. The Lasso regularization approach automatically selects the relevant variables and excludes the non-relevant variables by shrinking their coefficients to zero. Lasso has two noticeable shortcomings (Zou and Hastie, 2005): (i) the number of selected predictors is bounded by the number of samples size as shown in Rosset et al. (2004), and (ii) the Lasso technique tends to select only one (or a few) predictors from a subset of correlated predictors and shrinks the rest to zero.

Table 7.3 Financial Ratios

Variable	Ratio	Explanation
Profitability		
x_1	NI/TA	Net Income/Total Assets
x_2	NI/Sales	Net Income/Sales
x_3	OI/TA	Operating Income/Total Assets
x_4	OI/Sales	Operating Income/Sales
Leverage		
x_5	OF/TA	Own Fund/Total Assets
x_6	CL/TA	Current Liabilities/Total Assets
x_7	TD/TA	Total Debt/Total Assets
Cost Structure		
x_8	INT/TD	Interest payment/Total Debt
x_9	EBIT/INT-paid	EBIT/Interest paid
Liquidity		
x_{10}	STD/TD	Short Term Debt/Total Debt
x_{11}	Cash/TA	Cash/Total Assets
x_{12}	Cash/CL	Cash/Current Liabilities
x_{13}	QA/CL	(Cash and cash equivalent - Inventories)/Current Liabilities
x_{14}	CA/CL	Current Assets/Current Liabilities
x_{15}	WC/TA	Working Capital/Total Assets
x_{16}	CL/TL	Current Liabilities/Total Liabilities
Activity		
x_{17}	TA/Sales	Total Assets/Sales
x_{18}	INV/Sales	Inventories/Sales
x_{19}	AR/Sales	Account Receivable/Sales
x_{20}	AP/C-Sales	Account Payable/Cost of Sales
Dynamics		
x_{21}	Sale-growth	1 year growth in Sales
x_{22}	NI-growth	1 year growth in Net Income
Size		
x_{23}	Log (TA)	Log of Total Assets
x_{24}	Log (Sales)	Log of Sales

Zou and Hastie (2005) introduced the elastic-net penalty to address the drawbacks of the Lasso. The elastic-net penalty is a mixture of the L_1-norm and of the L_2-norm penalties. The two advantages of the elastic-net penalty are: (i) the number of selected predictors is not limited by the sample size, and (ii) group of correlated predictors can be selected together (group selection). The L_1 penalty plays the role of predictors selection, while the L_2 penalty helps in group selection. We expect the L_2 penalty can select the subset of correlated financial ratios in the credit risk analysis framework.

The elastic-net penalty, a compromise between ridge and lasso, is defined as (Friedman et al., 2010):

$$R_\gamma(\beta) = (1 - \gamma)\frac{1}{2}||\beta||_2^2 + \gamma||\beta||_1 \qquad (7.2)$$

$$= \sum_{j=1}^{p}\left\{(1 - \gamma)\frac{1}{2}\beta_j^2 + \gamma|\beta_j|\right\}, \qquad (7.3)$$

with the weight $0 < \gamma < 1$ that should be optimized simultaneously joint with the tuning parameter λ. If $\gamma = 0$ then the penalty $R_\gamma(\beta)$ boils down to the ridge penalty. The Lasso regularization is employed when $\gamma = 1$. For a very small $\varepsilon > 0$, the elastic-net penalty with $\gamma = 1 - \varepsilon$ performs like the Lasso, but removes any degeneracies and wild behavior caused by high correlations between predictors. As γ increases from zero to one, for a given λ, the sparsity of the solution to Eq. (7.1) increases monotonically from zero to the sparsity of the Lasso solution (Friedman et al., 2010).

7.3.2 Regularization on Logit Model

The regularization technique is now applied to the logit model. The probability of default and of non-default, respectively, for ith company given by default predictor x_i is formulated as:

$$P(y_i = 1|x_i) = \frac{e^{\beta_0 + x_i^T\beta}}{1 + e^{\beta_0 + x_i^T\beta}} \qquad (7.4)$$

$$= \frac{1}{1 + e^{-(\beta_0 + x_i^T\beta)}},$$

and

$$P(y_i = 0|x_i) = 1 - P(y_i = 1|x_i)$$
$$= \frac{1}{1 + e^{\beta_0 + x_i^T\beta}}.$$

The log odds ratio is a linear regression model:

$$\log \left\{ \frac{P(y_i = 1|x_i)}{P(y_i = 0|x_i)} \right\} = \beta_0 + x_i^T \beta. \tag{7.5}$$

The task is now maximizing regularized log-likehood function:

$$\max_{\beta_0, \beta} \left\{ \ell(\beta_0, \beta) - \lambda R_\gamma(\beta) \right\}, \tag{7.6}$$

where the log-likelihood is:

$$
\begin{aligned}
\ell(\beta_0, \beta) &= n^{-1} \sum_{1=1}^{n} [y_i \, \log \, P(y_i = 1|x_i) + (1 - y_i) \, \log\{1 - P(y_i = 1|x_i)\}] \\
&= n^{-1} \sum_{1=1}^{n} \{I(y_i = 1) \, \log \, P(y_i = 1|x_i)\} + I(y_i = 0) \, \log \, P(y_i = 0|x_i) \quad (7.7) \\
&= n^{-1} \sum_{1=1}^{n} I(y_i = 1) \left[(\beta_0 + x_i^T \beta) - \log \left\{ 1 + e^{\beta_0 + x_i^T \beta} \right\} \right].
\end{aligned}
$$

The unpenalized log-likelihood function in (7.7) is a concave function with respect to the parameters. The regularization yields sparse solution. Maximizing the penalized log-likelihood, for a given constant λ, singles out a certain number of non-zero estimates. If we relax the penalty by reducing the value λ, then more predictors of dimension $p^*(\lambda)$ will surface. Wu et al. (2009) stated that $p^*(\lambda)$ is basically a decreasing function of λ with jumps of size one, although minor exception occurs. The entry order of the predictors tends to be related to its marginal significance. This rule of thumb is violated though when the predictors are correlated.

The Eq. (7.7) is maximized using the Newton-Raphson algorithm which amounts to an iteratively reweighted least squares (IRLS) scheme. We follow the algorithm of Friedman et al. (2010) which used the similar approach to IRLS, i.e. using cyclical coordinate descent which is computed along a regularization path. They concluded that the coordinate descent performed best among the several competing algorithms. In cyclic coordinate descent, each estimate of the parameter is updated in turn. Wu and Lange (2008) developed greedy coordinate descent algorithm which update the parameter leading to the largest increase in the objective function. However, the algorithm slightly suffers from excess overhead, although it makes faster initial progress. Shevade and Keerthi (2003) also developed an algorithm to estimate the logit model with Lasso penalty based on the Gauss-Siedel method using coordinate-wise descent approach.

There are three steps in the cyclic coordinate descent algorithm: outer, middle, and inner loop. In the outer loop, we set up the value of λ yielding $(\tilde{\beta}_0, \tilde{\beta})$. In the middle loop, we update the quadratic approximation (Taylor expansion) of the log-likelihood function about current estimates $(\tilde{\beta}_0, \tilde{\beta})$:

$$\ell_Q(\beta_0, \beta) = -\frac{1}{2n} \sum_{i=1}^{n} \omega_i \left(z_i - \beta_0 - x_i^{\mathrm{T}} \beta \right)^2 + C(\tilde{\beta}_0, \beta), \tag{7.8}$$

with working response and weight:

$$z_i = \tilde{\beta}_0 + x_i^{\mathrm{T}} \tilde{\beta} + \frac{y_i - \tilde{P}(y_i = 1|x_i)}{\tilde{P}(y_i = 1|x_i)\tilde{P}(y_i = 0|x_i)},$$

and

$$\omega_i = \tilde{P}(y_i = 1|x_i)\tilde{P}(y_i = 0|x_i),$$

where $\tilde{P}(y_i = 1|x_i)$ and $\tilde{P}(y_i = 0|x_i)$ are evaluated at the current estimates and $C(\tilde{\beta}_0, \tilde{\beta})$ is a constant. The first term in $\ell_Q(\beta_0, \beta)$ is a weighted least square. In the inner loop, the coordinate descent algorithm is used to solve the following penalized weighted least squares (PWLS) problem:

$$\min_{\beta_0, \beta} \left\{ -\ell_Q(\beta_0, \beta) + \lambda R_\gamma(\beta) \right\}. \tag{7.9}$$

Each inner coordinate descent loop continues until the maximum change in Eq. (7.9) is less than a very small threshold. We set the threshold used in this study is 1E-7. The next step is to decrease the value of λ and repeat the three loops until the estimates are convergent. Once the final estimates are obtained, the sparse representation with selected relevant predictor is used to predict the default as well as PD.

7.4 EMPIRICAL RESULT

For simplicity of computation the predictors x_{ij} were standardized and the estimates are always returned on the original scale. We optimize γ and λ in the following way: for a fixed γ, the tuning parameter λ is optimized based on the value of area under the curve (AUC) from the receiver operating characteristic (ROC) curve, Sobehart and Keenan (2001). We increase the value of γ from 0.1 to 0.9 for elastic-net and obtain the optimum corresponding λ for each γ. We choose the best pair (γ, λ) which maximizes the AUC. The AUC reflects the performance of any method and is robust with respect to unbalance class. This is the case in our analysis where the proportion of default is smaller than of non–default.

Table 7.4 summarizes the performance for different γ and its corresponding optimum λ for all countries. For the logit model with Lasso regularization, the optimum λ

Table 7.4 Model Performance Based on Different Tuning Parameter Accuracy

	γ									
	0.1	0.2	0.3	0.4	0.5	0.6	0.7	0.8	0.9	1
Indonesia										
λ	2.6E−3	5.0E−4	0.0186	**7.0E−4**	**5.5E−5**	0.0148	2.0E−4	1.4E−3	3.0E−4	**6.0E−4**
$\log \lambda$	−5.958	−7.488	−3.986	−7.158	−9.801	−4.214	−8.462	−6.549	−8.156	−7.423
$\log \{\lambda(1se)\}$	−1.865	−7.303	−2.219	−5.205	−6.172	−3.098	−7.253	−5.433	−7.504	−6.214
AUC	0.991	0.994	0.976	**0.994**	**0.996**	0.975	0.994	0.992	0.994	0.994
p^*	20	21	9	**18**	**20**	6	18	13	12	12
Malaysia										
λ	**1.2E−5**	9.5E−5	6.0E−4	1.0E−4	4.0E−4	5.5E−5	9.1E−5	3.0E−4	7.7E−5	**3.0E−4**
$\log \lambda$	−11.362	−9.264	−7.437	−9.120	−7.762	−9.805	−9.308	−8.232	−9.466	−8.269
$\log \{\lambda(1se)\}$	−6.989	−5.543	−6.134	−6.701	−6.831	−6.176	−6.889	−7.301	−7.140	−7.245
AUC	**0.871**	0.864	0.851	0.864	0.855	0.869	0.868	0.859	**0.870**	0.861
p^*	**24**	24	22	23	21	24	23	22	**22**	21
Singapore										
λ	9.0E−4	1.3E−3	5.7E−3	1.9E−3	2.6E−3	1.9E−3	1.8E−3	**1.2E−3**	1.7E−3	**2.3E−3**
$\log \lambda$	−7.045	−6.622	−5.167	−6.292	−5.957	−6.232	−6.293	−6.706	−6.359	−6.092
$\log \{\lambda(1se)\}$	−4.905	−4.668	−4.422	−5.361	−5.119	−5.487	−4.804	−6.147	−5.149	−5.254
AUC	0.975	0.982	0.958	0.975	0.970	0.973	0.974	**0.978**	0.974	0.969
p^*	21	20	13	16	13	13	12	**14**	11	9
Thailand										
λ	2.6E−3	7.5E−3	1.8E−3	6.6E−3	0.0122	5.3E−3	5.9E−3	3.9E−3	**3.0E−4**	**0.0001**
$\log \lambda$	−5.962	−4.887	−6.316	−5.022	−4.408	−5.242	−5.117	−5.529	−8.159	−8.916
$\log \{\lambda(1se)\}$	−5.217	−4.701	−3.711	−3.813	−3.757	−4.497	−4.372	−4.227	−6.112	−6.869
AUC	0.982	0.970	0.982	0.963	0.934	0.960	0.937	0.962	**0.991**	0.993
p^*	21	16	20	12	7	11	8	10	**20**	19

of Indonesian, Malaysian, Singaporean, and Thailand, respectively, are 0.0006, 0.0003, 0.0023, and 0.0001. In the elastic-net approach we apply parsimonious principle, i.e. we choose smaller selected default predictor when the AUC values only differ very small. For Indonesia we choose $\gamma = 0.4$ instead of $\gamma = 0.5$ since it selects two less predictors. The optimum λ for the corresponding γ is 0.0007. For Malaysia we choose $\gamma = 0.9$ instead of $\gamma = 0.1$ for the same reason with optimum λ is 0.000077. The optimum γ for Singapore and Thailand are 0.8 and 0.9, respectively, with optimum λ are 0.0012 and 0.0003 for each corresponding γ. The number of selected default predictor, denoted as p^*, in the Lasso approach are much smaller than the one in elastic-net particularly for Indonesia, Singapore and Thailand.

Table 7.4 reports the value of log $\{\lambda(1se)\}$ which expresses the largest value of log λ such that the cross-validation (5-fold) error is within one standard-error of the minimum. This approach is the so called "one-standard-error" rule. This value is represented by the right vertical line in Figures 7.1 and 7.2. The left vertical line in each plot corresponds to mean cross-validated error curve or equivalently mean AUC. The fixed values of left and right vertical lines can be drawn from Table 7.4. The top of each plot is annotated with the number of predictors selected. For $p^* \geq 7$ on Indonesia data set, both Lasso and elastic-net yield very high accuracy where the AUC almost close to one. This is not the case for Malaysia data set where even $p^* \geq 18$ the AUC value are ranging from 0.85 to 0.87. Singapore and Thailand data set result in very high accuracy of default prediction in term of AUC. Singapore has smaller number of default predictors with little higher AUC values than Thailand.

Figures 7.3 and 7.4 show the solution paths of the estimates with respect to the value of log λ. The larger λ imply more number of estimates shrink to zero. The solution path seems alike decreasing function of log λ with minor exceptions particularly for Malaysia data set. This may affect its default prediction accuracy which is less accurate compare to the other three countries. The upper and lower paths correspond to the relevant predictors with positive and negative, respectively, sign estimate. The best estimates corresponding to these relevant predictors are reported in Table 7.5.

The Lasso selected predictors are in most cases a subset of the elastic-net variables. This clearly visible for each country particularly for Indonesia. For each country the sign of the estimates are identical with the exception own fund ratio (OF/TA) Thailand. Across the countries, only 9 out of 24 financial ratios have a consistent sign: OI/TA, OI/Sales, EBIT/INT-paid, Cash/CL, WC/TA, INV/Sales, AR/Sales, NI growth, and log (TA). These financial ratios are highlighted in Table 7.5. The remaining financial ratios have different sign across countries. This is in line with Balcaen and Ooghe (2006) who found that the default prediction based on logit model is country specific.

The inconsistency sign estimates are mostly exhibited in Singapore, i.e. five ratios: net profit margin (NI/Sales), average cost of debt (INT/D), sort term debt (STD/D),

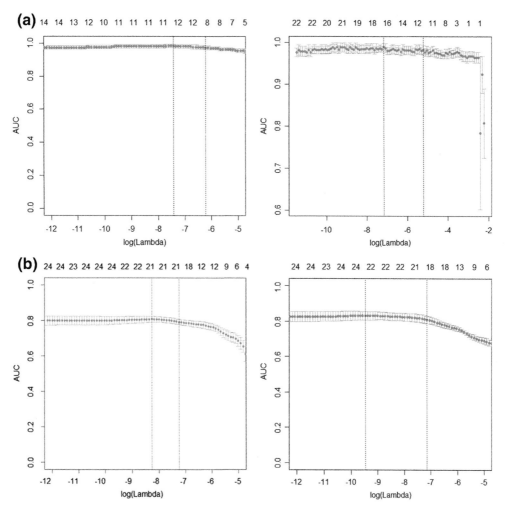

Figure 7.1 AUC values for lasso (left) and elastic-net (right): (a) Indonesia and (b) Malaysia. The γ values for elastic-net penalty are: (a) $\gamma = 0.4$, (b) $\gamma = 0.9$.

quick ratio (QA/CL), and current ratio (CA/CL), followed by Indonesia with four ratios: return on assets ratio (NI/TA), cash to total assets ratio (Cash/TA), account payable turnover (AP/C-Sales), and Sales growth. Malaysia and Thailand show inconsistency sign estimate for each one ratio, i.e. Log (Sales) and assets turnover ratio (TA/Sales), respectively.

The inconsistent picture across countries may be caused by the quality of the data. One source of the distortion may be creative accounting, i.e. accounting practices that follow required laws and regulations, but deviate from what those standards intend to accomplish. This practice is intended to portray a nice image of the company. Defaulting

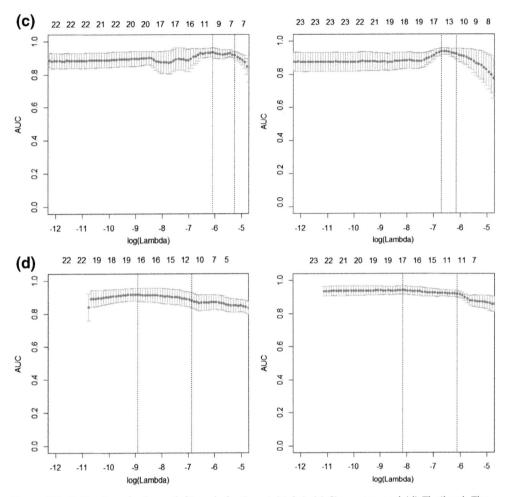

Figure 7.2 AUC values for lasso (left) and elastic-net (right): (c) Singapore and (d) Thailand. The γ values for elastic-net penalty are: (c) $\gamma = 0.8$ and (d) $\gamma = 0.9$.

companies adjust their income upwards and provide a more positive financial report particularly when the default event is coming. However, when companies indulge in creative accounting they often distort the value of the information that their financials provide.

Let us focus on the nine financial ratios with consistent signs across countries: OI/TA, EBIT/INT-paid, Cash/CL, INV/Sales, and NI growth (negative sign) and OI/Sales, WC/TA, AR/Sales, and log (TA) (positive sign). Negative signs of parameter imply the higher the corresponding financial ratio the lower the PD. It is not a surprise that the higher operating income on asset ratio (OI/TA) will reduce the PD.

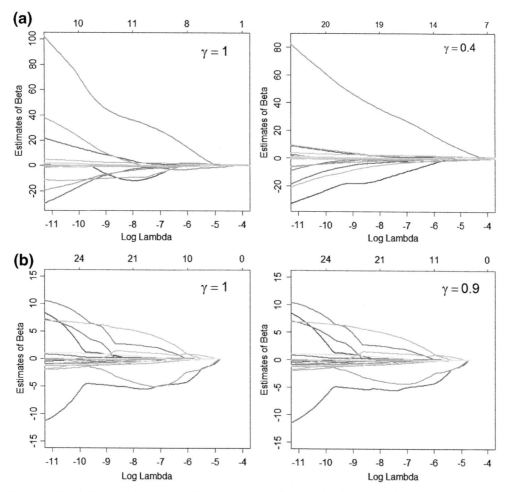

Figure 7.3 Solution path for lasso (left) and elastic-net (right): (a) Indonesia and (b) Malaysia.

The PD decrease for the higher interest coverage ratio (EBIT/INT-paid). An increase in cash ratio (Cash/CL) will reduce PD. Cash constitutes a substantial portion of current liabilities such that increase of the numerator is followed by a likewise increase of the denominator. Inventory turnover ratio (INV/Sales) alike has a counterintuitive sign. Keeping inventories as non-productive assets relatively high to sales should increase PD. This should provide positive sign coefficient. However, this adjustment is not fully applicable since too low inventory turnover (INV/Sales) leads to a higher PD represented by negative sign estimate. The relationship between inventory turnover and PD has a U-shaped therefore the magnitudes of the estimates across countries are close to zero. The higher 1 year net income growth not surprisingly decreases the PD.

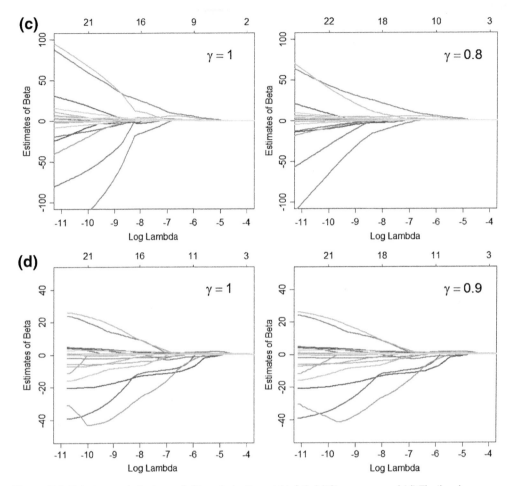

Figure 7.4 Solution path for lasso (left) and elastic-net (right): (c) Singapore and (d) Thailand.

A predictor with a positive sign has a monotone increasing effect on the PD. It is counterintuitive that the higher operating profit margin (OI/Sales) ratio increases the PD. The same problem happens for the WC/TA ratio. The higher account receivable turnover (AR/Sales) increases the PD. This ratio can be attributed to the inability to collect payments from its clients on time and show a weak position of a company. It is a surprise that the larger the firm the higher the PD since log (TA) has a positive sign estimate. The relationship between company size and PD may not be monotone where the increasing assets of small and medium size company may does not decrease PD. There are non-accounting and qualitative failure indicators affect the default.

Table 7.5 Estimates of the Selected Predictors for Indonesia (ID), Malaysia (MY), Singapore (SG), and Thailand (TH)

Ratios	Lasso				Elastic-Net			
	ID	MY	SG	TH	ID	MY	SG	TH
λ	6.0E−4	3.0E−4	2.3E−3	1.0E−4	7.0E−4	7.7E−5	1.2E−4	3.0E−4
γ	1	1	1	1	0.4	0.9	0.8	0.9
Intercept	−6.270	−3.880	−15.001	−3.470	−9.801	−6.066	−19.485	−5.984
Profitability								
NI/TA	−9.582	–	–	−17.916	−10.987	1.212	–	−13.458
NI/Sales	–	0.023	–	3.311	–	–	−0.014	1.709
OI/TA	–	−5.234	–	−29.140	–	−4.988	–	−12.532
OI/Sales	1.770	0.175	–	2.490	1.028	0.209	–	0.051
Leverage								
OF/TA	−1.587	–	–	0.034	−2.071	3.272	–	−0.055
CL/TA	–	2.581	–	14.312	−0.911	6.227	−0.469	9.285
TD/TA	–	−0.810	5.899	−2.371	0.510	−0.536	9.280	−1.841
Cost Structure								
INT/D	–	−0.207	–	0.170	–	−0.536	−0.040	0.106
EBIT/INT-paid	–	−0.002	–	–	–	−0.006	–	–
Liquidity								
STD/D	−0.160	−0.613	0.803	−0.527	−2.384	−0.893	2.062	−0.101
Cash/TA	31.707	−4.105	–	−40.429	29.143	−1.790	–	−27.327
Cash/CL	–	−0.394	–	–	–	−1.237	–	–
QA/CL	–	−0.220	0.064	−5.475	−0.377	−0.264	–	−4.011
CA/CL	−2.443	−1.028	–	−5.054	−1.383	−1.261	0.088	−1.494

(*Continued*)

Table 7.5 Continued

Ratios	Lasso				Elastic-Net			
	ID	MY	SG	TH	ID	MY	SG	TH
λ	6.0E−4	3.0E−4	2.3E−3	1.0E−4	7.0E−4	7.7E−5	1.2E−4	3.0E−4
γ	1	1	1	1	0.4	0.9	0.8	0.9
WC/TA	–	5.266	4.149	19.074	0.212	6.248	5.323	9.429
CL/TL	−8.497	1.249	–	−8.854	−3.571	–	0.029	−6.776
Activity								
TA/Sales	–	−0.004	–	–	–	−0.014	–	0.002
INV/Sales	–	−0.018	–	−0.276	−0.010	−0.029	−0.085	−0.040
AR/Sales	2.104	–	0.824	2.602	2.061	0.002	0.904	2.085
AP/C-Sales	−0.792	0.002	0.399	0.888	−0.911	0.006	1.134	0.785
Dynamics								
Sale-growth	–	1.0E−4	0.008	0.012	−1.9E−5	1.0E−4	0.007	0.011
NI-growth	−0.014	−5.0E−4	–	–	−0.015	−0.001	–	–
Size								
Log (TA)	0.029	0.534	0.662	0.643	0.224	0.843	0.681	0.528
Log (Sales)	0.311	−0.782	0.439	–	0.227	−1.087	0.791	–
AUC	0.994	0.861	0.970	0.993	0.994	0.870	0.978	0.991
p^*	12	21	9	19	18	22	14	20

7.5 CONCLUSION

Regularized logit model is able to simultaneously estimate and select default predictors with very high accuracy prediction particularly for Indonesia, Singapore, and Thailand industry. For the same level of accuracy, the number of default predictors selected by Lasso for Indonesia and Singapore data are significantly smaller than those selected by elastic-net penalty. Almost all predictors selected in the Lasso are also selected in the elastic-net. The relevant default predictors vary over the country which is in line with related studies which conclude that the default prediction analysis is sample specific.

ACKNOWLEDGMENT

This research was supported by the Deutsche Forschungsgemeinschaft through the SFB 649 "Economic Risk," Humboldt-Universität zu Berlin. Dedy Dwi Prastyo was also supported by Directorate General for Higher Education, Indonesian Ministry of Education and Culture through Department of Statistics, Institut Teknologi Sepuluh Nopember (ITS), Indonesia. The support under Credit Research Initiative (CRI) project, Risk Management Institute (RMI) at the National University of Singapore (NUS) is gratefully acknowledged by Härdle and Prastyo, respectively.

REFERENCES

Altman, E., 1968. Financial ratios, discriminant analysis and the prediction of corporate bankruptcy. Journal of Finance 23 (4), 589–609.

Altman, E.I., Hotchkiss, E., 2006. Corporate Financial Distress and Bankruptcy: Predict and Avoid Bankruptcy, Analyze and Invest in Distressed Debt, third ed. John Wiley & Sons Inc., Hoboken, New Jersey.

Altman, E., Marco, G., Varetto, F., 1994. Corporate distress diagnosis: comparison using linear discriminant analysis and neural network (the Italian experience). Journal of Banking and Finance 18, 505–529.

Balcaen, S., Ooghe, H., 2006. 35 years of studies on business failure: an overview of the classic statistical methodologies and their related problems. British Accounting Review 38, 63–93.

Beaver, W., 1966. Financial ratios as predictors of failures. Journal of Accounting Research Empirical Research in Accounting: Selected Studies 4, 71–111.

Chen, S., Härdle, W., Moro, R., 2011. Modeling default risk with support vector machines. Quantitative Finance 11, 135–154.

Friedman, J., Hastie, T., Tibshirani, R., 2010. Regularization path for generalized linear models via coordinate descent. Journal of Statistical Software 33 (1), 1–22.

Härdle, W., Lee, Y.-J., Schäfer, D., Yeh, Y.-R., 2009. Variable selection and oversampling in the use of smooth support vector machine for predicting the default risk of companies. Journal of Forecasting 28, 512–534.

Härdle, W., Prastyo, D.D., Hafner, C., 2014. Support vector machines with evolutionary model selection for default prediction. In: Racine, J.S., Su, L., Ullah, A. (Eds.), The Oxford Handbook of Applied Nonparametric and Semiparametric Econometrics and Statistics. Oxford University Press Inc., New York, NY.

Henley, W.E., Hand, D.J., 1996. A k-Nearest neighbour classifier for assessing consumer credit risk. Journal of the Statistical Society. Series D (The Statistician) 45 (1), 77–95.

Lau, A.H.-L., 1987. A five-state financial distress prediction model. Journal of Accounting Research 25 (1), 127–138.

Lo, A.W., 1986. Logit versus discriminant analysis: a specification test and application to corporate bankruptcies. Journal Econometrics 31 (2), 151–178.

Martin, D., 1977. Early warning of bank failure: a logit regression approach. Journal of Banking and Finance 1, 249–276.

Ohlson, J., 1980. Financial ratios and the probabilistic prediction of bankruptcy. Journal of Accounting Research 18 (1), 109–131.

Platt, H., Platt, M., Pedersen, J., 1994. Bankruptcy discrimination with real variables. Journal of Business Finance and Accounting 21 (4), 491–510.

Rosset, S., Zhu, J., Hastie, T., 2004. Boosting as a regularized path to a maximum margin classifier. Journal of Machine Learning Research 5, 941–973.

Shevade, S.K., Keerthi, S.S., 2003. A simple and efficient algorithm for gene selection using sparse logistic regression. Bioinformatics 19, 2246–2253.

Sobehart, J., Keenan, S., 2001. Measuring default accurately. Risk 14, 31–33.

Steinwart, I., Christmann, A., 2008. Support Vector Machine. Springer, New York, NY.

Tam, K., Kiang, M., 1992. Managerial applications of neural networks: the case of bank failure predictions. Management Science 38, 926–947.

Tibshirani, R., 1996. Regression shrinkage and selection via the Lasso. Journal of the Royal Statistical Society, Series B 58, 267–288.

Vapnik, V., 1998. Statistical Learning Theory. John Wiley, New York, NY.

Wilson, R.L., Sharda, R., 1994. Bankruptcy prediction using neural network. Decision Support System 11, 545–557.

Wu, T.T., Lange, K., 2008. Coordinate descent algorithms for lasso penalized regression. Annals of Applied Statistics 2 (1), 224–244.

Wu, T.T., Chen, Y.F., Hastie, T., Sobel, E., Lange, K., 2009. Genome-wide association analysis by lasso penalized logistic regression. Bioinformatics 25 (6), 714–721.

Zhang, J.L., Härdle, W., 2010. The bayesian additive classification tree applied to credit risk modelling. Computational Statistics and Data Analysis 54, 1197–1205.

Zou, H., Hastie, T., 2005. Regularization and variable selection via the elastic net. Journal of the Royal Statistical Society, Series B 67 (2), 301–320.

CHAPTER 8

Demand for International Reserve and Monetary Disequilibrium: Evidence from Emerging Asia

Chandan Sharma[a] and Sunny Kumar Singh[b]
[a]Indian Institute of Management Lucknow, Noida Campus, Noida 201307, India
[b]Indian Institute of Management Lucknow, Lucknow 226013, India

8.1 INTRODUCTION

Since the collapse of Bretton wood system in early 1970s, many countries have adopted flexible or more precisely managed floating exchange rate system. The theoretical considerations underpinning suggest for zero requirements of foreign reserves under a pure floating regime. In the case of managed floating regime, countries need to hold some reserves to limit the fluctuations in the exchange rate market. But in reality, no matter what exchange rate system prevails, there has always been certain demand for international reserves over time. Moreover, the demand for reserves has increased many folds in emerging Asian economies[1] after the painful financial crisis of late 1990s and since then the reserves hoarding has outpaced all traditional benchmark levels in these countries (IMF, 2010).

The standard literature offers two arguments which have explained motives behind holding a large pile of reserves in the emerging Asian countries. First, these countries desire for self-protection against possible sudden shocks in the external sector and holding reserves is considered to be a tool in fulfilling their desire (e.g., Aizenman and Marion, 2003; Kim et al., 2005; Aizenman and Lee, 2007). It is widely argued that during the 1997–1998 crisis the East Asian countries have suffered severely, and therefore, a larger amount of international reserves holding serves to protect these economies against sudden shortages of international liquidity thus preventing from occurrence of such crisis again in future (Park and Estrada, 2009). Consequently, this argument assigns precautionary motive behind holding reserves. On the other side, intentions behind stimulating export growth and FDI inflows through a large reserve buildup are assigned under the mercantile motive (Calvo and Reinhart, 2002; Dooley et al., 2004; Aizenman and Lee, 2007). Dooley et al. (2004) argue that to promote employment and growth, the emerging Asian countries have adopted strategies of undervaluing their exchange rates

---

[1] China, Indonesia, South Korea, Malaysia, Philippines, Singapore, and Thailand are considered as emerging Asia.

and managing sizable foreign exchange interventions and these strategies have been successfully pursued over time as these countries have accumulated a pile of reserves.[2]

Maintaining a high stock of international reserves often supports the growth process and provides confidence and safety to the domestic economy. However, holding of reserves is not without a cost and central banks of these countries have to pay a hefty price for accumulating reserves. Deployment of reserves generates very little return therefore the spread between the interest earned on reserves and the interest paid on the country's public debt is over and over again negative and increasing with more accumulation. Thus, hoarding the excess reserve causes heavy sterilization costs. Furthermore, it could also create inflationary pressure in the country in the case of non-sterilized foreign capital flows (Gosselin and Parent, 2005). The holding reserves also have serious negative implications on welfare, if the cost of holding an additional reserve is larger than the benefit. Therefore, the issue of adequacy and analysis of demand of reserves have become issues of debate in the literature and these issues are widely unsettled and still open. Furthermore, considering its serious implications for possible currency crisis and welfare measures, it also creates dilemma among the policy makers for a policy standpoint on the issue (Mishra and Sharma, 2011).

Against this background, this study has twin objectives. First, using a set of established benchmarks of adequacy we attempt to examine the level of reserves appropriateness in the emerging Asian countries. Second, we also attempt to estimate the determinants of international reserve in these countries. Our analyses focus on seven emerging Asian countries, namely China, Indonesia, South Korea, Malaysia, The Philippines, Singapore, and Thailand. This study contributes to promising line of the standard research by several ways. First, emerging Asian countries have become powerhouse for world growth in the recent years; however, the experience of the East Asian crisis has shown the vulnerability of these economies from possible external crisis. Also these countries are somewhat interlinked having similar business cycle. Therefore, we consider these economies for investigation in a single panel data framework. Second, previous studies based on panel data widely ignore the issues of non-endogeneity, serial correlation, and non-stationarity, which might have some serious consequences on reliability of statistical inference as inference based on unadjusted standard errors (see Gosselin and Parent, 2005). We make significant econometric improvement and analyzed the issue in the panel cointegration framework. For obtaining an unbiased estimator of the long-run parameters, we employ the Dynamic OLS (DOLS) estimator in panel context, which effectively corrects aforementioned problems in the econometrics analysis. Third, the demand for international reserves cannot be studied in isolation from the movements of country's money market as the monetary approach to the balance of payments crucially

---

[2] Some commenters also argued that there could also be political vendettas of holding excess amount of reserves especially in the case of China (see, e.g., Lindsay, 2003).

hypothesizes that disequilibrium in the national money market explains into the movement of reserve changes (Elbadawi, 1990). Barring a few, most of the previous studies on the emerging Asia have not given any attention on the role of national monetary disequilibrium in demand for international reserves. In this study, following Badinger (2004) and Mishra and Sharma (2011) we estimate and incorporate the national monetary disequilibrium using the time series cointegration analysis. Finally, to understand the demand for reserves, we use important measures of uncertainty and risk as well as opportunity cost in our analysis, which help us in quantifying the motive of holding reserves in these countries.

The remainder of the chapter is organized as follows: Section 8.2 reviews some empirical literatures on the determinants of international reserve. Section 8.3 provides some stylized facts and adequacy of reserves. Section 8.4 deals with data-related issues. Section 8.5 presents the empirical models and the estimation results. The final section concludes the study with some recommendations.

8.2 LITERATURE REVIEW

A strand of the standard literature on the international reserves around the world discussed about determinants of international reserve and successfully established a relatively stable long-run demand for international reserve based on a set of explanatory variables. The models of reserves holdings consider mainly precautionary factors. Nevertheless, some key indicators of mercantile motive and factors of cost of holding reserves are also included in the models.

Studies of Flood and Marion (2001), Aizenman and Marion (2004), and Delatte and Fouquau (2012) expect reserves holding increase with economic size as the volume of international financial transactions is crucially related to reserves demand of the country. Therefore, the level of the size of the economy measured in terms of GDP or per capita GDP is included in the reserves demand functions.

Learning lessons from recent crises including the Asian crisis, studies have gradually started including measures of capital account vulnerabilities (e.g., Aizenman et al., 2004). Broad money to reserves or GDP is frequently included in the empirical models to capture the risks from probable currency mismatches, which may lead to capital flight and finally affect the country's reserves holdings (e.g., Calvo, 1996). Acknowledging that high exposures increase vulnerability to financial crises, some studies have also considered variables of financing exposures such as FDI and portfolio flows in the models (e.g., Radelet and Sachs, 1998; Aizenman et al., 2004). However, the association between capital flows and reserves accumulation is not well established as of now perhaps because the linkage depends on the type of flow of capital (e.g., IMF, 2011).

Measures of the current account vulnerabilities are also modeled as crucial factors of determinants of reserves. Size of imports bill and export earnings are typically used indicators to capture the external shocks to the current account of the country. The literature has found imports and the volatility of real earnings to be positively correlated with reserves holdings (Aizenman and Marion, 2003; Flood and Marion, 2002). Some studies, for instance, Aizenman et al. (2004), used trade openness as an extensive measure, of current account vulnerability.

The exchange rate regime is also importantly linked with quantity of reserves holding in the literature. For example, pegged and managed exchange rate regimes need a large reserve hoarding to guard the parities of the currency (Edwards, 1985). However, Calvo and Reinhart (2000) have argued that some countries categorized as floaters are in reality peggers; in such cases using exchange rate regime as an indicator in the empirical models could lead to yield unexpected findings. Some recent research, for instance, Mishra and Sharma (2011) have shown that volatility of reserves increases vulnerabilities of the external sector therefore reserve accumulation is positively related to the volatility.

The related theories indicate that international reserves holdings should be inversely correlated with the opportunity cost of holding them. Recently, Gosselin and Parent (2005) and Mishra and Sharma (2011) have found that opportunity cost of holding (proxied by interest rate differential) is an important factor in explaining the reserves movement. However, due to difficulty in measuring opportunity cost, some others have argued that the effect of this indicator is quite undecided in the literature (e.g., Flood and Marion, 2002). A fiscal opportunity cost is also argued to be a key variable in reserves holdings mainly because it could otherwise be cast off to finance public capital expenditure or to pay down external debt and reduce the interest bill (Hauner, 2006).

Edwards (1984) synthesized the demand for reserves theory and the monetary theory. Linking these two different explanations explicitly, Edwards (1984) incorporates an additional variable, excess money demand in the empirical models. He argued that reserves holdings can be affected by money market disequilibria in the short run, which feasibly arises from a domestic economic disequilibrium. He employed the reduced form of the demand for reserves equation which includes money market disequilibrium. Although the monetary approach focuses on money market disequilibria effects on effect on the demand for reserve, Elbadawi (1990), Huang and Shen (1999), and Badinger (2004), and very recently, Mishra and Sharma (2011) examined whether or not money market disequilibria guide the reserves movements in the long-run specifications. Importantly, most of these studies have found encouraging results regarding disequilibrium of money market in the analysis of empirical models of reserves.

Some other studies have also included indicators of a currency crisis, a banking crisis or a twin crisis on international reserves accumulation (Eichengreen et al., 1996), while, Aizenmann and Marion (2004) considered the quality of institutions in the demand equations. It is argued that countries with weaker institutions are required to hold more reserves with the purpose of shoring up confidence. However, one can also argue that weaker institutions are related with lesser holdings of reserves as inefficient and corrupt governments often utilize reserves.

Recently, some studies have exclusively focused on emerging or developing countries of Asia in panel framework. Gosselin and Parent (2005) attempted to answer to the question that how far the current level of reserves is predicted by the standard macroeconomic determinants in the emerging Asia. Using panel cointegration framework it was found that the actual level of reserves accumulated during early 2000s was still in excess relative to that predicted reserves by the established models. Therefore, it is expected that as long as historical relationships hold, a slowdown in the rate of accumulation of reserves is likely. Park and Estrada (2009) attempted to estimate size of excess reserves in developing Asia. The results of their both informal and formal tests indicate that there are incidences of large and growing excess reserves since 2002 in the region.

8.3 STYLIZED FACTS AND ADEQUACY OF RESERVES

8.3.1 Stylized Facts

In this section, we present some important stylized facts on international reserves in the Asian region. Subsequently, we discuss issue of adequacy of reserves in the region. Prior to the wave of globalization, developing countries of the region used to hold international reserves mainly to accomplish foreign exchange demand and supply gap rising from deficit of current account transactions. Most of these countries of the region followed restrictive foreign trade policies and used its reserves for import of indispensable items like petroleum and food grains. Since early 1980s, these countries have experienced major shift in the external policy and export promotion has become the core of economic policy which replaced conventional import substitution policy. To succeed the new policy, sufficiency of international reserves was a major requirement. However, except Singapore other countries of the region were reluctant to hold adequate level of reserves. Thus in the beginning of the crisis when capital flight started the countries failed to protect their external sector from consequences of it. Only after the crisis these economies started building up reserves stockpile.

Figures 8.1 and 8.2 show the trend and growth rate of real international reserve in the emerging Asian countries during the period 1980–2011. During the period as whole, the emerging Asia's reserve has grown significantly from around USD46 billion in 1980 to USD4100 billion in 2011 (around 90 times). More importantly, it grew from USD319 billion at the time of East Asian crisis of 1997–1998 to USD4100 billion in 2011. During the post-crisis periods, the growth rate of reserve accumulation was much higher than that of the pre-crisis period.

To some extent, the growth of reserves in absolute terms over time simply mirrors the growth of emerging Asia's output over time. Hence, it is important to scale the

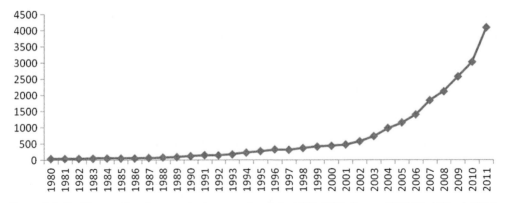

Figure 8.1 Real international reserve in the emerging Asia: 1980–2011. *Source:* WDI, World Bank, 2013, Value in billion USD, 2000.

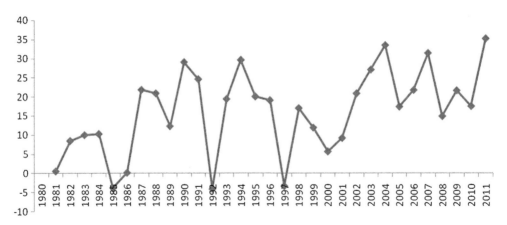

Figure 8.2 Annual growth rate of real international reserve in the emerging Asia: 1980–2011. *Source:* WDI, World Bank, 2013.

international reserves by GDP. Figure 8.3 presents the reserve as percentage of GDP in the emerging Asian countries. It reveals that growth of reserves accumulation is much higher than the output growth, as amount of growth in reserves has outpaced the GDP almost in all countries of the consideration in the post-crisis period.

A significant rise in the emerging Asia's share would lend further credibility to the global significance of their reserve buildup. Therefore, it is important to consider the share of emerging Asia's reserve in the world's reserves. Figure 8.4 shows that the share of emerging Asia's reserves has increased from 34% in 2003 to 59% in 2011. This suggests that emerging Asia has been accumulating reserves at a relatively faster rate than the rest of world.

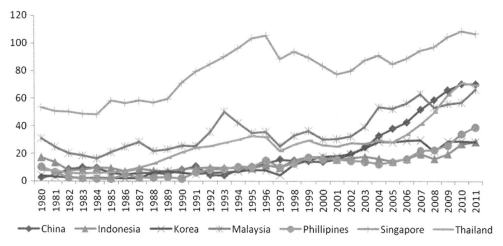

Figure 8.3 International reserve as percentage of GDP in the emerging Asia: 1980–2011. *Source:* WDI, World Bank, 2013.

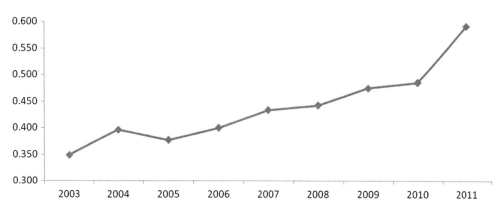

Figure 8.4 Share of the emerging Asia's reserve to world's reserve (%): 2003–2011. *Source:* WDI, World Bank, 2013 and authors' calculation.

8.3.2 Adequacy of Reserves

The issue of reserve sufficiency has gained importance in the aftermath of a series of currency and financial crises, for example Mexican crisis (1995), Asian crisis (1997–1998), Russian default (1998), Brazilian crisis (1999), and Argentina crisis (2002). These crises created turmoil in the international financial system and challenged the established system of international macroeconomic policies. And now, recent capital outflows from emerging Asia, which led to depreciation of currencies and depletion of reserves, further emphasized that the level of reserves can be an important factor in explaining and predicting a currency crisis. In the related literature, there are various methods which measure the reserve adequacy of a nation. In this study, we consider three conventional and popular rules of thumb for measuring reserve adequacy in our sample countries.

International reserves in months of import

Traditionally the ratio of reserves to import is considered to be a standard way to quantify reserves adequacy because of its operational simplicity. It is argued that where uncertainty in the external sector is mainly instigated from the current account or more specifically from trade deficit, evaluating the level of reserves acceptability using the value of imports to reserves holding seems to be a convincing measure (Bird and Rajan, 2003). Using this measure as a rule of thumb, it is generally recommended that the stock of reserves should be sufficient enough to finance at least three to four months of imports (Fischer, 2001). However, the surge in foreign capital flows in recent years has made capital account equally or even more important, which has made this measure redundant as a sole measure of adequacy. Figure 8.5 reveals that the stock of most of the emerging Asian countries' international reserve have crossed the benchmark of 3 months of imports in 1997–1998 and since then it stayed continuously above the minimum required level including during the American crisis.

International reserve and short-term debt

The ratio of reserves to imports was considered suitable in case of restrictive capital flow environment. The crisis of the East Asia reflected several insufficiencies involved in keeping import-to-reserves ratio as an important criteria of reserves adequacy. Furman

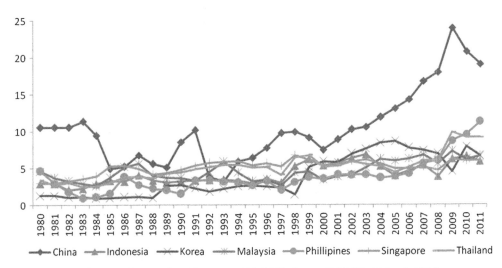

Figure 8.5 Total reserve in months of import: 1980–2011. *Source:* WDI, World Bank, 2013.

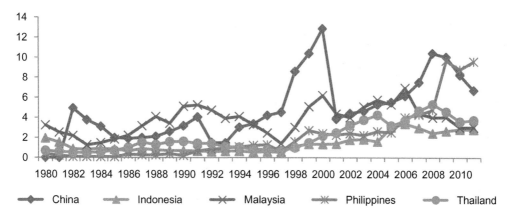

Figure 8.6 International reserve to short-term external debt ratio: 1980–2010. *Source:* WDI, World Bank, 2013.

et al. (1998) and Radelet and Sachs (1998) have highlighted that the excess burden of short-term external debt is a common story of all recent crises. Therefore, short-term external debt to reserves could be a useful measure of risks associated with the country's balance of payment. For optimal internal reserve, the Greenspan–Guidotti rule of thumb suggests that the ratio of international reserves to short-term external debt should be equal to 1. This rule of thumb will allow a country to survive without any foreign borrowings for at least one year, which significantly reduces the occurrence of the possible currency crisis (De Beaufort Wijnholds and Kapteyn, 2001). Figure 8.6 shows that all the countries in our study have crossed this benchmark level after the East Asian crisis.

International reserve and broad money

Short-term external debt to reserves is a useful indicator of the vulnerability of the external sector. However, this indicator is insufficient to gauge the risk of an "internal drain" accompanied with capital outflows (Bird and Rajan, 2003). The issue of capital flight and the associated domestic risks are effectively predicted by the indicator based on broad money supply. Generally, a low and dipping reserve to broad money ratio is said to be a leading indicator of a currency crisis and a conventional range for this ratio is suggested to be 5–15% (Kaminsky and Reinhart, 1999). According to this rule, all our sample countries are in the safe zone and possibility of the currency crisis seems to be highly unlikely. Finally, we can conclude that all the three measures of reserve adequacy indicate that Emerging Asia's stock of international reserves is much higher than the minimum required limit. Moreover, it is evidently indicated by the standard benchmarks that these countries have stockpiled excess reserves after the 1997–1998 crisis (see Figure 8.7).

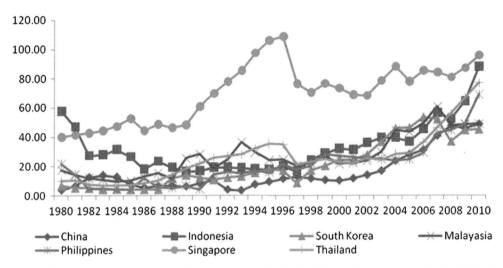

Figure 8.7 International reserve to broad money ratio (M2): 1980–2010. *Source:* WDI, World Bank, 2013.

8.4 DATA DESCRIPTION

Now we shift our attention to test the determinants of international reserves in the emerging Asia. For the empirical investigation, the data of seven emerging Asian countries—China, Indonesia, South Korea, Malaysia, the Philippines, Singapore, and Thailand—comes mainly from the World Development Indicator (WDI). We focus on the period 1980–2011 for the analysis. 1980 is considered as beginning year as after the collapse of the Bretton wood system, most of these economies have started economic reforms which include the open external economic policy and they also experienced remarkable economic growth in the last three decades. We select countries on the basis of size and importance. We could not consider some small emerging Asian countries mainly because of unavailability of the required data. Details of data series, their definitions, and sources are presented in Table 8.1.

8.5 EMPIRICAL MODELS AND RESULTS

To assess the determinant of international reserve in the emerging Asia during 1980–2011, we specify the following standard panel regression model:

$$RES_{it} = \beta_0 + \beta_1 finopen_{it} + \beta_2 tradeopen_{it} + \beta_3 GDPpercap_{it} + \beta_4 ExportVOL_{it} + \beta_5 XVOL_{it} + \beta_6 MDISQ_{it} + \beta_7 Interestdiff_{it} + \mu_{it} \tag{8.1}$$

$$\text{where } i = 1, 2, \ldots, 7 \text{ and } t = 1, 2, \ldots, 32$$

Table 8.1 Data Description

Variables	Definition and Measurements	Sources
Endogenous Variables		
International reserve (*RES*) (Dependent variable)	Log of total international reserve minus gold deflated by constant USA GDP, 2000	WDI
GDP per capita (*GDPpercap*)	Log of GDP per capita in US Dollar	WDI
Trade openness (*tradeopen*)	Export plus import divided by GDP at constant GDP	WDI
Financial openness (*finopen*)	Total external assets plus liabilities divided by current GDP	Lane and Milesi-Ferretti (2007) & WDI
Exogenous Variables		
Exchange rate volatility (*XVOL*)	Square of mean-adjusted relative change in Official exchange rate (per US Dollar)	WDI
Export volatility (*ExportVOL*)	Square of mean-adjusted relative change in export receipt	WDI
Opportunity cost of holding international reserve (*Interestdiff*)	Short-term domestic deposit rates minus USA 10 years T-bill rate	WDI & Federal reserve, USA
Monetary disequilibrium (*MDISQ*)	Money Supply (*t*−1) minus money demand (*t*)	WDI and Authors' construction

These variables are as defined in Table 8.1. Our first task is to estimate demand for money for the sample countries so that we can compute monetary disequilibrium (*MDISQ*). The demand for money, as empirically specified by macro studies, is positively determined by the income (measured as GDP) and negatively related to its opportunity cost (measured by deposit rate). Therefore, our money demand equation is as follows:

$$M_{2t} = \alpha_0 + \alpha_1 GDP_t + \alpha_2 DepRate + \varepsilon_t \tag{8.2}$$

where M_{2t} is the real money supply, GDP is the gross domestic product, *DepRate* is the short-term deposit rate, and ε_t is the error term.[3] All variables, except deposit rate, are in logarithmic form. All the variables in the equation are non-stationary in nature and hence applying simple ordinary least square may provide spurious relationship. To avoid spurious result, we follow the time series procedure starting with the testing of unit root of all the non-stationary variables followed by Johansen's (1988) cointegration technique for long-term relation between dependent and independent variables. The result

[3] Data source of these variables are WDI online, World Bank, 2013.

Table 8.2 Unit Root Test: Money Demand Function (1980–2011)

Variables	ADF		Phillip-Perron	
	At Level	At 1st Diff	At Level	At 1st Diff
DepRate_china	−1.811	−4.463**	−1.350	−4.372**
GDP_china	0.498	−3.903**	0.185	−3.285*
M2_china	−2.168	−4.394**	−3.375	−4.112**
DepRate_indo	−2.449	−5.709**	−2.449	−6.118**
GDP_indo	−1756	−4.040**	−1.691	−4.040**
M2_indo	−1.234	−3.527**	−0.904	−3.446**
DepRate_skor	−3.466	−4.938**	−3.415	−5.65**
GDP_skor	−0.727	−6.029*	−0.36	−9.794**
M2_skor	−1.942	−3.338*	−1.471	−3.385**
DepRate_mal	−1.634	−5.171**	−1.602	−4.823**
GDP_mal	−1.194	−4.531**	−1.378	−4.541**
M2_mal	−2.974	−5.216**	−3.076	−6.503**
DepRate_phil	0.671	−6.753**	−2.306	−4.972**
GDP_phil	−1.123	−7.012**	−1.341	−3.458*
M2_phil	−2.160	−5.588**	−2.160	−5.597**
DepRate_sgp	−2.191	−6.276**	−2.309	−6.279**
GDP_sgp	−1.805	−5.180**	−1.878	−5.176**
M2_sgp	−2.337	−5.125**	−2.455	−5.234**
DepRate_thai	−1.027	−5.229**	−0.900	−5.583**
GDP_thai	−1.319	−3.362*	−0.942	−3.382*
M2_thai	−0.969	−5.961**	−0.961	−5.961**

*Significance at 10%.**Significance at 5%.

Notes: (i) Optimal lags for ADF is determined based on AIC and for PP test it is Newey–West bandwidth selection using Bartlett kernel. (ii) Probability values for ADF and PP test are as per MacKinnon one-sided *p*-values. (iii) china—China, indo—Indonesia, skor—South Korea, mal—Malaysia, phil—the Philippines, sgp—Singapore, thai—Thailand.

of unit root is provided in Table 8.2. As expected, all the variables included in the model are found to be integrated of order 1, i.e., I (1). The results of Johansen cointegration have been presented in Table 8.3 which show that the null hypothesis of no cointegration is rejected in favor of at least one cointegrating relationship (see Table 8.4).

Using the long-run relationship provided by the normalized equation in Table 8.2 and following Badinger (2004), we estimate the following model to compute monetary disequilibrium (M_t^{dis}):

$$M_t^{dis} = M2_{t-1} - M2_t^* \tag{8.3}$$

where $M2_t^*$ is the equilibrium value of money demand. The calculated positive (negative) values of M_t^{dis} indicate an excess demand (supply) of money.

Now we focus on estimation of our reserves Eq. (8.1). Variables in consideration in Eq. (8.1) are subject to non-stationarity of the time series, which might lead to biased estimation of the coefficients. To test the non-stationarity problem, we used the Im-Pesaran-Shin (IPS) panel unit root test which is based on the simple averages of the

Table 8.3 Johansen Cointegration Test: Money Demand Function (1980–2011)

Trace Test			Max. Eigenvalue Test		
Rank	Eigenvalue	Trace Statistics	Rank	Eigenvalue	Max. Stat
China					
$r=0$	0.693374	51.7252*	$r=0$	0.693374	35.46384*
$r\leq 1$	0.298767	16.26135	$r\leq 1$	0.298767	10.64747
$r\leq 2$	0.170664	5.613882	$r\leq 2$	0.170664	5.613882
Cointegrating vector	M2	GDP	DEPRATE	Trend^2	C
Unrestricted	−3.895702	−26.06724	0.088489	3.047154	
Normalized (beta11=1)	1	4.175*	−0.023*	−0.539*	−61.042*
Malaysia					
$r=0$	0.597512	38.78912*	$r=0$	0.597512	26.39264*
$r\leq 1$	0.275617	12.39648	$r\leq 1$	0.275617	9.350633
$r\leq 2$	0.099702	3.045846	$r\leq 2$	0.099702	3.045846
Cointegrating vector	M2	GDP	DEPRATE	Trend	C
Unrestricted	−8.875505	10.87761	0.263768		
Normalized (beta11=1)	1	−1.225*	−0.030*		2.52*
The Philippines					
$r=0$	0.613119	33.37778*	$r=0$	0.613119	27.5395*
$r\leq 1$	0.180306	5.838273	$r\leq 1$	0.180306	5.765913
$r\leq 2$	0.002492	0.07236	$r\leq 2$	0.002492	0.07236
Cointegrating vector	M2	GDP	DEPRATE	Trend	C
Unrestricted	3.301351	1.100591	0.412843		
Normalized (beta11=1)	1	0.333*	0.125*		−15.4*
Indonesia					
$r=0$	0.611344	56.71742*	$r=0$	0.611344	27.40676*
$r\leq 1$	0.560797	29.31066*	$r\leq 1$	0.560797	23.86099*
$r\leq 2$	0.171319	5.449671	$r\leq 2$	0.171319	5.449671
Cointegrating vector	M2	GDP	DEPRATE	Trend	C
Unrestricted	4.30197	−15.27792	0.060452	0.552346	
Normalized (beta11=1)	1	−3.551*	0.0140*	0.1284*	28.819*

(Continued)

Table 8.3 Continued

Trace Test			Max. Eigenvalue Test		
Rank	Eigenvalue	Trace Statistics	Rank	Eigenvalue	Max. Stat
South Korea					
$r=0$	0.618391	43.63286*	$r=0$	0.618391	27.9374*
$r \leq 1$	0.357624	15.69547	$r \leq 1$	0.357624	12.83484
$r \leq 2$	0.093933	2.860624	$r \leq 2$	0.093933	2.860624
Cointegrating Vector	M2	GDP	DEPRATE	Trend	C
Unrestricted	7.462434	−15.10588	1.907769	0.638038	
Normalized (beta11 = 1)	1	−2.024*	0.255*	0.085*	10.51*
Singapore					
$r=0$	0.594324	40.34043*	$r=0$	0.594324	27.06601*
$r \leq 1$	0.27851	13.27441	$r \leq 1$	0.27851	9.793107
$r \leq 2$	0.109564	3.481308	$r \leq 2$	0.109564	3.481308
Cointegrating vector	M2	GDP	DEPRATE	Trend	C
Unrestricted	6.465002	−6.833817	0.768631		
Normalized (beta11 = 1)	1	−1.057*	0.118*		0.343*
Thailand					
$r=0$	0.48322	37.12442*	$r=0$	0.48322	19.80416
$r \leq 1$	0.391448	17.32026	$r \leq 1$	0.391448	14.9002
$r \leq 2$	0.077501	2.420065	$r \leq 2$	0.077501	2.420065
Cointegrating vector	M2	GDP	DEPRATE	Trend^2	C
Unrestricted	−7.968728	18.99907	−0.832794		
Normalized (beta11 = 1)	1	−2.214*	0.092*	0.078*	12.07*

*Significance at 5% level.

Notes: (i) VAR specification: optimal lag length (4) selected using AIC, (ii) deterministic trend assumptions of the cointegration test: intercept and trend in cointegrating relationship and no trend in VAR, and (iii) r denotes the assumption about the number of cointegration vectors.

individual cross-sectional augmented Dicky-Fuller statistics (Im et al., 2003). The result of panel unit root shows that the null hypothesis of unit root cannot be rejected at level form but can be rejected in the first differenced form.[4] Since all our endogenous variables are found to be I (1), we can employ the panel cointegration test. We apply

[4] Results of the Im-Pesaran-Shin panel unit root is not reported here due to space constraints but our result shows that the variables log of deflated international reserve, trade openness, financial openness and log of GDP per capita are stationary at first difference and export volatility, exchange rate volatility, monetary disequilibrium and interest rate differential are stationary at level form. The results can be made available on request.

Table 8.4 Pedroni's Panel Cointegration Test Results

Types	Statistics (Individual Intercept)	*p*-Value
Panel v-Statistic (within dimension)	−1.09*	0.08
Panel rho-Statistic	−0.88	0.18
Panel PP-Statistic	−1.75**	0.04
Panel ADF-Statistic	−1.65**	0.05
Group rho-Statistic (between dimension)	0.06	0.52
Group PP-Statistic	−1.96**	0.02
Group ADF-Statistic	−1.80**	0.04

**Significance at 5% level. *Significant at 10% level.
Note: Lag selection is based on SIC.

Pedroni's (1999) test, an extension of the Engle–Granger construction, to test the cointegration relationship. Results of the cointegration test are reported in Table 8.4, which clearly indicate that our endogenous variables form a long-term relationship as out of seven cases, the null hypothesis of no cointegration is rejected in five cases.

After establishing the long-term relation among our variables, we shift our attention to estimate the long-run estimates of the empirical model. Since the serial correlation and the endogeneity are likely problems in estimation, we employ the Dynamic OLS estimator in panel context, which effectively corrects these problems. Kao and Chiang (2000) propose dynamic OLS (DOLS) to panel cointegration estimation, which is an extension of Stock and Watson's (1993) estimator. For obtaining an unbiased estimator of the long-run parameters, the DOLS estimator uses parametric adjustment to the errors by including the lead and lag values of the differenced I (1) regressors. Results of the DOLS estimates of the determinants of the international reserves are reported in Table 8.5, which include both endogenous as well as exogenous variables.

The estimated results indicate that the determinants of international reserve are not uniform across the countries. Overall, export volatility, trade openness, GDP per capita, and interest rate differential (opportunity cost) are significant factors explaining the determinant of international reserves. The impact of country size measured as GDP per capita is quite significant in explaining the determinant of international reserves which is quite intuitive. The result shows that 1% increase in the GDP per capita will tend to increase the international reserve by almost 2.5% for the sample countries. Except for the Philippines, findings are very similar for almost all countries. Subsequently, trade openness measured as ratio of export and import divided by GDP and export volatility is positively related to international reserves. Results imply that countries with high degree of openness in trade or volume of trade would tend to have large amount of international reserves holding. Financial openness is estimated to be statistically

Table 8.5 Dynamic Ordinary Least Square (DOLS) Results: Determinant of International Reserve (1980–2011)

Country	Export Volatility	Exchange Rate Volatility	Financial Openness	Trade Openness	GDP Per Capita	Interest Rate Differential	Monetary Disequi-librium
China	0.68	1.12	1.32	0.10	1.87**	−0.11**	−1.20**
	(0.27)	(0.92)	(1.18)	(0.14)	(4.45)	(−2.91)	(−2.22)
Indonesia	5.34**	0.99	0.29	−0.32	2.32**	−0.11*	0.15
	(3.47)	(1.45)	(0.75)	(−0.47)	(8.22)	(−2.79)**	(0.79)
S. Korea	1.92	6.42*	−0.92*	2.25*	1.82**	−0.14**	1.44**
	(0.26)	(1.74)	(−1.83)	(1.81)	(4.14)	(−3.14)	(3.11)
Malaysia	−2.29	−2.66	0.84**	−0.21	2.17**	−0.14	0.05
	(−0.72)	(−0.98)	(2.75)	(−0.41)	(2.72)	(−0.88)	(0.34)
Philippines	0.12	−3.83	2.22*	2.92**	4.87**	0.05	−0.15
	(0.10)	(−1.17)	(2.81)**	(4.64)	(4.47)	(1.19)	(−1.43)
Singapore	3.15*	0.44	−0.04**	−0.15	2.84**	0.03	0.29**
	(1.87)	(0.31)	(−5.34)	(−1.21)	(19.12)	(1.49)	(2.16)
Thailand	2.26	−8.67	0.31	0.59	2.57**	0.12	−0.11
	(0.49)	(−1.48)	(0.77)	(0.48)	(3.41)	(1.52)	(−0.44)
Overall	3.03**	−1.47	0.51*	1.44**	2.52**	−0.03**	−0.02
	(2.67)	(−0.13)	(1.84)	(2.88)	(16.52)	(−1.94)	(−0.31)

**Significance at 5% level. *Significance at 10% level.
Note: We have treated export volatility, exchange rate volatility, interest rate differential, and monetary disequilibrium as exogenous variables to test the long-term impact on international reserves.

significant for overall sample however only at 10% significance level. Nevertheless for majority of countries the variable is found to be significant, which indicate that financial openness or size of the country's external liabilities is a crucial factor in explaining the reserves accumulation.

Now focusing on the opportunity cost of holding reserves, results indicate that the central banks do consider this aspect in accumulating reserves. Our estimate shows that one unit increase interest rate differential will tend to decrease the reserve by 0.03%. Hence, increase (decrease) in the spread between short-term deposit rates and US T-bill rate will tend to decrease (increase) the amount of international reserve held by the emerging economies of region. This makes sense as hoarding reserves becomes expensive (inexpensive), if the interest spread increases (decreases).

Considering the issue of exchange rate volatility, our result shows that this is somewhat an insignificant factor; perhaps exchange rate volatility is a reflection of other macroeconomic factors which are already captured by other variables in our empirical model. At last, the monetary disequilibrium, though statistically insignificant overall, is significant for three sample countries explaining that excess demand (supply) for money results in an increase (decrease) in international reserves (excess demand of money for South Korea and Singapore and excess supply for China). This is quite a new finding in this study. Furthermore, this result implies that monetary disequilibrium indicates that the central banks in these countries take measures to clear the money-market disequilibrium by making appropriate changes in both the interest rate and domestic credit.

8.6 CONCLUSION

A battery of reserves adequacy indicators shows that after the 1997–1998 Asian crisis emerging Asian countries have accumulated sufficient reserves, which effectively brings down probability of a currency crisis in these countries. Since these countries have hoarded a large pile of reserves we subsequently attempt to test the determinants of reserves holding in a panel data framework. Our results show that trade openness, country size, export volatility, and opportunity cost of reserve accumulation are significant factors explaining the determinants of international reserves in emerging Asia. Since all these countries are highly trade oriented, they require huge amount of reserve to fulfill their trade commitments and due to uncertainty in the global market they need more than sufficient amount of reserves holding. Hence, with expanding external sector, we can expect the reserve accumulation to increase further in these countries. Our findings also crucially indicate that high opportunity cost of reserves holding is a significant determinant of reserves demand. Results regarding monetary disequilibrium are also estimated to be one of the important factors for some countries, where central banks have been proactive in the external sector. Furthermore, evidently it seems that the central banks in these countries take measures to clear the money market by making appropriate changes in both the interest rate and domestic credit. Overall it seems that the reserves holding in the region is mainly for self-insurance as it is used as a buffer against future financial crises or shocks. Thus these countries need to acknowledge that stockpiling reserves cannot act as a substitute for appropriate domestic policy reforms, as such reforms effactually reduce the probability of a currency crisis, in turn, lesser requirements of reserves holding in the country.

ACKNOWLEDGMENT

The authors thank Greg N. Gregoriou for his useful comments and helpful suggestions on the previous version of this chapter.

REFERENCES

Aizenman, J., Lee, Y. Rhee, Y., 2004. International reserves management and capital mobility in a volatile world: Policy considerations and a case study of Korea. Working Paper No. 10534, National Bureau of Economic Research.

Aizenman, J., Lee, J., 2007. International reserves: precautionary versus mercantilist views, theory and evidence. Open Economies Review 18 (2), 191–214.

Aizenman, J., Marion, N., 2003. The high demand for international reserves in the Far East: What is going on? Journal of the Japanese and International Economies 17 (3), 370–400.

Aizenman, J., Marion, N., 2004. International reserve holdings with sovereign risk and costly tax collection. Economic Journal 114 (497), 569–591.

Badinger, H., 2004. Austria's demand for international reserves and monetary disequilibrium: the case of a small open economy with a fixed exchange rate regime. Economica 71 (281), 39–55.

Bird, G., Rajan, R., 2003. Too much of a good thing? The adequacy of international reserves in the aftermath of crises. World Economy 26 (6), 873–891.

Calvo, G.A., 1996. Capital flows and macroeconomic management: Tequila lessons. International Journal of Finance & Economics 1 (3), 207–223.

Calvo, G.A., Reinhart, C.M., 2000. Fixing for your life. Working Paper No. w8006. National Bureau of Economic Research.

Calvo, G.A., Reinhart, C.M., 2002. Fear of floating. Quarterly Journal of Economics 117 (2), 379–408.

De Beaufort Wijnholds, J.A.H., Kapteyn, A., 2001. Reserve adequacy in emerging market economies. Working Paper No. 01/43, IMF.

Delatte, A.L., Fouquau, J., 2012. What drove the massive hoarding of international reserves in emerging economies? A time-varying approach. Review of International Economics 20 (1), 164–176.

Dooley, M.P., Folkerts-Landau, D., Garber, P., 2004. The revived Bretton woods system. International Journal of Finance and Economics 9 (4), 307–313.

Edwards, S., 1984. The demand for international reserves and monetary disequilibrium: some evidence from developing countries. Review of Economics and Statistics 66, 496–500.

Edwards, S., 1985. On the interest-rate elasticity of the demand for international reserves: some evidence from developing countries. Journal of international Money and Finance 4 (2), 287–295.

Eichengreen, B., Rose, A.K., Wyplosz, C., 1996. Contagious currency crises. Working Paper No. 5681, National Bureau of Economic Research.

Elbadawi, I.A., 1990. The Sudan demand for international reserve: a case of a labour-exporting country. Economica 57 (225), 73–89.

Fischer, S., 2001. Opening Remarks. IMF/World Bank International Reserves: Policy Issues Forum, Washington DC, 28 April.

Flood, R., Marion, N., 2001. Holding international reserves in an era of high capital mobility. Brookings Trade Forum 2001 (1), 1–68.

Flood, R., Marion, N., 2002. Holding international reserves in an era of high capital mobility. In: Collins, Rodrik, (Eds.), Brookings Trade Forum: 2001. Brookings Institution Press, Washington, pp. 1–68.

Furman, J., Stiglitz, J.E., Bosworth, B.P., Radelet, S., 1998. Economic crises: evidence and insights from East Asia. Brookings Papers on Economic Activity 1998 (2), 1–135.

Gosselin, M.A., Parent, N., 2005. An Empirical Analysis of Foreign Exchange Reserves in Emerging Asia. Bank of Canada.

Hauner, D., 2006. A fiscal price tag for international reserves*. International Finance 9 (2), 169–195.

Huang, T.H., Shen, C.H., 1999. Applying the seasonal error correction model to the demand for international reserves in Taiwan. Journal of International Money and Finance 18 (1), 107–131.

Im, K.S., Pesaran, M.H., Shin, Y., 2003. Testing for unit roots in heterogeneous panels. Journal of Econometrics 115 (1), 53–74.

IMF, 2010. Reserve Accumulation and International Monetary Stability. Prepared by the Strategy, Policy and Review Department, International Monetary Fund. <http://www.imf.org/external/np/pp/eng/2010/041310.pdf>.

IMF, 2011. Assessing Reserve Adequacy. Prepared by Monetary and Capital Markets, Research, and Strategy, Policy, and Review Departments, International Monetary Fund. <http://www.imf.org/external/np/pp/eng/2011/021411b.pdf>.

Johansen, S., 1988. Statistical analysis of cointegration vectors. Journal of Economic Dynamics and Control 12 (2), 231–254.

Kaminsky, G.L., Reinhart, C.M., 1999. The twin crises: the causes of banking and balance-of-payments problems. American Economic Review, 473–500.

Kao, C., Chiang, M.-H., 2000. On the estimation and inference of a cointegrated regression in panel data. In: Baltagi, B.H. (Ed.), Advances in Econometrics: Nonstationary Panels, Panel Cointegration and Dynamic Panels, vol. 15, pp. 179–222.

Kim, J.S., Li, J., Rajan, R., Sula, O., Willett, T.D., 2005. Reserve adequacy in Asia revisited: new benchmarks based on the size and composition of capital flows. In: Claremont-KIEP Conference Volume on Monetary and Exchange Rate Arrangements.

Lane, P.R., Milesi-Ferretti, G.M., 2007. The external wealth of nations mark II: Revised and extended estimates of foreign assets and liabilities, 1970–2004. Journal of International Economics 73 (2), 223–250.

Lindsay, L., 2003. The Political Economy of Asian Exchange Rates. Center for Strategic and International Studies, Mimeo, October 15. <https://csis.org/files/attachments/031015%20China's%20economic%20development.pdf>.

Mishra, R.K., Sharma, C., 2011. India's demand for international reserve and monetary disequilibrium: reserve adequacy under floating regime. Journal of Policy Modeling 33 (6), 901–919.

Park, D., Estrada, G., 2009. Are developing Asia's foreign exchange reserves excessive? An empirical examination. Economics. Working Paper Series No. 170, Asian Development Bank, Manila, Philippines.

Pedroni, P., 1999. Critical values for cointegration tests in heterogeneous panels with multiple regressors. Oxford Bulletin of Economics and Statistics 61 (S1), 653–670.

Radelet, S., Sachs, J., 1998. The East Asian financial crisis: diagnosis, remedies, prospects. Brookings Papers on Economic Activity 1, 1–74.

Stock, J.H., Watson, M.W., 1993. A simple estimator of cointegrating vectors in higher order integrated systems. Econometrica 61 (4), 783–820.

PART Two

Market Developments and Governance Issues

CHAPTER 9

Singapore's Financial Market: Challenges and Future Prospects

David Lee Kuo Chuen and Kok Fai Phoon
Singapore Management University, Lee Kong Chian School of Business,
50 Stamford Road, Singapore 178899, Singapore

9.1 INTRODUCTION

This chapter explains the history and discusses the future prospects and challenges facing Singapore's financial markets. Singapore's financial sector is unique in that government played a major role in creating an ecosystem that nurtured quality growth. The Monetary Authority of Singapore (MAS), the de facto central bank of Singapore, was instrumental in developing Singapore as a financial center. Since Singapore's independence in 1965, the economy in general and the financial sector in particular have experienced high and sustained growth. Recent statistics provided in the next paragraph and in the next section are impressive given the unstable global environment. It is therefore not surprising that the MAS have received well-deserved accolades for its prudential macroeconomic management and for creating and sustaining a vibrant ecosystem to support growth.

Singapore has become the largest foreign exchange trading center in Asia and ranks second in interest rate derivatives trading. In April 2013, reported daily trading volume in foreign exchange grew 44% to USD 282 billion from 3 years ago. In fund management, there are more than 500 asset managers managing USD 1.1 trillion of assets. Singapore has also done well in other areas such as wealth management, real estate investment via private equity and publicly listed REITs, investment banking, insurance, treasury management, and risk management.

Issues that we will discuss in this chapter will be the impact of capital flows on Singapore's financial sector. Specifically, the discussion centers on the impact of large capital inflows in a time-compressed manner and how possible negative impacts can be mitigated through the use of prudential policies by the MAS. In an open economy like Singapore, global flows can have negative longer-term impact with symptoms of such potential malaise that include growth mainly driven by the real estate sector and the accumulation of liquid foreign capital resulting in increasingly higher debt to GDP ratios.

9.2 GROWTH OF THE FINANCIAL SECTOR

Singapore has developed to be a leading global financial center. Since 1965, Singapore's GDP has grown 32 times, while the financial (Finance and Insurance) sector has grown 280 times with a share of the GDP of 12.2% in 2011 (Figure 9.1). The growth of this sector averaged 13.6% p.a. as compared to the 8.1% p.a. overall GDP growth. The financial sector also outperformed the overall GDP growth for 30 years out of the 47 years since Singapore's independence.

On examining the plot of valued-add of the financial sector as a proportion of GDP in Figure 9.1, the share of GDP over time and the gradient of the share ratio, we can observe three distinct periods for the evolution of the financial sector in Singapore. These three sub-periods can be categorized and described as the Development, Regulatory, and Supervisory phases: the Development phase from 1965 to 1980; the Regulatory phase from 1981 to 1998, and the Supervisory phase from 1999 to the present.

The table in Figure 9.1 shows that the average financial sector growth has been declining over the three sub-periods from 20.8% to 12.6% and then down to 6.10%. This is not surprising as we can see from the fourth row that the sector has grown 16.5 times, 4.7 times, and 1.3 times in the respective sub-periods.

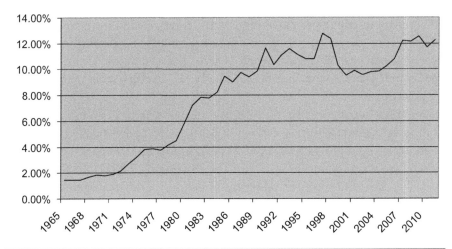

Period	Development	Regulatory	Supervisory
Years	1965–1980	1981–1998	1999–2011
No of Years	16	18	13
Growth (times)	16.5x	4.7x	1.3x
Average	20.80%	12.60%	6.10%

Figure 9.1 The financial (Finance and Insurance) sector's share of GDP.

The average sector growth has been declining due to the larger base effect. Moreover, between the years 1998 and 2004, the sector suffered a reduction in share of GDP due to the Asian financial crisis and the SARs episodes. But the financial sector has since bounced back strongly from the 10% share of overall GDP in 1998 to 12% in 2007.

9.2.1 Singapore's Financial Sector Success Factors

What are the success factors of Singapore's financial sector? Kuah (2008) has attributed the financial sector's success to "clustering." On the other hand, the MAS (2012) provided an interesting account of 40 years of history outlining the sector's competitive strength. General consensus is that the success of the Singapore's financial sector is built on prudence with a wide array of competitive advantages.

The current global financial environment is characterized by the interactions between complex, fast changing, and closely connected financial markets. These financial markets are volatile with free capital flow, while technological improvement has given rise to specialization. Given that the financial markets are complex, closely connected, open to rapid flow of capital and highly specialized, few central banks have a clear understanding of the workings of these markets. Even fewer countries have the necessary policy instruments to anticipate, mitigate, and deal with possible malfunctions. It is therefore not surprising that there were so many crises in the last 40 years. Interestingly, Singapore has weathered these crises well that would lead us to believe that the regulators have a good understanding of its financial market and were able to leverage on its competitive strengths. The next section will clarify Singapore financial sector's competitive strengths that have fueled its growth.

9.2.2 The Development, Regulatory, and Supervisory Phases
The development phase
The Development phase for Singapore's financial sector was the years from 1965 to 1980. In the 1960s and 1970s, Singapore took the opportunity to provide foreign exchange services to its neighbors. It leveraged on its position as a trading hub in resource-rich Southeast Asia to support the increasing need for foreign currency transactions. Singapore established the Asian Dollar Market during that period. While the economy grew rapidly, the financial sector, with strong demand for domestic and offshore banking activities, grew even faster.

The strong growth was made possible by Singapore's geographically strategic position that made Singapore a burgeoning entre-port within a time zone that overlapped the opening trading hours of Europe and the after trading hours of the US markets.

The regulatory phase
The Regulatory Phase was from the years 1981 to 1998. In April 1977 and in November 1984, the Insurance Act and Security Industry Act, respectively, were

brought within the regulatory purview of the MAS. In the 1980s and 1990s, Singapore was able to leverage on the increasing importance of free capital flow and took advantage of technological advancement to shorten settlement duration. More importantly, ease of capital flows was set within a clear regulatory environment that local and foreign institutions were not only comfortable to operate in, but also to expand their financial activities.

Within this supportive environment, capital flows increased in speed and volume, resulting in exponential growth in the financial sector. The country continued its efforts to embrace an impartial judiciary to ensure certainty of property rights and the enforceability of contract. The clearer rules of law and the regulatory environment increased investors' confidence and trust. The increase in the number of legal and finance professionals along with the promulgation of Section 47 of the Banking Act on client confidentiality played important supportive roles as well.

The supervisory phase

The next phase from the year 1999 until now focused on liberalization and on the supervisory role of the regulator with a key objective to promote increasing foreign participation. The banking and other sectors were liberalized, allowing for new banking licenses, greater access to the domestic market and greater percentage of foreign ownership. For example, tax and other incentives, together with the abolition of estate duties promoted the rapid growth in Real Estate Investment Trusts (REITs), and assets in wealth and fund management. These activities were complemented by an increased pool of professionals with different financial market and technical skills.

9.3 THE PROSPECTS

Singapore possesses a clear set of positive factors underpinning its future development. It is located advantageously along with a broad base of financial professionals and entrepreneurs who are supported by the right physical and regulatory infrastructure. Menon (2013) has postulated that smart regulation, diverse ecosystem, pan-Asia focus, and deep talent pool are value propositions for future growth. Indeed, the prospects have never been better after 2008 given that there has been huge capital inflow. Singapore has taken advantage of technological change in the financial sector that allows for free capital flow. The development policies have encouraged very specialized concentrations that include REITs (Koh et al., 2013), wealth (Koh and Tan, 2013), and fund management to grow. Beside banks and fund management companies, more than 190 insurance institutions are located in Singapore to provide services in the area of marine, energy, aviation, credit, and political insurance, beyond the protection needs of the economy (Menon, 2013). Many of the development strategies have been initiated in proposals by the Financial Services Working Group in 2002 (Economic Review Committee, 2002).

Policy makers have been able to leverage on Singapore's competitive advantages by creating an ecosystem for the financial industry to grow.

Looking forward, Singapore's financial sector is set to benefit from the growth in consumption and trade in Asia and the increase in use of the Renminbi (RMB) in trade and investments. A preview of this development is illustrated in the bilateral swap facility for the offshore RMB or Chinese Yuan market (with up to CNY 300 billion in Chinese Yuan liquidity made available to eligible financial institutions operating in Singapore as a full-fledged Yuan trading center). We expect that Singapore's reputation as a safe haven for wealth management will ensure it will garner a significant share of such activities compared with other financial centers. We expect Singapore to maintain or even increase its competitive advantages that had taken years to develop resulting in its continued viability and growth in the years ahead. The financial sector has grown because of its openness, judicious use of advanced technology and systems; and specialization and focus. These same factors that have contributed to growth may have also increased the vulnerability of the financial sector to extreme circumstances that result in a huge outflow of capital. I shall elaborate below with more details on such risks that may arise due to the long-term structural problems of the USA, Europe, Singapore, and the short-term problems of a slowdown in the emerging markets especially China. There are also associated problems brought about by a change in the composition of the Singapore's investment portfolio due to its aging population and a bias to invest in real estate in Singapore. It is important to analyze the impact and guard against possible capital outflow during extreme events, especially when the financial sector and economy is heavily dependent on real estate along with a growth strategy driven by increased issuance of debt and use of derivatives.

Since the 2000s there have been huge global imbalances in fiscal deficits, foreign reserves, income growth, and structural issues that cannot be resolved over a short span of time. Creating jobs remains the main problem with advances in technology giving rise to increasing efficiency. Lower overall economic growth driven mainly by domestic consumption may be the norm for countries with foreign reserves in the near future. The countries that fail in creating enough jobs to offset domestic mandatory consumption will face huge challenges. Fortunately, despite an aging population, Singapore has official reserves in excess of USD 300 million to withstand short-term fluctuations. However, Singapore is highly vulnerable to the global economic environment given its open economy. Essentially, global developments, especially in the developed world, can have a huge impact not only on Singapore's economy, but also on its financial sector.

Specifically, the fiscal gap in the world's largest economy, the USA has widened over the past few years following the 2008 debt crisis. There has been a clear divergence between the US Federal Government current receipts and the Federal Government current expenditures over that period. Furthermore, there seems to be no feasible solution to narrow this fiscal gap even in the long term. The "Fiscal Cliff" created great consternation when the tax holiday expired at the end of 2012, reducing federal spending and the US deficit in FY2013. Fortunately, the US economy demonstrated great resilience and while the GDP growth was projected to shrink by 0.5% previously, the economy grew fairly well at 1.1% and 2.5% for first and second quarters of FY2013, respectively. Unemployment that was projected to increase to 9.1% from 8%, instead, reduced to below 8%. All may seem well and capital began flowing back from emerging markets to the USA, reversing the trend since 2008. However, clear impediments remain with no solutions to balance the budget with deficits projected to be as high as 5% of the US GDP for 2013 and beyond. While attempts have been made to focus on micro- and macroprudential policies, the long-term structural problems of the USA will continue to affect the global financial markets, increasing volatility and affecting the stability of the global financial system. While QE III (Quantitative Easing) has been stabilizing financial markets in the USA and even globally; however, by linking the policy with the official unemployment threshold of 6.5% as the trigger for tapering has again temporarily raised fears of financial markets corrections, leading to increased market volatility.

Over in Europe, the debt crisis was more severe than that of the USA, as building a consensual solution in a divided Euro zone was much harder to achieve. Micro- and macroprudential policies may have calmed markets, but the long-term structural problems resulting from excessive spending and debts continue to be a drag on the economies. It has been well documented that the debt crisis and budget deficits in Europe will take more than a decade to resolve. While debt and budget deficits issues are being addressed, progress remains very slow. According to Eurostat, the statistical office of the European Union, the 2012 government deficit to GDP ratio of EA17 and EU27 both decreased from 4.2% to 3.7% and 4.4% to 4.0% compared with 2011, respectively. However, over the same period, the government debt to GDP ratios increased from 87.3% to 90.6% of the EA17 and 82.5% to 85.3% for the EU27. The good news is that EU27 external current account has recorded a surplus of 36 billion Euros or 1.1% of GDP as at 2013Q2 as compared to only 0.2% of GDP at end 2012.

But, the inability to create jobs, especially for youths below 25 years of age, coupled with increased social spending for an aging population will be a heavy drag on the economies. High youth unemployment can potentially lead to increasing social unrest. In mid-2013, the unemployment rate remains above 27% (62% for under 25s) and 26% (56% for under 25s) in Greece and Spain, respectively. These rates compare with the average of 11% (23% for under 25s) for the EU28. New Euro zone addition Croatia (member on 1 July 2013) has a youth unemployment rate of 55% for under 25s. The stabilizing factor for the European markets had been the announcement of outright monetary transactions (OMTs) by the European Central Bank, promising unlimited support for vulnerable countries in the Euro zone. While Singapore has low exposure to European sovereign debt, banking activities resulting from trading activities can slow considerably if problems in the Euro zone flare up or worsen.

Since the beginning of 2013, Brazil, Russia, India, and China (the BRIC countries) are all experiencing economic slowdown with shrinking manufacturing activities and lower commodity prices resulting from the anemic global environment. An aging population and income inequality have emerged as social issues not only in the developed economy, but are expected to become a serious problem in the next 10–15 years for many of the emerging economies where the impacts of urbanization will be felt. In the short-term, the fear of the FED tapering its USD 85 billion a month buying of bonds has resulted in an exodus of capital from the emerging markets since mid-2013 and the reverse trend of normalization of interest rates with the draining of excess liquidity created by Quantitative Easing I–III may continue for 6–8 quarters. Coupled with the slowdown and self-imposed structural reform, especially in Asia, the Asian growth story may subside for a while. But knowing that the slowdown has resulted from deliberate micro- and macroprudential policies by government to mitigate the adverse impact of excess liquidity from easy money policy of the developed world gives comfort that the long-term Asian growth story is intact.

Furthermore, with the lessons learned from the Asian financial crisis, central bank reserves had been built up to reduce the need for USD borrowing as compared to pre-crisis levels in 1997. Nevertheless, the recent funds outflows from emerging markets had impacted Indonesia and India severely with their currencies weakening more than 20% as at September 2013. Despite the current high debt to GDP ratios in many countries, the difference this time is that high levels of borrowing are not purely for infrastructure and manufacturing, but mainly for construction, commercial, and residential real estate. Therefore, the type of crisis that Asia experienced in 1997 is unlikely to repeat itself, though the speed of outflow of capital may result in significant damage to the heavily debt laden economies.

Another stabilization factor for Asia has been the ambitious plans of the newly elected Japanese government to try to reflate the economy using fiscal policy and aggressive monetary easing, thus giving a temporary boost to the Asian markets. The Yen as a consequence has depreciated substantially against other major currencies along with economic growth accelerating, spurred by consumption spending and higher net exports.

Singapore has so far avoided the high debt, high mandatory spending, and high unemployment crises faced by many developed countries. However, like the many countries that have experienced rapid economic growth and urbanization in the past 50 years, its population is aging. The 2011 fertility rate of 1.2 births per woman is one of the lowest in the world. This development will have major consequences for economic growth and dependency providence, especially for participation rates due to the availability of financial professionals in segments of the financial markets and the need for retirement investment capital in Singapore. To discuss the demographic impacts on Singapore's financial markets, we will first look at the experiences of the USA. This will allow us to draw inferences on the likely scenario for the Singapore, where symptoms of likely impacts are already showing in the trading volume in its exchanges.

Life cycle investment patterns have shown that as one grows older, the willingness to take risk declines. Equity markets are expected to be under pressure worldwide because of the aging demographics. Exposure to equities has also declined among most 401(k) participants (Investment Company, 2011, 2012). Consequently, on a global basis, we expect to see lower flow into equity funds and perhaps reduced trading volume of equities on exchanges. Furthermore, traditional exchanges will be affected by competition from alternate platforms.

Since 2007, net new cash flow into equity funds has been on the decline and the rebound in the market after 2008 was not accompanied by continuous and large cash inflows, according to the Investment Company Institute (Investment Company, 2011, 2012). This finding is troubling. Net withdrawals from equity funds amounted to USD 153 billion in 2012, USD 28 billion more than 2011. While there is a positive correlation between funds inflow and market performance, the relation has weakened over the years suggestive of a long-term downtrend. While there is an increase in inflow into mutual fund companies in the region of between USD 40 and 50 billion in recent years, the flows away from equity have been increasing. Considering that mutual funds account for 57% of household defined contribution retirement accounts and in aggregation that funds hold around 28% of US corporate equity, the downtrend signals lower trading volume ahead. As for direct holdings of equities, the net outflow totaled USD 225 billion from 2009 to 2012, after a period of substantial inflow of USD 1271 billion from 2004 to 2008. The turnover rate—the percentage of a fund's holdings that have changed over a year—is a measure of a fund's trading activities and the rate has been declining from an average of 62% for 1980–2012 to around 48% (Investment Company, 2012).

In the USA, factors such as lower investor risk tolerance, product development, and greater investment diversification have been found to play an important role in the investors' reduced demand for domestic equity mutual funds. However, investor demographic is likely to be the major factor as a decline in investors' willingness to take above-average or substantial investment risk as investors grow old is a key finding for the USA. More importantly, there seems to be less of an appetite to take risk even for the same cohort that was found when comparing the 50–64 age-group over time. The percentage of those willing has declined from 23% to 19% from 2001 to 2012. Similarly, for those above 65, the percentage willing to take higher risk decreased from 9% to 7%.

On a separate note, shrinking trading volume in traditional and domestic exchanges is a concern. Mergers and acquisitions of exchanges have also proven difficult to improve economy of scales. After all, most of the mergers were driven by the competition from alternative trading platforms such as dark pools. Indeed, in the USA, the rise of high-frequency trading has fragmented trading volumes rather than increased trading volume in traditional exchanges. Moreover, the growth in cash flow to bond funds has been mostly positive since year 2000 with the exceptions of years 2003 and 2009. The same secular and demographic factors that reduce funds flow to equity may have served to boost flows into bond funds. With the baby boomers retiring coupled with a reduced appetite for risk, more investment allocations have been in fixed income funds.

Based on the previous observations, the prospects for equities are not likely to be rosy and the growth in transactions is expected to slow. However, as long as economies continue to grow, we may see continual growth in the foreign exchange, derivatives markets, debt markets, and other non-equity sectors. Given Singapore's aging population and the corresponding reduced appetite for equities, it is not surprising that we will observe similar patterns as the USA going forward. There, however, remain bright spots where the fixed income market and derivatives market in Singapore have flourished.

While the FX market is growing in single digits to above USD 261 billion in October 2012, the derivatives market has grown at double digit pace. The SGX (Singapore Exchange) has more than 770 listed companies of which 40% are foreign and is the largest securities market in Southeast Asia with approximately SGD 1 trillion in total market capitalization. The SGX is known as the derivative supermarket as it has become the offshore venue for Japan, China, Taiwan, India, and ASEAN futures. More than 90% of derivative volume is of index derivative of key markets mentioned above. Furthermore, the SGX provides clearing not only for exchange-traded securities and derivatives, it also provides clearing for over-the-counter derivatives given that it is among the first in the world to comply with CPSS-IOSCO (the Committee on Payment and Settlement System and the International Organization of Securities Commission) principle and certified under Basel III as qualifying counterparty. In this environment with regulators pushing for OTC products to be cleared through the exchanges, Singapore is well equipped to take advantage of the redirection of offshore business. For example, SGX AsiaClear experienced healthy growth in transactions of 77% for 2012 in energy, freight, and dry bulk-related derivatives. Singapore leads in Iron ore derivatives with 109.7 million metric tonnes of iron ore swaps and options cleared. SGX also cleared SGD 340 billion in notional values of SGD and USD interest rate swaps and Asian FX forwards in 2012.

Given the experience of the USA, we examine the securities and the derivatives business on the Singapore Exchange. While the SGX generated comparatively low revenue of SGD 715 million and net profit of SGD 336 million in FY2013, its contribution to the financial sector is still significant. A breakdown of SGX's revenue shows that the securities business is the largest revenue generator with SGD 279 million accounting for 38% share, with derivatives at SGD 201 million and a share of 28%. The average daily trading volume of futures contracts after the crisis of 2008 in Singapore increased from 238,000 contracts in 2009 to 308,000 contracts in 2012. The increase in the volume can be mainly attributed to the introduction of China A50 futures and Nikkei options. Algorithmic trading has increased from an average daily market share of 15%–35% per day in 2012, more than twofold. At this rate of growth, it is not unreasonable to conjecture that algorithmic trading will double to 70% in fewer than 3 years with the introduction of the fast trading platform REACH at the SGX. The proportion forecasted is also in line with trading patterns in the USA. While derivatives accounted for 26% of SGX's revenue, its growth was 23% over the previous year compared with 9% growth in equities revenue. We expect that demand for derivatives as risk management tools along with the potential of further product development will continue to support Singapore's leading position as a derivative market.

Singapore's corporate debt market has seen an upward trend in the amount of outstanding long-term SGD and Non-SGD corporate debt. At the end of 2012, the outstanding amount of Singapore corporate debt reached SGD 231 billion with an annual growth rate of 14% (MAS Annual Report, 2013). In 2012 alone, the issuance was SGD 134 billion with SGD 30.5 billion in SGD Bonds. The weighted average maturity of these newly issued SGD bonds increased to 12.9 years from 7.5 years compared with 1 year ago with 22% from foreign issuers. The corporate debt sector is another high growth area with 90% of bond listings from overseas. The major development in the bond market has been the introduction of the 30-year government bond (30Y SGS—30 year Singapore Government Securities) to extend the yield curve as a benchmark for pricing of corporate bond. A SGD corporate bond index was launched in June 2013. To widen and deepen the market, bond borrowing facilities will eventually be introduced and the MAS is already providing swap liquidity to primary dealer banks handling SGD debt.

For the equities market, of the thirty new offerings in the first three quarters of 2013 that raised USD 8.1 billion, 6 were REITs and business trusts. There are 38 REITs and business trusts listed on the exchange with a market value of SGD 67 billion, making Singapore the largest cluster in the Asia Pacific region excluding Japan. The recent trend is interesting given the challenging market conditions worldwide. For 2013Q3, Singapore was ranked number 2 in the world behind the USA for IPO fund raising (Ernst and Young, 2013). USD 1.7 billion was raised representing an increase of 39% from the previous quarter. The SGX Catalist Board, targeted at less established companies, also saw an increase in new offerings from USD 4 million to USD 137.9 million from 7 deals in recent quarters. Out of the USD 1.7 billion, USD 1.27 billion was from 3 REITs. For the first 9 months in 2013, equity deals from the real estate sector were dominant with 86% of the USD 2.9 billion new listings, and 39% or USD 5.8 billion of in total.

In addition, Phang et al. (2013) have proposed to introduce listed REITs with public residential housing assets which accounts for more than 80% of Singapore's housing units. If such an idea eventuates, public housing REITs and hedging instruments based on daily traded Housing REITs can be another growth area. There is no doubt that real estate is expected to outpace others including sectors like financial and oil and gas.

With the start of the RMB clearing operations by Industrial and Commercial Bank of China in Singapore, SGX has started offering depository services for RMB Bonds. REITs, wealth, and fund management will also continue to grow amidst margin squeeze. The assets under management (AUM) grew 21.5% to above SGD 1.6 trillion in 2012 with more than 80% from outside Singapore and 70% invested in the Asia–Pacific region. Together with derivatives, these sectors offset the single digit 4.8% growth to SGD 9.3 billion in the non-life insurance sector. The real estate and related sectors will continue to be a growth area given the short supply of freehold land above ground, and the potential increase in population to over 6 million or more. Construction and property loans will continue to increase in tandem given that construction underground will typically be more costly. Such property and construction loans have already increased substantially at double digit growth rates as reported in the MAS Annual Report (2013). The Asian Dollar Market, while growing at a much slower pace of 7.4%, has the potential to see growth boosted once lending in RMB increases.

The biggest impetus will likely be business and finance activities associated with the RMB bilateral swap arrangement with China. The RMB is seen to be undervalued and will continue to appreciate in the long term. Foreign businesses have increased their willingness to pay their suppliers in RMB with Chinese companies accepting RMB to avoid currency volatility. In less than 2 years, trade using the RMB has risen from almost zero to RMB 600 billion accounting for 12% of China's total trade. Capital control has provided stability to China's financial system. In addition, China's urbanization has still a long way to go being currently below 20% compared with US urbanization rate of above 40%. Urban consumption in China is estimated at three times rural consumption. Trade and burgeoning consumption growth highlight the potential for RMB transactions. China's per capita GDP was USD 9233 (GDP of USD 8.22 trillion) compared with USD 49,965 (GDP of USD 15.68 trillion) in the USA in 2012. China's per capita GDP is projected to reach 20% of the US USD 50,000 in 2020. With 1.4 billion people compared with 315 million in the USA in 2012; assuming that China's economy continues to grow at a pace faster than 6% p.a., then its GDP will surpass the USA by 2020.

9.4 THE CHALLENGES

The focus for MAS has been to strengthen the framework for robust protection of depositors, insurance policy holders, consumers of financial services, and of course, financial stability. The MAS constantly reviews and refines rules governing the insurance industry, financial advisory firms, fund managers and banks promulgating various MAS (Amendment) Bills, and other legislations. Similar to most regulators, MAS has initiated actions to increase statutory reserves, to enhance risk management process and internal controls, to combat money laundering. The most interesting and significant development was the launch in May 2013 of RMB clearing services in Singapore by the Singapore Branch of Industrial and Commercial Bank of China. As of July 2013, Singapore has SGD 28.5 billion RMB deposits, a growth of 40% since December 2012. Singapore can continue to serve the international trading companies based in the country and as an intermediary for RMB flows between China and its trading partners. The Bank of China signed a memorandum of understanding with the SGX in September 2013 to develop Yuan products and services. Given that the SGX has already supported 141 companies from China in their fund-raising efforts, this will only grow over time.

We expect such initiatives to provide more opportunities for RMB trades, finance, and especially bilateral swaps. These are areas that are definitely worth exploring given the resilience and competencies inherent in the Singapore financial sector. Historically, given the constraints of a small economy and its many short comings, Singapore has demonstrated its ability to take a new financial infrastructure and architecture and move it ahead of the curve among its competitors not only in the region, but on a global basis as well. One excellent and recent example is the emergence of other exchanges that rode on the China listing and left Singapore behind with smaller Chinese companies for listings on the SGX. However, regulations to boost fund management via a common market using the Asia Region Funds Passport (ARFP) are to be introduced in 2016. This creates a common platform making it easier for fund managers to launch the same product across four countries, namely Australia, New Zealand, South Korea, and Singapore. Other new innovations via derivatives and REITs, together with the ability to take advantage of new trading platforms and RMB internationalization in the fixed income market, have moved the financial sector a notch higher.

The greatest challenge confronting Singapore's financial sector is not from within. Ironically, it is what it has enjoyed the most, i.e., the external environment in an open economy, and the free flow of capital in large volume. The danger arises from the technological improvements resulting in specialization in a time-compressed world. With quantitative easing, easy credit, low interest environment, asset price inflation, changing pattern of reduced long-term investment of an aging population, more reliance on derivatives and foreign debts as a growth strategy, the Singapore financial sector is vulnerable to a rapid withdrawal of huge foreign capital, as in the case during the Asian Financial Crisis (Forbes and Warnock, 2011; Rozhkov, 2009). This is especially crucial as the housing market is a major component of individual debt and has been increasing rapidly over time. The consolation is that many property cooling measures (Lee et al., 2013) and consumer loan measures (especially for car and credit card) have been introduced. With the revised MAS Notice 637 to implement the Basel III capital framework, Singapore-incorporated banks are required to maintain a ratio of no less than 9% (inclusive of a capital conservation buffer requirement of 2.5%) for Common Equity Tier 1 capital with effect on 1 January 2013. This is higher than the requirement set by the Basel Committee on Banking Supervision of 7%. Given that the debt to GDP ratio has crossed 100%, this buffer will provide some comfort.

The rapid GDP growth in Singapore over the past several years has been attributed to an increasing foreign and immigrant workforce, a more flexible regime for lending to real estate investment, pro market regulations to develop the debt market for SGD and foreign currencies for non-Singapore incorporated entities, an open door policy for professionals and high net worth and their liquid assets, as well as investment in infrastructure and facilities to attract tourism dollars. This is not to underplay the contribution of investment in manufacturing, especially in pharmaceutical, oil and gas, shipping, education, logistic, commerce, and other economic sectors. The focus of this chapter is to discuss the challenge and potential issues of having an open economy that may be vulnerable to rapid capital flow, fast information flow, large volume transaction, and speedy technological change.

Being a very open economy, Singapore's fate is closely linked to its Asian neighbors and trading partners. According to Rozhkov (2009) and IMF estimates (IMF, 2009), when Asian economies were under financial stress during the Asian crisis, the recession lasted a median of four quarters with cumulative output loss of more than 27% for Asia as a whole. It is also noted that 30% of credit to the private sector evaporated 8 quarters after the peak of the recession.

The Pan-Electric crisis (MAS, 2004), the Baring crisis, the Asian Crisis, and the recent debt crisis did not result in systemic banking crisis. Regulations had already been in place for foreign institutions to increase their capital base in their branches in Singapore. However, over time, greater economic and financial integrations have resulted in higher correlation among the Asian economies and financial markets. Coupled with a lower likelihood for strong export led recovery due to the malaise in the developed economies, capital outflow will have a negative impact for Singapore's private sector as demonstrated in 2008.

The market value of Singapore reserves is not known precisely although it is reported officially by MAS that the foreign reserves are valued at USD 262 million as at August 2013. The uncertainty created by market perception of the total reserve size is ironically an important stabilizing force. Uncertainty over the size of a country's reserves can be argued to be an effective part of Singapore's armory to defend the SGD, reducing the probability of its collapse. Along with the central bank's reputation of providing confidence with liquidity to investors and the private sector, the SGD has traditionally been viewed as a safe haven currency during crises. This perception was slightly dented during the Asian Crisis, and furthermore, the new global financial architecture has made the central banks' mission of maintaining stability of their currencies more complicated than before. This is not in any way a problem faced by MAS alone, but the consequence of time compression risk caused by a combination of advanced technology, rapid information flow, as well as huge and free flow of capital.

In this new era, the rapid free flow of capital (both capital inflows and outflows) is more difficult to manage. The magnitude of such flows can be in the ten or hundred billions USD over a short time span, creating instability in the financial system, with massive asset inflation and deflation. Historical evidence has shown that the extent of the surge and stop episodes on capital inflows prior to 1997 and 2008 along with the sharp withdrawals during the two crises can be very damaging to the economy.

The potential danger of global contagion brought about by the complexity inherent in the leveraged financial system flushed with liquidity is a real and constant danger. Leverage, illiquidity, and concentration are the most toxic cocktails one can have. There are many examples of institutions self-organizing themselves into a critical situation when they are heavily leveraged, holding on to illiquid assets with great concentration. Real estate, bank lending, and individual ability to service debts are a real issue for the financial sector in Singapore. Let me give a few specific isolated examples of how this can happen in order to illustrate the challenges we are facing, but not only in Singapore.

9.4.1 The Flood, the Reservoir, and Finance

In this section, we explain a concept related to complexity in financial markets and development. In finance, we are always looking for a law of nature and to recognize patterns in other sciences as a way to understand problems. Consider the reservoir in the diagram with inflow and outflow of water. Persistent rainfall will fill our drains and eventually our reservoir. An intense rainfall within a short period of time when the water level is high will lead to flooding (see Figure 9.2).

The letter R is the range and the lines indicate the minimum and maximum of the water level. In order to prevent flooding and that we have enough water during a drought, we must have an idea of the potential maximum and minimum level of the reservoir. We need to know the range R and its volatility σ. Hurst (1951) developed the relation of the form:

$$R = C\sigma T^{H}$$

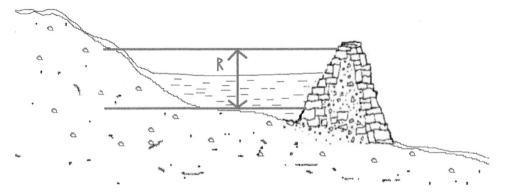

Figure 9.2 The flood and the Hurst coefficient.

where R is the range, C is a constant, σ is the standard deviation of R, and T is the period ahead. What this means is that we will know what R is T periods ahead if we know the Hurst coefficient H, which is between 0 and 1. We also know that the larger the H, the larger the R, and the more persistent is the rainfall.

We can relate the massive printing of money that can be moved around freely with the impact of heavy rainfall. Unlike the weather change that happens over a longer period, the printing of money is close to instantaneous. What is even more disturbing is the speed of capital flow via wired transfer or via the Internet. This has the same impact of smoothing the flow of the drain and increasing the speed of flow to fill up the reservoir thereby increasing the volatility. It is quite obvious from the diagram that if you fill the reservoir quicker than you can drain, the water will overflow and cause severe damage to surrounding areas. In that case, you will have an H higher than 0.5 and around possibly 0.8 or higher. This has the same effect of a bubble forming. Eventually, the bursting of the bubble will have very damaging consequences not only on our own Wall Street in Raffles Place (Singapore), but also the Main Street like the shopping centers and housing estates in Orchard Road, Boon Lay, and Bukit Timah.

It is interesting to note that the quarterly Property Price Indices for Singapore in various functional forms are anti-persistent with H between 0.3 and 0.5. If you look at the plots of the Urban Redevelopment Authority (URA) Residential Property Price Index (RPPI) in Figure 9.3, the series is smoother than a random walk suggesting that it reverts to its mean more often. In Figure 9.4, we have plotted the log returns of URA RPPI year on year (Series 1) and quarter on quarter (Series 2) series.

A possible explanation is that the visible hand is doing a good job in countering the rapid outflow and inflow of capital out of and into the property market whenever extreme events occur. Contrary to current belief that the property market is out of

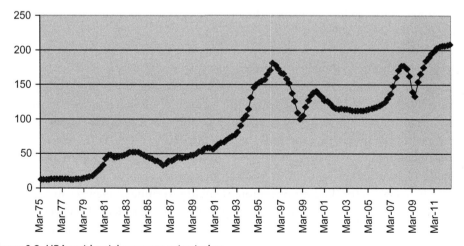

Figure 9.3 URA residential property price index.

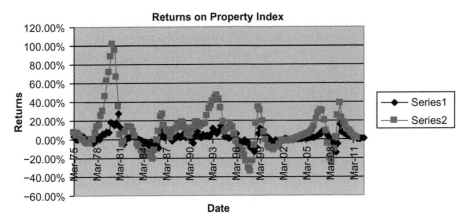

Figure 9.4 URA returns of residential property price index (Series 1: year on year log return, Series 2: quarter on quarter log return).

control and that there is a bubble, the results suggest that despite the peaks and troughs, the policy instruments have worked fairly well to reduce instability. If the housing prices do not exhibit mean reversion and continues to exhibit a persistent uptrend, then there is a likelihood that a bubble has formed. This is clearly not the case for Singapore as the time series exhibit more mean reversion than a persistent uptrend. It is also interesting to note that it is not the price increase or level that will directly induce instability; it is the amount of potential bad debts that is the key trigger. Therefore, if households and mortgage debts continue to increase to a level that poses danger when there is a rapid withdrawal of capital, then macro–prudential measures have to be introduced. It is important to note that if a bubble is allowed to form in the housing market, any intervention will be very damaging. It is the ability to use macro prudential policies to avert a bubble and therefore to reduce the probability of a potential voluminous capital outflow that is more important.

Bubble detection techniques are self-defeating. If a bubble is allowed to build up, a soft landing is extremely difficult as any proactive policy actions will result in being perceived negatively resulting in dire consequences. At the wrong time, introducing prudential policies will only invite unwanted attention that can result in a mass exodus of capital from the sector or country to preserve portfolio performance. This self-interest behavior of participants will always result in self-organized destructive behavior collectively. The job of a policy maker is to prevent a bubble from forming so as to avert likely rapid withdrawal of voluminous funds by investors, triggered by a fear of illiquidity in a highly leveraged financial sector. The co-operation of multigovernment agencies in Singapore has successfully averted a bubble from forming using macro prudential policies.

Both the MAS and URA have been successful in preventing a serious problem from forming especially in the area of mortgage finance. However, if the debt ratio linked to real estate continues to increase over time, if affordability is not correspondingly increased and if the economy is perceived to be heavily reliant on real estate, then such a "real estate"—driven economy becomes vulnerable to risks of capital outflow. More specific discussions of liquidity flow using the concept of flooding and self-organized activities are as follows.

9.4.2 High-Frequency Trading and H

High-power computers have brought about a new form of trading: the emergence of High-Frequency Trading (HFT), a special case of algorithmic trading with lightning speed of execution. HFT is supposedly a supplier of liquidity, lowers transaction costs and lowers the bid-ask of financial assets. HFT is using technology to increase the flow of capital in the shortest possible time such as a micro-second. The round-trip latent time, or the time taken to give an order, to execute, and to inform the executor, has decreased from 20s from a few years ago to 250μs in NASDAQ OMX INET. Things are occurring faster than the time we have to think, to strategize, and to react. Technology has brought about efficiency beyond the optimal point and this is starting to trouble us, as we have seen in many mini crashes of stock market and bond market around the world. HFT did not cause crashes, but it exaggerated volatility.

During the Flash Crash in 2010, the machines sold US stocks to 1 cent and bid up a few others to USD 99999.99, because those are the two limit prices that can be executed. While transaction cost of trading has decreased in recent years with high-frequency trading as provider of liquidity, it has also become a competing consumer of liquidity during extreme periods of volatility. Financial markets expect these traders to provide trading volume during both normal times and extreme events. But the fact is that in extreme events, such traders would on the same sell side as everyone else. There will be no liquidity provided by these traders as there would be no buyers of decent size. On the contrary, these traders would be the ones with the speed and size to sell when markets expect them to be on the buy side with decent bid size. There is simply no free lunch, and lower transaction costs brought about by HFT traders would be repaid with higher volatility during a crisis.

9.4.3 Asian Crisis: Lesson Learned

We have learned from the last few crises that rapid inflow and outflow of capital occur when the profit and loss or balance sheets of banks are badly affected. At other times, when credit is tightened, trades will fall dramatically resulting in a wave of withdrawals from the debt and equity markets.

After the Asian Crisis, Asian bank's reserves were increased substantially along with improved regulation of banks and lowered toxic assets on their balance sheets. China took this a step further to control the speed of flow of information and capital by shutting down the Internet at times. Despite its efforts, in the 12 months through September 2012, an estimated USD 225.7 billion fled the country. The outflow would have been much greater if there were no capital controls in China given this race to zero (trading) time. Fortunately, capital control in China prevented a much larger volume of funds flowing out during the current downturn.

It is well-known that domestic owned banks in Singapore play a crucial role in providing liquidity during crises as foreign institutions would likely have many problems to deal with and focus outside Singapore, especially if they were taken over by other institutions or by their own central bank. As a small red dot (that is what Singapore is known as to its neighbors), Singapore can only impose higher capital requirements and other liquidity requirements so that during a crisis, lending to businesses in Singapore would not be affected. Alternatively, more liquidity can be injected by the central bank. Another risk during a crisis situation is posed by lending to foreign institutions. If such lending is not carefully monitored and if the ability to repay by foreign entities is suspect, a loss in confidence in the financial sector can be triggered.

This is one of the two empirical examples that tail risk has increased in Singapore. The Hurst exponent H is getting larger for shorter holding periods with the volatility becoming larger resulting in a thinner tail distribution. The volume is displaying a higher H and when you cannot clear the market with a huge amount of outstanding buy or sell orders, toxic volume shows up. Persistence in returns and volume of asset prices lead to thicker tail distribution with Power Law characteristics. Complexity and behavioral factors are affecting the market in a more prominent way than ever before. What is worrying is that the initial advantage from lower cost and increased liquidity may overtime self-organize into a concentrated group of players and impose greater risk to the world financial markets across all asset classes, especially to those markets that have no barriers to capital flow. During the crisis, portfolios are highly correlated and become concentrated, and these cause great instability in the market turbo charged with leverage.

9.4.4 Spain's Banking Crisis

Another example is the recent banking crisis in Spain. As the European Central Bank printed money with the objective of strengthening the capital base and liquidity of Spanish banks, the banks in performing their task efficiently purchased more Spanish sovereign debt, thinking it would be the most liquid and the safest asset. When the market realized that there were further austerity measures to come and that banks were not providing loans to SMEs to grow the economy, a sovereign debt crisis was triggered by fears of stagnant growth and rising non-performing loans. The Spanish banking sector suddenly found that it became a concentrated reserve portfolio of Spanish sovereign debt that had to be marked-to-market under Basel III and became a crisis sector.

The correlation with sovereign debt on the balance sheets of banks had increased even though the exposure was only 6%, way below the historical high of 12%. This is another example of doing a job too well, but unwittingly being put into a critical situation. What we now see is related to the power law and complexity phenomena and that a self-organized behavior becomes a real issue. The major problem in applying the law of nature to finance is behavioral. Take the case of prediction, if we were to ask where the earth would be next year, we would know roughly where we are relative to the sun. However, if I were to ask: "Where the market index will be next year at this time?" We will not have a clue as perhaps a wide range of outcomes is probable. In addition, if we knew the outcome, our action may render our original forecast to be inaccurate. We simply cannot forecast the absolute magnitude, but we can have a good idea about of the range or volatility of outcomes. We are surely in a chaos that is not deterministic. Likewise, we will never know how correlated or concentrated a bank's portfolio is until the crisis erupts (or maybe not even then). In addition, we will never know how illiquid our portfolio will be until the crisis hits. We may have self-organized ourselves into more correlated and concentrated portfolios as a whole and once we are in a crisis, it is hard to get out of that situation. These are the main challenges of an open economy that Singapore's financial sector serves given the chaotic state and complexity of the world today.

As mentioned previously, the mixture of leverage, illiquidity, and concentration is deadly. Financial innovation may seem to have reduced or redistributed risk at the micro-level, but systemic risk may not be reduced at the macrolevel. There are already great efforts in increasing the capital base, reserve requirements and margins to tackle leverage. The markets, unlike the orbit of the earth, are gravely affected by human behavior. Bubbles can be formed easily given an open economy, but by monitoring debt and reducing leverage, hopefully we can avoid greater instability. While excess liquidity is a major issue, the reverse is as dangerous and illiquidity during crisis can instill greater instability. It would be important to prevent the supplier of liquidity from turning into a consumer of liquidity thereby causing great damage.

When it comes to the concentration of assets and participants, it is prudent to ensure that markets are not dominated by a small group of participants with the same set of instruments or strategies. The strong linkages among participants and their portfolios can propagate weaknesses in a single or small number of entities into a systemic failure. In a small economy such as Singapore where the domestic market is limited in size with the economy wide open to many international investors, along with a group of SMEs without any economies of scale, the concentration of strategies and market structure will make Singapore a great deal more vulnerable than if the country is larger in size and less open.

9.5 THE INSTABILITY PARADOX

Her Majesty the Queen Elizabeth visited the London School of Economics in November 2008 and demanded an answer to the question from top economists: "Why had nobody noticed that the credit crunch was on its way?" The collective answer from

33 top academics in the UK was summarized by the following sentence: "principally a failure of the collective imagination of many bright people." In other words, everyone was taking care of their own interest and executed their own mandate so well that they failed to realize they had put the whole economy and system at great risk.

Clearly, communication and the exchange of information are sometimes detrimental to self-interest or profit maximization because narrow interests are competing. With advanced technology, we have even more specialized, as each task is difficult on its own. In addition, we are now given a short time to think, to strategize, and to react. Machines are faster than human beings in a time-compressed world. The profit-based financial institutions will always move faster and ahead of the regulators who are cost based.

There is already a call to limit the speed of everything to the speed of human understanding or a speed that we can handle so as to minimize the damage. This can also be done by constant balancing of competition and cooperation, whether it is among policy makers, government, corporations, and people. Constant communication, making different parties aware of the constraints of others as well as the impact of collective actions, is important. Given the low cost of funds and the flexibility to extend the loan tenure to 30–35 years will likely cause many borrowers to be over extended. The banking system may be sound, and prudential policies are in place to maintain stability, but the combination of surging property prices, increased lending to private, local, and foreign corporations, low interest rates, growing leverage of consumers and corporations, pose significant risks to financial stability.

Mortgages account for 46% of Singapore's GDP and is an increase of 35% from 2010 (see Figure 9.5). The total loan amount has been increasing at 18% for the past 3 years. If interest payments are to increase by 3%, MAS estimates that 10–15% of the borrowers

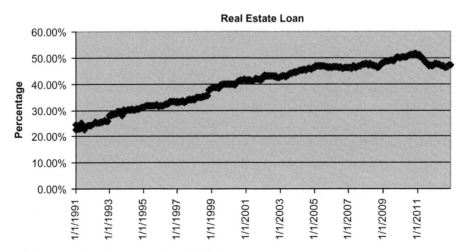

Figure 9.5 Percentage of real estate loan to GDP.

may be at risk as repayment accounts for more than 60% of their salary. While the 3% increase in interest payment for the vulnerable group of borrowers is not likely in the near future, it does signal a potential risk given that 2011 and 2012 saw the highest property transaction values and total debt servicing ratios. Tighter loan to value as a prudential policy tool has limited the buildup of an even higher leverage ratio. On the other hand, Singapore government debt to GDP was reduced from 103.4% of GDP to 97.9% in 2013, and most government debt is internal borrowing and used for investments by the government. Development strategies are well thought through to leverage on Asian and global growth, albeit they are not without risk.

Given the concerns over the increase in mortgage loans and property price inflation, the Singapore government has introduced macroprudential policies, usually making minor changes each time to gauge the policy response of and impact on participants with diverse interests. No fewer than 17 property measures have been introduced since 1981 in Singapore. The "more often, less drastic" approach to sense the reaction of the market, before introducing a more drastic approach where necessary, has been successful in Singapore. This inching approach has given the policy maker a "good feel" of the market and time to study the reactions of vested parties. Obviously, such a strategy can only be employed way before any potential bubble is formed as once it is formed, a time-compressed policy reaction may well exacerbate the damage.

9.6 MICRO- AND MACROPRUDENTIAL POLICIES

History has shown the keys to Singapore's success and resilience include being at the right place at the right time, being well supported by human resource and infrastructure. We also learned that these factor can be sustained, leading us to conclude that prospects for Singapore remain positive when compared with other financial centers despite a tight labor market. Professional, postgraduate, and leadership training programs will continue to play an important role to develop the perquisite talents to support Singapore's financial sector.

We have learned that the most of the challenges faced by Singapore may not be within its control given the open economy that relies on free mobility of capital and advanced technology with ever-increasing specialization. Uncertainty is aggravated by the rapid and voluminous flow of capital in an environment of multiple interests.

Given that the episodes of quantitative easing by the FED have widened the income distribution gap through asset price inflation, the competing interests of the entire spectrum of income groups are now even more diverse. Balancing the interests of many groups in a time-compressed world requires more than monetary and fiscal policy response. Imposing capital control is not necessarily an optimal option for Singapore. Better options would be the use of micro- and macroprudential policies that include strengthening the capital base, lowering leverage and increasing transaction tax to slow flows, transactions, and asset price appreciation. In a time-compressed world with multiple interests, we expect that these modern policy instruments may dampen and possibly reduce the damage, but are unlikely to prevent future bubbles and crashes. It is insufficient to monitor exchange rate/consumer price inflation; it is more important to both target asset inflation and maintain financial stability to ensure not only economic growth, but to ensure a right balance of social equity.

Gradual change to deal with uncertainty is the right policy for now. Singapore is faced with the need to deal with uncertainty in a state of indeterministic chaos. It has become harder to quantify what risk is, and therefore, it is difficult and even impossible to manage what is not known. The implications are that one should only make small gradual changes to policy to prevent the butterfly effect. In times of great uncertainty, slowing the policy response may be the best approach and a small step is better than subscribing to the ideal of creative destruction. MAS has been working within this framework especially with regard to asset price inflation, and many rounds of cooling measures have been introduced. This has the advantage of gauging the behavior of the adaptive agents and gathering feedback to further refine the measures step by step. The measures have so far been successful in molding the "desired" behavior of market participants.

Ironically, we have to put up obstacles during a normal period to induce inefficiency in order to avoid concentration and high correlation. Intense competition will lead to a tug-of-war among regulated firms. It is important to ensure intense competition does not lead to survival of the fittest or result only in the survival of organizations that employ the same strategy, thus leading to concentration. To avoid too big to fail is to avoid concentration of organizations that account for substantial employment and value added in a small economy, perhaps leading to sub-optimal economy of scale for organizations to compete internationally. This balance between concentration and economy of scale is a major challenge for a financial city that is also a city state. This balance have further implications for policy options that include the employment of local versus foreign talents, to allocate resources on MNCs versus SMEs, domestic versus regional businesses, and private versus public enterprises.

The mindset of efficiency and profit maximization may have to take a backseat in periods of instability and social inequity caused by leverage, illiquidity, and concentration. In response, some regulators in other parts of the world are already calling for reform with urgent execution of even more micro- and macroprudential policies such as lowering the leverage of financial institutions, banning short selling during crises, and making OTC derivatives trading transparent. Others in Europe have called for circuit breakers to slow down trading speed during crises to ease the consumption of liquidity and correlation across all asset classes and markets. Yet more have called for prudential policies to slow down asset inflation, to lower debt ratios, and to prevent huge capital outflows during crises. However, not many countries can execute the "right" prudential policies as easily as Singapore. Prudential policies are not new, but Singapore has been known to take the lead in implementing many of these prudential policies (MAS, 2010; Oh, 2013; BBA, 2010; Kawai and Morgan, 2012). The effectiveness and implementation issues of such policies in other Asian countries can be found in HKMA (2012).

This ease of introduction of prudential policies is an advantage. But Singapore does face other social issues. There are social equity issues of employing locals versus engaging foreign talents, taxing rich versus subsidizing the lower and middle classes, and many other non-financial considerations. Singapore has addressed many of these financial and social issues and notably has done well in managing the development of the financial sector for 40 years. The challenges remain to balance the need to regulate or to allow market forces to work in achieving growth within a set of social objectives. More importantly, the Singapore government needs to demonstrate that it understands how the markets work so that the implemented policy achieves the right results. Only by maintaining the trust and social capital can the government continue to earn the right to implement new policies with ease, which is a major competitive advantage for Singapore.

9.7 CONCLUSION

The future of Singapore's financial markets lies in its stability in a time-compressed world of complexity and so far, it has been very successful! Singapore is already in the right place and in the right time by being in an advantageous location in Asia. It possesses the relevant human capital of very competent professionals with strong political leadership that promote an embracing culture for global talents. To maintain growth with financial and social stability, the key political and economic focus will be to provide a satisfactory balance between the ever-increasing interests with possibly divergent objectives. Given a strong track record where policy makers have demonstrated good understanding of how the markets function and the ability to create and maintain an ecosystem for growth, future prospects of Singapore's financial sector and its markets remain positive. The key risk to such a future is clearly Singapore's vulnerability given its openness to global economic developments and funds flows. Macro- and micro-prudential policies need to be considered and implemented carefully, to prevent the development of bubbles and imbalances in its various financial markets. Excessive credit in domestic loan and loans to foreign entities need to be carefully managed. Capital flows and especially significant reversals over a short time span do not only increase market volatility; but under more extreme scenarios exacerbate real imbalances that can result in systemic failures of both the financial and real sectors.

REFERENCES

BBA, 2010. A Possible Macro-Prudential Approach. British Bankers' Association.

Economic Review Committee, 2002. Positioning Singapore as a Pre-eminent Financial Centre in Asia. In: Sub-Committee on Services Industries. Financial Services Working Group.

Ernst and Young, 2013. Global IPO Trends Report. Ernst and Young Q32013 Report.

Forbes, K.J., Warnock, F.E., 2011. Capital flow waves, Macroeconomic Review. Monetary Authority of Singapore.

HKMA, 2012. Loan-to-value ratio as a macroprudential tool – Hong Kong SAR's experience and cross-country evidence. BIS Papers No 57, Bank of International Settlement.

Hurst, H.E., 1951. Long term storage capacity of reservoirs. Transactions of the American Society of Civil Engineering 116, 770–808.

IMF, 2009. Regional Economic Outlook. Asia and Pacific, May.

Investment Company, 2011. Investment Company Fact Book. Investment Company Institute, USA.

Investment Company, 2012. Investment Company Fact Book. Investment Company Institute, USA.

Kawai, M., Morgan, P.J., 2012. Central banking for financial stability in Asia. Public Policy Review 8 (3), 215–246.

Koh, F., Tan, P., 2013. Wealth Management – A Comparison Between Switzerland, Singapore and Hong Kong. Preprint and chapter in this book.

Koh, F., Lee, D., Phoon, K.F., Seah, E.S., 2013. Market Structure and Growth Potential of Singapore REITs. Preprint and a chapter in this book.

Kuah, A.T.H., 2008. Managing competitive advantage: clustering in the Singapore financial centre. Manchester Business School Working Paper No 549.

Lee, D.K.C., Phang, S.Y., Cheong, A, Phoon, K.F., Wee, K., 2013. Evaluating the effectiveness of cooling measures on property prices: an exploration of alternative econometric techniques. Paper presented to the 2013 Asian Meeting of the Econometric Society, August 2–4, 2013.

MAS, 2004. Case study on pan-electric crisis. MAS Staff Paper No. 32, June, Monetary Authority of Singapore.

MAS, 2012. Sustaining Stability: Servicing Singapore. MAS 40th Anniversary Publication. Monetary Authority of Singapore.

MAS, 2013. Annual Report. Monetary Authority of Singapore.

Menon, R., 2013. Singapore's financial centre in the new landscape. In: Keynote Address at the Investment Management Association of Singapore 14th Annual Conference on March 13, 2013.

Oh, H.S., 2013. Loan-to-value as macro-prudential policy tool: experiences and lessons of Asian emerging countries. DSF Policy Paper Series, No. 33, Duisenberg School of Finance.

Phang, S.Y., Lee, D.K.C., Cheong, A., Phoon, K.F., Wee, K., 2013. Housing policies in Singapore: evaluation of recent measures and proposals for reform. Paper presented to the Singapore Economic Review Conference, August 6–8, 2013.

Rozhkov, D., 2009. Recessions and recoveries in Asia lessons from the past, Macroeconomic Review. Monetary Authority of Singapore.

CHAPTER 10

Wealth Management: A Comparison of Switzerland, Singapore, and Hong Kong

Francis Koh[a] and Peggan Tan[b]

[a]Singapore Management University, Lee Kong Chian School of Business, 50 Stamford Road, Singapore 178899, Singapore
[b]DBS Bank, 12 Marina Boulevard, Level 6, DBS Asia Central, MBFC Tower 3, Singapore 18982, Singapore

10.1 INTRODUCTION

Wealth management is generally defined as the provision of investment services by financial institutions to high net worth individuals (HNWIs). HNWIs are clients with investible assets of more than a million US dollars. They are normally served by relationship managers from Private Banks. Other clients with less investible funds are served by "premier banking" or "retail banking" units within a consumer bank.

Private banks provide a host of services which includes asset management, client advisory, and wealth planning to both onshore and offshore clients. An offshore bank is a financial institution which is "located outside the country of residence of the depositor." It is estimated that HNWIs hold about one-third of their wealth in offshore banks. Switzerland has USD 2.8 trillion in assets under management with USD 2.1 trillion coming from offshore wealth. It accounts for about 34% of total global wealth. Singapore is said to be the fastest growing wealth management center in the world, with USD 550 billion of assets under management of which about USD 450 billion is offshore wealth (CNBC, 2013).

The longer-term outlook is for wealth to grow faster in Asia-Pacific, estimated at 9.8% p.a. than Europe at 6.2% p.a. (see Figure 10.1). Hence, more and more European Private Banks have been looking east and setting up operations in Singapore and Hong Kong. In recent years, some reports have mooted the possibility for Switzerland to lose its current pole position as the "mecca" of private banking, with Singapore advancing as the premier offshore global banking center. This chapter discusses the key factors favoring wealth management in the three financial centers focusing on the economic-social-political and legal/tax environments.

10.2 SWITZERLAND

Switzerland has been one of the most stable and developed market economies in the world. The financial sector is a major pillar of the economy and contributes significantly to the country's Gross National Product. Swiss banks contributed 9.3% to the overall

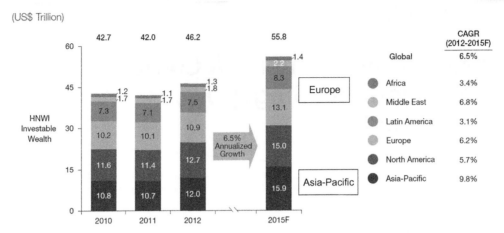

Figure 10.1 High net worth individual (HNWI) wealth forecast 2010–2015 (by region). *Source:* Capgemini—RBC Wealth Management, World Wealth Report 2013, p. 7.

Swiss economy in 2011 (Swiss Bankers Association, 2012a). The growth of the financial sector in Switzerland can be attributed to a few key factors. Firstly, Switzerland has a strong and stable economy with stable economic growth while maintaining a low rate of inflation. Secondly, it is geographically well-located, being a close neighbor of many countries in the European Union (EU) while being politically neutral. Consequently, it has evolved historically as a banking center for wealthy individuals to place their funds for professional management.

Further, the Swiss education system, which has vocational training and an apprenticeship system, annually grooms a large pipeline of young bankers. Many banking professionals begin their apprenticeships after high school and are comprehensively trained in banking which lasts three or more years, in programmes accredited by the Swiss Bankers Association. At the tertiary level, students can choose to read practice-oriented diplomas or enroll in degree programmes at universities and technical colleges (MarketLine, 2012). Through various talent development pathways, Switzerland has put in place a sustainable pipeline of wealth managers.

Switzerland has a very established legal framework regulating financial institutions and has a regulatory environment helpful for business. From the taxation angle, Switzerland does not tax its residents excessively. There are Swiss cantons that are known to offer generous tax concessions to wealthy individuals (Groux and Jesswein, 2011). The legal and business environment encourages HNWIs to move their residence to Switzerland.

However, the 2008 global financial crisis caused numerous countries to step up efforts to combat tax evasion. Switzerland, in particular, faced immense pressure from its European neighbors. Subsequently, Switzerland went on to conclude a large number of bilateral withholding tax agreements with many countries, including United Kingdom and Austria. Under these agreements, Switzerland forwards the tax owed directly to the country involved without releasing a client's information (Swiss Federal Department of Finance, 2013). The withholding tax arrangement was preferred over agreements for exchange of information, which would compromise client privacy.

Yet, Switzerland faces many uncertainties in the near and medium term. As Switzerland is economically and geographically linked with countries in the European Union, the unresolved sovereign debt crisis in the Euro zone and an on-going, prolonged economic slowdown have direct negative impact on the Swiss economy. In May 2012, the International Monetary Fund (IMF) warned that "the Swiss economy is threatened by the Euro zone debt crisis," and faces the risk of a recession if the crisis becomes more severe.

Since the 2008 global financial crisis, the Swiss private banking industry has been operating in an increasingly difficult environment, especially the issues of increased regulatory pressure and banking secrecy. Further, many Swiss banks had to pay hefty fines to the US government because of alleged illegal banking transactions, suspected money laundering or gross violation of cross-border banking rules (Barrett and Novack, 2009). This has led to increased regulation, loss of business reputation and higher compliance costs, issues which have plagued the Swiss banking industry.

10.3 SINGAPORE

The active promotion of Singapore as an international financial center gained traction in the 1960s. With excellent infrastructure, a well-educated workforce and an efficient legal system, many financial institutions were attracted to establish operations in Singapore. This growth was also helped by the surge in the increase in wealth and millionaires in the region. Over the years, with consistent promotion by the Monetary Authority of Singapore, Singapore has established itself as a leading financial center of international reputation. With its strategic location, excellent infrastructure and leisure attractions, many leading global financial institutions and companies have set up their Asian offices in the city-state (Koh, 2012). According to Singapore's Department of Statistics, the financial sector generated total revenue of about USD S$30 billion which forms about 12% of Gross Domestic Product in 2011.

Singapore has grown to become a major wealth management center offering both onshore and offshore banking services. There are at least 40 financial institutions offering private banking services. According to the Monetary Authority of Singapore, total assets managed exceeded USD 1 trillion as at 2011. This represents a 5-year average growth rate of about 11% p.a. Private Banks, as a sector, have assets under management of about USD 500 billion.

According to the World Bank's 2012 Doing Business Report, Singapore was globally ranked first out of 183 nations in terms of the ease of doing business. Singapore also has well-crafted regulations to protect investor rights. With pro-business policies in place, Singapore has continued to attract foreign investment and business entrepreneurs providing sustained economic growth and stability.

Socially, Singapore offers an excellent expatriate lifestyle with world-class infrastructure and a convenient transport system while having a secure and safe environment to live in. The government consistently invests in education and the development of human resources. In addition, it has a far-sighted game plan to build a competent workforce and a pipeline of wealth managers across all levels. In 2003, the Wealth Management Institute (WMI) was established with the support of the Monetary Authority of Singapore, Temasek Holdings, and the Government of Singapore Investment Corporation (GIC), to offer superior wealth management training. In collaboration with the Singapore Management University (SMU), WMI offers the MSc in Wealth Management Program. Besides this Master's degree, WMI also offers other programs leading to the award of Certificates in Private Banking and Trust Services.

Legally, like Switzerland, Singapore has strict bank secrecy regulations which protect client privacy. The Monetary Authority of Singapore takes a proactive approach to oversee a regulatory framework which facilitates, accommodate, and promote the growth of wealth management. Singapore has a competitive tax regime, with one of the lowest personal and corporate tax rates in Asia. Any income received in Singapore from outside the state is not taxable, and estate duties have been removed facilitating wealth succession.

However, the growth of wealth management services in Singapore has led to a number of challenges. With the arrival of more private banking units in Singapore and the increased number of high net worth clients, there is a severe shortage of competent wealth managers. Instead of in-house training and development, banks tend to choose the quicker route of "poaching" experienced staff from other banks. The aging population and low birth rates of Singaporeans have added to the current and future human capital problem. Banks also face a very competitive environment to offer suitable products and services to their demanding clients.

With the accelerated growth of offshore banking services, there is an urgent need for Singapore to remain a competent, clean and trusted financial center and avoid reputational risks from accepting funds from dubious clients. Recent legacy problems in Switzerland have motivated some clients to transfer their funds to be managed in Singapore. Some wealthy Asians, with accounts in Switzerland, now view Singapore as a feasible alternative. The challenge for Singapore is to adhere strictly to a gold standard in monetary transactions and strenuously avoid accepting funds from suspicious sources, including funds linked to "undeclared" taxes or "money laundering." In recent years, Singapore has signed many bilateral agreements with other countries to implement the international standard for the exchange of information (Jek and Tan, 2010).

Another challenge for Singapore wealth managers relates to the current low interest rate environment and the slow economic recovery in developed markets. These have affected the rate of investment returns to clients. Clients are also increasingly more risk averse during uncertain periods and commit much less of their investible funds, resulting in lower revenue for banks. The outcome is that banks have very high cost-to-income ratios which have risen from an average of about 64% in 2007 to 80% or more.

10.4 HONG KONG

In contrast to Singapore and Switzerland, the development of Hong Kong as a private wealth management center is largely market-driven. The Hong Kong government has adopted "a relatively laissez-faire approach, leaving the growth of the industry to market forces and the effort of the market participants" (Jek and Tan, 2010). However, because of its proximity to China, Hong Kong remains well-positioned to be a hub for North Asia. According to Meyer (2009), "the growth of China will generate an enormous demand for sophisticated financial services which Hong Kong firms can provide ... and will cement the city's rank as (one of) the three great global International Financial Centers (IFCs)."

Hong Kong, like Singapore, has a competitive tax regime, strict regulatory environment, bank secrecy rules, and extensive "social network of capital." Meyer (2009) explained that the network includes not only commercial and investment banks, but also the insurance companies, private equity and hedge funds that thrive in Hong Kong, as well as the huge trading firms and regional offices. The continued strengthening of the financial linkages between China Mainland and Hong Kong ensures the latter's continued success into the longer term.

However, Hong Kong has its share of challenges as a wealth management center, including the high cost of doing business. One key drawback is its linkage to China, a double-edged sword, as some Chinese HNWIs viewed it negatively. Although China has consistently sought to remove any doubts of latent "political risks" linked to the status of Hong Kong as a sovereign state, this remains a lingering issue into the longer term. This issue has required the need for repeated affirmation by senior Chinese leaders (Meyer, 2009). On this important issue, Singapore is a normally preferred over Hong Kong to manage the assets of HNWIs from North Asia.

10.5 A COMPARISON OF SWITZERLAND, SINGAPORE, AND HONG KONG

In 2012, Credit Suisse published a comprehensive study on the competitiveness of Switzerland as a financial center. The study examined Switzerland's current position and compared its strengths and weaknesses with other international financial centers. The study noted that in recent years, "gross margins (of the wealth management sector) have come under pressure as investors have moved toward lower-margin assets, transaction volumes have declined and interest rates have fallen to historic lows ... increasing challenges due to government efforts to enhance transparency in taxation matters" (Credit Suisse, 2012, p. 6). Credit Suisse identified 17 key success factors for financial centers under 5 broad categories:

(a) **People** (openness to new talents; competitive income; education infrastructure; and quality of life).

(b) **Business Environment** (extent of bureaucracy; openness of entry; and capitalization of banks).

(c) **Market Access** (equity exchanges, commodity and derivative markets, security markets, and trade and insurance services).

(d) **Infrastructure** (political system; rule of law; legal framework).

(e) **Competitiveness** (safe haven; use of English; appropriate regulation).

Tabulating the scores of the 17 success factors for Switzerland, Singapore, and Hong Kong, an interest picture emerges. Switzerland has scores broadly in line with Singapore and Hong Kong (see Figure 10.2) but Singapore is marginally ahead.

Singapore was analyzed as having similar strengths as Switzerland but has an edge over Switzerland because of its location in Asia. Singapore was complimented for having a strong economy, well-developed infrastructure, responsive tax environment, an industry-derived code of conduct, and nurturing professional competencies. Consequently, Singapore enjoys three advantages over Switzerland: faster pace of wealth accumulation, absence of legacy issues like taxes, and facing relatively less political pressure from neighboring countries. As expected, Hong Kong was analyzed as benefiting from the rapid growth of the economies of the Greater China region. Hong Kong also gains from the overseas expansion of Chinese businesses abroad and the offshore Renminbi market.

The Credit Suisse Study is useful in documenting what has been the perception in the industry that Switzerland leads in private banking but is facing serious and real competition from Singapore and Hong Kong. In particular, implementation of the new Swiss tax agreements with countries in the EU will result in short-term asset outflows and structural revenue loss. The total funds outflow and revenue loss has been estimated at about 47 billion CHF and 1 billion CHF, respectively (Carlos, 2012). However, the losses are short-term, one-off, and not likely to be devastating. Thus, there is no reason to believe that these new tax agreements and regulations will be catastrophic for the Swiss banks.

10.6 VOICES OF PRACTITIONERS IN SINGAPORE

Focused interviews were conducted with various private bankers in Singapore to obtain their views of the wealth management scene in Singapore. The discussions focus on:

(a) contemporary issues facing private banks;

(b) challenges for Singapore to be a leading wealth management hub; and

(c) the competitive advantages of Switzerland over Singapore.

FACTORS	Singapore	Hong Kong	Switzerland
1. People			
Open immigration for highly qualified people	7	7	7
Competitive income (and capital gains) tax, particularly for high earners	7	7	6
Strong university and business school infrastructure	6	5	6
Good quality of life and real estate	5	5	7
2. Business environment			
Limited bureaucracy for establishing new financial/investment companies and banks	9	9	7
Open policy for non-bank financial companies, i.e., hedge funds, private equity, infrastructure funds and real estate	9	8	8
Well-capitalized banks with limited systemic risk	6	6	6
3. Market access			
Liquid and deep debt and equity exchanges, open for foreign IPOs	6	6	5
Exchanges for derivatives and commodities	7	7	6
Global products in FX, fixed income and equities independent of and not correlated with domestic banks	7	8	6
Trade and insurance hub linked to bank trade finance	7	8	7
4. Infrastructure			
Stability of macroeconomic and political system	6	6	7
Strong rule of law for protecting asset ownership	9	8	9
Strong legal framework for mutual funds, investment funds and ETFs	6	6	7
5. General competitiveness			
Safe-haven status	7	5	8
English as the main language, or widely used	9	8	7
Clear and appropriate regulation, and measured enforcement	6	6	7
Overall Score	**119**	**115**	**116**

Figure 10.2 Seventeen success factors for international financial centers. *Source:* Credit Suisse, "Switzerland as a Financial Center," September 2012, p. 9.

Many respondents interviewed concurred that the main drivers shaping Singapore's wealth management landscape are its political stability, geographical location, and the stringent regulatory framework which engender trust. One private banker specifically mentioned that Singapore's location in Asia is a safe haven, away from any fallout emanating from the European crisis. With the ongoing crisis in Europe, some European HNWIs are considering or have shifted their assets into Asia as a form of geographical diversification. They also want to invest in Asia's growth as well as to protect their assets and real purchasing power over time.

Another banker analyzed the growth of private banks in Singapore from "push" and "pull" factors. The push factors include the global financial and economic crises in USA and Europe. These factors are aggravated by the unfriendly tax and regulatory regulations introduced by US and Europe authorities, creating severe difficulties for HNWIs to manage their assets. The commonly cited pull factor relates to the ambience and location of Singapore in the midst of Asia, especially its proximity to growth countries in Southeast Asia. Additionally, Singapore has a time zone which straddles the US and Europe, allowing it to efficiently service clients and manage their investments in both continents.

The most pressing challenge in Singapore cited by the respondents is the issue of talent shortage. With the exponential growth of millionaires in Asia, there are not enough senior client advisors. Hence, there is a merry-go-round as private bankers are lured to move from one bank to another. Another challenge for Singapore bankers is to keep up with the constant changes in the regulatory framework within the wealth management industry. With the global spotlight on tax evasion, there is a tighter control of money inflows into Singapore which impacts revenue. This imposes a conflict between increasing near-term revenue generation and incurring potential longer-term reputation risks.

There is a consensus that there is relatively more "old" wealth in Switzerland compared to Asia. More wealth in Europe has passed from one generation to the next. Hence, the Swiss wealth management market is more stable and robust. On the other hand, wealth in Asia is relatively "new," and a large part of the investible wealth comes from the nouveau riche like successful entrepreneurs. As such, clients in Asia normally tend to be more hands-on: they want to know specific products recommended and make more decisions. On the other hand, European clients are more inclined to entrust their relationship manager with "discretionary mandates." With these fairly distinct differences between the wealth markets in Singapore and Switzerland, it would seem that the two markets are complementary. Thus, the challenge lies in the ability of the private bankers to manage the different types of clients from Europe to Asia.

There were diverse views on how fast and far Singapore will grow as a wealth management hub. Some private bankers felt that there is a potential for Singapore to overtake Switzerland as a wealth management hub but not in the near future—perhaps in another 10 years or more. The impetus is the rapid growth of wealth in Asia. In addition, with the many initiatives implemented by the authorities to promote wealth management, Singapore, it can be a strong magnet for the inflows of funds. In recent years, there are more Family Offices established in Singapore as well as external asset managers (Hubbis, 2012; Camden, 2012). However, there are also many skeptics who view Singapore merely as a regional player for the foreseeable future.

10.7 CONCLUSION

While Switzerland may be facing an erosion of business in wealth management resulting from legacy issues and the weak economic prognosis in Europe, Singapore, and Hong Kong are charging ahead, attracting more new funds from within and outside of Asia. Against this backdrop, Singapore is likely to grow further and be a big significant wealth management hub in Asia, serving both Asian and non-Asian clients. However, in the foreseeable future, Switzerland will continue to retain its position as the premier global wealth management center, especially in serving European clients. We conclude that Singapore will not replace but be able to complement Switzerland to serve high net worth individuals from around the world. The challenge for Singapore is having more competent managers who can provide suitable wealth solutions for global clients in an increasingly complex and uncertain economic as well as legal environment.

REFERENCES

Barrett, W., Novack, J., 2009. UBS Agrees To Pay $780 Million. 18 February. <www. Forbes.com>.
Camden Research, 2012. Growing Towards Maturity: Family Offices in Asia-Pacific Come of Age. Singapore.
Carlos, E.A. et al., 2011. The Future of Swiss Offshore Private Banking. Booz & Company.
CNBC, 2013. Singapore Will Replace Switzerland as Wealth Capital, April 22, 2013. Singapore.
Credit Suisse, 2012. Switzerland as a Financial Center. Credit Suisse, Zurich, Switzerland.
Credit Suisse Research Institute, 2012. Global Wealth Report 2012. Singapore.
Groux, S., Jesswein, K., 2011. The continuing role of Switzerland and the Swiss franc in international finance. Proceedings of the Academy for Economics and Economic Education 14 (1), 11–15 (Orlando, Florida, USA).
Hubbis, 2012. The Guild to External Asset Management. Singapore.
Jek, A.L., Tan, D., 2010. The growth of the private wealth management industry in Singapore and Hong Kong. Capital Markets Law Journal 6 (1), 104–126.
Koh, F., 2012. Wealth Management in Singapore—Current Landscape and Strategic Challenges. In: Frick, R. et al. (Eds.), Asset Management. Haupt Verlag, Bern, Switzerland, pp. 79–90.
MarketLine, 2012. Country Analysis Report—Switzerland. In-Depth PESTLE Insights. New York, USA.
Meyer, D.R., 2009. Hong Kong's transformation as a financial centre. In: Schenk, C.R. (Ed.), Hong Kong SAR's Monetary and Exchange Rate Challenges: Historical Perspectives. Palgrave, London, U.K.
Swiss Bankers Association, 2012a. The Economic Significance of the Swiss Financial Centre. Basel, Switzerland.
Swiss Bankers Association, 2012b. The Importance of the Swiss Banking Sector. Basel, Switzerland.
Swiss Federal Department of Finance, 2013, Taxation of Savings Agreement with the EU. Available at: www. efd.admin.ch/themen/steuern
Tan, C.H., 2011. Financial Services and Wealth Management in Singapore. Ridge Books, Singapore.

CHAPTER 11

Asian Market Reactions to US Macroeconomic News Surprises

Natàlia Valls[a] and Helena Chuliá[b]

[a]CAIXABANK, Risk Analysis and Capital Optimization, Avenida Diagonal,
621–629, Tower I, 8th floor, Barcelona 8028, Spain
[b]University of Barcelona, Department of Econometrics and Riskcenter-IREA,
School of Economics and Business, Avenida Diagonal, 690, Barcelona 8034, Spain

11.1 INTRODUCTION

Interrelations between the US and Asian markets have strengthened in recent years due to their developing financial relations. However, before investing, good portfolio managers need to know the characteristics of a geographical area, and should analyze the factors that can influence the behavior of assets in a given financial market. Traditionally, one of the factors that can affect the behavior of the equity markets is macroeconomic news announcements. This study analyzes the impact of US macroeconomic news releases in several Asian countries, primarily the emerging markets of Southeast Asia.

The specific Asian countries examined here are the following: first, Japan, representative of the mature Asian market; second, the emerging economies of Southeast Asia divided into two groups—the Asian Tigers (hereinafter *tigers*) of Taiwan, Singapore, Hong Kong, and South Korea (hereinafter Korea), and the Tiger Cub countries (hereinafter *cubs*), comprising the Philippines, Indonesia, Malaysia and Thailand; and third, China, a growing economy with a great influence worldwide.

Southeast Asia is characterized by its high population growth rate, political instability and the fact that it is enjoying a marked economic boom (of the countries analyzed here, Indonesia and Singapore show the greatest development potential). However, the Southeast Asian economies remain vulnerable to economic decisions taken abroad, given that their domestic markets are small and they are heavily dependent on their exports and on foreign energy and technology. The *tigers* emerged between 1945 and 1990, and they present a broad range of characteristics that are similar to those found in the economies of China and Japan. The *tigers'* economies underwent great growth, not only in quantitative terms, but also in terms of the quality of the low-price products they were able to introduce into international markets. The *cubs* achieved industrialization at a later date, following a similar path to that taken by the *tigers*. Subsequently, all these countries have managed to maintain high rates of industrialization and development, becoming attractive destinations for foreign investment.

The Southeast Asian region makes an interesting case study as both *tigers* and *cubs* are growing economies that offer major opportunities for international industry. As developing countries, they are following the lead set by China, the motor of growth in Asia, and, in recent decades, the financial and commercial ties established with the USA have been strengthened considerably, since these countries are making an increasing contribution to global economic development while establishing themselves as key players in international industrialization. Although investors on non-US stock markets are interested in US news releases, their general importance can be expected to vary across economic regions as a result of differences in dependence on international trade, size of the market, foreign ownership and the industrial and economical structures.

The domestic impact of US macroeconomic news announcements has been widely studied in the financial literature (see Bomfim, 2003; Bernanke and Kuttner, 2005; Boyd et al., 2005; Cristiansen and Ranaldo, 2007; Andersen et al., 2007; Zebedee et al., 2008; Brenner et al., 2009; Chuliá et al., 2010; Wongswan, 2006, among others); however, the effect of US news releases on the emerging Asian economies has not been as extensively discussed. For example, Kim (2003) explores the spillover effects of US and Japanese scheduled announcements in the advanced Asia-Pacific stock markets of Australia, Hong Kong and Singapore between the years 1991 and 1999. His results show that both US and Japanese news releases significantly impact on the returns of the other markets. Similarly, Wongswan (2006) finds a significant transmission of information from the US and Japan to Korean and Thai equity markets. Using high-frequency intraday data, this author finds a significant relation between emerging-economy equity volatility and trading volume and developed-economy macroeconomic news announcements at short-time horizons. Finally, Vrugt (2009) studies the impact of US and Japanese macroeconomic news announcements on stock market volatility in Japan, Hong Kong, Korea, and Australia. He finds that overnight conditional variances are significantly higher on announcement days and significantly lower on days before and after announcements, especially for US releases.

This chapter analyzes whether the release of US macroeconomic news announcements affects the returns and volatility of the 10 Asian financial markets analyzed and their correlations with the US market. Moreover, the chapter also studies whether there is an asymmetric effect of news, so that the surprise (computed as the difference between the observed and the expected data) affects the returns, volatility, and correlation differently depending on its sign (good or bad). Finally, the chapter examines whether the pattern observed changed following the onset of the financial crisis in August 2007.

Our study makes a number of contributions to the relevant literature. First, we explore the entire emerging region of Southeast Asia, grouping countries with similar characteristics to determine whether they present any differences in behavior. Second, our sample period incorporates the recent global financial crisis. Third, we also look at the effect of US news announcements on the correlations between the respective markets while the previous literature has focused solely on returns and volatility.

Following Brenner et al. (2009), the methodology for testing the effect of US macroeconomic news announcements on conditional returns, return volatility, and the correlation between the US and the Asian markets is based on the Dynamic Conditional Correlation (DCC) multivariate model of Engle (2002). Our main findings can be summarized as follows. First, our results indicate significant heterogeneity in the impact of the release of "good" and "bad" news announcements on Asian market returns and volatility. Second, there appears to be a relation between the response shown by returns and volatility and a country's level of development. Third, our evidence suggests that the co-movement between the US and the Asian markets is unchanged when US news announcements are released. Finally, we find that the financial crisis has not changed the response of Asian market returns, volatility, and correlations to US macroeconomic news announcements.

The remainder of the chapter is organized as follows. Section 11.2 describes our data. Section 11.3 outlines the methodology we use. Section 11.4 discusses the empirical results and, finally, Section 11.5 concludes.

11.2 DATA

11.2.1 Stock Market Data

We use daily data covering the period from January 1, 2003, until February 29, 2012.[1] The data has been obtained from Bloomberg. The S&P 500 Index and the Nikkei 225 Index are used as benchmarks for the US and Japanese markets, respectively. Among the emerging markets of Southeast Asia, the four *tigers* include South Korea (Kospi Index), Taiwan (Taiwan Stock Exchange Index), Hong Kong (Hang Seng Index), and Singapore (Straits Time Index), and the four *cubs* are made up of Malaysia (FTSE Bursa Malaysia Kuala Lumpur Composite Index), Thailand (FTSE SET Shariah Index), Indonesia (Jakarta Composite Index), and the Philippines (Philippine Stock Exchange Index). Finally, China is represented by the Shanghai A-Share Stock Price Index.

It should be stressed that trading in the US and Asian markets is non-synchronous, so when the US market is operating, the Asian markets are closed, and the latter start negotiating when the US market has already closed. Table 11.1 shows the time (Greenwich Mean Time) in the different countries included in this analysis, indicating that the trading times of the US and Asian markets do not overlap.

As the minimum time difference between any of the Asian countries and the USA is 11 hours, when a news announcement is released in the USA on calendar date t, the

---

[1] The earliest data available for Indonesia and Thailand are from 1 April 2004.

Table 11.1 GMT Hours

Country	Time
USA	GMT −5:00
JAPAN	GMT +8:00
HONG KONG	GMT +7:00
SOUTH KOREA	GMT +8:00
SINGAPORE	GMT +7:00
TAIWAN	GMT +7:00
THE PHILIPPINES	GMT +7:00
INDONESIA	GMT +6:00
MALAYSIA	GMT +7:00
THAILAND	GMT +6:00
CHINA	GMT +7:00

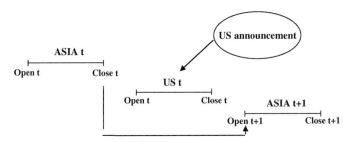

Figure 11.1 Timeline of the US and Asian financial markets.

Asian markets are already closed. When the USA market closes, therefore, the Asian markets open on calendar date $t+1$. As such, the opening price of the Asian markets on calendar date $t+1$ incorporates the information that was released in the USA on calendar date t. We can therefore take the close-to-open (t to $t+1$) returns of the Asian markets to analyze the impact of US news releases on the returns, volatility and correlation of the Asian markets (spillover effects). The timeline described is shown in Figure 11.1.

The market returns that capture the impact of US macroeconomic news releases are calculated over the closing price on the calendar day before the announcements and the opening price one calendar day after for the Asian markets (overnight return on calendar date $t+1$, $\ln(P_{t+1}^{Open}/P_t^{Close})$).

The summary statistics of the overnight returns on the Asian markets are shown in Table 11.2. It can be seen that the means are fairly close to zero, that the return series are leptokurtic and the Jarque–Bera test rejects normality of the returns. These characteristics are typical of high-frequency financial return series.

Table 11.2 Statistical Properties of Overnight Stock Market Index Returns

	Mean	Standard Deviation	Skewness	Kurtosis	Normality
Japan	0.0004	0.0078	0.4413	9.222	3932.348 (0.000)
Hong Kong	0.0005	0.0117	−0.3703	10.307	5370.992 (0.000)
Korea	0.0008	0.0101	−0.5764	8.287	2915.454 (0.000)
Singapore	0.0004	0.0104	−0.5076	8.721	3361.635 (0.000)
Taiwan	0.0014	0.0101	−0.9036	11.584	7662.886 (0.000)
The Philippines	0.0003	0.0063	0.5259	23.502	41966.590 (0.000)
Indonesia	−0.0002	0.0069	0.6405	36.383	96027.360 (0.000)
Malaysia	0.0001	0.0042	−1.0142	22.297	37492.150 (0.000)
Thailand	0.0008	0.0078	−1.0739	15.671	14210.930 (0.000)
China	−0.0010	0.0077	0.9681	27.279	59074.490 (0.000)

Note: *p*-values displayed as (·).

11.2.2 Announcement Data

The announcement data have also been obtained from Bloomberg. For each macroeconomic announcement, we obtain a time series of the real values as well as of the market forecasts based on survey expectations. In line with the literature, the "surprise" is computed as the difference between the real value and the survey median. It should be stressed that, depending on the nature of the macroeconomic news announcement, the sign of the surprise will indicate either "good" or "bad" news. The information provided by the survey is traditionally taken to represent unbiased estimates of the anticipated portion of macroeconomic announcements.[2] Therefore, the survey data enable us to identify the unexpected component in the news when released to the public.

The macroeconomic news announcements that have been analyzed concern the following fundamentals: Gross Domestic Product (GDP), the Consumer Price Index (CPI), the unemployment rate and the Federal Open Market Committee (FOMC) decisions on the federal funds target rate. The GDP is an aggregate indicator describing

[2] See Balduzzi et al. (2001) and Andersen et al. (2003, 2007), among others.

domestic production. It acquires particular relevance here, however, as the aggregate indicator of economic performance. A positive (negative) surprise indicates that the GDP has either increased (decreased) by a surprising amount or decreased (increased) surprisingly little with respect to the previous announcement, and so this is good (bad) news.

The CPI measures the change in prices of a basket of goods and services considered representative of the general consumption of the population. Controlling the CPI is particularly relevant since the price evolution of an economy has a direct influence on monetary policy decisions. A positive (negative) surprise means that the CPI has either increased (decreased) by a surprising amount or decreased (increased) surprisingly little with respect to the previous announcement, and so this is bad (good) news.

The unemployment rate indicates the number of unemployed out of a country's total labor force. As with the CPI announcement, a positive (negative) surprise means that the unemployment rate has either increased (decreased) by a surprising amount or decreased (increased) surprisingly little with respect to the previous announcement, and so this is bad (good) news.

Finally, the announcements of FOMC decisions on the federal funds target rate are analyzed. The committee's decisions regarding the target rate have a major impact on international capital markets, since they provide a broad picture of the economic situation of the country and the expectations of its monetary authority. A positive (negative) surprise indicates that the FOMC announced either a surprisingly large rate increase (cut) or a surprisingly small rate cut (increase), and so this is bad (good) news.

Table 11.3 reports summary statistics for the macroeconomic news surprises. The number of surprises during the sample period is higher for announcements concerning

Table 11.3 Descriptive Statistics of News Announcement Surprises

	Mean	Median	Max	Min	Standard Deviation	N
GDP	−0.700	−0.600	2.200	−3.200	1.165	36
GDP+	0.670	0.500	2.200	0.100	0.617	10
GDP−	−1.227	−1.100	−0.200	−3.200	0.852	26
CPI	0.044	0.100	0.700	−0.400	0.251	80
CPI+	0.236	0.200	0.700	0.100	0.186	42
CPI−	−0.168	−0.100	−0.100	−0.400	0.090	38
Unemployment rate	−0.029	−0.100	0.400	−0.400	0.186	77
Unemployment rate+	0.183	0.200	0.400	0.100	0.089	29
Unemployment rate−	−0.156	−0.100	−0.100	−0.400	0.082	48
Interest rate	−0.007	0.005	0.140	−0.229	0.076	30
Interest rate+	0.027	0.012	0.140	0.001	0.034	21
Interest rate−	−0.086	−0.072	−0.002	−0.229	0.090	9

Note: N is the number of observations for each macroeconomic announcement surprise. Max and Min are the maximum and minimum for the surprise, respectively. + (−) refers to positive (negative) surprises.

the CPI and the unemployment rate. Good news announcements were more common regarding the unemployment rate (62% of releases), and bad news announcements were more frequent in the case of the GDP, the CPI and the FOMC decisions (72%, 52.5%, and 70% of releases, respectively).

11.3 METHODOLOGY

Following Brenner et al. (2009), the methodology for testing the effect of US macroeconomic news announcements on conditional returns, volatility, and the correlation between the US and the Asian markets is based on the Dynamic Conditional Correlation (DCC) multivariate model of Engle (2002). The DCC model has the flexibility of univariate GARCH models but does not suffer from the "curse of dimensionality" as do multivariate GARCH models. The estimation consists of two steps. First, the conditional variance of each variable is estimated using a univariate GARCH procedure. Second, the standardized regression residuals obtained in the first step are used to model conditional correlations that vary over time.

To analyze the response of Asian markets to the arrival of US macroeconomic news, the evolution in the returns and volatility of country i is modeled as

$$r_t^i = \mu_i^e + \rho_i r_{t-1}^i + sr_t^i + \varepsilon_t^i$$
$$\varepsilon_t^i = \sqrt{h_t^i} e_t^i \qquad e_t^i \big| F_{t-1} \sim N(0, 1) \qquad \qquad (11.1)$$
$$h_t^i = sh_t^i \left[\omega_i^e + \alpha_i^e \left(e_{t-1}^i \right)^2 + \beta_i^e h_{t-1}^i \right]$$

where r_t^i is the overnight return on calendar day $t+1$ of the Asian market i, F_{t-1} denotes the information set at time $t-1$, $sr_t^i = (\gamma_i^{+e} I_t^{+e} + \gamma_i^{-e} I_t^{-e}) S_t^e$ and $sh_t^i = 1 + (\delta_i^{+e} I_t^{+e} + \delta_i^{-e} I_t^{-e}) |S_t^e|$. In the above specification, $I_t^{+e}(I_t^{-e})$ is a dummy variable equal to one if a positive (negative) surprise macroeconomic event of type e occurred at time t and equal to zero otherwise and, finally, S_t^e are news surprises. As standard in the finance literature, Eq. (11.1) specifies a first-order autocorrelation model to control for microstructure effects and gradual convergence to equilibrium.

The above specification enables us to identify the asymmetric effects of surprises on conditional returns and volatilities. The coefficient $\gamma_i^{+e}(\gamma_i^{-e})$ captures the impact of a positive (negative) surprise announcement on the mean returns. Similarly, the dummy coefficient $\delta_i^{e+}(\delta_i^{e-})$ proxies for the impact of positive (negative) absolute macroeconomic news surprises on conditional volatility.[3]

[3] Following Brenner et al. (2009), macroeconomic news announcement surprises enter the variance equation as absolute values due to the existence of evidence (Jones et al., 1998; Bomfim, 2003, among others) that it is the mere occurrence of a macroeconomic announcement surprise, regardless of its sign, that impacts conditional return variance.

Finally, to analyze the impact of news announcements on conditional correlations the following exponential smoothing function is used:

$$q_t^{ij} = sq_t^i \left[\lambda q_{t-1}^{ij} + (1 - \lambda) \eta_{t-1}^i \eta_{t-1}^j \right] \tag{11.2}$$

where $sq_t^i = 1 + (\theta_{i,j}^{+e} I_t^{+e} + \theta_{i,j}^{-e} I_t^{-e}) |S_t^e|$.[4] To deal with the problem identified by Forbes and Rigobon (2002) that shocks to the conditional covariance among asset returns in proximity of certain macroeconomic announcements may be due to shocks to return volatility, the residuals are standardized as follows:

$$\eta_t^i = \frac{\varepsilon_t^i}{\sqrt{sh_t^i \cdot h_t^i}} \quad \text{and} \quad \eta_t^i = \frac{\varepsilon_t^j}{\sqrt{sh_t^j \cdot h_t^j}} \tag{11.3}$$

In Eq. (11.2), the coefficient $\theta_{i,j}^{+e} (\theta_{i,j}^{-e})$ captures the impact of a positive (negative) surprise announcement on the conditional covariance between any pair of standardized residuals (countries i and j).

The above model enables us to examine the effect of US news releases on the returns, volatilities and correlations of Asian markets. Moreover, we can also observe whether there exists an asymmetric effect, that is, if the impact of the news differs depending on whether the surprise is positive or negative.

In order to estimate the model a conditional normal distribution for the innovation vector is assumed and the quasi-maximum likelihood method is applied. Bollerslev and Wooldridge (1992) show that the standard errors calculated by this method are robust even when the normality assumption is violated.

11.4 EMPIRICAL RESULTS

Tables 11.4–11.7 display the estimation results. An inspection of the coefficients shows that, in general, the number of significant coefficients increases as the level of development of the country falls. Of the potentially significant values (16 coefficients for each country), Japan presents 1 significant coefficient, Hong Kong 3, Singapore 5, Korea 6, Taiwan 7, The Philippines 5, Indonesia 12, Malaysia 8, Thailand 10, and China 9. Given that *tigers*, *cubs*, and China are more exposed to the global economy with exports representing a very high percentage of their GDP, these results could be explained by the fact that export-oriented firms weigh heavily in the Asia-Pacific market indexes.

Japan is only affected by announcements concerning GDP. Bad news in relation to GDP (lower than expected data) increases the volatility of the Nikkei 225 by 18.6%.

---

[4] In order to estimate conditional correlations, the return and variance equations in (11.1) are also estimated for the US market. In this case, r_t^i refers to the over night return on calendar day t of the US market calculated as $\ln(P_t^{Open}/P_{t-1}^{Close})$.

Table 11.4 Estimates of the DCC Model for the GDP

	Impact on Returns		Impact on Variance		Impact on Correlation	
	γ_i^{+e}	γ_i^{-e}	δ_i^{+e}	δ_i^{-e}	θ_i^{+e}	θ_i^{-e}
Japan	0.001270	0.000357	0.747520	0.185660*	−0.874121	1.192541
	(0.68)	(0.77)	(0.05)	(0.00)	(0.15)	(0.26)
Hong	−0.000300	0.000625	0.171500	0.179400*	(1.589632)	(0.896521)
Kong	(0.94)	(0.66)	(0.52)	(0.02)	(0.65)	(0.81)
Korea	−0.002854	−0.000868	−0.239600*	0.050600	3.569003	0.122303
	(0.68)	(0.62)	(0.01)	(0.44)	(0.63)	(0.80)
Singapore	−0.001983	0.000074	−0.245600*	0.109400	−0.080853	0.269842
	(0.52)	(0.92)	(0.00)	(0.1)	(0.25)	(0.14)
Taiwan	−0.002945	−0.000218	−0.274100*	−0.179500*	−0.059647	0.098721
	(0.11)	(0.83)	(0.01)	(0.00)	(0.82)	(0.25)
The	−0.004348*	−0.000897	−0.049400	−0.038000	0.012547	1.254863
Philippines	(0.00)	(0.36)	(0.71)	(0.33)	(0.89)	(0.48)
Indonesia	−0.000421	−0.001133*	5.714933*	0.100044*	−0.158725	0.048523
	(0.96)	(0.03)	(0.00)	(0.02)	(0.82)	(0.12)
Malaysia	−0.000303	−0.000231	−0.405600*	−0.003466	0.987235	0.542186
	(0.76)	(0.69)	(0.00)	(0.91)	(0.85)	(0.74)
Thailand	−0.002091	0.002041*	2.360752*	0.366151*	0.498532	0.215525
	(0.66)	(0.00)	(0.00)	(0.00)	(0.82)	(0.04)
China	0.003880*	−0.000988	1.519956*	2.760999*	−0.869571*	0.596452*
	(0.00)	(0.11)	(0.00)	(0.00)	(0.00)	(0.00)

*Significant coefficients at the 5% level.
Note: p-values displayed as (·).

Japanese stock market returns and volatility remain indifferent to all other US news announcements. This result is in line with the findings reported by Kim (2003), who likewise finds that the response of Japan to US news announcements is not as great as that of Hong Kong and Singapore.

Among the *tigers*, the news announcements that have most impact on Hong Kong are primarily those that report signs of possible recession in the USA. These include worse than expected GDP data (bad news), which increase the volatility of the Hang Seng Index, or a higher than anticipated unemployment rate (bad news), which increase volatility in the Hong Kong market. Good news, such as a lower than expected interest rate, increases the returns of the benchmark index in Hong Kong. Korea and Singapore are more markedly influenced by news announcements in the USA. In the case of news releases related to GDP, a higher than expected outcome (good news) decreases market volatility in both countries, while bad news about the US GDP has no impact. The volatility of both the Kospi and Straits Time Indexes falls after reports of a lower than expected inflation rate. Good news regarding the unemployment rate is well received, as market volatility in Korea decreases and the returns of the benchmark index

Table 11.5 Estimates of the DCC Model for the CPI

	Impact on Returns		Impact on Variance		Impact on Correlation	
	γ_i^{+e}	γ_i^{-e}	δ_i^{+e}	δ_i^{-e}	θ_i^{+e}	θ_i^{-e}
Japan	−0.001153	0.000869	−0.075800	0.205500	−1.387669	1.034019
	(0.75)	(0.82)	(0.82)	(0.56)	(0.56)	(0.11)
Hong Kong	−0.003647	0.001037	0.232500	0.024300	−0.3978631	3.187014
	(0.48)	(0.87)	(0.28)	(0.95)	(0.57)	(0.12)
Korea	0.001072	−0.006707	0.511000	−0.617000*	0.254125	0.154821
	(0.83)	(0.41)	(0.05)	(0.04)	(0.26)	(0.25)
Singapore	0.001828	0.003527	0.252700	0.169800	(0.318547)	0.985621
	(0.79)	(0.60)	(0.32)	(0.67)	(0.95)	(0.52)
Taiwan	−0.002700	−0.012100*	−0.060100	−0.331200	0.289641	0.364527
	(0.53)	(0.01)	(0.79)	(0.30)	(0.83)	(0.62)
The Philippines	−0.001955	−0.005931	−1.076626*	−0.109816	0.564218	0.736212
	(0.34)	(0.05)	(0.00)	(0.65)	(0.39)	(0.25)
Indonesia	−0.006151*	−0.001938	0.476500*	0.678800*	0.269512*	0.821541
	(0.00)	(0.61)	(0.00)	(0.00)	(0.04)	(0.23)
Malaysia	−0.000550	−0.001534	−0.683700*	0.650000*	0.900235	0.062512
	(0.61)	(0.33)	(0.00)	(0.00)	(0.89)	(0.15)
Thailand	0.003641*	0.010923*	0.070975*	−0.378907*	0.492355	1.018961
	(0.00)	(0.00)	(0.00)	(0.00)	(0.22)	(0.62)
China	0.002145*	0.009534*	−0.417172*	2.097830*	0.552321	0.864251
	(0.02)	(0.00)	(0.00)	(0.00)	(0.13)	(0.11)

*Significant coefficients at the 5% level.
Note: p-values displayed as (·).

in Singapore increase. Bad news about the unemployment rate increases the volatility of both markets. Lower than predicted interest rates (good news) increase returns and diminish the volatility of the Korean market. Finally, Taiwan is the *tiger* that is affected by most events. Good news about US GDP reduces market volatility in Taiwan, and somewhat unexpectedly, bad news about US GDP also decreases the volatility of the Taiwanese economy. Good news about the CPI decreases the index returns and good news about the unemployment rate decreases its volatility. As for the interest rate, bad news increases both the returns and the volatility of the index, while good news decreases the market volatility.

In the case of the *cubs*, positive GDP news reduces the returns of the benchmark index while negative CPI news reduces index volatility in the Philippines. Bad news regarding the unemployment rate increases financial market volatility whereas good news reduces it. Finally, lower than anticipated interest rates increase the volatility of the Philippine Stock Exchange Index. Twelve coefficients are found to be positive in the case of Indonesia. For example, both positive and negative news announcements concerning GDP and CPI increase market volatility, while negative news releases about

Table 11.6 Estimates of the GARCH Model for the Unemployment Rate

	Impact on Returns		Impact on Variance		Impact on Correlation	
	γ_i^{+e}	γ_i^{-e}	δ_i^{+e}	δ_i^{-e}	θ_i^{+e}	θ_i^{-e}
Japan	−0.011100	0.002163	0.686800	0.296000	−0.638440	0.907516
	(0.24)	(0.71)	(0.30)	(0.57)	(0.25)	(0.49)
Hong Kong	−0.017593	0.008899	1.130583*	−0.190983	0.424799	0.30545*
	(0.12)	(0.15)	(0.01)	(0.52)	(0.20)	(0.00)
Korea	−0.017029	0.000165	1.463060*	−0.973817*	−0.417070	0.61198*
	(0.25)	(0.97)	(0.00)	(0.00)	(0.41)	(0.00)
Singapore	−0.004297	0.014300*	0.937200*	−0.382300	−0.326841	0.841511
	(0.67)	(0.00)	(0.04)	(0.26)	(0.32)	(0.23)
Taiwan	0.006531	−0.001186	0.179100	−0.814000*	0.896512	0.524143
	(0.49)	(0.74)	(0.60)	(0.00)	(0.11)	(0.14)
The Philippines	−0.003869	0.001297	3.654532*	−1.308812*	−0.348851	0.727411
	(0.60)	(0.37)	(0.00)	(0.00)	(0.25)	(0.23)
Indonesia	−0.002613	−0.001058	1.889536*	−1.690238*	−0.844275	−1.700112
	(0.77)	(0.28)	(0.00)	(0.00)	(0.11)	(0.44)
Malaysia	−0.007200	0.000322	4.196010*	−0.797554*	−0.30014*	0.258141
	(0.00)	(0.80)	(0.00)	(0.00)	(0.03)	(0.39)
Thailand	−0.007804	0.008466	−0.736383*	1.255180*	0.314785	0.992121
	(0.17)	(0.35)	(0.00)	(0.00)	(0.71)	(0.59)
China	−0.001114	−0.003509	0.516497	3.893653*	0.009821	0.965111
	(0.78)	(0.05)	(0.10)	(0.00)	(0.66)	(0.38)

*Significant coefficients at the 5% level.
Note: p-values displayed as (·).

these two macroeconomic variables reduce market returns. Negative and positive news releases about the unemployment rate affect the market volatility of the Jakarta Index. Good news about GDP reduces market volatility in Malaysia, while both good and bad news about inflation and unemployment affect the volatility of the benchmark index in this country. As for the interest rate, a lower than expected data improves market performance and reduces its volatility. Finally, in Thailand, announcements about US GDP, both positive and negative, increase market volatility. Additionally, both negative and positive news about inflation affect the returns and the volatility of this market. As for the unemployment rate, both good and bad news have an impact on financial market volatility. Finally, lower than expected interest rates reduce market volatility.

US macroeconomic news releases also have an effect on the Chinese market. Announcements, both good and bad, regarding US GDP affect the volatility of the financial market. A higher than anticipated GDP outcome increases the returns of the Shanghai Index. Similarly, both good and bad news about inflation affect the returns and the volatility of the Chinese benchmark index. Finally, good news about the unemployment rate and higher than expected interest rates increase the volatility of this market.

Table 11.7 Estimates of the GARCH Model for the Interest Rate

	Impact on Returns		Impact on Variance		Impact on Correlation	
	γ_i^{+e}	γ_i^{-e}	δ_i^{+e}	δ_i^{-e}	θ_i^{+e}	θ_i^{-e}
Japan	0.055479	0.037867	0.639483	−1.619943	0.826241	−1.402871
	(0.53)	(0.12)	(0.85)	(0.12)	(0.15)	(0.29)
Hong Kong	−0.017274	0.099444*	−1.137140	−1.348582	0.252181	1.030454
	(0.73)	(0.00)	(0.64)	(0.14)	(0.68)	(0.45)
Korea	0.051459	0.095780*	−3.851420	−2.110422*	−0.206874	−0.87451
	(0.32)	(0.00)	(0.06)	(0.00)	(0.21)	(0.19)
Singapore	0.041635	0.074877*	−0.661143	−2.938556*	1.451691	−0.148989*
	(0.46)	(0.00)	(0.82)	(0.00)	(0.50)	(0.03)
Taiwan	0.085453*	0.055063	6.591156*	−2.269191*	0.09851	0.105141
	(0.00)	(0.11)	(0.00)	(0.00)	(0.18)	(0.31)
The Philippines	0.044919	0.020911	0.512860	3.851027*	0.206981	−0.727154
	(0.13)	(0.39)	(0.79)	(0.00)	(0.39)	(0.62)
Indonesia	0.002350*	0.093844*	−7.142857*	−3.574224*	1.074554	−1.285211
	(0.00)	(0.00)	(0.00)	(0.00)	(0.45)	(0.99)
Malaysia	−0.009912	0.024525*	0.919318	−2.724842*	−1.267711	−0.032882
	(0.60)	(0.01)	(0.65)	(0.00)	(0.33)	(0.41)
Thailand	0.025715	0.045006	3.139486	−3.376319*	−1.191455	−0.011254
	(0.67)	(0.10)	(0.40)	(0.00)	(0.50)	(0.51)
China	−0.019703	0.017141	3.988248*	−1.139869	0.152210*	−0.480091
	(0.54)	(0.70)	(0.01)	(0.10)	(0.00)	(0.97)

*Significant coefficients at the 5% level.
Note: p-values displayed as (·).

An examination of news release types shows that the response tends to vary across markets. Thus, the announcement that has the greatest impact on markets is a lower than expected (good news) interest rate, which causes a decrease in the volatility of six of the 10 markets analyzed (the *tigers* of Korea, Singapore and Taiwan and the *cubs* of Indonesia, Malaysia and Thailand). Similarly, a lower than expected interest rate increases the returns of five markets, three *tigers* (Hong Kong, Korea, and Singapore), and two *cubs* (Indonesia and Malaysia).

As regards news announcements concerning the GDP, negative surprises (i.e., the GDP has fallen by a surprising amount or increased only slightly with respect to the previously reported figure) increase the volatility of five markets (Japan, Hong Kong, Indonesia, Thailand, and China). Conversely, positive surprises reduce market volatility in three of the *tigers* (Korea, Singapore, and Taiwan) and in one of the *cubs* (Malaysia).

Bad news regarding the unemployment rate increases market volatility in three of the *tigers* (Hong Kong, Korea, and Singapore) and three of the *cubs* (The Philippines, Indonesia, and Malaysia) and good news reduces volatility in two of the *tigers* (Korea and Taiwan) and in three of the *cubs* (The Philippines, Indonesia, and Malaysia). Finally, news releases concerning the CPI have a varied and uneven impact across the countries.

An examination of the impact of US news announcements on correlations indicates that overall the co-movement between the US and the Asian markets is unchanged when the US news releases are made. In the case of Japan, our result is in line with the findings reported in Karolyi and Stulz (1996) who also find that macroeconomic announcements do not significantly affect co-movements between US and Japanese share returns. In the case of the Asia-Pacific countries (i.e., those that are more exposed to the global economy), our results are more closely in line with Albuquerque and Vega (2009), who analyze the effects that real-time domestic and foreign news about fundamentals have on the co-movement between stock returns of a economy exposed to the global economy, Portugal, and a large economy, USA. They find that US macroeconomic news does not affect stock market co-movements.

Finally, to determine whether the responses of the Asian markets to US macroeconomic news releases have changed after the global financial crisis, the sample was split into two subsamples. The first subsample covers the period January 1, 2003 until July 31, 2007 and the second subsample runs from August 15, 2007 until February 29, 2012.[5] Our results (not reported) show that responses to macroeconomic news announcements have not changed notably.

11.5 CONCLUSION

This chapter analyzes the effect of US macroeconomic news releases on the returns and volatility of several Asian countries, primarily the emerging economies of Southeast Asia, and their correlations with the US market. The study covers the period from January 2003 until February 2012, examining the impact of news releases concerning the gross domestic product, the consumer price index, the unemployment rate, and the Federal Open Market Committee decisions on the target rate. To carry out this study, a Dynamic Conditional Correlation model is used, which incorporates the possibility that the response of returns, volatility, and correlations might be asymmetric depending on the sign of the news item.

The results provide interesting insights into the effects of US macroeconomic news announcements on Asian markets. First, there appears to be a relation between the response shown by returns and volatility and a country's level of development. Japan, representative of a mature market, remains quite indifferent to US news arrivals. However, as the level of market maturity falls, the effect of US macroeconomic news announcements becomes greater; hence, the *tigers* are more strongly influenced by US

---

[5] Results (not reported) remain unchanged when we fix the start of the financial crisis as coinciding with the collapse of Lehman Brothers.

news releases than Japan, while the *cubs* are even more susceptible to them. Finally, China is very strongly affected by US macroeconomic news releases. Given that the *tigers, cubs*, and China are more susceptible to the vagaries of the global economy, their export earnings representing a very high percentage of their GDP, these results could be explained by the fact that export-oriented firms weigh heavily in the Asia–Pacific market indexes.

Our results also show that on average the conditional correlations do not change on news announcement days. Finally, we find that the financial crisis has not necessarily increased the sensitivity of Asian market returns, volatility and correlations to macroeconomic news releases. Market participants should be careful in picking markets in the emerging Asia as the results show that these markets are also dependent on the US economy.

ACKNOWLEDGMENT

The authors are grateful to the Spanish Ministry of Economy and Competitiveness support Grant ECO2012-35584.

REFERENCES

Albuquerque, R., Vega, C., 2009. Economic news and international stock market co-movements. Review of Finance 13 (3), 401–465.

Andersen, T.G., Bollerslev, T., Diebold, F.X., Vega, C., 2003. Real-time price discovery in global, stock, bond, and foreign exchange markets. Journal of International Economics 73 (2), 251–277.

Andersen, T.G., Bollerslev, T., Diebold, F.X., Vega, C., 2007. Micro effects of macro announcements: real-time price discovery in foreign exchange. American Economic Review 93 (1), 38–62.

Balduzzi, P., Elton, E., Green, C., 2001. Economic news and bond prices: evidence from the U.S. treasury market. Journal of Financial and Quantitative Analysis 36 (4), 523–543.

Bernanke, B.S., Kuttner, K.N., 2005. What explains the stock market's reaction to federal reserve policy? Journal of Finance 60 (3), 1221–1257.

Bollerslev, T., Wooldridge, J.M., 1992. Quasi-maximum likelihood estimation and inference in dynamic models with time-varying covariances. Econometric Reviews 11 (2), 143–172.

Bomfim, A.N., 2003. Pre-announcement effects, news, and volatility: monetary policy and the stock market. Journal of Banking and Finance 27 (1), 133–151.

Boyd, J.H., Jagannathan, R., Hu, J., 2005. The stock market's reaction to unemployment news: why bad news is usually good for stocks. Journal of Finance 60 (2), 649–672.

Brenner, M., Pasquariello, P., Subrahmanyam, M., 2009. On the volatility and comovement of U.S. financial markets around macroeconomic news announcements. Journal of Financial and Quantitative Analysis 44 (6), 1265–1289.

Christiansen, C., Ranaldo, A., 2007. Realized bond-stock correlation: macroeconomic announcement effects. Journal of Futures Markets 27 (5), 439–469.

Chulia, H., Martens, M., Dijk, D., 2010. Asymmetric effects of federal funds target rate changes on S&P100 stock returns, volatilities and correlations. Journal of Banking and Finance 34 (4), 834–839.

Engle, R., 2002. Dynamic conditional correlation -- a simple class of multivariate GARCH models. Journal of Business and Economic Statistics 20 (3), 339–350.

Forbes, K.J., Rigobon, R., 2002. No contagion, only interdependence: measuring stock market comovements. The Journal of Finance 57 (5), 2223–2261.

Jones, C.M., Lamont, O., Lumsdaine, R.L., 1998. Macroeconomic news and bond market volatility. Journal of Financial Economics 47 (3), 315–337.

Karolyi, G.A., Stulz, R.M., 1996. Why do markets move together? an investigation of US-Japan stock return co-movements. Journal of Finance 51 (3), 951–985.

Kim, S.J., 2003. The spillover effects of US and Japanese public information news in advanced Asia-pacific stock markets. Pacific-Basin Finance Journal 11 (5), 611–630.

Vrugt, E.B., 2009. U.S. and Japanese macroeconomic news and stock market volatility in Asia-pacific. Pacific-Basin Finance Journal 17 (5), 611–627.

Wongswan, J., 2006. Transmission of information across international equity markets. Review of Financial Studies 19 (4), 1157–1189.

Zebedee, A.A., Bentzen, E., Hansen, P.R., Lunde, A., 2008. The Greenspan effect on equity markets: An intraday examination of US monetary policy announcements. Financial Markets and Portfolio Management 22 (1), 3–20.

CHAPTER 12

Monetary Policy in Taiwan: The Implications of Liquidity

Logan Kelly[a], Jane Binner[b], Chia-Ling Chang[c], and Yi-Heng Tseng[d]
[a]University of Wisconsin, College of Business and Economics, 23D South Hall,
410 S. Third Street, River Falls, WI 54022, USA
[b]University of Birmingham, Birmingham Business School, University House, Birmingham, B15 2TT, UK
[c]National Chengchi University, Department of Economics, No. 64, Sec. 2, ZhiNan Rd., Taipei City,
Wenshan District, 11605, Taiwan, ROC
[d]Yuan Ze University, College of Management, No. 135, Neicuo Rd., Zhongli City, Taoyuan County 320, Taiwan, ROC

12.1 INTRODUCTION

With apologies to Mark Twain, reporting practices of modern central banks beg the expression, "Lies, damn lies *and monetary data.*" Although demonstrably wrong in their construction, simple-sum measures of the money stock continue to be the official data published by most central banks around the world and are used to guide policy decisions whenever monetary quantity variables are part of that process. Moreover, "whether by tradition or ease of access, academic research also persists in using simple sum monetary quantity aggregates to test hypotheses about the effects of money on economic activity" (Belongia, 2000, Chapter 1, p. 1).

We are confident in our belief that conventional wisdom changes only slowly. As Belongia (2000) states, p. 1, little more that 40 years have passed since Friedman and Schwartz, in *Monetary Statistics of the United States* (1970) ended their discussion of the potential usefulness of weighted monetary aggregates by concluding that, so far there is only the barest of answers [of how to do it properly], p. 152. Papers by Andersson and Jordan (1968) reporting a primary linkage between money and nominal spending (and the ineffectiveness of fiscal actions) marked a mid-point of sweeping change in orthodox economics. By the end of the 1970s, the demand for money appeared to be a stable function of a few key macroeconomic variables, changes in the supply of money appeared to have significant short-run effects on output, and inflation appeared to be closely related to the trend rate of money growth (see, e.g., Belongia, 1996 for more details). Many economists, however, believe that the link between monetary growth and inflation has weakened over the last two decades. This is thought to be due in part to rapid innovations in the financial sector, see Crowder (1998). By the mid 1980s, it had become apparent throughout the developed world that increased competition within the banking sector and the computerization of the financial world was beginning to have substantial effects on the relative user costs (prices) of bank liabilities and the ever-increasing array of substitutes for them. It is now well established that the substantial financial innovations of the 1980s introduced instability into estimated demand functions for broad money. It was largely for this reason that the case for monetary targeting was discredited (see, e.g., Friedman, 1996).

Recent empirical work (Belongia and Chrystal, 1991; Drake and Chrystal, 1994, 1997) puts forward the view that the breakdown in the demand for money function during the 1980s outlined above is mainly attributable to the use of conventional simple sum aggregates that assume the assets that comprise the aggregate are perfect substitutes. It is now widely acknowledged that the simple sum procedure traditionally used by central banks to aggregate monetary assets is inappropriate in the absence of perfect substitutability between the component assets (see, e.g., Drake et al., 2000). Simply summing the constituent component assets to form the aggregate creates flawed index numbers because aggregating any set of commodities with equal weights implies that each good is a perfect substitute for every other good in the group.

The simple sum aggregation method will lead to particularly severe mismeasurement of monetary services during periods of significant financial development, since it is during these times that interest rate yields on the various components of broad money are changing most over time. The introduction of new instruments and technological progress in making transactions has almost certainly had diverse effects on the productivity and liquidity of monetary assets; thus, the use of equal weights for the user costs of the constituent component assets is wholly inappropriate during periods of high financial innovation.

Barnett (1980) first applied index number formulation devised by Divisia (1925) to the problem of measuring a monetary price and quantity aggregate. A Divisia quantity index of money measures the flow of monetary services from a stock of money holdings. The underlying assumption is that individuals hold monetary assets both for the liquidity services they provide and the return they yield. Thus, monetary assets that yield return are the joint product of a transaction vehicle and investment asset. Therefore, any proper measurement of the monetary service flow must account for the investment service provided by component assets which cannot in any economic sence be considered money. The Divisia index belongs to a class of superlative indices that provide a third-order approximation of the first difference of any unknown aggregator function (see Diewert, 1976, 1978).

The Divisia index has its roots firmly based in microeconomic aggregation theory and statistical index number theory. Belongia (2000) provide a survey of the relevant literature, while Fisher et al. (1993), and more recently, Hancock (2005) review the construction of Divisia indices and associated problems. An empirically weighted monetary aggregate has been developed for the UK by Drake and Mills (2005) and extensions of Divisia to incorporate the risk of assets have been derived by Barnett and Liu (2000) for the USA and Elger and Binner (2004) for the UK.

The financial system of an advanced economy provides an array of monetary assets, which vary considerably in their ability to facilitate transactions, term to maturity, and rates of return. In other words, monetary assets differ in terms of the kinds of monetary services they provide, their ability to provide transactions services, and their ability to serve as stores of value. A Divisia index formulation is able to overcome the drawbacks of the simple sum provided the marginal rates of substitution between all asset pairs within the aggregate are independent of quantities consumed of goods not in the aggregate; that is, as above, the asset represents a weakly separable commodity group.

The Bank of Taiwan long ago realized the importance of the theoretical developments in the monetary aggregation literature (Shih, 2000, p. 227). The principles outlined in the monetary aggregation literature have gained widespread acceptance among economists as well as practitioners around the world. Lucas (2000, p. 271), for example, considers US data and states that "I share the widely held opinion that M1 is too narrow an aggregate for this period [the 1990s], and I think that the Divisia approach offers much the best prospects for resolving the difficulty." Seminal work on the performance of UK household sector money was conducted by Drake and Chrystal (1997), who concluded that there "was a stable underlying demand for monetary assets on the part of the UK household sector, when Divisia aggregates are used, for a period stretching from the mid-1970s to the early 1990s—a period of substantial change in the UK financial system." In a later study using a UK MSI (Divisia) aggregate, Drake et al. (2000) concluded that "the behavior of Divisia monetary aggregates be taken seriously by both policy-makers and academic economists who use 'money' in their research." Recent evidence using a Euro Divisia further finds that the Divisia index outperforms the Simple Sum index when evaluated in a nonlinear framework (see Binner et al., 2008 for details).

Our hypothesis developed over a series of studies and summarized in Gazely and Binner (2000) is that measures of money constructed using the Divisia index number formulation are superior indicators of monetary conditions when compared to their simple sum counterparts. This hypothesis is reinforced by a growing body of evidence from empirical studies around the world which demonstrate that weighted index number measures may be able to overcome the drawbacks of the simple sum. Ultimately, such evidence could reinstate money as a meaningful macroeconomic variable, which should not be ignored when setting policy.

We offer an exploratory study of the relevance of the Divisia monetary aggregate for Taiwan over the period 1970 to date. We explore the potential of Divisia monetary aggregates in a small macroeconomic model, using vector autoregressive models. The results of our simple monetary experiment using vector autoregressions to evaluate the link between money growth and inflation are presented in Section 12.4 while Section 12.5 concludes and offers suggestions for future research.

12.2 FINANCIAL INNOVATION AND THE DIVISIA MONETARY AGGREGATE IN TAIWAN

The banking system in Taiwan was heavily regulated by the Central Bank and the Ministry of Finance until September 1989, which saw the introduction of the revised Banking Law. At the beginning of the 1980s, drastic economic, social, and political changes took place creating a long-term macroeconomic imbalance. Rising oil prices caused consumer prices to rise by 16.3% in 1981, followed by a period of near-zero inflation in the mid-1980s, although from the 1990s onwards inflation has fluctuated around 5%. The control of inflation has not been the mainstay of recent economic policy in Taiwan, in contrast to the experience of the western world. Rather, policy has focused more on achieving balanced economic and social development.

Major financial liberalization measures were implemented in Taiwan in the late 1980s. In July 1987, trade-related foreign exchange controls were abolished and capital flow-related foreign exchange controls greatly relaxed. The entry of new securities firms was permitted in January 1988, with the result that the number of securities firms increased from 60 to 150 within the first year (Shih, 2000, p. 227). The limit on daily fluctuations in stock prices was raised from 3% to 5% in 1988 and to 7% the following year. In December 1990, foreign institutional investors were allowed to invest directly in the local stock market. In respect of the banking sector, the revised Banking Law in September 1989 resulted in bank interest rates on deposits and loans being completely liberalized and new private commercial banks were allowed to be established. As of the end of 1993, 16 new private banks had begun operating.

This financial revolution in Taiwan over the last three decades has yielded new types of financial assets and liabilities and new markets have been created, as outlined above. These changes have manifested themselves throughout the global economy in the emergence of competition and merger activity between the traditional commercial banks and previously distinct financial institutions. For example, the banks introduced interest payments on formerly non-interest bearing cheque accounts together with a wide range of new financial products, stimulating product innovation.

Along with the process of price and entry deregulation, local financial markets expanded rapidly and financial price variables (such as interest rates, exchange rates, and stock prices) became flexible and increasingly sensitive to market conditions. The resultant volatility in these financial prices in the second half of the 1980s which was unparalleled in Taiwanese post-Second World War history, deeply affected the portfolio behavior of households and firms. Consequently, the narrowly defined monetary aggregate, M1B, which is vulnerable to deposit-shift behavior, fluctuated significantly, Shih (2000, p. 227).

Faced with the increasing instability of money demand for M1B, in 1990 the central bank replaced M1B with the broadly defined monetary aggregate M2 as the intermediate target variable of monetary policy. Since differing degrees of monetary services are provided by the component assets under the definition of the broad aggregate, M2, this shift to M2 as a policy target has aroused concern as to whether the traditional M2, which sums the balances of component assets with equal weights, can serve as an appropriate measure of monetary service flows in society. One solution to this is to apply a Divisia weighting strategy to the component assets to create admissible monetary aggregates.

We explore the econometric performance of Divisia indices in Taiwan, extending the work of Shih (2000) and Binner et al. (2002). Our objective is to provide an updated picture of the policy relevance of Divisia monetary aggregates and to offer insights into how liquidity measurement and management can be enhanced in the future across different asset risk classes and different risk regimes as a comparative approach to obtain valuable feedback for policy implementation in Taiwan.

12.3 DATA AND METHODOLOGY

12.3.1 Divisia Aggregation

Following Anderson and Jones (2011) and Barnett (1980), we construct Divisia money using the Törnqvist-Theil discrete time approximation of the Divisia service flow index number (see Törnqvist, 1936; Theil, 1967),

$$M_t = M_{t-1} \prod_{n=1}^{N} \left(\frac{m_{n,t}}{m_{n,t-1}} \right)^{\frac{\omega_{n,t} + \omega_{n,t-1}}{2}}, \tag{12.1}$$

where $m_{n,t}$ is the quantity of monetary asset n held in period t, and

$$\omega_{n,t} = \frac{\psi_{n,t} m_{n,t}}{\sum_{i=1}^{N} \psi_{i,t} m_{i,t}} \tag{12.2}$$

is the total expenditure share on monetary asset n held in period t. The Törnqvist-Theil index is simply Simpson's rule applied to the Divisia index number.

Key to the construction of this aggregate is $\psi_{n,t}$, the user cost of monetary asset n held in period t,

$$\psi_{n,t} = \frac{R_t - r_{n,t}}{1 + R_t}, \tag{12.3}$$

which was formally derived by Barnett (1978). The user cost of a monetary asset is a function of $r_{n,t}$, which is the own rate of return on of monetary asset n held in period t, and R_t, which is the rate of return of a pure investment asset, i.e., a "benchmark asset" that provides no liquidity service. While the own rate of return on such a benchmark asset is not available as an observable series, we proxy the benchmark rate by adding a liquidity premium of 100 basis points to the maximum own rate of return of the monetary assets included in the aggregate (see, e.g., El-Shagi and Kelly (2013) for more on the construction of the benchmark rate).

12.3.2 Divisia Money and the Official Aggregates

Kelly (2009) and Kelly et al. (2011) showed that the simple sum monetary stock can be decomposed into the following two stocks

$$SSUM_t = CSM_t + ISM_t, \tag{12.4}$$

where CSM_t is the current stock of money, i.e., the present value of the contemporaneous and future monetary service flows, and ISM_t is the investment stock of money, i.e., the present value of the contemporaneous and future investment returns. Thus, simple sum aggregates conflate monetary and investment stocks.

Kelly (2009) further showed that the conflation of the monetary and investment stocks of money causes simple sum aggregates to obfuscate the dynamics of the money-interest rate relationship. To see this, Kelly examined the first derivative of each stock with respect to the return yielded by each monetary asset. Those derivatives are repeated here:

$$\frac{\partial}{\partial r_{nt}} CSM = -\frac{m_{nt}}{R_t} \quad \forall n = 1 \ldots N, \tag{12.5}$$

$$\frac{\partial}{\partial r_{nt}} ISM = \frac{m_{nt}}{R_t} \quad \forall n = 1 \ldots N. \tag{12.6}$$

Note that (12.5) and (12.6) are identical, except that they have opposite signs. Figure 12.1 demonstrates how the simple sum money stock obscures the dynamics of the monetary stock. Both the Divisia money stock (CSM), i.e., the money stock implied by the Divisia

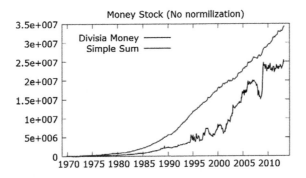

Figure 12.1 Simple sum and Divisia money stock (CSM).

service flow, and the simple sum stocks are plotted. As can be shown, simple sum is smoother and overstates the true money stock, both results are as expected given (12.4).

12.3.3 Data

In order to construct Divisia monetary aggregates for Taiwan, component assets based on the definition of M2 have been classified into the following categories provided in Table 12.1. According to the historical definitions of money in Taiwan, M2 comprises all

Table 12.1 List of Component Assets and Associated Rates of Return for Central Bank of Taiwan Monetary Aggregates

Taiwanese Central Bank Grouping	Quantity Description	Description of Interest Rate or Interest Rate Proxy
Deposit money	Currency held by the public	Interest rate is zero
	Checking accounts[a]	Interest rate is zero
	Passbook deposits	Interest rate on passbook deposits of 1st Commercial Bank
	Passbook savings deposits	Interest rate on passbook saving deposits of 1st Commercial Bank
Quasi-money	Postal savings deposits[b]	Interest rate on passbook saving deposits of Chunghwa Post Co.
	1 month to 3 year N.T. Dollar deposits by non-residents[c]	3 month interest rate on time saving deposits of Chunghwa Post Co.
	Time & savings deposits	3 month interest rate on time saving deposits of Chunghwa Post Co.
	Money market mutual funds[d]	Commercial paper rate in the primary market (31–90 days to maturity)
	Repurchase agreements[e]	Commercial paper rate in the primary market (31–90 days to maturity)
	Foreign currency deposits	3 month interest rate on US dollar deposits of 1st Commercial Bank

[a]Checking Accounts include cashier's checks, certified and traveler's checks. [b]Postal savings deposits include giro accounts, passbook savings deposits, and time savings deposits of Chunghwa Post Co. [c]Non-residents N.T. dollar deposits include demand and time deposits held by foreign non-financial institutions. [d]Money market mutual funds represents net present value of money market mutual funds, issued since October 2004, held by enterprises, individuals, and non-residents. [e]Data on represents repurchase agreements sold to enterprises and individuals by monetary institutions and Chunghwa Post Co. prior to January 1994 is not available.

assets, that is, deposit money plus Quasi-money listed here in each of the ten categories. All data are monthly and seasonally adjusted and are available from DataStream and the Central Bank of the Republic of China (Taiwan) online database, please see http://www.cbc.gov.tw/ct.asp?xItem=1869&ctNode=511&mp=2.

Unlike the earlier work of Shih (2000) we have adjusted the interest rate on foreign currency deposits as follows; before the 1990Q1, we assume the assumption of perfect foresight will be held; from the beginning of 1990Q1, we assume the assumption of Uncovered Interest Rate Parity will be held. Detailed descriptions of each component are provided in Shih (2000).

12.4 RESULTS AND DISCUSSIONS

In this section, we will demonstrate the usefulness of this new data set by applying it to a simple VAR framework inspired by the system used by Leeper and Gordon (1992) and Kelly et al. (2011).

12.4.1 Data Selection

We choose variables similar to those used in the system estimated by Leeper and Gordon (1992), Kelly et al. (2011). Variables and transformations used are as follows:

- IP   The natural log of the seasonally adjusted industrial production index for Taiwan
- CPI   The natural log of the seasonally adjusted consumer price index for Taiwan
- ONR   The average interest rate on overnight interbank loans published by the Central Bank of the Republic of China (Taiwan)
- SSUM   The natural log of the official simple sum monetary aggregate for Taiwan (seasonally adjusted)
- DIV   The natural log of the Divisia liquidity aggregate for Taiwan (seasonally adjusted)

Figure 12.2 plots each of the variables used in this analysis.

12.4.2 VAR Identification

We use a block-recursive identification scheme similar to that first used by Christiano et al. (1999) and later applied to liquidity aggregation by Keating et al. (2013). Let

$$Z_t = \begin{pmatrix} X_{1t} \\ X_{2t} \\ X_{3t} \end{pmatrix} \tag{12.7}$$

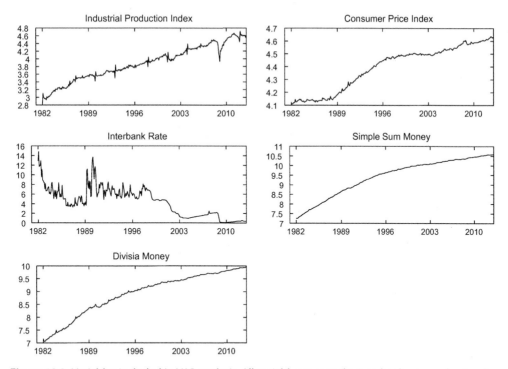

Figure 12.2 Variables included in VAR analysis. All variables except the interbank rate are log levels.

be the vector of variables for which we estimate

$$Z_t = A + B(L)Z_{t-1} + u_t, \quad u_t \sim N(0, \Sigma), \tag{12.8}$$

where we subdivide Z_t into three groups, X_{1t}, X_{2t}, and X_{3t} and follow Christiano et al. (1999) by specifying that X_{2t} contains a single variable designated to be the policy indicator. Then, as was shown by Christiano et al. (1999), the responses to the policy variable, X_{2t}, can be found by applying a Cholesky decomposition to residuals covariance matrix, and are invariant to the internal orderings of X_{1t}, and X_{3t}.

We begin our investigation with a standard four variable model, which we will label Model 1, where

$$Z_t = \left(IP_t, CPI_t, ONR_t, SSUM_t\right)' \tag{12.9}$$

and ONR_t is considered to be the policy variable. The impulse responses to a one-standard deviation shock to the policy variable are reported in Figure 12.3. Model 1 clearly exhibits price and output puzzles that are common to many Christiano et al. type models of monetary models.

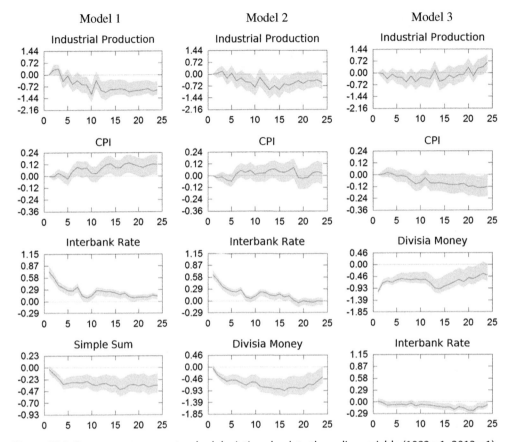

Figure 12.3 Responses to a one-standard deviation shock to the policy variable (1982m1–2013m1).

In Model 2, we replace the theoretically inferior simple sum monetary aggregate with a Divisia Money. Notice that the output puzzle in Model 2 (see Figure 12.3) is all but eliminated and the price puzzle is greatly reduced. In our final model, Model 3, the interbank rate and Divisia money are switched so that Divisia money is designated the policy indicator and the vector, Z_t, becomes

$$Z_t = \left(IP_t, CPI_t, DIV_t, ONR_t\right)'. \tag{12.10}$$

Model 3 exhibits neither a price puzzle nor an output puzzle. Thus, simply by using Divisia money as the policy indicator and removing the flawed simple sum monetary aggregates we are able to correct for two of the most vexing problems in empirical monetary policy analysis. Note, reversing the ordering of Divisia money and the interbank rate in Model 3 negates the influence of the interbank rate. We surmise that in

Table 12.2 Forecast Error Variance Decomposition for Model 3

	12 Months Ahead	24 Months Ahead	60 Months Ahead
Industrial Production	2.35	1.60	1.13
	(0.85, 6.30)	(0.75, 4.86)	(0.63, 4.32)
CPI	2.45	8.39	27.21
	(0.67, 7.23)	(3.15, 16.84)	(16.71, 39.69)
Divisia Money	60.94	47.65	30.63
	(46.82, 74.82)	(33.02, 66.28)	(17.80, 49.78)
Interbank Rate	5.98	6.82	6.90
	(1.37, 15.90)	(1.51, 17.20)	(1.68, 16.85)

Note: Numbers in parentheses are the boundaries of the associated 90% confidence interval.

this case the influence of the interbank rate has already been internalized within the construction of Divisia money.

Table 12.2 presents the forecast error variance decomposition for a policy shock in Model 3. The confidence intervals reported are calculated by bootstrapping with 10,000 repetitions. From the forecast error variance decomposition, we see that a Divisia money policy shock has a small effect on price level in the short run but much greater effect on price level in the long run. This delayed reaction to monetary policy is a fairly common result (see, e.g., Keating et al., 2013).

12.5 CONCLUSION

Our work has revisited the early questions asked by Shih (2000) and Binner et al. (2002). Because these studies have not been re-examined for over 11 years, we returned to the basic question: Is Taiwan monetary policy still linked closely with variations in money growth? More precisely, we asked whether Divisia aggregates in Taiwan could be employed productively in setting monetary policy in Taiwan.

The theoretical case for weighted monetary aggregates never has been challenged seriously. Their potential for use in practice, however, has been questioned on three fronts. First, criticisms about the choice of a benchmark rate of return and the treatment of risk when measuring monetary user costs (both of which affect index weights) suggest that such an index is subject to unknown, and presumably large, measurement error. Second, if the money stock were measured as the sum of its components, with each weighted by its share of total expenditures on monetary services, it has been alleged (without evidence) that central banks would be unable to influence the behavior of such an index in the pursuit of a monetary policy objective. Most commonly, however, the case against the construction, publication, and use of any superlative index of money has been grounded in empirical evidence showing that an official simple sum measure, in the context of a particular model, time period, or set of tests, performs as well as or better than a weighted index of the same asset collection. In sum, these perceived shortcomings have led most monetary economists and policymakers to conclude that the practical difficulties associated with finding empirical proxies for a weighted index's theoretical components and explaining the behavior of such an index to authorities who monitor central bank actions more than offset the small marginal gains (if any) from use of the index itself (Belongia, 2005).

These are matters that need to be examined in greater detail in further experimentation. Work is also on-going to enhance the construction of Divisia money in line with recent financial innovations, see, for example, Binner (2009), Binner et al. (2004), and Anderson and Jones (2011). Thus the destabilization of the money demand function may be attributed to the financial innovations and deregulations revealing flaws in the construction of monetary aggregates. It has been suggested that it might be appropriate, given the increased financial innovations in the way money is held and utilized, to include risky assets, e.g., equities, bonds, and unit trusts, into the construction of monetary aggregates (see, e.g., Barnett and Zhou, 1995; Elger and Binner, 2004). The latter estimated a demand system over both capital certain and risky assets held by the UK personal sector and showed that risky assets are substitutes for more liquid assets. Money velocity appears to depend on the degree of risk in the returns on monetary assets and the level of risk aversion. With continual innovation in financial markets, the impact on the measurement of monetary aggregates will continue to present problems in empirical studies. More sophisticated Divisia monetary aggregates have the potential to make a valuable contribution to future studies and should ideally focus on finding enhanced methods of capturing the true user cost of money by, e.g., finding enhanced ways of incorporating the risk of holding the asset and more thorough theoretical treatment of the modeling of the opportunity costs for Divisia money, including improvements on measuring the benchmark rate of return in the construction along the lines proposed by Binner et al. (2010). The relationship between monetary policy and long-term interest rates is currently in hot debate, see, e.g., Beckworth et al. (2012), and of great concern to proponents of Divisia money where the role of the Divisia price dual is under—researched and neglected, Belongia (2005); and hence a natural topic for further investigation. Future models should also make full use of the relevant theory, as emphasized by Belongia and Ireland (2012). We echo Carlstrom and Fuerst (2004) who state "…we think the current de-emphasis on the role of money may have gone too far. It is important to think seriously about the role of money and how money affects optimal policy." In a similar vein, the former Governor of the Bank of England King (2002) stated "My own belief is that the absence of money in the standard models which economists use will cause problems in future, and that there will be profitable developments from future research into the way in which money affects risk premia and economic behavior more generally. Money, I conjecture, will regain an important place in the conversation of economists."

In keeping with Barnett and Chauvet (2011), we conclude that the use of simple sum monetary aggregates is indefensible in a modern economy. These are matters that need to be examined in greater detail in further experimentation. Taken together, our results indicate that future research into improved constructions of monetary aggregates is promising and is a worthwhile route to pursue.

REFERENCES

Andersen, L.C., Jordon, J.L., 1968. Monetary and fiscal actions: a test of their relative importance in economic stabilisation. Federal Reserve Bank of St. Louis Review, November, pp. 11–23.

Anderson, R.G., Jones, B., 2011. A comprehensive revision of the monetary services (Divisia) indexes for the United States. Federal Reserve Bank of St. Louis, Review, September/October 93 (5), pp. 325–359.

Barnett, William A., 1978. The user cost of money. Economics Letters 1 (2), 145–149. Reprinted in: Barnett, W.A., Serletis, A. (Eds.), The theory of monetary aggregation. In: Contributions to Economic Analysis, vol. 245. North Holland, Amsterdam, 2000, pp. 6–10 (Chapter 1).

Barnett, W.A., 1980. Economic monetary aggregates: an application of index number and aggregation theory. Journal of Econometrics 14 (1), 11–48. Reprinted in: Barnett, W.A., Serletis, A. (Eds.), The theory of monetary aggregation. In: Contributions to Economic Analysis, vol. 245. North Holland, Amsterdam, 2000, pp. 11–48 (Chapter 2).

Barnett, W.A., Chauvet, M., 2011. How better monetary statistics could have signalled the systemic risk precipitating the financial crisis. Journal of Econometrics 161 (1), 6–23.

Barnett, W.A., Liu, Y., 2000. Beyond the risk-neutral utility function. In: Belongia, M.T., Binner, J.M. (Eds.), Divisia Monetary Aggregates: Theory and Practice. Palgrave Macmillan, pp. 11–27.

Barnett, W.A., Zhou G., 1995. Mutual funds and monetary aggregates: commentary. Federal Reserve Bank of St. Louis, Review, 76, November/December, pp. 53–62. Reprinted in: Barnett, W. Serletis, A. (Eds.), The Theory of Monetary Aggregation. North Holland, Amsterdam, 2000, pp. 307–322 (Chapter 15).

Barnett, W.A., Chae, U., Keating, J.W., 2005. The discounted economic stock of money with VAR forecasting. Annals of Finance 2 (2), 229–258.

Barnett, W.A., Keating, J.W., Kelly, L.J., 2008. Toward a bias corrected currency equivalent index. Economics Letters 100 (3), 448–451.

Beckworth, D., Moon, K.P., Toles, J.H., 2012. Can monetary policy influence long term interest rates? It depends. Economic Inquiry 50 (4), 1080–1096.

Belongia, M.T., 1996. Measurement matters: recent results from monetary economics re-examined. Journal of Political Economy 104 (5), 1065–1083.

Belongia, M.T., 2000. Introductory comments, definitions, and research on indexes of monetary services. In: Belongia, M.T., Binner, J.M. (Eds.), Divisia Monetary Aggregates: Theory and Practice. Palgrave, New York, pp. 1–10 (Chapter 1).

Belongia, M.T., 2005. The neglected price dual of monetary quantity aggregates. In: Belongia, M.T., Binner, J.M. (Eds.), Money Measurement and Computation. Palgrave McMillan, London. ISBN: 978-1-4039-4793-2 and 10: 1-4039-4793-7 (Chapter 10).

Belongia, M.T., Chrystal, K.A., 1991. An admissible monetary aggregate for the United Kingdom. The Review of Economics and Statistics 73 (3), 497–503.

Belongia, M.T., Ireland, P.N., 2012. The Barnett critique after three decades: a new Keynesian analysis (No. w17885). National Bureau of Economic Research.

Binner, J.M., 2009. Financial innovation in the UK: new tier-adjusted household sector monetary services indexes. Global Business and Economics Review 11 (1), 44–64.

Binner, J.M., Gazely, A.M., Chen, S.H., 2002. Financial innovation in Taiwan; an application of neural networks to the broad monetary aggregates. European Journal of Finance 8 (2), 238–247.

Binner, J.M., Gazely, A.M., Chen, S.H., Chie, B.T., 2004. Financial innovation and Divisia money in Taiwan: comparative evidence from neural networks and vector error correction forecasting models. Contemporary Economic Policy 22 (2), 213–224.

Binner, J.M., Gazely, A.M., Kendall, G., 2008. Evaluating the performance of a EuroDivisia index using artificial intelligence techniques. International Journal of Automation and Computing 5, 58–62.

Binner, J.M., Tino, P., Tepper, J., Anderson, R., Jones, B., Kendall, G., 2010. Does money matter in inflation forecasting? Physica A: Statistical Mechanics and its Applications 389 (21), 4793–4808.

Bissoondeeal, R., Binner, J.M., Bhuruth, M., Gazely, A., Mootanah, V., 2008. Forecasting exchange rates with linear and nonlinear models. Global Business and Economics Review 10 (4), 414–429.

Carlstrom, C., Fuerst, T., 2004. Thinking about monetary policy without money. International Finance 7 (2), 325–347.

Christiano, L., Eichenbaum, M., Evans, C., 1999. Monetary policy shocks: what have we learned and to what end?. In: Handbook of Macroeconomics, Vol. 1. Elsevier, pp. 65–148.

Crowder, W.J., 1998. The long run link between money growth and inflation. Economic Inquiry 36 (2), 229–243.

Diewert, E., 1976. Exact and superlative index numbers. Journal of Econometrics 4 (2), 115–146.

Diewert, E., 1978. Superlative index numbers and consistency in aggregation. Econometrica 46 (4), 883–900.

Divisia, F., 1925. L'indice monétaire et al théorie de la monnaie. Review d'Economy Politique 39, 980–1008.

Drake, L., Chrystal, K.A., 1994. Company sector money demand: new evidence of a stable long run relationship in the UK. Journal of Money Credit and Banking 26 (3).

Drake, L., Chrystal, K.A., 1997. Personal sector money demand in the UK. Oxford Economic Studies 49 (2), 188–206.

Drake, L., Mills, T.C., 2005. A new empirically weighted monetary aggregate for the United States. Economic Inquiry 43 (1), 138–157.

Drake, L., Chrystal, K.A., Binner, J.M., 2000. Weighted monetary aggregates for the UK. In: Belongia, M.T., Binner, J.M. (Eds.), Divisia Monetary Aggregates: Theory and Practice. Palgrave, New York, pp. 47–78 (Chapter 3).

Elger, T., Binner, J.M., 2004. The UK household sector demand for risky money. In: Topics in Macroeconomics Series, vol. 4 (1). Berkeley Electronic Press <http://www.bepress.com/bejm/topics/vol4/iss1/art3>.

El-Shagi, M., Kelly, L.J., 2013. What can we learn from country level liquidity in the EMU. Working Paper, University of Wisconsin-River Falls, USA.

Fisher, P., Hudson, S., Pradhan, M., 1993. Divisia indices for money: an appraisal of theory and practice. Bank of England Quarterly Bulletin 33 (2), 240–255.

Friedman, M., Schwarz, A.J., 1970. Monetary Statistics of the United States. Columbia University Press, New York.

Friedman, M., 1996. The rise and fall of money growth targets as guidelines for US monetary policy. NBER Working Paper, pp. 54–65.

Gazely, A.M., Binner, J.M., 2000. A neural network approach to the Divisia index debate: evidence from three countries. Applied Economics 32 (12), 1607–1615.

Hancock, M., 2005. Divisia money. Bank of England Quarterly Bulletin (Spring), 39–46.

Keating, J.W., Kelly, L.J., Smith, A.L., Valcarcel, V., 2013. A model of monetary policy shocks for financial crises and normal conditions. Working Paper, University of Wisconsin-River Falls, USA.

Kelly, L.J., 2009. The stock of money and why you should care. In: Binner, J.M., Edgerton, D.L., Elger, T. (Eds.), Measurement Error: Consequences, Applications and Solutions. In: Fomby, T.B., Carter Hill, R. (Eds.), Advances in Econometrics, vol. 24. Emerald Group Publishing Limited, pp. 237–250. ISBN: 978-1-84855-902-8.

Kelly, L.J., Barnett, W.A., Keating, J.W., 2011. Rethinking the Liquidity Puzzle: application of a new measure of the economic money stock. Journal of Banking and Finance 35 (4), 768–774.

King, M., 2002. No money, no inflation: the role of money in the economy. Bank of England Quarterly Bulletin (Summer), 162–177.

Leeper, E.M., Gordon, D.B., 1992. In search of the liquidity effect. Journal of Monetary Economics 29 (3), 341–369.

Lucas Jr., R., 2000. Inflation and welfare. Econometrica 68 (2), 247–274.

Shih, Y.C., 2000. Divisia monetary aggregates for Taiwan. In: Belongia, M.T., Binner, J.M. (Eds.), Divisia Monetary Aggregates: Theory and Practice. Palgrave, New York, pp. 227–248 (Chapter 10).

Theil, H., 1967. Economics of Information Theory. North-Holland, Amsterdam.

Törnqvist, L., 1936. The bank of Finland's consumption index. Bank of Finland Monthly Bulletin 10, 1–8.

CHAPTER 13

Comparative Financial Development in Asia-Pacific Since the Asia Crisis

Kym Brown, Jonathan A. Batten, Michael Skully, and Yen N. Nguyen
Department of Banking and Finance, 900 Dandenong Road, Caulfield East, Victoria 3145, Australia

13.1 INTRODUCTION AND BACKGROUND

Prior to 1997, economic growth in Asia was due in part to the late adoption of developing technologies, in addition to relative cheap labor. Countries, such as Malaysia, Thailand, and South Korea, were touted as "Asian Tigers" with huge development potential. They benefited considerably from Japan's efforts to move production to countries with lower costs. The decision to retain pegged or otherwise fixed exchange rates, however, eventually caused much of Asia's market-based systems to falter in the 1990s, and the devaluation of the Baht in Thailand on 2 July 1997 is often viewed as the start of the Asian financial crisis. Given the prior stability in exchange rates, countries such as Indonesia and Thailand had borrowed overseas, often short term, in foreign currency positions that were unhedged. The IMF, World Bank, and Asian Development Bank assisted Asian governments in their recovery efforts. The aim of course was to prevent any future occurrences, so reform of Asia's financial systems appeared a necessity to stabilize markets.

In this chapter we investigate the recovery process given it appears the Asian region has better survived the 2007 global financial and European debt crises than many other regions both developed and developing. The irony of this situation is of course what followed in 2007–2010 with the global and European global crises. While developed nations faced volatile markets, one of the biggest areas of concern for the Asian region were initially inflationary pressures, followed with some contractions especially by developed nation investors (felt greatest in China, Taiwan, Korea, and Malaysia), falling stock markets and trade flows, but with much milder financial impacts than in developed markets (Filardo et al., 2010).

This study uses a sample of 10 large economies in the Asia-Pacific region. It provides the basis for intra-regional analysis and should facilitate the identification of those financial sector features relevant for economic development. These economies include China, Hong Kong (China), Indonesia, Japan, Malaysia, the Philippines, Singapore, South Korea, Taiwan (China), and Thailand. Indonesia, the Philippines, Thailand, and South Korea were the most affected countries as a result of the crisis. It should be noted that Hong Kong returned to Chinese rule on 1 July 1997 after being a British colony. Section 13.2 looks at the reforms in response to the Asian and global crises.

Section 13.3 examines various macroeconomic and type of financing across the region to determine whether financial development has improved. The findings suggest that there has been a remarkable improvement in financial development especially with China, but with domestic debt financing the government sector has tended to crowd out the corporate sector. Section 13.4 concludes the chapter.

13.2 THE ASIAN FINANCIAL CRISIS AND GLOBAL FINANCIAL CRISIS REFORMS

The Asian financial crisis identified specific areas for academic investigation and attention. These included corporate governance, creditor rights, and accounting standards (Szilagyi and Batten, 2004). Several countries also developed government bond markets to help finance their huge debt burdens from saving their banking systems, but also as an alternative to bank financing. The Asian crisis exposed large levels of non-performing loans, and governments merged banks, set up asset management companies (AMCs) to recover on poorly performing loans and injected capital. In Japan, banks were tied to the historical convoy system, which required surviving banks to merge with failing ones (Nakaso, 2001). By the early 1990s this became too difficult given the number of bank failures (with deflating asset prices as well). Their Jusen companies, effectively non-bank home loan vehicles, were also impacted by the deflationary pressure on asset prices including housing, but the government and other banks did not bail them out. NPLs of Japanese banks rose to 6–8% by the early 1990s. This impact was mainly felt in 1993–1996. Japan was also not without a banking scandal. By September 1995, a rogue Daiwa bank employee produced some US$1.1 billion of losses by skimming client accounts due to poor internal controls. Note this was the same year that Nick Leeson was found corrupting the internal control systems at Barings in Singapore.

Each country in the region of course has its own unique culture and currency, and this needs to be considered more carefully than in other regional areas such as Europe or Latin America. Obviously there are some parallels with the development of Eastern Europe from socialist control to market-based systems, but the Chinese progression to financial market development has taken a long-term incremental approach. With increased sophistication and maturity in financial services, financial markets in Asia should be more developed than before. It is expected that the resolution process as part of the Asian crisis increased public confidence in regional financial systems and their associated restructuring efforts have had prolonged effects. Therefore, we hypothesize that as a result, Asia's financial markets, especially those of crisis affected countries, have become and remained more diversified.

Regardless of the specific cause of the Asian financial crisis, the fiscal impact on regional economies was enormous. The burden was felt hardest on impoverished people with females and farmers in Thailand and Indonesia having difficulties with school, petrol and food expenses (AusAID, 2009). As shown in Table 13.1 Indonesia,

Table 13.1 Episodes of Systemic Financial Crises in the Asia-Pacific Region

Economy	Scope of Crisis	Estimated Losses or Costs
China 1990s	Four large state-owned commercial banks (68% banking system assets deemed insolvent, 1998). Non-performing Loans (NPLs) estimated 50%	$428 billion or 47% GDP in 1999
Indonesia 1997–2002	Bank Indonesia had closed 70 banks & nationalized 13, of a total of 237. NPLs estimated 65–75% at peak of crisis: 12% by February 2002	55% GDP
Japan 1990s	In 1995 estimate of NPLs was 40 trillion yen ($469 billion, or 10% of GDP). An unofficial estimate put NPLs at $1 trillion, equivalent to 25% of GDP. At the end of 1998 banking system NPLs were estimated at 88 trillion yen ($725 billion, or 18% of GDP)	More than $100 billion (1996). 1998 the Obuchi Plan, provided 60 trillion yen ($500 billion, or 12% of GDP) in public funds
Korea 1997–2002	March 1999, 2 of 26 commercial banks—accounting for 12% of banking system assets—were nationalized. Five banks—accounting for 8% of banking system assets—were closed. 303 financial institutions closed including 215 credit unions. Bank system NPLs peak during crisis at 30–40%	28% of GDP
Malaysia 1997–2002	Finance sector reduced from 39 to 10 institutions. NPLs estimated 25–35% (1998): 10.8% by March 2002. Further banks merged to just 8 banks	16.4% of GDP
The Philippines 1998–2002	Since January 1998 one commercial bank, 7 of 88 thrifts, and 40 of 750 rural banks have been placed under receivership. NPLs 12% November 1998 and 20% 1999	$4 billion or 7% GDP (1999)
Taiwan, China 1997–1998	NPLs estimated 15% end 1998	$26.7 billion or 11.5% GDP (1999)
Thailand 1997–2002	Through March 1999 the Bank of Thailand (BOT) closed 59 (of 91) finance companies that together accounted for 13% of financial system assets and 72% of finance company assets. At peak of crisis NPLs were 33%: 10.3% by February 2002	34.8% of GDP

Source: Caprio et al. (2005), World Bank Datasets.

Thailand, South Korea, and the Philippines were all heavily affected. Malaysia too was impacted but its defensive actions helped to minimize the effects. The cost of the crisis for Taiwan was also significant, at around 11.5% of GDP in 1999. Meanwhile not related specifically to the Asian financial crisis, Japan had overriding banking problems with asset devaluation of the stock market and real estate sectors resulting in high non-performing loans in the 1990s. In addition, China throughout the 1990s and early 2000s continued its transformation from a state-controlled banking system that predominantly only directed state finances to state-owned enterprises (SOEs), to commercial bank style lending but creating high levels of NPLs in the process. The entry of foreign banks into China is likely to have the added advantage of stimulating further reform of banking systems and to improve efficiency.

Within the major Asian financial crisis affected countries of Malaysia, Thailand, Korea, Indonesia, and the Philippines, Bongini et al. (2002) found that some 42% of banks experienced distress after July 1997 and that 13% of their sample banks and non-bank financial institutions had closed by July 1999. As part of their resolution process, banks connected with business groups or influential families were more likely to fail. Smaller banks in Asia were more often closed while distressed larger banks tended to remain indicating the too big to fail (TBTF) attitude of regulators. Another interesting finding from the Bongini et al. (2002) study was that no foreign controlled banks were closed and the higher the foreign ownership level the lower the probability of distress. Basically that finding alone supports the liberalization of the banking markets in the Asian region and further foreign bank entry.

The shock of the crisis in 2007 clearly impacted Asia. Sovereign debt credit default swap premia peaked in late 2008 with Indonesia recording levels of 1000 bps while Korea, the Philippines, and Malaysia close behind (Filardo, 2012). Central banks in Asia also had to deal with the severe shortage of US dollars by offering higher rates on US dollars domestically. Korean firms were especially hit given their contract exposures in US dollars. Table 13.2 illustrates some of the policy actions suggested for each country to survive the Global Financial Crisis. It is evident that Korea was the most robust in their approach perhaps due to the implications they faced.

13.3 MACROECONOMIC ASIA AND FINANCIAL SYSTEMS

GDP has continued to grow across the region. Before the Asian crisis Japan stood as the regional powerhouse with some US$4.7 trillion GDP output compared to US$856 million for China. The regional leading economy has since changed in 2010 and by 2012 China had GDP output of some US$8.2 trillion surpassing Japan at US$5.9 trillion (IMF/IFS Statistics). One of the major vulnerabilities before the Asian financial crisis was the negative current account imbalances Thailand, the Philippines, Korea, Malaysia, and Indonesia. As shown in Table 13.3 these imbalances were rectified,

Table 13.2 Policy Actions Proposed as a Result of the Global Financial Crisis (as at July 2009)

	CH	HK	ID	JP	KR	MY	PH	SG	TH
Ease monetary policy	X	X	X	X	X	X	X	X	X
Introduce fiscal stimulus		X	X	X	X	X	X	X	X
Liquidity assistance in local currency	X	X	X	X	X		X		
Lend foreign exchange	X		X	X	X		X	X	
Expand deposit insurance		X	X		X	X	X	X	X
Guarantee non-deposit liabilities					X				
Prepare bank capital injection	X	X		X	X				X
Create demand for assets	X		X	X	X	X			
Impose short sale restrictions	X	X	X	X	X			X	
Relax mark to market rules	X		X	X	X	X	X		

Source: Filardo et al. (2010).
CH=China, HK=Hong Kong, ID=Indonesia, JP=Japan, KR=Korea, MY=Malaysia, PH=The Philippines, SG=Singapore, TH=Thailand.

Table 13.3 Current Accounts of Selected Asian Countries Percentage of GDP

Country	1996	1997	1998	2000	2002	2008	2012
Korea	−4.2	−2	13	2	1.3	0.34	3.74
Indonesia	−3.5	−2	4.7	6	4.2	0.02	−2.75
Thailand	−7.6	−2	13	7.5	6.0	0.8	0.75
The Philippines	−4.7	−4.8	2.5	12	3.8	2	2.85
Malaysia	−4	−4	−5.5	16	7.7	16.84	11*

*2011 data.

Source: The World Bank, (2002) World Bank Development Indicators, International Bank for Reconstruction and Development, Washington, pp. 263.

which assisted countries in dealing with the Global Financial Crisis in 2007/2008, but since Indonesia has trended into a deficit by 2012. Some economic problems in India in 2013 have led to fears of another region-wide Asian crisis. So far, the proponents of macroeconomic stability have quelled these concerns with cited improvements in current account balances in developing Asian nations.

Investigating the financial markets across the region allows a bird's eye perspective of the extent of financial development. Certainly at the time of the Asian financial crisis, region-wide analyses were lacking. Some of the innate differences can be captured when making such comparisons. Beginning with banking sector domestic credit, it is apparent that the Japanese market has the most dominant banking system with the

Philippines and Indonesia markets still struggling to fully recover to the levels pre-Asian financial crisis (Table 13.4). For the Philippine and Indonesian markets this is offset with growth in equity market capitalization, which suggests growth in the overall financial market, but suggests that these economies still have high levels of unbanked or under-banked people. A surprising result is for the Chinese banking system, which reports lower levels of bank finance, but an increase in equity markets. This may also be supported by growth in other financial markets such as bonds. Hong Kong stands out both in terms of the growth of the banking sector credit, but also to the nearly sixfold increase in equity market size. This can be attributed to the listing of mainland Chinese companies in Hong Kong with its better governance and common law protection.

A major impact of the Asian financial crisis, which was not widely publicized, was the bursting of the equity bubble in Malaysia. In 1996 the Malaysian equity market size was an incredible 303% of GDP, with the bubble bursting down to 128% by 1997. Initially a similar concern may allay for Hong Kong, but its role as an offshore financial center with mainland Chinese companies listings helps ensure a strong banking sector and so access to credit. A threat to the development of the Chinese market for instance is the huge and rapidly growing shadow banking market. The Financial Stability Board estimated the size to be some 2–3 trillion yuan in November 2012 (FSB, 2012). The concern with shadow banking is the lack of regulation. Small and medium enterprise owners for instance demonstrated against these lenders in Zhejiang province in coastal China due to the exorbitant fees and charges. Concerns also remain over China's large state-owned banks (SOBs), which although listed, retain high exposures to state-owned enterprises (SOEs) and the influence of local and provincial governments. Past state bank problems resulted in a massive bailout of over US$50 billion equivalent in the early 1990s, and again there is further speculation of similar occurrences (The Economist, 2013).

Table 13.4 Domestic Credit and Equity Market Capitalization (%GDP)

	Domestic Credit by Banking Sector				Equity Market Capitalization			
	1996	1997	2002	2012	1996	1997	2002	2012
China	97	106	170	155	14	26	37	45
Hong Kong	154	165	143	200	286	238	284	1075
Indonesia	55	58	61	42	40	21	15	45
Japan	130	129	142	346	66	53	51	61
Korea	60	69	108	168	26	15	43	104
Malaysia	111	130	118	133	303	128	100	156
The Philippines	67	78	55	50	97	51	24	105
Singapore	67	73	77	99	168	127	110	150
Taiwan	160	n/a	143	n/a	98	99	93	155
Thailand	100	131	102	169	52	22	36	104

Source: BIS (2001, 2003) World Federation of Exchanges, Table 1.3.a, exchange rates, IFS statistics.

The Thai market has seemingly improved remarkably from the Asian financial crisis and through the global financial crisis. With banking sector credit of some 169% and equity market capitalization of 104% by December 2012, this has been an amazing feat in recovery. The spiked increase in equity market capitalization for Indonesia and the Philippines could point to the interest by mutual funds from developed nations looking for higher returns than with the mature markets of Singapore, Hong Kong, and Taiwan for instance.

The externalities of foreign bank borrowings and deposits are provided in Table 13.5. Focussing on the bank sector column it is evident that Hong Kong moved from a net borrowing to a net lender from 1997 to 2001. The handover back to the Chinese government occurred on the 1 July 1997 in the midst of the Asian crisis. The Indonesian and Filipino banks had limited transactions in the international banking markets but tended to be net borrowers. The Japanese and Taiwanese banks were net lenders in the international banking markets, while China, Hong Kong, and Singaporean banks became net lenders post the Asian financial crisis. The major changes in the non-bank corporate sector loan to deposit ratios illustrate huge imbalances in the international banking market for Asia at December 1997. The crisis-related countries of Indonesia, Korea, and Thailand, along with China and Japan, had very high corporate exposures to international bank borrowings. By 2012 in all cases except Indonesia's 534% loan/deposit ratio, this imbalance had been rectified. Based on overall dollar size of loans and deposits Japan has remained the largest, followed by Hong Kong and Singapore.

Another signal of more developed financial markets is often the level of growth of bond or securities market financing. Table 13.6 highlights the amazing expansion of the Chinese domestic and international debt issues. For all countries, but Hong Kong, the bond markets have increased. This is a positive signal as to the development of the financial markets in Asia. So by 2013, the Korean and Japanese markets have well-developed bond markets. Japan and China also have much larger domestic debt bond markets.

An overview of the government, banking and corporate sector financing via international bank borrowing, domestic debt securities, and international debt securities is provided in Table 13.7. China has the most significant growth in all funding types and for all three sectors. Focussing first on government financing, the largest growth is in domestic debt securities/bonds especially with the Japanese government funding some US$10.5 trillion with domestic issues, with much less international debt. The Indonesian and Malaysian governments also witnessed good growth in international debt issues.

As with the government sector, banks have increased their domestic debt issuance for funding. Chinese banks actually outstripped the Chinese government domestic issues. Still, it could be argued that as the large Chinese banks are state owned and so not distinctly distant from the government. The impact of the Asian financial crisis is clearly shown in the banking sector with a substantial decline in international bank

Table 13.5 Bank Finance: Foreign Loans and Deposits of Reporting Banks on Individual Countries (Billions USD)

	Year End	All Sectors			Bank Sector			Non-Bank Corporate Sector		
		External Loans	External Deposits	Loans/Deposits (%)	External Loans	External Deposits	Loans/Deposits (%)	External Loans	External Deposits	Loans/Deposits (%)
China	1997	82.7	64.5	128	66.9	60.7	110	15.8	3.8	415
	2001	46.2	93.8	49	35.5	81.9	43	10.7	11.9	90
	2012	395.1	354.3	111	n/a	n/a		150.4	117.6	127
Hong Kong	1997	464.7	297.8	156	448.8	230.7	194	15.9	67.1	145
	2001	147.2	295.8	49	120.0	253.1	47	27.2	42.7	63
	2012	413.7	434.9	95	n/a	n/a		102.9	95.8	107
Indonesia	1997	62.2	12.0	518	25.4	8.3	306	36.8	3.7	994
	2001	31.6	13.2	239	10.1	9.9	102	21.5	3.3	651
	2012	63.7	20.3	313	n/a	n/a		33.7	6.3	534
Japan	1997	840.4	725.4	115	585.7	686.2	85	254.7	39.2	649
	2001	445.5	445.2	100	385.9	393.6	98	59.6	51.6	115
	2012	924.7	629.8	146	n/a	n/a		235.1	141.4	166
Korea	1997	88.6	41.8	212	70.4	39.5	178	18.2	2.3	791
	2001	48.3	28.7	168	36.0	26.7	135	12.3	2.0	615
	2012	127.4	56.2	226	n/a	n/a		25.7	10.3	249
Malaysia	1997	25.3	13.1	193	21.6	9.6	225	3.7	3.5	105
	2001	15.7	12.7	123	12.2	9.6	127	3.5	3.1	112
	2012	40.7	28.8	141	n/a	n/a		17.0	13.1	129

The Philippines	1997	14.5	9.7	149	9.3	6.5	143	5.2	3.2	162
	2001	14.2	10.8	131	7.4	7.0	105	6.8	3.8	179
	2012	24.2	21.2	114	n/a	n/a		10.3	5.5	187
Singapore	1997	292.3	221.3	132	285.4	206.1	138	6.9	15.2	45
	2001	204.5	276.3	74	195.5	252.2	77	9.0	24.1	37
	2012	477.1	462.1	103	n/a	n/a		55.4	76.5	72
Taiwan	1997	20.6	36.7	56	18.5	27.5	67	2.1	9.2	22
	2001	14.9	67.7	22	10.3	46.8	22	4.6	20.9	22
	2012	74.2	113.9	65	n/a	n/a		15.9	58.1	27
Thailand	1997	74.4	9.5	783	64.2	7.5	856	10.2	2.0	510
	2001	19.9	15.3	130	13.5	11.7	115	6.4	3.6	177
	2012	46.3	25.1	184	n/a	n/a		16.3	11.4	142

Source: BIS (2002, 2013) BIS Quarterly Review, June, Table 7A and 7B.

Table 13.6 Domestic and International Debt Securities (Billions of US Dollars)

	Domestic Issues			International Issues		
	December 1997	December 2001	December 2012	December 1997	December 2001	December 2012
China	161.6	238.0	3766.5	17.4	17.4	172.8
Hong Kong	38.2	43.6	–	22.8	35.5	110.9
Indonesia	1.5	43.3	130.4	17.8	9.1	53.8
Japan	5054.7	6161.8	14,404.7	316.8	257.2	374.8
Korea	130.3	292.7	1280.2	51.2	47.1	167.6
Malaysia	57.0	81.8	351.8	12.5	16.0	50.5
The Philippines	16.7	24.1	84.5	10.0	15.5	45.2
Singapore	13.0	28.9	116.5	4.7	15.5	79.3
Taiwan	105.2	124.4	310.8	6.3	7.7	12.3
Thailand	1.0	18.4	290.5	14.5	11.0	16.6

Source: BIS (2001, 2013), "BIS *Quarterly Review: International Banking and Financial Market Developments*," Table 16B. BIS (2002), "BIS *Quarterly Review: International Banking and Financial Market Developments*," Table 16A–B. BIS (2002), "BIS *Quarterly Review: International Banking and Financial Market Developments*," Table 12A–D.

borrowings for crisis affected countries of Indonesia, Malaysia, the Philippines, Thailand, and even Hong Kong and Taiwan in 2002. By 2012 most economies had recovered or used other funding sources, but the Filipino banks appear to have the most long reaching impacts of the Asian crisis lingering. The Indonesian banking sector was able to raise some US$13.5 billion of domestic debts in 2012, which counteracted its reduction in international bank borrowings. Clearly the Japanese banks have moved to more insular funding via domestic debt funding.

The strength of any financial system can be measured by examining the ability of the corporate sector to raise funds. Comparing the total amount of corporate sector international bank borrowings to that of the government sector, the former has had good access with some 11.5 times government levels in 1997 but reducing to nearly 2 times by 2012. On a similar comparison but with domestic debt securities corporates had approximately 5.5 times the government sector levels in 1997, but this changed to a mere 18.4% by 2012. This suggests government issues are dominating, although the banking sector can also access this market. For international debt issues the corporates had some 4.6 times the level of government international debt in 2007, but this decreased to 2.11 times by 2012. As with the other sectors, the corporate sector favored domestic debt issues over international bank borrowings and then international debt issuance. For corporates borrowing via international debt markets the crisis affected countries of Indonesia, the Philippines, and Thailand were severely impacted in 2002, with the latter two recovering by 2012.

Table 13.7 Outstanding Sector Financing Across Asia (Billions of US Dollars)

Sector/Country	International Bank Borrowings			Domestic Debt Securities			International Debt Securities		
	December 1997	December 2002	December 2012	December 1997	December 2002	December 2012	December 1997	December 2002	December 2012
Government									
China	7.2	6.1	67.1	112.6	201.3	1283.6	9.0	5.4	13.6
Hong Kong	1.4	1.3	120.4	13.4	15.1	–	–	–	1.3
Indonesia	6.8	7.5	23.4	–	–	109.7	0.7	0.9	29.1
Japan	n/a	48.9	280.9	3082.8	4837.5	10,552.8	23.6	4.4	3.8
Korea	3.9	6.2	82.1	25.4	95.7	411.5	19.7	5.1	7.1
Malaysia	1.7	4.0	46.3	19.4	34.0	146.5	1.5	5.0	4.1
The Philippines	2.4	3.2	14.6	–	–	81.1	1.5	11.7	29.7
Singapore	0.6	0.6	73.4	13.1	32.8	116.6	–	0.3	–
Taiwan	0.4	1.0	51.2	–	–	176.6	–	–	–
Thailand	1.8	1.5	31.8	–	28.9	100.6	2.1	3.7	0.3
TOTALS	26	80	791	3266	5245	12,979	58.1	36.5	89
Banking									
China	46.0	18.4	217.4	42.7	200.7	1687.5	4.4	9.5	41.2
Hong Kong	126.3	32.4	53.6	22.2	24.7	–	6.9	28.1	8.3
Indonesia	12.4	2.4	12.6	–	–	13.5	3.9	7.8	1.6
Japan	n/a	259.8	255.4	814.1	1157.8	3034.6	108.4	204.2	164.0
Korea	58.3	36.7	72.4	51.7	134.0	370.3	12.8	29.0	52.8
Malaysia	9.9	2.9	13.0	16.8	10.6	75.6	0.7	7.8	6.8
The Philippines	9.1	4.7	5.9	–	–	–	2.7	4.8	2.6
Singapore	165.1	56.4	40.6	–	18.7	–	0.4	11.2	28.0
Taiwan	15.2	8.2	19.8	–	–	43.3	0.5	3.4	1.1
Thailand	25.0	3.2	18.7	–	11.9	144.3	6.8	5.0	5.5
TOTALS	467	425	709	947	1558	5369	147	310	311

(Continued)

Table 13.7 Continued

Sector/Country	International Bank Borrowings			Domestic Debt Securities			International Debt Securities		
	December 1997	December 2002	December 2012	December 1997	December 2002	December 2012	December 1997	December 2002	December 2012
Corporates									
China	30.0	17.9	209.4	6.3	10.4	805.4	4.1	2.5	15.0
Hong Kong	82.9	47.0	390.6	2.5	4.8	–	15.9	13.6	20.5
Indonesia	39.7	18.0	64.4	–	–	7.3	13.2	0.8	7.9
Japan	n/a	60.8	249.5	502.4	752.7	817.4	184.8	49.5	46.1
Korea	34.0	16.9	164.2	53.2	151.2	498.4	18.6	21.2	47.7
Malaysia	15.9	12.8	96.1	20.8	38.0	129.7	10.2	9.6	5.7
The Philippines	8.3	7.8	15.9	–	–	3.5	5.8	3.9	8.6
Singapore	38.6	27.9	205.3	2.3	6.1	–	4.3	5.6	20.8
Taiwan	11.1	8.2	80.2	–	–	91.0	5.9	10.2	9.1
Thailand	39.2	12.3	42.7	–	6.5	45.7	5.6	3.4	6.2
TOTALS	300	230	1518	588	970	2398	268	120	188

Source: BIS, Table 12B (2013, 2003, 1998), BIS Quarterly Review.

13.4 CONCLUSION

This chapter examined the financial development of 10 economies across the Asian region from pre-1996 Asian financial crisis to post-2007 Global Financial Crisis. The general consensus of the findings supports the proposition that the lessons learned from the Asian financial crisis allowed Asian nations to become more resilient in the face of financial market volatility that confronted most developed markets from 2007 onwards.

Most of the region's banking sectors have also recovered to their pre-Asian financial crisis levels, with the key exceptions being Indonesia and the Philippines, the latter being compensated by an increased level of equity market capitalization. Table 13.7 also shows that corporations in both of these countries improved their access to international bank finance. Although limited, by 2012, both countries reported that corporates had some access to domestic debt finance and wider access to international debt securities. The sovereign ratings for Indonesia and the Philippines have improved, which further supports our findings.

Japan remains a bank-dominated economy but one also with the ability of the government and banking sectors to raise significant domestic debt funds. Across the region although funding via international intermediated and debt markets increased with continued access for the corporate sector, domestic debt issuances have moved from being corporate and banking dominated to government issued. With further progression of financial systems it would be expected that banks and corporates could access a wider share.

The Asian region is at a pivotal point in its development, with diverse financial systems and an ever growing middle class. Nevertheless, the Asian market structure appears to have been rigorous in surviving the Global Financial Crisis. This structure is changing and as we witness China's move to the largest economy in the region, with an expanding consumer-based economy, instead of its earlier manufacturing focussed model. China's international trade will also become increasing denominated and settled in RMB, with banks in Hong Kong, Singapore, and Australia already allowed to do so. This should further internationalize the RMB and expand it into an important vehicle currency in addition to the USD and the Euro. Long term this should help improve regional stability and the process its financial development.

REFERENCES

AusAID, 2009. Lessons from the Asian financial crisis, Issues Note. February, Australian Government.

BIS, 2001. Quarterly Review: International Banking and Financial Market Developments, Bank for International Settlements.

BIS, 2002. Quarterly Review: International Banking and Financial Market Developments, Bank for International Settlements.

BIS, 2003. Quarterly Review: International Banking and Financial Market Developments, Bank for International Settlements.

Bongini, P., Claessens, S., Ferri, G., 2002. The political economy of distress in East Asian financial institutions. Journal of Financial Services Research 19 (1), 5–25.

Caprio, G., Klingebiel, D., Laeven, L., Noguera, G., 2005. Banking crisis database. In: Honohan, P., Laeven, L. (Eds.), Systemic Financial Crises. Cambridge University Press, Cambridge.

Filardo, A., 2012. Ensuring price stability in post-crisis Asia: lessons from the recovery. BIS Working Paper No. 378, April.

Filardo, A., George, J., Loretan, M., Ma, G.N., Munro, A., Shim, I., Wooldridge, P., Yetman, J., Zhu, H.B., 2010. The international financial crisis: timeline, impact and policy responses in Asia and the Pacific. BIS Papers No. 52, July.

(FSB) Financial Stability Board, 2012. Global Shadow Banking Monitoring Report, November.

Nakaso, H., 2001. The financial crisis in Japan during the 1990s: how the bank of Japan responded and the lessons learnt. BIS Papers No. 6, October.

Szilagyi, P., Batten, J., 2004. Corporate governance and financial system development. Journal of Corporate Citizenship 13, 49–65.

The Economist, 2013. Giant Reality Check: Four of the Worlds' Biggest Lenders Must Face Some Nasty Truths, August 31.

World Bank, 2002. World Bank Development Indicators, International Bank for Reconstruction and Development, Washington, DC.

CHAPTER 14

Does Asia Really have Poorer Governance? Evidence from International Variations in Self-Dealing Transparency

Raj Aggarwal[a] and John W. Goodell[b]
[a]7380 Sherman Rd., Chesterland, OH 44026, USA
[b]Department of Finance, University of Akron, 325 Buchtel Common, OH 44107, USA

14.1 INTRODUCTION

Corporate governance is the system of rights in a corporation exercised by various stakeholders, such as the majority shareholders, minority shareholders, debt holders, employees, and the community. Thus, it is a critical aspect of how corporations relate to the rest of society. Prior international studies on governance have noted that Asian countries are characterized by poor corporate governance with widespread use of pyramid ownership structures and family control of Asian companies as parts of closely interrelated business groups (e.g., Mitton, 2002; Claessens and Fan, 2002; Perkins et al., 2008). However, there is relatively little attention paid to the governance environment in Asia. This contrast in attention may help explain why Asian capital markets are thriving and growing in spite of poor corporate governance. It seems poor corporate governance in Asia is at least partially offset by good national governance environments and related laws and regulations.

Further, a considerable body of literature has shown that efficient financial systems and easy access to finance are important for economic development (Levine, 2005). Further, Beck and Demirguc-Kunt (2008) note that there are other broad social benefits to an efficient financial system. Beck et al. (2007), for instance, find that nations with better developed financial systems and easier access to finance not only have faster economic growth but also have reduced economic inequality (and greater benefits for the poorer population). Concomitant with this, however, as noted by Williamson (1988) and others, e.g., Aggarwal and Zhao (2009), Transaction Cost Economics (TCE) suggests that the costs involved with resolving the asymmetric information inherent in financial contracting have a direct bearing on the health of financial systems.

Self-dealing is the act of an agent acting in their own interest rather than in the interest of shareholders, beneficiaries, or clients during the conducting of a transaction. Economic transactions between parties can be adversely influenced by undisclosed self-dealing, when an economic entity owns other parties in a transaction but does not disclose that fact to some parties in a transaction. Given the central role of opportunistic behavior in transactions costs, the transparency of self-dealing can be expected to be an important determinant of transactions costs in a country. For instance, it is expected that greater self-dealing transparency lowers the cost of market financing by lowering the transaction costs of resolving asymmetric information (e.g., Ergungor, 2004; Kwok and Tadesse, 2006; Aggarwal and Goodell, 2009a, 2010). In short, governance and transparency are important at least for financial intermediation and financial development.

In this chapter, using an index of self-dealing disclosure for over 60 countries, we empirically examine the cultural determinants of the level of national self-dealing transparency, with a view toward whether there really is inherently less governance transparency in Asia. We document that higher self-dealing transparency is positively associated with the Asian region. We also find that governance disclosure is negatively associated with uncertainty avoidance and positively associated with an English legal origin and greater economic inequality. It does seem that poor corporate governance in Asia is offset by better laws and regulations regarding governance disclosure. Our findings shed important light on the assessment of governance practices in Asia, given that the Asian region has often been regarded as having poor governance. Our findings regarding the determinants of self-dealing disclosure have important implications for international variation with regard to the role of opportunistic behavior and the level of transactions costs in countries.

14.2 CORPORATE GOVERNANCE, TRANSPARENCY, AND TRANSACTION COSTS

Corporate governance, corporate transparency, and transactions costs are intimately connected. The quality of corporate governance depends critically on corporate transparency as information asymmetry between stakeholders determines the nature of corporate governance. The institutional environment is instrumental in how this information asymmetry feeds into transactions costs that in turn determine the nature of corporate governance. In this section, we examine these relationships in greater detail.

Corporate governance is the system through which various stakeholders exercise their rights. Naturally, this exercise is critically dependent on the level of information asymmetry faced by these stakeholders. This level of information asymmetry clearly varies internationally and depends on, among other factors, the level and nature of disclosure and transparency with respect to governance issues.

14.2.1 The Nature of Corporate Governance

Corporate governance is an important global topic that has received much attention in finance, economics, management, and international business. However, the state of the art in corporate governance does not seem uniformly advanced as there is little agreement even in how corporate governance is defined. For example, according to most finance literature on corporate governance "Corporate governance deals with the ways in which suppliers of finance to corporations assure themselves of getting a return on their investment" (Shleifer and Vishny, 1997). In contrast, according to the management literature, corporate governance more broadly concerns "the structure of rights and responsibilities among the parties with a stake in the firm" Aoki (2000) and there seem to be three major stakeholder groups involved in corporate governance: capital, labor, and management.

Subsequent to Shleifer and Vishny (1997) scholars have traditionally studied corporate governance within the framework of agency theory, viewing the corporation as a nexus of contracts between principals (risk-bearing shareholders) and agents (managers with specialized expertise). Comparative corporate governance is usually conceived of in terms of the mechanisms available to minimize agency problems arising out of asymmetric information (Denis and McConnell, 2003). Thus, the corporate governance literature has mostly taken a fairly narrow perspective focusing on the rights of the shareholders in a dyadic shareholder-manager relationship. This narrow agency problems-based perspective has proven to be inadequate in many different ways.

First, different types of investors (such as banks, institutional investors, families, etc.) are likely to pursue different interests, particularly when some of these investors are actually organizations governed by their own rules. Similarly, managers most likely also have varied interests. Comparative governance research must address these variations in interests within categories of stakeholders in different countries (Aguilera and Jackson, 2003). Second, international governance must consider important interdependencies among various stakeholders in the firm, and the exclusive focus on bilateral contracts between principals and agents is inadequate. For example, agency theorists treat employment relations as exogenously determined by labor markets despite important employee voice within corporate boards of many European and some US firms. Similarly, interfirm ownership prevalent in many countries may create networks that condition business competition, cooperation, and innovation (Aguilera and Jackson, 2003).

Second, agency theory has only a thin view of the institutional environment surrounding corporate governance (Roe, 2000). For example, shareholder rights do not adequately capture the entire complexity of institutional domains in limiting actors' financial behavior to the effects of law (La Porta et al., 1998). Firms must adapt to multiple features of their institutional environment, and their behavior is unlikely to be explained by a single force such as agency costs. Thus, corporate governance needs to be understood in the context of a wider range of institutional environments (Aggarwal et al., 2008; Aoki, 2000).

Third, with the rise of internationalization, there has been much interest in global and comparative corporate governance. Country location of a firm matters for corporate governance because it influences the costs that firms incur to promise good governance (Doidge et al., 2007). Better governance reduces a firm's cost of capital when investors expect the firm to be well governed so a firm must commit itself credibly to higher-quality governance. However, mechanisms to do so could be unavailable or prohibitively expensive in countries with poor investor protection, poor economic and financial development, or otherwise poor institutional environment. In such cases, good governance may provide better access to capital markets. But, firms in countries with low financial and economic development will find it uneconomic to invest in governance, and the rights of minority shareholders will be mostly determined at the country level (Coffee, 1999).

However, the diversity of governance practices around the world seems inconsistent with a common global definition of corporate governance (Aggarwal et al., 2008). Internationalization has also sparked corporate and policy debates over the transferability of best practices and has given rise to studies on international convergence (Guillen, 2000; Coffee, 1999). National differences in corporate governance and how they should best be conceptualized remain debated (O'Sullivan, 2000; Shleifer and Vishny, 1997; Denis and McConnell, 2003). It is worth noting that internationalization has not led to convergence of corporate governance but to a *hybridization* of corporate governance models, where practices developed in one national setting are transferred to another where they undergo adaptation through their specific new institutional environment.

14.2.2 Corporate Governance in Asia

Most Asian countries suffered from major currency and financial market crises in the late 1990s. One major conclusion from this crises period in Asia was that Asian systems of corporate governance were inadequate. Indeed, it was contended that poor corporate governance in Asia was a major contributor to the crises (Johnson et al., 2000). Since then, Asian countries have grown at higher than average rates and now Asian economies are some of the largest in the world. Consequently, there has been much effort at reform of corporate governance systems in Asia with an attempt to transplant western corporate governance systems in Asian countries. Such attempts resulted in systems of corporate governance that were hybrids of the western systems adapted to institutional and cultural conditions in each of the Asian countries (Aggarwal et al., 2008).

But, Asia is different. Asian corporate governance systems differ greatly from US or European systems (Aoki, 2000). Further, systems of corporate governance in Asia are of course different in different countries. Nevertheless, they all seem to share a couple of common concerns. First, Asian corporate governance systems must account for sometimes family-controlled pyramidal business groups (Khanna and Yafeh, 2007). Included in this broad category are the widely known business groups, the Japanese *Kieretsu,* the Korean *Chaebols,* the Southeast Asian *family (ethnically)-controlled businesses*, and the *Indian Business Houses.* All of these Asian business groups are characterized by significant inter-firm stock holdings, important inter-firm business relations, and control of the group through pyramidal holdings. Second, given the evidence of tunneling, Asian systems of corporate governance all seem to be concerned with protecting minority shareholders and other stakeholders from possible expropriation of resources by the controlling shareholder (Bertrand et al., 2002; Johnson et al., 2000).

As assessed by previous literature such as Claessens and Fan (2002), Rajan and Zingales (1998), corporate governance in Asia is colored heavily by an emphasis on controlling family ownership, business groups, and boards that lack independence. Past research has often focused on single region or single country studies (see for example, Joh, 2003 on business groups in Korea; Claessens et al., 2000 on East Asia; Yeh et al., 2001 on Taiwan; Chhibber and Majumdar, 1999 for Indian firms; Qi et al., 2000 for Chinese firms; and Khanthavit et al., 2004 on Thailand). More comprehensive studies include Durnev and Kim (2005), Klapper and Love (2005).

And yet, as important as the Asian markets are to the world there has been relatively little research that directly investigates Asian governance compared to the rest of the world and even less that focuses on the legal environment of Asia. An exception is Durnev and Kim (2005), who suggest that firms adopt better governance in response to poor legal environments. On the other hand, Krishnamurti et al. (2005) find firms adopting better governance in countries with better legal systems. Interestingly, a number of papers suggest that better country-level governance promotes market-based financing over bank financing (e.g., Ergungor, 2004; Kwok and Tadesse, 2006; Aggarwal and Goodell, 2009a). However, Aggarwal and Goodell (2009b) find, ceteris paribus, that if an emerging market is Asian then equity financing is more preferred over bank financing. Obviously there is much that is unsettled.

As the brief review of corporate governance in general and corporate governance in Asia suggests international variations in corporate governance can be overwhelming; with innumerable combinations of institutions, culture, law, ownership structure, and stakeholder structure with each unique combination of these factors giving rise to a unique system of corporate governance. In order to simplify, we contend that focusing a few significant factors can provide fresh insights. We suggest an important factor in understanding international variations in corporate governance is the role of governance transparency and how it influences transactions costs.

14.2.3 Corporate Governance Transparency

Transparency of firms is important for financial and economic development. The development of financial markets especially depends on the transparency of firms, and partially as a consequence, so does economic development. Our focus on transparency is also closely relevant to past studies on governance (e.g., Guillen, 2004; Rubach and Sebora, 1998; Thomas III and Waring, 1999; Gedajlovic and Shapiro, 1998; Pedersen and Thomsen, 1997; Shleifer and Vishny, 1997). Denis and McConnell (2003), a survey of research on corporate governance systems around the world, notes that there has been a shift over time from research focused on firm characteristics in individual countries to cross-national corporate governance research that considers the possible impact of country-level characteristics such as differing legal systems. Quality of governance seems to vary from country to country. Doidge et al. (2007) develop and test a model of how country characteristics, such as legal protections for minority investors and the level of economic and financial development, influence firms' governance and transparency. They find that country characteristics explain much more of the variance in governance ratings than firm characteristics. It is natural to therefore consider that country-level factors are very important in determining cross-natural differences in transparency.

Efficient capital markets depend critically on reliable disclosure and the cost of capital and market mispricing decline with increased disclosure. For instance, Bailey et al. (2006) examine market behavior around earnings announcements to understand the consequences of the increased disclosure faced by non-US firms when listing in the USA. They find that absolute return and volume reactions to earnings announcements are positively associated with firms cross-listing in the US. Alford et al. (1993) find that improvement in disclosure and governance leads to improvement in, and is positively associated with, the usefulness of accounting earnings. Almazan et al. (2003) find that absolute return and volume reactions to earnings announcements typically *increase* significantly once a company cross-lists its shares in the US. Aggarwal and Kyaw (2006) find that transparency affects firms' capital structure and cost of capital. Sengupta (1998) documents that increased disclosure is associated with lower cost of debt and this association is stronger when market uncertainty is higher. Similarly, Leuz and Verrechia (2000) interpret their results to show that greater transparency reduces the cost of capital. In addition to these examples of the shareholder advantages of transparency, literature also shows that other stakeholders also benefit from transparency (Aguilera and Jackson, 2003). Clearly, the nature of transparency matters for corporate governance (Doidge et al., 2007).

14.2.4 Opportunistic Behavior and Transaction Costs

As noted by Williamson (1988) and others more recently (e.g., Aggarwal and Zhao, 2009; Aggarwal and Goodell, 2009a), Transaction Cost Economics (TCE) suggests that the overall costs of market exchange has a significant impact on respective financial systems. Hart (1995, 2001) recognize that the primary transactions costs of market exchanges stem from the uncertainties of contracts. Especially since the publication of Williamson (1975), the transaction cost approach to the study of firms and other governance structures has become recognized as a major theory. Further, since Williamson (1975), opportunistic behavior of individuals has been identified as an important and fundamental component of transaction costs. Williamson (1975) suggests that under conditions of imperfect information, all transactions are affected by the problem of "self-interest seeking with guile." He later offered the alternative definition of opportunistic behavior as the "incomplete or distorted disclosure of information, especially to calculated efforts to mislead, distort, disguise, obfuscate, or otherwise confuse." What is meant by this is that, given the opportunity, agents are likely to serve their own interests rather than those of the other party to the contract (see also Jensen and Meckling, 1976; Fama, 1980). Therefore, the potential for opportunistic behavior is inherently a primary cause of a need to reconcile the asymmetric information central to contracts. It is then the subsequent cost of reconciling asymmetric information that is the central cost of contracting (Hart, 1995, 2001). Absent the likelihood of opportunistic behavior, there would be little consequent pecuniary need to expensive information gathering. Here in this chapter, we examine the determinants of laws that mandate disclosure of potential opportunistic behavior. In so doing we feel we address a fundamental aspect of determinants of transaction costs in respective financial systems.

14.2.5 Country Determinants of Governance Transparency

The effect of country-level variables on corporate transparency and disclosure, especially financial disclosure, has been extensively considered in the literature. Of seminal interest is the work of Gray (1988), who hypothesizes that the "secrecy of firms" is partially determined by respective national cultures. For instance, Gray (1988) suggests a positive association of disclosure and the masculinity cultural dimension of Hofstede (2001). Gray (1988) contends that as more masculine societies would be more concerned with the position of one entity versus another, a more masculine social environment would encourage disclosing more information about its financial position and performance to enable comparisons of the level of performance of different entities. Gray (1988) proposes that secrecy is also positively related with uncertainty avoidance. He reasons that in societies with more ambiguity aversion less information is expected to avoid conflict and competition. Gray (1988) also suggests a positive association of individualism and a negative association of power distance with transparency. Gray (1988) contends that less information is conducive to preserve power inequalities.

Building on Gray (1988), subsequent investigation of the association of transparency and national culture have also been undertaken by, for example, Taylor Zarzeski (1996), Jaggi and Low (2000), Hope (2003), Archambault and Archambault (2003), and Santema et al. (2005). Taylor Zarzeski (1996) find that masculine societies are more transparent. In addition, Taylor Zarzeski (1996) documents significant a positive relation between secrecy and uncertainty, as well as a negative relationship between individualism and secrecy.

Jaggi and Low (2000) document a negative relation between masculinity and financial disclosure. Jaggi and Low (2000) also find a significant positive relation between secrecy and uncertainty and a negative association of secrecy and individualism.

Archambault and Archambault (2003) find a positive relation between uncertainty avoidance and financial disclosure. Archambault and Archambault (2003) also find a negative relation between masculinity and financial disclosure and a positive association of individualism with disclosure. Hope (2003) find significant positive relation between secrecy and uncertainty. Further, Hope (2003) finds a negative relation between masculinity and financial disclosure. Salter and Niswander (1995) also find a significant positive relation between secrecy and uncertainty.

Both Jaggi and Low (2000) and Hope (2003) investigate the effect of legal origin on the impact of culture on transparency. Jaggi and Low (2000) find that in countries with an English legal origin, culture does influence disclosure levels, but not in civil-law countries. Hope (2003) find that culture matters more than legal origin in determining transparency. Bushman et al. (2004) find that transparency is positively related to a country's legal system and political-economic factors. Similarly, we expect that better regulation and less corruption are associated with better transparency.

Previous literature has also investigated other cross-country determinants of firm-level behavior related to financial reporting. For instance, past literature covers cross-country variation in earnings management and the value-relevance of earnings (e.g., Alford et al., 1993; Ali and Huang, 2000; Francis et al., 2003; Guenther and Young, 2000; Land and Lang, 2002. Previous research has also examined cross-country determinants of earnings management (e.g., Leuz et al., 2003; Bhattacharya et al., 2003; Kinnunen and Koskela, 2003). Other research has examined cross-national differences in earnings timeliness (Ball et al., 2000) and disclosure intensity and audit quality (Francis et al., 2003; Jaggi and Low, 2000). Bushman et al. (2004) find that transparency is positively related to a country's legal system and political-economic factors. While there is little direct evidence of the influence of national characteristics on self-dealing transparency, we use these prior findings regarding financial and general transparency to guide us regarding the possible national variables that may be important in determining national self-dealing transparency levels.

14.2.6 Contribution

The corporate environment in Asia may well be described as by Claessens and Fan (2002) and others as typified by business groups, family ownership, and questionable independence of boards. However, previous research on Asian corporate governance has not considered the impact of disclosure about the potential for opportunistic behavior. We investigate in this chapter whether or not Asia is characterized by more openness about respective potential for opportunistic behavior. If Durnev and Kim (2005) suggest that firms adopt better governance in response to poor legal environments, it is important to investigate the quality of disclosure in Asia as it compares with the rest of the world. As the primary focus of this chapter is to investigate the quality of governance disclosure in Asia relative to the rest of the world. We consider the following set of hypotheses:

H1: Governance disclosure is lower in Asia than elsewhere.

H2: Governance disclosure is higher in Asia than elsewhere.

H3: Governance disclosure is independent of being in Asia.

We note tension in our hypotheses regarding the association with Asia and governance disclosure. Perhaps, there is more potential for opportunistic behavior in Asia. But is it also true (or not) that they disclose this potential more?

14.3 METHODOLOGY

14.3.1 Dependent Variable

Our dependent variable for transparency is the anti-self-dealing index of Djankov et al. (2008) (GOVERNANCE_DISCL). This index was compiled with the aide of Lex Mundi law firms in 72 countries, based on prevailing laws and reported in Djankov et al. (2008) (this is the latest such data available). Self-dealing is the act of an agent acting in their own interest rather than in the interest of shareholders, beneficiaries, or clients during the conducting of a transaction.

In this section, drawing heavily from Djankov et al. (2008), we describe in detail the variables used in forming the index of anti-self-dealing. The index of anti-self-dealing is built from other indices that capture ex-ante and ex-post disclosure and the quality of enforcement. According to Djankov et al. (2008), the "Disclosures by Buyer" is an "index of disclosures that are required before the transaction may be approved." This ranges from 0 to 1.

"One-third point if each of the following items must be disclosed by Buyer to the public or its shareholders before the transaction is approved: (1) Mr. James owns 60% of Buyer; (2) Mr. James owns 90% of Seller; and either (3) all material facts or the following three items: (a) description of the assets; (b) nature and amount of consideration; and (c) explanation for the price." "Disclosures by Mr. James" is an index of disclosures that Mr. James must make before the transaction may be approved. This index ranges from 0 to 1 and is assigned "0" if no disclosure is required. It is assigned "0.5" if only the existence of a conflict of interest must be disclosed, without details. The index is assigned "1" if all material facts must be disclosed. "Independent Review" is an index that is assigned "1" if a positive review by a financial expert or independent auditor is required before the transaction may be approved and "0" otherwise. According to Djankov et al. (2008), Ex-Ante Disclosure is the arithmetic average of "Disclosures by Buyer," "Disclosures by Mr. James," and "Independent Review."

"Approval by Disinterested Shareholders" is an index that is assigned "1" if the transaction must be approved by disinterested shareholders and "0" otherwise. "Ex-Ante Disclosure of Self-Dealing" is an index formed as the arithmetic average of Ex-Ante Disclosure and Approval by Disinterested Shareholders. "Disclosures Required in Periodic Filings" ranges from 0 to 1. 0.20 point is granted for each of the following items: "(1) Mr. James owns 60% of stake in Buyer; (2) Mr. James owns 90% of Seller; (3) shares held beneficially by Mr. James (i.e., shares held and/or managed via a nominee account, trust, brokerage firm, or bank); (4) shares held indirectly by Mr. James (e.g., via a subsidiary company or holding); and either (5) all material facts about the transaction or the following three items: (a) description of the assets; (b) nature and amount of consideration; and (c) explanation for the price." According to Djankov et al. (2008), Standing to Sue is assigned "1" if a 10% shareholder may sue derivatively Mr. James or the approving bodies or both for damages that the firm suffered as a result of the transaction, and "0" otherwise.

"Ease in Rescinding the Transaction" ranges from 0 to 1. It is assigned "0" when rescission is unavailable or only available in case of bad faith, or when the transaction is unreasonable or causes disproportionate damage. It is assigned 0.5 when rescission is available when the transaction is oppressive or prejudicial. It is assigned "1" when rescission is available when the transaction is unfair or entails a conflict of interest. According to Djankov et al. (2008), "Ease in Holding Mr. James Liable for Civil Damages" ranges from 0 to 1. It is assigned "0" when the interested director is either not liable or liable in case of bad faith, intent, or gross negligence. It is assigned "0.5" when the interested director is liable if he/she either influenced the approval or was negligent. And it is assigned "1" if the interested director is liable if the transaction is unfair, oppressive, or prejudicial.

According to Djankov et al. (2008), "Ease in Holding Members of the Approving Body Liable for Civil Damages" ranges from 0 to 1. It is assigned "0" when members of the approving body are either not liable or liable in case of intent, bad faith, or gross negligence. It is assigned "0.5" when members of the approving body are liable if they acted negligently. It is assigned "1" if members of the approving body are liable if the transaction is unfair, oppressive, or prejudicial. "Index of Access to Evidence" ranges from 0 to 1. One-quarter point is added to the measure for each of the following four rights: "(1) a shareholder owning at least 10% of the shares can request that the court appoint an inspector to investigate Buyer's affairs; (2) the plaintiff can request any documents relevant to the case from the defendant (without specifying which ones); (3) the plaintiff may examine the defendant without the court approving the questions in advance; and (4) the plaintiff may examine non-parties without the court approving the questions in advance." One-eighth point is added to the measure for each of the following two rights: "(1) the plaintiff may examine the defendant but questions require prior court approval; and (2) the plaintiff may examine directly the non-parties but questions require prior court approval."

"Ease of Proving Wrongdoing" is the arithmetic average of Standing to Sue, Ease in Rescinding the Transaction, Index of the Ease in Holding Mr. James Liable for Civil Damages, Index of the Ease in Holding Members of the Approving Body Liable for Civil Damages, and Access to Evidence., "Ex-post Private Control of Self-Dealing" is the arithmetic average of Disclosure in Periodic Filings and Ease of Proving Wrongdoing. Finally, the "Anti-Self-Dealing Index" is the arithmetic average of Ex-Ante Private Control of Self-Dealing and Ex-Post Private Control of Self-Dealing.

14.3.2 Statistical Specification

Our empirical models and their estimates are based on the following equation.

$$GOVERNANCE\_DISCL_i = \alpha_i + \sum \beta_1 * ASIA + \sum \beta_{2i} * X_i + e_i \quad (14.1)$$

In Eq. (14.1), GOVERNANCE_DISCL is the anti-self-dealing index, ASIA is a dummy variable that is assigned "1" if the country is in Asia and "0" otherwise, and X_i represents a vector of relevant country-level control variables that are discussed next.

14.3.3 Independent Control Variables

We control for a number of country-level variables that have been found by previous studies of transparency to be of importance. This includes controlling for the effect of national culture on cross-national differences in the transparency of corporate reporting. Among country-level variables, previous literature has identified national culture as having an important role in determining cross-country differences in financial disclosure and corporate reporting (see, for instance, Taylor Zarzeski, 1996; Jaggi and Low, 2000; Hope, 2003; Archambault and Archambault, 2003; Gray, 1988; Lainez and Gasca, 2006). From a sociological perspective, De Jong et al. (2006) find a positive association of "openness" with individualism and negative association of openness with uncertainty avoidance and power distance. Consequently, we include as independent variables the six cultural dimensions of Hofstede et al. (2010): uncertainty avoidance (UAI), individualism versus collectivism (IDV), power distance (PDI), and masculinity or gender differentiation (MAS), indulgence versus restraint (IVR), and long-term orientation (LTOWVS). To improve sample sizes, Hofstede et al. (2010) employ World Value Surveys to assist in forming their estimates of this last dimension. We consider the following hypothesis with regard to the association of national culture and self-dealing transparency.

H5: There is a negative association of self-dealing transparency with uncertainty avoidance.

De Jong et al. (2006) find a negative association of openness with uncertainty avoidance. Gray (1988) proposes that secrecy is positively related with uncertainty avoidance, equating to hypothesizing a negative association between transparency and uncertainty avoidance. Gray (1988) suggests that in societies with more ambiguity aversion less information is expected to avoid conflict and competition. In other words, a negative correlation between uncertainty avoidance and financial disclosure is expected. Consistent with this, Salter and Niswander (1995), Taylor Zarzeski (1996), Jaggi and Low (2000), and Hope (2003) find significant positive relation between secrecy and uncertainty (and so inferring a negative relation to uncertainty avoidance). However, in contrast to other research, Archambault and Archambault (2003) find a positive relation between uncertainty avoidance and financial disclosure.

Among the other independent variables, we include a dummy variable that is assigned "1" if the legal origin of the respective home country is English and "0" otherwise

(LEGAL_ORIGIN). This data is compiled from La Porta et al. (2006). This variable is included because first many theorize that common law systems offer better investor protection especially against self-dealing (e.g., Johnson et al., 2002). We wish to differentiate a region effect of Asia from a legalorigins effect. Secondly, Djankov et al. (2008) note a high correlation between the index of anti-self-dealing and English common law.

Both Jaggi and Low (2000), Hope (2003) investigate the effect of legal origin on the impact of culture on accounting transparency. Jaggi and Low (2000) find that in countries of an English legal origin culture does influence accounting disclosure levels, but not in civil-law countries. Hope (2003) find that culture matters more than legal origin in determining transparency. We do not hypothesize about the sign of this independent variable as previous research has been inconclusive. Does English legal origin concomitantly improve self-dealing transparency?

In addition, in order to control for cross-national differences in wealth we include as an independent variable, GDP per capita in constant US dollars. As is usual for this variable, to make it better behaved we take the log of this value because of its large variation and size compared with the other independent variables (LNGDP). We also control for wealth inequality with the Gini Index (GINI) from the *World Development Indicators*. As noted by Bjornskov (2008) and others, inequality establishes societal fractionalization which can impact social trust. Gini has been included in a vast number of studies that have political economy aspects.

We also control for cross-national differences in measures against corruption from the World Bank (Kaufmann et al., 2010). We include this variable, ANTI-CORRUPTION, because previous research, e.g., Bushman et al. (2004), finds that accounting transparency is positively related to a country's legal system and political economic factors. We expect that better regulation and less corruption are associated with better governance disclosure, as legal requirements for disclosure is a part of the respective overall regulatory emphasis.

H4: Home country control of corruption is positively associated with governance disclosure.

14.3.4 Additional Statistical Correction

In order to reduce any effects of multi-collinearity and to correct for associations between the Asian region and governance disclosure, we orthogonalize LEGAL_ORIGIN against national culture and the Asian region. To form this variable we first orthogonalize LEGAL_ORIGIN against national culture and the Asian regional dummy variable. Orthogonalization is done by first regressing the main independent variable against national culture variables and ASIA according to Eq. (14.2) below and then using the residuals from Eq. (14.2), RESID_LEGAL_ORIGIN, as substitutes for the independent variable LEGAL_ORIGIN in the regressions.

$$\text{LEGAL\_ORIGIN}_i = \alpha_i + \beta_{1i}\text{UAI} + \beta_{2i}\text{PDI} + \beta_{3i}\text{IDV} + \beta_{4i}\text{MAS} \\ + \beta_{4i}\text{LTOWVS} + \beta_{5i}\text{IVR} + \beta_{6i}\text{ASIA} + \varepsilon_i \tag{14.2}$$

14.4 RESULTS

14.4.1 Descriptive Statistics and Preliminary Analysis

Table 14.1 displays the mean, standard deviation and sources for our dependent and independent variables. Table 14.2 displays the Pearson correlations coefficients for our dependent and independent variables. Our sample includes all of the major Asian countries such as China, Hong Kong, India, Indonesia, Japan, Korea, Malaysia, Pakistan, Philippines, Singapore, Taiwan, and Thailand. Examining Table 14.2, we see that the correlation between GOVERNANCE_DISCL and ASIA is positive, suggesting a positive relation between disclosure of the potential for opportunistic behavior and the Asian region.

Table 14.1 International Governance Disclosure: Descriptive Statistics and Summary of Data Sources

Variable	Mean	Standard Deviation	Source
GOVERNANCE_DISCL	0.444	0.234	Index of Anti-Self-Dealing from Djankov et al. (2008) This index was compiled with the aide of Lex Mundi law firms in 72 countries, based on prevailing laws in 2003. Self-dealing is the act of an agent acting in their own interest rather than in the interest of shareholders, beneficiaries or clients during the conducting of a transaction
ASIA	0.183	0.340	Dummy variable that is assigned "1" is the nation is from the Asian region and "0" otherwise
ANTI_CORRUPTION	0.517	1.116	Anti-Corruption measure of World Bank
LNGDP	8.901	1.464	PPP GDP per capita 2003
LEGAL_ORIGIN	0.324	0.471	Dummy variable that is assigned "1" if the nation has English language origin and "0" otherwise
GINI	38.224	9.291	Gini coefficient from World Development Indicators 2003
PDI	58.429	21.797	Power Distance Hofstede et al. (2010)
UAI	64.968	23.434	Uncertainty Avoidance Hofstede et al. (2010)
IDV	44.508	23.721	Individualism versus Collectivism Hofstede et al. (2010)
MAS	50.492	20.092	Masculinity Hofstede et al. (2010)
LTOWVS	46.703	24.561	Long-Term Orientation incorporating World Value Surveys Hofstede et al. (2010)
IVR	48.238	22.977	Indulgence versus Restraint Hofstede et al. (2010)

This table lists the mean, and standard deviations, and sources of variables used in regressions which are reported in Table 14.2. All other data dates reflect consistency with the latest available data on governance disclosure.

Table 14.2 International Governance Disclosure: Pearson Correlation Coefficients

		1	2	3	4	5	6	7	8	9	10	11	12
1	GOVERNANCE_DISCL	1.000											
2	ASIA	0.399	1.000										
3	ANTI_CORRUPTION	0.057	−0.168	1.000									
4	LNGDP	0.020	−0.258	0.802	1.000								
5	LEGAL_ORIGIN	0.661	0.351	−0.050	−0.159	1.000							
6	GINI	0.375	0.219	−0.401	−0.485	0.295	1.000						
7	UAI	−0.487	−0.314	−0.297	−0.165	−0.564	0.036	1.000					
8	IDV	0.003	−0.441	0.558	0.681	0.105	−0.485	−0.266	1.000				
9	PDI	0.009	0.327	−0.665	−0.661	0.015	0.440	0.223	−0.668	1.000			
10	MAS	0.013	0.093	−0.261	−0.071	0.155	0.102	0.075	0.067	0.190	1.000		
11	LTOWVS	0.041	0.375	0.192	0.363	−0.262	−0.322	0.006	0.119	−0.018	0.155	1.000	
12	IVR	0.003	−0.361	0.207	0.254	0.110	0.132	−0.171	0.221	−0.293	−0.060	−0.412	1.000

14.4.2 Results of Regressions of Bounded Tobit Regressions

First, the statistical properties of the results give us confidence that the results are reliable and dependable. All estimated models have variance inflation factors (VIF) of less than 10 for all regressors indicating that any multi-collinearity is unlikely to be a significant problem. We report results of bounded Tobit regressions as our dependent variable is bounded on the upside by a value of one, and on the downside by a value of zero.

Table 14.3 reports the results of regressions using four different sets of independent variables on the dependent variable GOVERNANCE_DISCL. The first

Table 14.3 Cross-National Determinants of Self-Dealing Transparency: The Role of Asia

Dependent Variable: GOVERNANCE_DISCL	Model			
	1	2	3	4
ASIA	0.216**	0.218**	0.222**	0.179**
	(0.044)	(0.041)	(0.011)	(0.043)
LNGDP	0.028	0.041	0.059	0.063*
	(0.411)	(0.345)	(0.103)	(0.079)
ANTI_CORRUPTION		−0.022	−0.017	−0.025
		(0.628)	(0.656)	(0.501)
RESID_LEGAL_ORIGIN			0.409***	0.333***
			(0.000)	(0.000)
GINI				0.010***
				(0.002)
UAI	−0.004**	−0.004**	−0.004***	−0.004***
	(0.014)	(0.012)	(0.002)	(0.003)
PDI	0.000	0.001	0.001	0.000
	(0.581)	(0.668)	(0.405)	(0.912)
MAS	0.000	0.000	0.000	−0.000
	(0.858)	(0.961)	(0.841)	(0.765)
IDV	0.000	0.000	0.000	0.001
	(0.908)	(0.908)	(0.906)	(0.542)
LTOWVS	−0.002	−0.002	−0.002	−0.001
	(0.352)	(0.323)	(0.117)	(0.382)
IVR	−0.000	−0.000	−0.000	−0.002
	(0.925)	(0.876)	(0.668)	(0.234)
INTERCEPT	0.361	0.361	0.361	−0.147
	(0.231)	(0.336)	(0.471)	(0.651)
OBS	58	58	58	58
Pseudo R-square	21.16%	15.71%	43.66%	63.64%
LR Chi square	23.20***	23.44***	47.87***	7.32***
	(0.003)	(0.005)	(0.0003)	(0.000)

*Significant at 10% level. **Significant at 5% level. ***Significant at 1% level.
Dependent variable is TRANSPARENCY. Dependent and independent variables defined in Table 14.1. Variance inflation factors (VIF) less than 10 for all variables and all models. Results of Tobit regressions with upper bound of 1 and lower bound of 0. p-Values in parentheses.

regression includes as independent variables the six dimensions of national culture of Hofstede et al. (2010), as well as LNGDP and our independent variable of primary interest ASIA. These results show that ASIA is significantly positive at 5%. This is consistent with improved governance disclosure associated with the Asian region. UAI is negatively significant at 5%, consistent with less governance disclosure in societies with more ambiguity aversion.

Model 2 of Table 14.3 adds to the independent variables of Model 1 the World Bank measures of the effectiveness of measures against corruption (ANTI_CORRUPTION). We include this variable to control for overall corruption while examining cross-national differences in governance disclosure. Again, ASIA is positively significant at 5%. UAI is again negatively significant at 5%. ANTI_CORRUPTION is not significant, consistent with cross-national differences in governance disclosure being independent of cross-national differences in the overall control of corruption.

Model 3 adds to the set of independent variables RESID_LEGAL_ORIGIN. This estimate also shows that ASIA is again positively significant at 5%. UAI is again negatively significant, now at 1%. RESID_LEGAL_ORIGIN is also positively significant (1%). The results of Model 3 are consistent with governance disclosure being more efficient in Asia even when controlling for cross-national differences in legal origin, overall control of corruption, wealth levels, and national culture.

Model 4 adds to the set of independent variables the Gini coefficient of economic inequality (GINI). This results in GINI being positively significant at 1%. This result is consistent with greater governance disclosure being positively associated with greater wealth inequality. ASIA is again positively significant at 5%. UAI is again negatively significant at 1%. RESID_LEGAL_ORIGIN is again positively significant at 1%.

14.4.3 Discussion

Overall, the results of Table 14.3 strongly support that governance disclosure is stronger in the Asia region: ASIA is positively significant at 5% in all four models of Table 14.3. Our results also evidence strong support in favor of H2 and against H1 and H3. We also find strong support for H5, that uncertainty avoidance and governance disclosure are negatively associated. We find UAI to be negatively significant in every model of Table 14.3.

These results are consistent with De Jong et al. (2006) who find a negative association of openness with uncertainty avoidance. Gray (1988) who suggests a negative association of transparency with uncertainty avoidance. Gray (1988) suggests that in societies with more ambiguity aversion less information is expected to avoid conflict and competition. A negative association of uncertainty avoidance or ambiguity aversion with transparency has also been found by Salter and Niswander (1995), Taylor Zarzeski (1996), Jaggi and Low (2000), Hope (2003). We also find a positive association in Model 4 of Table 14.3 of the Gini coefficient with governance disclosure, consistent with more efficient regulation in high inequality countries engendering financial development and concomitant wealth inequality. These results are consistent with Aggarwal and Goodell (2013) who suggest less pension wealth is intermediated in more redistributed superannuation systems.

We also find a positive association of English common law with governance disclosure. RESID_LEGAL_ORIGIN is positively significant in every model of Table 14.3. These results are consistent with Djankov et al. (2008) who note a high correlation between the anti-self-dealing index and common law and with La Porta et al. (1998) who contend that common law provides more efficient investor protection (see also Johnson et al., 2002). However, having used an orthogonalized variable for legal origin, our evidence shows unambiguously that the positive association of common law with governance disclosure is independent of region and national culture.

14.5 CONCLUSION

Given the recent rise of the Asian economies and increasing globalization, there is much interest in Asian corporate governance. Prior research on Asian corporate governance has noted the special features of Asian business that include the widespread prevalence of business groups controlled by families and ethnic groups through pyramidal structures. In addition, given the evidence of tunneling, studies of Asian systems of corporate governance all seem to be concerned with mechanisms to protect minority shareholders and other stakeholders from possible expropriation of resources by the controlling shareholder. Consequently, corporate governance in Asia has widely been considered to be poorer than in other parts of the world. However, prior research on Asian corporate governance has not considered the impact of the institutional disclosure environment.

This paper is an attempt to correct that deficiency. It examines the determinants of governance disclosure activity in 60 countries, focusing especially on the impact of national culture and Asian countries. We document that higher governance disclosure in the form of self-dealing transparency is positively associated with the Asian region. We also find that governance disclosure is negatively associated with uncertainty avoidance and positively associated with an English legal origin and greater economic inequality. Thus, prior contentions of corporate governance being poorer in Asia may not be justified as poor ownership practices in Asia are offset by better self-dealing disclosure. Consequently, our study will be of considerable interest to managers and policy makers.

ACKNOWLEDGMENTS

The authors are grateful to their colleagues for useful comments but remain solely responsible for the contents.

REFERENCES

Aggarwal, R., Goodell, J.W., 2009a. Markets and institutions in financial intermediation: national characteristics as determinants. Journal of Banking and Finance 33 (10), 1770–1780.

Aggarwal, R., Goodell, J.W., 2009b. Markets versus institutions in developing countries: national attributes as determinants. Emerging Markets Review 10 (1), 51–66.

Aggarwal, R., Goodell, J.W., 2010. Financial markets versus institutions in European countries: influence of culture and other national characteristics. International Business Review 19 (5), 502–520.

Aggarwal, R., Goodell, J.W., 2013. Political-economy of pension plans: impact of institutions, gender, and culture. Journal of Banking and Finance 37 (6), 1860–1879.

Aggarwal, R., Kyaw, N.A., 2006. Transparency and capital structure in Europe: evidence of firm, industry, and national institutional influences. In: Oxelheim, L. (Ed.), Corporate and Institutional Transparency for Economic Growth in Europe. Elsevier, Netherlands.

Aggarwal, R., Zhao, S., 2009. The diversification discount puzzle: empirical evidence for a transactions cost resolution. Financial Review 44 (1), 113–135.

Aggarwal, R., Dow, S., Choi, J.J., 2008. Probing corporate governance globally: impact of business systems and beyond. International Finance Review 9 (1), 3–31.

Aguilera, R., Jackson, G., 2003. The cross-national diversity of corporate governance: dimensions and determinants. Academy of Management Review 28 (3), 447–465.

Alford, A., Jones, J., Leftwich, R., Zmijewski, M., 1993. The relative informativeness of accounting disclosures in different countries. Journal of Accounting Research 31 (Suppl.), 183–223.

Ali, A., Huang, L.-S., 2000. Country specific factors related to financial reporting and the value relevance of accounting data. Journal of Accounting Research 38 (1), 1–21.

Almazan, A., Suarez, J., Titman, S., 2003. Stakeholder, transparency, and capital structure. NBER Working Paper No. 10101.

Aoki, M., 2000. Information, Corporate Governance, and Institutional Diversity: Competitiveness in Japan, the USA, and the Transnational Economies. Oxford University Press, Oxford, UK.

Archambault, J.J., Archambault, M.E., 2003. A multinational test of determinants of corporate disclosure. International Journal of Accounting 38 (2), 173–194.

Bailey, W., Karolyi, A.G., Salva, C., 2006. The economic consequences of increased disclosure: evidence from international cross-listings. Journal of Financial Economics 81 (1), 175–213.

Ball, R., Kothari, S.P., Robin, A., 2000. The effect of international institutional factors on properties of accounting earnings. Journal of Accounting and Economics 29 (1), 1–51.

Beck, T., Demirguc-Kunt, A., 2008. Access to finance: an unfinished agenda. World Bank Economic Review 22 (3), 383–396.

Beck, T., Demirguc-Kunt, A., Levine, R., 2007. Finance, inequality and the poor. Journal of Economic Growth 12 (1), 27–49.

Bertrand, M., Mehta, P., Mullainathan, S., 2002. Ferreting out tunneling: an application to Indian business groups. Quarterly Journal of Economics 117 (1), 121–148.

Bhattacharya, U., Daouk, H., Welker, M., 2003. The world price of earnings opacity. Accounting Review 78 (3), 641–678.

Bjornskov, C., 2008. Social trust and fractionalization: a possible reinterpretation. European Sociological Review 24 (3), 271–283.

Bushman, R.M., Piotoski, J.D., Smith, A.J., 2004. What determines corporate transparency? Journal of Accounting Research 42 (2), 207–252.

Chhibber, P.K., Majumdar, S.K., 1999. Foreign ownership and profitability: property rights, control, and the performance of firms in Indian industry. Journal of Law and Economics 42 (1), 209–238.

Claessens, S., Fan, J.P.H., 2002. Corporate governance in Asia: a survey. International Review of Finance 3 (2), 71–103.

Claessens, S., Djankov, S., Lang, L.H.P., 2000. The separation of ownership and control in East Asian corporations. Journal of Financial Economics 58 (1–2), 81–112.

Coffee, J.C., 1999. The future as history: the prospects for global convergence in corporate governance and its implications. Northwestern University Law Review 93 (3), 641–708.

De Jong, E., Smeets, R., Smits, J., 2006. Culture and openness. Social Indicators Research 78 (1), 111–136.

Denis, D.K., McConnell, J.J., 2003. International corporate governance. Journal of Financial and Quantitative Analysis 38 (1), 1–36.

Djankov, S., La Porta, R., Lopez-de-Silvanes, F., Shleifer, A., 2008. The law and economics of self-dealing. Journal of Financial Economics 88 (3), 430–465.

Doidge, C.G., Karolyi, A.G., Stulz, R.M., 2007. Why do countries matter so much for corporate governance? Journal of Financial Economics 86 (1), 1–39.

Durnev, A., Kim, H.E., 2005. To steal or not to steal: firm attributes, legal environment, and valuation. Journal of Finance 60 (3), 1461–1493.

Ergungor, O.E., 2004. Market- vs. bank-based financial systems: do rights and regulations really matter? Journal of Banking and Finance 28 (12), 2869–2887.

Fama, E.F., 1980. Agency problems and the theory of the firm. Journal of Political Economics 88 (2), 288–307.

Francis, J.R., Khurana, I.K., Pereira, R., 2003. The role of accounting and auditing in corporate governance and the development of financial markets around the world. Asia-Pacific Journal of Accounting and Economics 10 (1), 1–30.

Gedajlovic, E.R., Shapiro, D.M., 1998. Management and ownership effects: evidence from five countries. Strategic Management Journal 19 (6), 533–553.

Gray, S.J., 1988. Towards a theory of cultural influence on the development of accounting systems internationally. ABACUS 24 (1), 1–15.

Guenther, D.A., Young, D., 2000. The association between financial accounting measures and real economic activity: a multinational study. Journal of Accounting and Economics 29 (1), 53–72.

Guillen, M.F., 2000. Corporate governance and globalization: is there convergence across countries? Advances in International Comparative Management 13, 175–204.

Guillen, M.F., 2004. Corporate governance and globalization: is there convergence across countries? In: Clarke, T. (Ed.), Theories of Corporate Governance: The Philosophical Foundations of Corporate Governance. Routledge, London and New York, pp. 223–242.

Hart, O., 1995. Firms, Contracts, and Financial Structure. Oxford University Press, New York.

Hart, O.D., 2001. Financial contracting. Journal of Economic Literature 39 (4), 1079–1100.

Hofstede, G., 2001. Culture's Consequences. Sage Publications, London.

Hofstede, G., Hofstede, G.J., Minkov, M., 2010. Cultures and Organizations: Software of the Mind. McGraw-Hill, USA.

Hope, O.-K., 2003. Firm-level disclosures and the relative roles of culture and legal origin. Journal of International Financial Management and Accounting 14 (3), 218–248.

Jaggi, B., Low, P.Y., 2000. Impact of culture, market forces, and legal system on financial disclosures. International Journal of Accounting 35 (4), 495–519.

Jensen, M., Meckling, W., 1976. Theory of the firm: managerial behavior, agency costs, and ownership structure. Journal of Financial Economics 3 (4), 305–360.

Joh, S.W., 2003. Corporate governance and firm profitability: evidence from Korea before the economic crisis. Journal of Financial Economics 68 (2), 287–322.

Johnson, S., Boone, P., Breach, A., Friedman, E., 2000. Corporate governance in the Asian financial crisis. Journal of Financial Economics 58, 141–186.

Johnson, S., La Porta, R., Lopez-de-Silvanes, F., Shleifer, A., 2002. Tunneling. In: Hopt, K.J. (Ed.), Capital Markets and Company Law. Oxford University Press, Oxford, pp. 22–27.

Kaufmann, D., Kraay, A., Mastruzzi, M., 2010. The world wide governance indicators: methodology and analytical issues. World Bank Policy Research Working Paper 5430.

Khanna, T., Yafeh, Y., 2007. Business groups in emerging markets: paragons or parasites? Journal of Economic Literature 45 (2), 331–372.

Khanthavit, A., Polsiri, P., Wiwattanakantang, Y., 2004. Did families gain or lose control after the East Asian financial crisis? In: Fan, J., Ianazaki, M., Teranishi, J. (Eds.), Designing Financial Systems for East Asia and Japan. Routledge, London and New York.

Kinnunen, J., Koskela, M., 2003. Who is miss world in cosmetic earnings management? A cross-national comparison of small upward rounding of net income numbers among eighteen countries. Journal of International Accounting Research 2 (1), 39–68.

Klapper, L.F., Love, I., 2005. Corporate governance, investor protection, and performance in emerging markets. Journal of Corporate Finance 10 (5), 703–728.

Krishnamurti, C., Šević, A., Šević, Ž., 2005. Legal environment, firm-level corporate governance and expropriation of minority shareholders in Asia. Economic Change and Restructuring 38 (1), 85–111.

Kwok, C.C., Tadesse, S., 2006. National culture and financial systems. Journal of International Business Studies 37 (2), 227–247.

La Porta, R., Lopez-de-Silvanes, F., Shleifer, A., Vishny, R.W., 1998. Law and finance. Journal of Political Economy 106 (6), 1113–1155.

La Porta, R., Lopez-de-Silvanes, F., Shleifer, A., 2006. What works in securities laws? Journal of Finance 61 (1), 1–32.

Lainez, J.A., Gasca, M., 2006. Obstacles to the harmonization process in the European union: the influence of culture. International Journal of Accounting, Auditing and Performance Evaluation 3 (1), 68–97.

Land, J., Lang, M.H., 2002. Empirical evidence on the evolution of international earnings. Accounting Review 77, 115–133 (Supplement Quality of Earnings Conference).

Leuz, C., Verrechia, R.E., 2000. The economic consequences of increased disclosure. Journal of Accounting Research 38, 91–124 (Supplement: studies on accounting information and the economics of the firm).

Leuz, C., Nanda, D., Wysocki, P.D., 2003. Earnings management and investor protection: an international comparison. Journal of Financial Economics 69 (3), 505–527.

Levine, R., 2005. Finance and growth: theory and evidence. In: Aghion, P., Durlauf, S.N. (Eds.), Handbook of Economic Growth. Elsevier, Amsterdam.

Mitton, T., 2002. A cross-firm analysis of the impact of corporate governance on the East Asian financial crises. Journal of Financial Economics 64 (2), 215–241.

O'Sullivan, M., 2000. Contests for Corporate Control: Corporate Governance and Economic Performance in the United States and Germany. Oxford University Press, Oxford, UK.

Pedersen, T., Thomsen, S., 1997. European patterns of corporate ownership: a twelve-country study. Journal of International Business Studies 28 (4), 759–778.

Perkins, S., Morck, R., Yeung, B., 2008. Innocents abroad: hazards of international joint ventures with pyrimidal group firms. Working Paper, NBER WP#13914.

Qi, D., Wu, W., Zhang, H., 2000. Shareholding structure and corporate performance of partially privatized firms: evidence from listed Chinese companies. Pacific Basin Finance Journal 8 (5), 587–610.

Rajan, R.G., Zingales, L., 1998. Which capitalism? Lessons from the East Asian crisis. Journal of Applied Corporate Finance 11 (3), 40–48.

Roe, M.J., 2000. Political preconditions to separating ownership from control. Stanford Law Review 53, 539–606.

Rubach, M.J., Sebora, T.C., 1998. Comparative corporate governance: competitive implications of an emerging converenge. Journal of World Business 33 (2), 167–184.

Salter, S.B., Niswander, F., 1995. Cultural influence on the evelopment of accounting systems internationally: a test of Gray's (1988) theory. Journal of International Business Studies 26 (2), 379–397.

Santema, S., Hoekert, M., van de Rijt, J., van Oijen, A., 2005. Strategy disclosure in annual reports across Europe: a study on differences between five countries. European Business Review 17 (4), 352–366.

Sengupta, P., 1998. Corporate disclosure policy and the cost of debt. Accounting Review 73 (4), 459–474.

Shleifer, A., Vishny, R.W., 1997. A survey of corporate governance. Journal of Finance 52 (2), 737–783.

Taylor Zarzeski, M., 1996. Spontaneous harmonization effects of culture and market forces on accounting disclosure practices. Accounting Horizons 10 (1), 18–37.

Thomas III, L.G., Waring, G., 1999. Competing capitalisms: capital investment in American, German and Japanese firms. Strategic Management Journal 20 (8), 729–748.

Williamson, O.E., 1975. Markets and Hierarchies: Analysis and Antitrust Implications. Free Press, New York.

Williamson, O.E., 1988. Corporate finance and corporate governance. Journal of Finance 43 (3), 567–592.

Yeh, Y.-H., Lee, T.-H., Woidtke, T., 2001. Family control and corporate governance: evidence from Taiwan. International Review of Finance 2 (1–2), 21–48.

CHAPTER 15

Attitudes Toward Tax Evasion in Korea: A Study in Public Finance

Robert W. McGee[a] and Yeomin Yoon[b]
[a]Fayetteville State University, School of Business and Economics, 1200 Murchison Road, Fayetteville, NC 28301, USA
[b]Seton Hall University, Stillman School of Business, 400 South Orange Avenue, South Orange, NJ 07079, USA

15.1 INTRODUCTION

The topic of tax evasion has been discussed and debated ever since the first tax was imposed. The subject is thousands of years old (Adams, 1982, 1993), and scholars over the centuries have been unable to agree on when evasion is unethical and when it is not (Crowe, 1944; McGee, 2012a).

The subject of tax evasion can be subdivided into several subtopics, including types of evasion, the widespread nature of evasion, how to prevent evasion, optimal tax evasion, and ethical aspects of tax evasion. The present chapter focuses on ethical issues.

Numerous empirical studies have been done on the various aspects of tax evasion, including opinion surveys. However, to date, to the authors' knowledge, no study has been done of South Korean opinion on this important topic. This study aims to help fill that gap in the literature.

The data used for the empirical part of the present study are from a South Korean sample. The data were gathered by social scientists as part of a much larger World Values Survey. The sample size is 1199, which is large enough to examine several demographic variables in addition to overall views on the topic.

15.2 PRIOR STUDIES

A number of theoretical, philosophical, and ethical studies have been conducted on the ethics of tax evasion. The first comprehensive study was done by Crowe (1944), who examined 500 years of Christian (mostly Catholic) literature on the subject, much of which was in Latin. It was Crowe who introduced this Latin literature to an English-speaking audience, and who assembled and revived the tax evasion debate that had been going on in the English language religious literature. The Crowe research was later expanded upon and updated by McGee (2004, 2006, 2012a). The scholars Crowe (1944) studied had differing views on the ethics of tax evasion. One area of relative agreement within the Catholic literature is that the duty to pay is reduced or eliminated in cases where the taxpayer is unable to pay.

At the other end of the spectrum, Marx (1875) took the view that those who are best able to pay should pay more just because they are more able to pay. This view could be criticized on several grounds. For one, such a policy is exploitative of the most productive members of society. Another criticism is based on the cost–benefit principle, which holds that the amount paid should be related to the benefits received. If some relatively wealthy people are forced to pay more than what they receive in benefits, the duty to pay ceases (McGee, 2012a).

There is support for the ability to pay principle in the religious literature (Crowe, 1944; LeCard, 1869). In the Christian Bible it says that the king taxed the people according to their ability to pay (2 Kings 23:35), but it did not say whether such a practice was moral. In another passage of the Christian Bible, Jesus is asked whether there is an obligation to pay taxes to the Roman Empire. His response was that one should give to Caesar what is Caesar's and to God what is God's (Matthew 22:21), but he did not elaborate on what either Caesar or God is entitled to (McGee, 2012b). Gronbacher (1998) has pointed out that Catholic theologians have not been consistent on their views regarding the duty to pay taxes. Traditional Catholic sources like Encyclicals and Bishops' letters take a more or less classical liberal view of taxation, whereas more recent views of American bishops take a more statist and collectivist approach.

The literature of other religions is also in disagreement as to whether, and under what circumstances, tax evasion is ethical or unethical. The Church of Jesus Christ of Latter-day Saints (a.k.a. Mormon) literature does not make any exceptions to the view that tax evasion is always unethical (Smith and Kimball, 1998). McGee (2012a) challenged this absolutist view by asking the question: Would it be unethical for a Jew living in Nazi Germany to evade taxes? A survey of Mormon students found that many Mormons also disagree with this absolutist position (McGee and Smith, 2012).

The literature of the Baha'i faith allows only one exception—in cases where members of the Baha'i religion are being persecuted. In all other cases, including the case where Hitler is the tax collector, there is a moral duty to pay (DeMoville, 1998). The Jewish literature is generally against tax evasion, although it makes some exceptions (Cohn, 1998; Tamari, 1998), especially in cases where the government is corrupt or oppressive. A survey of Jewish students found that Jews believe there is some duty to pay taxes even to Hitler, although the duty is less than absolute (McGee and Cohn, 2008).

The Islamic literature is absolutist in one sense, but relativist in another sense. Ahmad (1995) and Yusuf (1971) take the position that there is no moral duty to pay a tax that is based on income or that causes prices to rise, which would include income taxes, sales taxes, excise taxes, value-added taxes and tariffs, among others. However, Jalili (2012) believes that there is an absolute duty to pay all taxes where the state follows Sharia law, because God is the tax collector. He also believes that the duty to pay is less than absolute in a secular state, although he does not go into further detail.

The studies mentioned above were mostly theoretical studies. Some empirical studies have also been done on the ethics of tax evasion. Torgler (2012) found that people who had a great deal of national pride had a lower probability of evading taxes.

In a series of studies, McGee (2012a), sometimes with co-authors, distributed a survey instrument that listed 15 or 18 arguments that had been given in the past to justify tax evasion. Participants were asked to choose a number from 1 to 7 to indicate the strength of their agreement or disagreement with each statement. The arguments were then ranked to determine which arguments justifying tax evasion were the strongest.

Many of these studies are summarized elsewhere (McGee, 2012a), so there is no need to do it again here. However, one can summarize the summary by mentioning the arguments that were generally considered to provide the strongest moral justification for tax evasion.

In many cases, the three strongest arguments to justify tax evasion all had to do with human rights abuses. Many of the surveys ranked the strongest argument as the one where Jews living in Nazi Germany were forced to pay taxes to Hitler. The other two human rights cases were where the government discriminates against a group on the basis of religion, race or ethnic background, or where the government imprisons people for their political opinions.

Some of the other strong arguments to justify tax evasion were the ability to pay argument, where the government is corrupt, where the system is perceived as unfair, where the government wastes money or spends it on projects that do not benefit the taxpayer.

A survey by Song and Yarbrough (1978) found that taxpayers thought people should pay based on ability rather than benefits received. They also found that those who fell they are paying more than their fair share tend to be middle aged people who work for a living, and who own their own home and who have higher than average incomes.

15.3 THE PRESENT STUDY

15.3.1 Methodology

The present study uses the data gathered by other social scientists as part of the most recent World Values Survey. The most recent surveys covered more than 50 countries. One of them was South Korea. The survey consisted of several hundred questions, including questions on some ethical issues. One of those ethical questions was on tax evasion. Specifically, it asked whether tax evasion could ever be justified. Participants were asked to select a number from 1 to 10 to signify the extent of their agreement or disagreement with this issue, where 1 represented Never Justifiable and 10 represented Always Justifiable.

The sample size was 1199. Some of the tables below had samples of slightly less than 1199, either because some respondents did not answer all of the demographic questions in the survey or because demographic groups were sometimes omitted because of small sample size.

15.3.2 Findings

Table 15.1 shows the data. More than 74% of the sample thought that tax evasion is never justified. Only three-tenths of 1% thought evasion was always justified.

15.3.3 Gender

Prior studies on the relationship of views on tax evasion to gender were mixed. Some studies found that women were more opposed to tax evasion than men (Baldry, 1987; Gerxhani, 2007; Lewis et al., 2009; McGee, 2012a), while others found men to be more opposed to tax evasion (Kirchler and Maciejovsky, 2001; McGee and Benk, 2011; McGee, 2012a). A third group of studies found men and women to be equally opposed to tax evasion (Grasmick et al., 1984; McGee, 2012a; Torgler, 2007). We decided to test the Korean sample for gender differences, since this demographic information was available.

Table 15.2 shows the statistics for gender. The mean scores were identical. The difference between male and female views was statistically insignificant ($p = 1.0000$). In other words, Korean men and women were equally opposed to tax evasion.

Table 15.1 Justifiability of Cheating on Taxes Overall Data

	n	(%)	Cumulative *n*	Cumulative (%)
Never justifiable	889	74.2	889	74.2
2	125	10.5	1014	84.6
3	84	7.0	1098	91.7
4	32	2.7	1130	94.3
5	28	2.3	1158	96.7
6	8	0.7	1166	97.3
7	16	1.3	1182	98.7
8	6	0.5	1188	99.2
9	6	0.5	1194	99.7
Always justifiable	4	0.3	1198	100.0
Base for mean	1199			
Mean	1.6			
Standard deviation	1.44			

Table 15.2 Gender

Rank		*n*	Mean	SD
1	Male	593	1.6	1.37
1	Female	606	1.6	1.51

15.3.4 Age

Some studies have examined age as a variable for various ethical issues. The studies generally find that people become more compliant, law abiding and moral with age (Gottfredson and Hirschi, 1990; Groenland and Veldhoven, 1983; Jackson and Milliron, 1986; Kaplan and Reckers, 1985; McGee, 2012a), although there are some exceptions (McGee, 2012a; Torgler, 2007; Wallschutzky, 1984). We decided to examine the age variable, since the data provided the information needed.

Table 15.3a shows the statistics for the age category. The two oldest groups had the strongest opposition to tax evasion and had identical mean scores.

Table 15.3b shows the p values. The 15–29 group was significantly less opposed to tax evasion than the other two groups. Differences are generally considered significant if the p value is 0.05 or less. Thus, the Korean sample results were similar to those of most other studies that found older people to be more law abiding and compliant than younger people.

15.3.5 Employment Status

A few studies have examined the relationship between tax compliance and employment status. Torgler (2012) and Song and Yarbrough (1978) found that there is no relationship. In a study of eight European countries, Torgler and Valev (2010) found that self-employed individuals were more likely to evade taxes. We decided to examine this demographic variable, since the data were available. Table 15.4a shows the statistics for employment status. The two groups most opposed to tax evasion were the self-employed and the housewives. The least opposed group was the unemployed. This finding is contra to that of the other studies mentioned above, which means there is a need for further research.

Table 15.4b shows the p values. Several of the differences in mean scores were significant.

Table 15.3a Age

Rank		n	Mean	SD
1	30–49	571	1.6	1.47
1	50+	368	1.6	1.18
3	15–29	260	1.9	1.69

Table 15.3b Age—p Values

	30–49	50+
15–29	0.0095	0.0090
30–49		1.0000

Table 15.4a Employment Status

Rank		n	Mean	SD
1	Self-employed	60	1.4	1.12
1	Housewife	309	1.4	1.31
3	Full-time	379	1.6	1.35
4	Retired	41	1.7	1.26
4	Other	142	1.7	1.53
6	Part-time	103	1.9	1.62
6	Students	116	1.9	1.64
8	Unemployed	49	2.3	1.97

Table 15.4b Employment Status—*p* Values

	Housewife	Full-Time	Retired	Other	Part-Time	Students	Unemployed
Self-employed	1.0000	0.2766	0.2120	0.1720	0.0361	0.0356	0.0034
Housewife		0.0506	0.1673	0.0329	0.0017	0.0012	0.0001
Full-time			0.6505	0.4686	0.0564	0.0475	0.0014
Retired				1.0000	0.4794	0.4789	0.0960
Other					0.3255	0.3129	0.0297
Part-time						1.0000	0.1872
Students							0.1800

15.3.6 Marital Status

Several studies have examined the relationship between marital status and attitude toward tax evasion. Song and Yarbrough (1978) and Torgler (2007, 2012) found that married people were more opposed to tax evasion than other groups. Other studies found similar results (McGee, 2012a). However, the studies are not unanimous in their findings. Some studies found that married people are less tax compliant (McGee, 2012a; Torgler, 2007). A study of more than 80 countries found that, in general, widows were most opposed to tax evasion, followed by married people, separated, living together as married, single, and divorced (McGee, 2012a).

Table 15.5a shows the statistics for marital status for the Korean sample. Widows were most opposed to tax evasion, followed by married and single individuals. Divorced

Table 15.5a Marital Status

Rank		n	Mean	SD
1	Widowed	62	1.3	0.71
2	Married	807	1.6	1.40
3	Single	300	1.8	1.65
4	Divorced	19	2.1	1.52

Table 15.5b Marital Status—*p* Values

	Married	Single	Divorced
Widowed	0.0952	0.0198	0.0021
Married		0.0447	0.1250
Single			0.4408

individuals were least opposed. Thus, the Korean population results were the same as those found in the 80+ country study.

Table 15.5b shows the *p* values. Several of the differences in mean scores were significant.

15.3.7 Religion

A few studies have examined the relationship between religion and attitude toward tax evasion. Song and Yarbrough (1978) found there was no correlation. A more recent study (McGee, 2012a) involving many countries found mixed results.

People who identified themselves as either Sunni or Shiite Muslims were more opposed to tax evasion than Buddhists, Catholics, or Protestants, whereas those who identified themselves merely as Muslims were less opposed to tax evasion than Buddhists, but more opposed to tax evasion than Catholics or Protestants. The reason for the difference was due to the way the question was asked in particular countries. In some countries, there were different categories for Sunni and Shiite Muslims, whereas in other countries the two groups were combined. Catholics were generally less opposed to tax evasion than members of other religions.

We decided to examine the relationship between religion and views on tax evasion, since the data were available. Table 15.6a shows the data for religion. Protestants and Roman Catholics were most opposed to tax evasion. Buddhists were least opposed. However, as Table 15.6b shows, the differences in mean scores were not significant for any of the comparisons.

Table 15.6a Religion

Rank		*n*	Mean	SD
1	Protestant	264	1.6	1.40
1	Roman Catholic	254	1.6	1.20
3	Buddhist	298	1.7	1.76

Table 15.6b Religion—*p* Values

	Roman Catholic	Buddhist
Protestant	1.0000	0.4602
Roman Catholic		0.4438

15.3.8 Social Class

Torgler (2012) found the relationship between social class and views on tax evasion to be curvilinear for a United States population. Those in the upper class were least opposed to tax evasion, and opposition to evasion grew as one moved to the lower middle class and upper middle class. A Malaysian study (Ross and McGee, 2011) found that the upper class and lower middle class were the two groups most opposed to tax evasion, whereas the lower class was least opposed. However, the differences in mean scores were generally not significant.

Table 15.7a shows the statistics for social class for the present study. Upper middle class, lower middle class, and working class had identical mean scores and were the three groups most opposed to tax evasion. The upper class was least opposed. The upper class was significantly less opposed to tax evasion than the other groups. All other differences in mean score were not significant. Table 15.7b shows the statistics.

15.3.9 Confidence in Government

Several studies have found that tax morale is lower in cases where people feel alienated from government (Cebula, 2001; Cebula and Saadatmand, 2005; Scholz and Lubell, 1998; Song and Yarbrough, 1978). Such a relationship seems reasonable, since people

Table 15.7a Social Class

Rank		n	Mean	SD
1	Upper Middle Class	253	1.6	1.44
1	Lower Middle Class	633	1.6	1.38
1	Working Class	217	1.6	1.11
4	Lower Class	86	1.8	2.04
5	Upper Class	8	4.2	3.48

Table 15.7b Social Class—p Values

	Lower Middle Class	Working Class	Lower Class	Upper Class
Upper Middle Class	1.0000	1.0000	0.3211	0.0001
Lower Middle Class		1.0000	0.2381	0.0001
Working Class			0.2749	0.0001
Lower Class				0.0038

Table 15.8a Confidence in Government

Rank		n	Mean	SD
1	None at all	125	1.5	1.58
2	A great deal	31	1.6	1.33
3	Quite a lot	515	1.7	1.47
3	Not very much	524	1.7	1.39

Table 15.8b Confidence in Government—p Values

	A Great Deal	Quite a Lot	Not Very Much
None at all	0.7458	0.1793	0.1600
A great deal		0.7117	0.6966
Quite a lot			1.0000

generally like to get good value for their money, whether it is tax payments of shopping. Where tax morale is low, there tends to be a higher probability to evade. We decided to test this relationship using the Korean data. Table 15.8a shows the data for confidence in government. Those who had no confidence in government were most opposed to tax evasion, which seemed like a strange result. One might expect just the opposite.

The two groups least opposed to tax evasion were the quite a lot and not very much categories. However, none of the differences in mean scores were significant, as is seen in Table 15.8b.

15.3.10 Feeling of Happiness

A Malaysian study of the relationship between happiness and attitude toward tax evasion (Ross and McGee, 2011) found that happy people were more averse to tax evasion than unhappy people, although the differences in mean score were not significant. A study of the Netherlands (Ross and McGee, 2012) found that that groups that were very happy and quite happy were significantly more opposed to tax evasion than people in the not very happy group. Table 15.9a shows the relationship between happiness and attitude

Table 15.9a Feeling of Happiness

Rank		n	Mean	SD
1	Not very happy	141	1.3	0.94
2	Quite happy	892	1.6	1.40
3	Very happy	155	2.0	1.77
4	Not at all happy	11	2.7	3.40

Table 15.9b Feeling of Happiness—*p* Values

	Quite Happy	Very Happy	Not at All Happy
Not very happy	0.0141	0.0001	0.0005
Quite happy		0.0017	0.0118
Very happy			0.2418

toward tax evasion for the Korean sample. Those with the strongest opposition to tax evasion are not very happy, while least opposed were not at all happy. The two unhappy groups were at the far ends of the spectrum, while the two happy groups were in the middle, making for a curvilinear relationship. Most of the differences in mean scores were significant, as is seen in Table 15.9b.

15.3.11 Longitudinal

Since South Korea data are available for all five waves of surveys, it is possible to see if there is a trend. Table 15.10a shows that opposition to tax evasion was strongest in 1990. Opposition eased somewhat for the other surveys. The year with the least opposition was 1996.

Table 15.10b shows that some of the differences in mean scores were significant.

Table 15.10a Longitudinal

Rank		*n*	Mean	SD
1	Wave 2—1990	1246	1.5	1.68
2	Wave 1—1982	916	1.6	1.35
2	Wave 4—2001	1199	1.6	1.38
2	Wave 5—2005	1199	1.6	1.44
5	Wave 3—1996	1245	1.8	1.66

Table 15.10b Longitudinal—*p* Values

	W2	W3	W4	W5
W1	0.1381	0.0028	1.0000	1.0000
W2		0.0001	0.1086	0.1148
W3			0.0012	0.0015
W4				1.0000

15.4 CONCLUSION

The South Korean people, as a group, were firmly opposed to tax evasion. However, their opposition was not uniform. Sometimes there were differences in attitude. These differences sometimes became pronounced when certain demographic variables were examined. The findings can be summarized as follows:

- Opposition to tax evasion was generally strong, although a significant percentage of the population was not totally opposed to tax evasion.
- Gender—Males and females were equally opposed to tax evasion.
- Age—Older people were significantly more opposed to tax evasion than younger people.
- Employment Status—The two groups most opposed to tax evasion were the self-employed and the housewives. The least opposed group was the unemployed. This finding is contra to that of some other studies.
- Marital Status—Widows were most opposed to tax evasion, followed by married and single individuals. Divorced individuals were least opposed.
- Religion—was not a significant variable.
- Social Class—The upper class was significantly less opposed to tax evasion than the other classes.
- Confidence in Government—was not a significant variable.
- Happiness—Those with the strongest opposition to tax evasion are not very happy, while least opposed were not at all happy. The two unhappy groups were at the far ends of the spectrum, while the two happy groups were in the middle, making for a curvilinear relationship.
- Longitudinal Trend—Attitude toward tax evasion has changed over time, but the change is not linear.

The social scientists who gathered the Korean data did not inquire as to the reason for the particular answer, which is reasonable, given the fact that the survey instrument contained hundreds of questions. One area for possible future research would be to find the reasons why the participants answered as they did. Since the surveys were anonymous, it is not possible to contact the participants to obtain this information. However, a more targeted survey that is more limited in scope could be used to gather this information.

REFERENCES

Adams, C., 1982. Fight, Flight and Fraud: The Story of Taxation. Euro-Dutch Publishers, Curacao.
Adams, C., 1993. For Good or Evil: The Impact of Taxes on the Course of Civilization. Madison Books, London, New York and Lanham.
Ahmad, M., 1995. Business Ethics in Islam. The International Institute of Islamic Thought and the International Institute of Islamic Economics, Islamabad, Pakistan.

Baldry, J.C., 1987. Income tax evasion and the tax schedule: some experimental results. Public Finance 42 (3), 357–383.

Cebula, R.J., 2001. Impact of tax-detection technology and other factors on aggregate income tax evasion: the case of the United States. Banca Nazionale Dela Lavoro Quarterly Review 53 (1), 101–115.

Cebula, R.J., Saadatmand, Y., 2005. Income tax evasion determinants: new evidence. Journal of the American Academy of Business 7 (2), 124–127.

Cohn, G., 1998. The Jewish view on paying taxes. Journal of Accounting, Ethics and Public Policy 1 (2), 109–120. Reprinted in McGee, R.W. (Ed.), The Ethics of Tax Evasion (pp. 180–189). Dumont, NJ: The Dumont Institute for Public Policy Research. 1998, pp. 180–189.

Crowe, M.T., 1944. The Moral Obligation of Paying Just Taxes. The Catholic University of America Studies in Sacred Theology, vol. 84. The Catholic University of America Press, Washington, DC.

DeMoville, W., 1998. The ethics of tax evasion: a baha'i perspective. Journal of Accounting, Ethics and Public Policy 1 (3), 356–368. Reprinted in McGee, R.W. (Ed.), The Ethics of Tax Evasion. The Dumont Institute for Public Policy Research., Dumont NJ, 1998, pp. 230–240.

Gerxhani, K., 2007. Explaining gender differences in tax evasion: the case of Tirana, Albania. Feminist Economics 13 (2), 119–155.

Gottfredson, M.R., Hirschi, T., 1990. A General Theory of Crime. Stanford University Press, Stanford.

Grasmick, H., Finley, N., Glaser, D., 1984. Labor force participation, sex-role attitudes, and female crime: evidence from a survey of adults. Social Science Quarterly 65 (3), 703–718.

Groenland, E., van Veldhoven, G., 1983. Tax evasion behavior: a psychological framework. Journal of Economic Psychology 3 (2), 129–144.

Gronbacher, G.M.A., 1998. Taxation: catholic social thought and classical liberalism. Journal of Accounting, Ethics and Public Policy 1 (1), 91–100. Reprinted in McGee, R.W. (Ed.), The Ethics of Tax Evasion. The Dumont Institute for Public Policy Research. Dumont, NJ, 1998, pp. 158–167.

Jackson, B.R., Milliron, V.C., 1986. Tax compliance research: findings, problems, and prospects. Journal of Accounting Literature 5 (1), 125–165.

Jalili, A.R., 2012. The ethics of tax evasion: an islamic perspective. In: McGee, R.W. (Ed.), The Ethics of Tax Evasion in Theory and Practice. Springer, New York, pp. 167–199.

Kaplan, S., Reckers, P., 1985. A study of tax evasion judgments. National Tax Journal 38 (1), 97–102.

Kirchler, E., Maciejovsky, B., 2001. Tax compliance within the context of gain and loss situations, expected and current asset position, and profession. Journal of Economic Psychology 22 (3), 173–194.

LeCard, S.E., 1869. Gousset, Theologie Morale I, p. 504, as cited in Crowe (1944) at 40.

Lewis, A., Carrera, S., Cullis, J., Jones, P., 2009. Individual, cognitive and cultural differences in tax compliance: UK and Italy compared. Journal of Economic Psychology 30 (3), 431–445.

Marx, K., 1875. A Critique of the Gotha Program.

McGee, R.W., 2004. The Philosophy of Taxation and Public Finance. Kluwer Academic Publishers, Norwell, MA and Dordrecht.

McGee, R.W., 2006. Three views on the ethics of tax evasion. Journal of Business Ethics 67 (1), 15–35.

McGee, R.W. (Ed.), 2012a. The Ethics of Tax Evasion in Theory and Practice. Springer, New York.

McGee, R.W., 2012b. Christian views on the ethics of tax evasion. In: McGee, R.W. (Ed.), The Ethics of Tax Evasion in Theory and Practice. Springer, New York, pp. 201–210.

McGee, R.W., Benk, S., 2011. The ethics of tax evasion: a study of turkish opinion. Journal of Balkan and Near Eastern Studies 13 (2), 249–262.

McGee, R.W., Cohn, G.M., 2008. Jewish perspectives on the ethics of tax evasion. Journal of Legal, Ethical and Regulatory Issues 11 (2), 1–32.

McGee, R.W., Smith, S.R., 2012. Ethics, tax evasion and religion: a survey of opinion of members of the church of Jesus Christ of latter-day saints. In: McGee, R.W. (Ed.), The Ethics of Tax Evasion in Theory and Practice. Springer, New York, pp. 211–226.

Ross, A.M., McGee, R.W., 2011. A demographic study of Malaysian views on the ethics of tax evasion. In: Published in the Proceedings of the 2011 Spring International Conference of the Allied Academies, Orlando, April 6–8, 2011. Reprinted as Attitudes toward Tax Evasion: A Demographic Study of Malaysia, in the *Asian Journal of Law and Economics* 2(3): 1–49 (2011). <http://www.bepress.com/ajle/vol2/iss3/5>.

Ross, A.M., McGee, R.W., 2012. Attitudes toward tax evasion: a demographic study of the netherlands. Journal of International Business Research 11 (2), 1–44.

Scholz, J.T., Lubell, M., 1998. Adaptive political attitudes: duty, trust and fear as monitors of tax policy. American Journal of Political Science 42 (3), 398–417.

Smith, S.R., Kimball, K.C., 1998. Tax evasion and ethics: a perspective from members of the church of Jesus Christ of latter-day saints. Journal of Accounting, Ethics and Public Policy 1 (3), 337–348. Reprinted in McGee, R.W. (Ed.), The Ethics of Tax Evasion. The Dumont Institute for Public Policy Research. Dumont, NJ, 1998, pp. 220–229.

Song, Y.-D., Yarbrough, T.E., 1978. Tax ethics and taxpayer attitudes: a survey. Public Administration Review 38 (5), 442–452.

Tamari, M., 1998. Ethical issues in tax evasion: a Jewish perspective. Journal of Accounting, Ethics and Public Policy 1 (2), 121–132. Reprinted in McGee, R.W. (Ed.), 1998. The Ethics of Tax Evasion. The Dumont Institute for Public Policy Research. Dumont, NJ, 1998, pp. 168–178.

Torgler, B., 2007. Tax compliance and tax morale: a theoretical and empirical analysis. Edward Elgar, Cheltenham, UK and Northampton, MA.

Torgler, B., 2012. Attitudes toward paying taxes in the USA: an empirical analysis. In: McGee, R.W. (Ed.), The Ethics of Tax Evasion in Theory and Practice. Springer, New York, pp. 269–283.

Torgler, B., Valev, N.T., 2010. Gender and public attitudes toward corruption and tax evasion. Contemporary Economic Policy 28 (4), 554–568.

Wallschutzky, I., 1984. Possible causes of tax evasion. Journal of Economic Psychology 5 (4), 371–384.

World Values Survey Data. <www.wvsevsdb.com/>.

Yusuf, S.M., 1971. Economic Justice in Islam. Kitab Bhavan Publishers, New Delhi, India.

CHAPTER 16

Attitudes Toward Accepting a Bribe: A Comparative Study of the People's Republic of China, Taiwan, and Hong Kong

Robert W. McGee

Fayetteville State University, School of Business and Economics, 1200 Murchison Road, Fayetteville, NC 28301, USA

16.1 INTRODUCTION

It is often assumed that bribery is always unethical, but a closer analysis finds that this assumption may not be correct. An analysis of bribery might involve the following matrix.

Party A solicits a bribe from Party B. Party A offers to do something if Party B pays	Party B offers to pay a bribe to Party A if Party A will do something
1 Is it unethical for Party A to solicit the bribe? **2** Is it unethical for Party B to pay the bribe?	**1** Is it unethical for Party B to attempt to bribe Party A? **2** Is it unethical for Party A to accept the bribe?

If one party is the victim of a bribe, it seems reasonable to argue that the victim may not be acting unethically if he or she pays the bribe. It might also be argued that if one party makes the other party a victim, the person who causes someone to be a victim is acting unethically, since victimizing someone is generally viewed as unethical conduct.

Does it make a difference if the person soliciting the bribe is offering to perform a valuable service in exchange for the bribe? For example, let us say that a California fruit and vegetable producer wants to sell fruits and vegetables in the Korean market and the Korean health inspectors have a policy of deliberately waiting 30 days to inspect the goods after they arrive at a Korean port (which has been the case in the past). It is a protectionist measure aimed at protecting Korean fruit and vegetable producers from foreign competition.

What if one of the Korean health inspectors offers to conduct the inspection a day or two after arrival instead of waiting 30 days, as is the normal procedure? Such an offer has value to the California producer, and the Korean inspector also benefits, as do hundreds or thousands of Korean fruit and vegetable consumers. The only losers are the few

285

Korean fruit and vegetable producers, who must now face a little more competition for their products, and who are not morally entitled to protection in the first place? Can it be said that either the Korean inspector or the California producer is acting unethically?

This chapter reviews the literature on the ethics of bribery and then analyzes opinion data gathered as part of a larger study on human beliefs and values to determine what the views are of people in the People's Republic of China, Taiwan, and Hong Kong on the question of whether it is ever acceptable to accept a bribe in the course of one's business.

16.2 PRIOR STUDIES

Bribery may be viewed from several ethical perspectives, which makes life more interesting. One strain of utilitarian ethics asserts that what is efficient is ethical (Posner, 1983, 1998). This approach may be criticized if one takes it as an absolute statement. For example, if one finds a more efficient way to kill people, the act does not become ethical just because someone has found a way to increase efficiency. However, one may argue that, if conserving resources is an ethical act, then dissipating resources is unethical. If one does not choose the most efficient way to do something, one is dissipating resources. Therefore, one must choose the most efficient way of doing something, provided the benefit exceeds the cost. Dissipating resources when one has a choice not to do so constitutes an unethical act.

Let us apply this view to bribery. If one applies economic efficiency to bribery, it is possible to conclude that a bribe may not be unethical if the result is increased economic efficiency. For example, where bribery reduces transaction costs, Johnsen (2009) has suggested that consumers may benefit. He even suggests a change in terminology to describe certain situations. Rather than label something as a bribe in cases where consumers benefit, one may call such transactions third-party payments, at least in cases where it is uncertain whether any harm has been done.

It is not always clear that grease payments increase efficiency. Kaufmann and Wei (2000) did a study that found that firms paying more in bribes also spent more time negotiating with bureaucrats, and that the cost of capital increased.

A problem inherent in any ethical analysis is that one may apply several different principles to ethical issues, sometimes with differing results. Utilitarian ethics is perhaps the most widely used ethical system, especially for economists and for many policy analysts (Goodin, 1995). But utilitarian ethics is only one of several accepted ethical systems. One may also apply rights theory, the theory of duty (Kant, 1952, 1983) or virtue ethics (Aristotle, 2002), to mention a few (Baron et al., 1997; Graham, 2004). Sometimes, results differ depending on which ethical principles one applies.

According to utilitarian ethics, an act or policy is good if the result is the greatest good for the greatest number, or at least that is the conclusion reached by the classical thinkers on the subject (Bentham, 1843; Mill, 1979). The problem with this approach is that it is impossible to maximize more than one variable at a time. Doing so violates basic mathematical principles (McGee, 2012). One may, perhaps, maximize the greatest good, or one may attempt to benefit the greatest number, but one may not do both at the same time.

Another problem with utilitarian ethical theory has to do with measurement. It is not possible to precisely measure gains and losses. One may rank preferences, but one may not say that one preference is 14.7% better than another preference. A corollary of this approach is that some individuals may gain or lose much from a certain policy, whereas others would stand to gain or lose little. For example, a protectionist trade policy that protects the domestic textile industry from foreign competition greatly benefits a few domestic textile producers and their employees, but it does so at the expense of every domestic consumer of clothes, not to mention all the foreign producers of textile products, who are not able to sell their goods in the domestic market at what would otherwise be the market price (McGee, 1994a). A few people benefit greatly by the protectionist measure, while the vast majority must pay a slightly higher price for textile products, and since they have to pay more for clothing, they have less money to spend on the products of every other industry, which means that the producers of all other industries suffer, as do their employees (Bastiat, 1968).

Another weakness with utilitarian ethics is that it is not always possible to identify all the winners and losers. Frederic Bastiat pointed out this inherent weakness in the 1840s (Bastiat, 1968). There may be obvious winners and obvious losers, but some winners and losers are more difficult, or even impossible to determine, as is illustrated in the textile example above.

Another inherent deficiency of utilitarian ethics is its total disregard of rights (Bentham, 1843; Brandt, 1992; Frey, 1984; Rothbard, 1970). According to utilitarian ethics, it is perfectly acceptable to violate someone's rights if the result is more winners than losers, or, as economists would say, if the result is a positive-sum game. A rights theorist to quickly assert that an act or policy is automatically unethical if anyone's rights are violated, regardless of whether the result is a positive-sum game (McGee, 1994b). (It might also be pointed out that, because of measurement problems, it is often not possible to determine with any degree of confidence whether the result is a positive-sum game).

In spite of all these inherent flaws in utilitarian ethics, it continues to be a dominant ethical view. A study by Premeaux and Mondy (1993) found that managers tended to be utilitarians. A follow-up study by Premeaux (2004) found that there had been somewhat of a shift in managers' viewpoint. Although the continued to apply utilitarian ethical principles, there was somewhat more emphasis on duty, or doing the right thing than there had been a decade earlier.

The two Premeaux studies also found that demographics did not make a difference. Views did not differ by gender, marital status, race, income, region, religion, education, political affiliation or size or type of firm.

Some scholars have taken the position that whatever is corrupt is unethical (Wong and Beckman, 1992), which requires one to first determine whether a particular practice is corrupt.

If one applies the principles of virtue ethics, one may ask the question, "Does the practice result in human flourishing?" If the answer is *yes*, then the policy or practice is ethical. If one applies this approach to the Korean fruit and vegetable case mentioned above, the conclusion is that bribing a Korean health inspector to accelerate the inspection process is an ethical act because thousands of Korean consumers benefit, as does the California producer.

Other studies of bribery in addition to those of Premeaux have looked at various demographic variables. Swamy et al. (2001) found that women were less involved in bribery and were less likely to approve of the practice. They also found that there was less corruption in countries where women held a larger share of seats in Parliament or held more senior government positions, or where women comprised a larger portion of the labor force.

Roy and Singer (2006) suggested some ways to reduce bribery and other forms of corruption in India. The Organization for Economic Cooperation and Development has addressed the topic of bribery (OECD, 2011), but the effectiveness of their main document on this issue has been subject to dispute (Bonucci and Moulette, 2007; Darrough, 2010).

A study of bribery in Latin America (Sanchez et al., 2008) found that regionally dominant cultural values helped determine the view of managers' tolerance for the practice. Their attitudes toward power distance and collectivism also played a part in determining their attitudes. A study of attitudes in South Africa, the United States, Colombia, and Ecuador (Bernardi et al., 2009) found that the individuals in the US study generally had views that were more ethical than those of the other groups included in the study.

16.3 THE PRESENT STUDY

The data used in the present study were collected as part of a much larger study of human beliefs and values. Data were collected by social scientists in dozens of countries. The survey instrument included hundreds of questions. One of those questions asked whether accepting a bribe in the course of one's business was ethically justifiable. Participants were asked to choose a number from 1 to 10, where 1 was never justifiable and 10 was always justifiable. The countries included in the present study are the People's Republic of China, Hong Kong, and Taiwan. Although all three countries have predominantly Chinese populations, the history of the three countries over the last 100 years or so has been much different, which could account for the fact that there are some differences in attitudes toward bribery. The People's Republic of China has been a communist country since the late 1940s, although its economy has become more market oriented in recent decades. The economy of Hong Kong is among the freest in the world and has remained relatively free even after the communist takeover in 1997. The economy of Taiwan is somewhere between these two extremes in terms of economic and political freedom. Thus, although the populations are homogeneous in some ways, recent cultural and political differences may have played a role in determining their attitudes toward the acceptability of bribery.

16.3.1 Methodology

Data were taken from the Human Beliefs and Values Survey data. Two-tailed t-tests were used to determine whether any differences between or among groups were significant at the 5% level.

16.3.2 Findings

The overall results for the three countries are summarized in Table 16.1.

Table 16.1 shows several interesting similarities and differences between and among the three samples. Although the vast majority of people in all three groups believe that

Table 16.1 Overall Findings

	PRC		Taiwan		Hong Kong	
	n	%	*n*	%	*n*	%
Never justifiable 1	1279	63.5	939	76.5	837	66.9
2	241	12.0	115	9.3	128	10.2
3	64	3.2	84	6.8	137	10.9
4	33	1.6	26	2.1	83	6.6
5	48	2.4	38	3.1	35	2.8
6	30	1.5	8	0.7	16	1.3
7	12	0.6	5	0.4	3	0.2
8	10	0.5	4	0.3	2	0.2
9	8	0.4	2	0.2	1	0.1
Always justifiable 10	26	1.3	4	0.3	3	0.2
Don't know	253	12.6	1	0.1	7	0.6
No answer	11	0.5	0	0.0	0	0
Total	2015		1227		1252	
Base for mean	1751		1226		1245	
Mean	1.7		1.5		1.8	
Standard deviation	1.68		1.28		1.33	

Overall Test of Significance (p values)
PRC vs. Taiwan = 0.0004
PRC vs. Hong Kong = 0.0808
Taiwan vs. Hong Kong < 0.0001

taking a bribe in the course of one's employment is never justifiable, a substantial minority of all three groups believe that taking a bribe is acceptable sometimes. Computing the ratio of never justifiable to sometimes justifiable for each group reveals the following relationship:

PRC 63.5/36.5 = 1.74.

Taiwan 76.5/23.5 = 3.26.

Hong Kong 66.9/33.1 = 2.02.

The Taiwan sample has the highest percentage of people believing that bribery is never justifiable, and this group also has the lowest mean score, indicating the strongest opposition to bribe taking. Two-tailed t-test comparisons showed that the difference between groups is significant, although the difference between the PRC and Hong Kong samples is significant only at the 10% level ($p = 0.0808$). Thus, it can be said that the Taiwan sample was most opposed to bribe taking and the Hong Kong sample was least opposed. The PRC sample fell somewhere in between.

Another interesting finding is the percentage of the sample that either did not have an opinion or did not know. While the percentage was negligible for Hong Kong and Taiwan, slightly more than 13% of the PRC sample either could not decide or chose not to answer. One possible explanation for this relative hesitancy might be that the PRC is a totalitarian dictatorship, whereas the residents of Hong Kong and Taiwan are freer to express their opinions.

Gender

Gender is perhaps the most frequently studied demographic variable for a wide range of social science studies. Studies have found that sometimes gender makes a difference in ethical attitude and sometimes it does not. Peppas and Peppas (2000) found that gender did not make a difference for Greek college students. Premeaux and Mondy (1993) found that it did not make a difference for managers. However, a study of Turkish managers (Serap et al., 1999) found that women were more ethical than men. Other studies have also found that women were more ethical than men (Harris, 1990; Callan, 1992; Ruegger and King, 1992; Beu et al., 2003; Roxas and Stoneback, 2004; Swaidan et al., 2006). A third group of studies found that men were more ethical than women (Barnett and Karson, 1987; Weeks et al., 1999).

The present study examined gender differences. However, it should be kept in mind that, just because women might be more opposed to taking a bribe, it does not mean that women are more ethical than men. That is because taking a bribe might not be considered unethical, especially in cases where the bribe may be described as giving a helping hand rather than a greedy hand.

The results are summarized in Table 16.2.

The gender comparison shows several interesting results. In the case of the PRC, although the sample sizes for the men and women were about the same, women were unable to decide on a response by a ratio of more than 2-to-1. The t-tests

Table 16.2 Gender Comparisons

		PRC		Taiwan		Hong Kong	
		Male	Female	Male	Female	Male	Female
Never justifiable	1	630	649	474	466	381	456
	2	103	138	64	51	65	63
	3	26	38	40	45	73	64
	4	17	16	12	14	41	42
	5	22	26	16	22	21	14
	6	9	21	5	2	9	7
	7	4	8	1	4	1	2
	8	4	6	2	2	2	0
	9	4	4	2	0	0	1
Always justifiable	10	18	8	2	3	1	2
Don't know		81	172	0	1	5	2
No answer		5	6	0	0	0	0
Total		923	1092	618	609	599	653
Base for mean		837	914	618	608	594	651
Mean		1.7	1.7	1.5	1.6	1.8	1.7
Standard Deviation		1.76	1.61	1.26	1.31	1.36	1.29

Gender Test of Significance (p values)
PRC = 1.0000
Taiwan = 0.1733
Hong Kong = 0.1834

found that the differences in male and female opinion were not significant at the 5% level.

The present study found that gender is not a significant variable when it comes to attitudes toward taking a bribe. A study of gender attitude of Chinese business students in Beijing toward tax evasion also found that gender attitudes are not significantly different (McGee and An, 2008). However, a study of Chinese law, business and philosophy students in Hubei (McGee and Guo, 2007) found that women were significantly more opposed to tax evasion. A comparative study of Southern China (Guangzhou) and Macau (McGee and Noronha, 2008) found that men and women were equally opposed to tax evasion. A Hong Kong tax evasion study (McGee and Butt, 2008) also found no significant gender differences. However, a study of Taiwanese attitudes toward tax evasion found women to be significantly more opposed to tax evasion (McGee and Andres, 2009). Because of these different outcomes, it seems that there is a need for additional research to determine whether gender is a significant variable for ethical issues in the three Chinese communities.

Age

Age is another variable that has been examined in the ethical literature. Mocan (2008) has stated that people under age 20 and over age 60 have more exposure to bribery situations, although it does not necessarily follow that individuals in these age categories are either more or less receptive to bribes than other groups. Peppas and Peppas (2000) found that the attitude of Greek college students toward ethical issues did not differ by age. However, most studies have found that people tend to be more ethical as they get older, or that they tend to be more opposed to tax evasion as they get older, which is not quite the same thing, since tax evasion may not always be unethical (McGee and Benk, 2011; Gupta and McGee, 2010; Ruegger and King, 1992; McGee, 2012).

The present study tests the age demographic. The Human Beliefs and Values surveys split age into three categories. Table 16.3 summarizes the results.

An examination of the means shows that older people tend to be more opposed to bribe taking than do young people. The p value comparisons show that the difference is usually significant. However, the differences were not significant at the 5% level for the PRC sample, which indicates that age is not a significant variable for the PRC, but is a significant variable for the Taiwanese and Hong Kong samples.

Marital status

The marital status variable was examined to determine whether it was a significant variable. Some other studies have tested this variable in connection with ethical attitudes.

Table 16.3 Age Comparisons

		PRC			Taiwan			Hong Kong		
		15–29	30–49	50+	15–29	30–49	50+	15–29	30–49	50+
Never justifiable	1	199	569	511	224	401	314	150	366	313
	2	39	128	74	36	46	33	27	64	37
	3	12	35	17	34	33	18	27	69	38
	4	7	17	9	10	10	6	17	30	34
	5	8	23	17	7	21	10	11	12	12
	6	4	20	6	3	4	0	8	4	4
	7	1	6	5	3	2	0	1	2	0
	8	4	1	5	3	1	0	1	0	0
	9	0	6	2	0	2	0	0	1	0
Always justifiable	10	7	7	12	4	1	0	1	1	1
Don't know		19	114	120	0	0	1	2	3	2
No answer		1	3	7	0	0	0	0	0	0
Total		301	929	785	325	521	382	245	552	441
Base for mean		281	812	658	325	521	381	243	549	439
Mean		1.8	1.7	1.6	1.8	1.6	1.3	2	1.7	1.7
Standard Deviation		1.87	1.6	1.7	1.59	1.3	0.86	1.57	1.24	1.24

Age Tests of Significance (p values)

	PRC	Taiwan	Hong Kong
15–29 vs. 30–49	0.3881	0.0424	0.0040
15–29 vs. 50+	0.1096	<0.0001	0.0062
30–49 vs. 50+	0.2468	<0.0001	1.0000

The results have been mixed. It was not a significant variable for a study of managers (Premeaux and Mondy, 1993). A bribery study of three Latin American countries (Hernandez and McGee, 2013) found that widows and married people were least accepting of bribery, whereas single and divorced people were most accepting of the practice. A tax evasion study that included many countries found that widows and married individuals were most opposed, and that divorced and single people were least opposed (McGee, 2012).

The results for the present study are summarized in Table 16.4.

Table 16.4 Marital Status Comparisons

	Ranking (Most Opposed to Least Opposed)	*n*	Mean	S.D.
PRC				
Married	2	1450	1.7	1.67
Divorced	4	25	2.3	2.39
Widowed	1	67	1.6	1.9
Single	3	164	1.9	1.91
Taiwan				
Married	2	774	1.5	1.09
Divorced	4	42	1.9	2.04
Widowed	1	61	1.3	0.83
Single	3	339	1.7	1.59
Hong Kong				
Married	3	771	1.7	1.19
Divorced	1	28	1.2	0.65
Widowed	2	70	1.4	0.89
Single	4	354	2.1	1.63

Tests of Significance (*p* values)	Divorced	Widow	Single
PRC			
Married	0.0776	0.6340	0.1525
Divorced		0.1471	0.3475
Widowed			0.2791
Taiwan			
Married	0.0293	0.1616	0.0152
Divorced		0.0414	0.4154
Widowed			0.0560
Hong Kong			
Married	0.0274	0.0400	<0.0001
Divorced		0.2836	0.0039
Widowed			0.0005

Widows and married people were the most strongly opposed groups for the PRC and Taiwan samples, but were in the second and third positions for the Hong Kong sample. The divorced category was least opposed to bribe taking in the PRC and Taiwan samples, whereas the least opposed group in the Hong Kong sample was the single group. It is not readily apparent why the Hong Kong single group would be least opposed, or why the Hong Kong sample results would be different from the results found in the PRC and Taiwan samples. More research is needed. An analysis of p values found that the differences between groups were not significant at the 5% level for the PRC sample, but that some differences were significant for the Taiwan and Hong Kong samples.

16.4 CONCLUSION

This study found several interesting relationships that were previously unknown. All three Chinese groups were significantly opposed to bribe taking. The Chinese population on Taiwan was significantly more opposed to bribe taking than were the populations of the PRC and Hong Kong. Men and women were equally opposed to bribe taking in all three jurisdictions. Older people tended to be more opposed to bribe taking than younger people, although the extent of opposition was not as pronounced in the PRC as it was in the other two jurisdictions. Marital status was a significant variable in some cases but not in others. It could be said that, in general, widowed people and married people tend to be more opposed to bribe taking than divorced and single people. The reasons for these differences between groups and between jurisdictions could not be determined from the Human Beliefs and Values data set. More research is needed to determine why there are differences in some cases but not in others. Another area for future research could be the examination of other variables, such as religion, employment status, social class, and political affiliation, among others, although political affiliation would not be a variable in the PRC, since the communist party has a monopoly at present.

REFERENCES

Aristotle, 2002. Nicomachean Ethics. Oxford University Press, Oxford, UK.
Barnett, J.H., Karson, M.J., 1987. Personal values and business decisions: an exploratory investigation. Journal of Business Ethics 6 (5), 371–382.
Baron, M.W., Pettit, P., Slote, M., 1997. Three Methods of Ethics. Blackwell Publishing, Malden, MA and Oxford, UK.
Bastiat, F., 1968. Selected Essays on Political Economy. Foundation for Economic Education, Irvington-on-Hudson, NY.
Bentham, J., 1843. Anarchical Fallacies. Reprinted as an ebook by Amazon Digital Services in 2011.
Bernardi, R.A., Witek, M.B., Melton, M.R., 2009. A four country study of the associations bribery and unethical actions. Journal of Business Ethics 84 (4), 389–403.
Beu, D.S., Buckley, M.R., Harvey, M.G., 2003. Ethical decision-making: a multidimensional construct. Business Ethics: A European Review 12 (1), 88–107.
Bonucci, N., Moulette, P., 2007. The OECD anti-bribery convention 10 years on. The OECD Observer No. 264/265.

Brandt, R.B., 1992. Morality, Utilitarianism, and Rights. Cambridge University Press, Cambridge, UK and New York.

Callan, V.J., 1992. Predicting ethical values and training needs in ethics. Journal of Business Ethics 11 (10), 761–769.

Darrough, M.N., 2010. The FCPA and the OECD convention: some lessons from the U.S. experience. Journal of Business Ethics 93 (2), 255–276.

Frey, R.G. (Ed.), 1984. Utility and Rights. University of Minnesota Press, Minneapolis.

Goodin, R.E., 1995. Utilitarianism as a Public Philosophy. Cambridge University Press, Cambridge, UK.

Graham, G., 2004. Eight Methods of Ethics. Routledge, Oxford, UK.

Gupta, R., McGee, R.W., 2010. A comparative study of New Zealanders' opinion on the ethics of tax evasion: students vs. accountants. New Zealand Journal of Taxation Law and Policy 16 (1), 47–84.

Harris, J.R., 1990. Ethical values of individuals at different levels in the organizational hierarchy of a single firm. Journal of Business Ethics 9 (9), 741–750.

Hernandez, T., McGee, R.W., 2013. Ethical attitudes toward taking a bribe: a study of three Latin American countries. International Journal of Business and Economics Perspectives 8 (1), 142–166.

Johnsen, D.B., 2009. The ethics of commercial bribery: integrative social contract theory meets transaction cost economics. Journal of Business Ethics http://dx.doi.org/10.1007/s10551-009-0323-6.

Kant, I., 1952. Fundamental principles of the metaphysics of morals, Great Books of the Western world, vol. 42. Encyclopedia Britannica, Chicago. pp. 251–287.

Kant, I., 1983. Ethical Philosophy (J.W. Ellington, Trans.). Hackett Publishing Company, Indianapolis and Cambridge, UK.

Kaufmann, D., Wei, S., 2000. Does "Grease Money" speed up the wheels of commerce? IMF Working Paper No. 64.

McGee, R.W., 1994a. A Trade Policy for Free Societies: The Case against Protectionism. Quorum Books, Westport and New York.

McGee, R.W., 1994b. The fatal flaw in NAFTA, GATT and all other trade agreements. Northwestern Journal of International Law and Business 14 (3), 549–565.

McGee, R.W. (Ed.), 2012. The Ethics of Tax Evasion: Perspectives in Theory and Practice. Springer, New York.

McGee, R.W., An, Y., 2008. A Survey of Chinese business and economics students on the ethics of tax evasion. In: McGee, Robert W. (Ed.), Taxation and Public Finance in Transition and Developing Economies. Springer, New York, pp. 409–421.

McGee, R.W., Andres, S.N.V., 2009. The ethics of tax evasion: case studies of Taiwan. In: McGee, Robert W. (Ed.), Readings in Business Ethics. ICFAI Press, Hyderabad, India, pp. 200–228.

McGee, R.W., Benk, S., 2011. The ethics of tax evasion: a study of Turkish opinion. Journal of Balkan and Near Eastern Studies 13 (2), 249–262.

McGee, R.W., Butt, Y.Y., 2008. An empirical study of tax evasion ethics in Hong Kong. In: Proceedings of the International Academy of Business and Public Administration Disciplines (IABPAD), Dallas, pp. 72–83. April 24–27. Reprinted in McGee, Robert W. (Ed.), 2012. The Ethics of Tax Evasion: Perspectives in Theory and Practice, Springer, New York, pp. 309–320.

McGee, R.W., Guo, Z., 2007. A survey of law, business and philosophy students in China on the ethics of tax evasion. Society and Business Review 2 (3), 299–315.

McGee, R.W., Noronha, C., 2008. The ethics of tax evasion: a comparative study of Guangzhou (Southern China) and Macau opinions. Euro Asia Journal of Management 18 (2), 133–152.

Mill, J.S. 1979. In: Sher, G. (Ed.), Utilitarianism. Hackett Publishing Company, Indianapolis.

Mocan, N., 2008. What determines corruption? International evidence from microdata. Economic Inquiry 46 (4), 493–510.

Organization for Economic Co-operation and Development, 2011. Convention on Combating Bribery of Foreign Public Officials in International Business Transactions and Related Documents, OECD, Paris.

Peppas, S.C., Peppas, G.J., 2000. Business in the European union: a study of Greek attitudes. Management Decision 38 (6), 369–376.

Posner, R.A., 1983. The Economics of Justice. Harvard University Press, Cambridge, MA.

Posner, R.A., 1998. Economic Analysis of Law, fifth ed. Aspen Law and Business, New York.

Premeaux, S.R., 2004. The current link between management behavior and ethical philosophy. Journal of Business Ethics 51 (3), 269–278.

Premeaux, S.R., Mondy, R.W., 1993. Linking management behavior to ethical philosophy. Journal of Business Ethics 12 (2), 337–349.

Rothbard, M.N., 1970. Man, Economy and State. Nash Publishing, Los Angeles, CA.

Roxas, M.L., Stoneback, J.Y., 2004. The importance of gender across cultures in ethical decision-making. Journal of Business Ethics 50 (2), 149–165.

Roy, A., Singer, A.E., 2006. Reducing corruption in international business: behavioural, managerial and political approaches. Journal of Economics and Social Policy (2) (Article 2).

Ruegger, D., King, E.W., 1992. A study of the effect of age and gender upon student business ethics. Journal of Business Ethics 11 (3), 179–186.

Sanchez, J.I., Gomez, C., Wated, G., 2008. A value-based framework for understanding managerial tolerance of bribery in Latin America. Journal of Business Ethics 83, 341–352.

Serap, A., Ekin, M.G., Tezölmez, S.H., 1999. Business ethics in Turkey: an empirical investigation with special emphasis on gender. Journal of Business Ethics 18, 17–34.

Swaidan, Z., Vitell, S.J., Rose, G.M., Gilbert, F.W., 2006. Consumer ethics: the role of acculturation in the U.S. immigrant populations. Journal of Business Ethics 64 (1), 1–16.

Swamy, A., Knack, S., Lee, Y., Azfar, O., 2001. Gender and corruption. Journal of Development Economics 64, 25–55.

Weeks, W.A., Moore, C.W., McKinney, J.A., Longenecker, J.G., 1999. The effects of gender and career stage on ethical judgment. Journal of Business Ethics 20 (4), 301–313.

Wong, A., Beckman, E., 1992. An applied ethical analysis system in business. Journal of Business Ethics 11, 173–178.

PART Three

Sovereign Wealth Funds

CHAPTER 17

The Emergence of Sovereign Wealth Funds in Asia

Donghyun Park and Gemma Esther B. Estrada
Asian Development Bank, Economics and Research Department, 6 ADB Avenue, Mandaluyong City,
Metro Manila 1550, Philippines

17.1 INTRODUCTION

Since the Asian financial crisis of 1997–1998, developing Asia has been running a sizable current account surplus vis-à-vis the rest of the world on a sustained basis, although the surplus has declined visibly since the global financial crisis of 2008–2009.[1,2] This has transformed the region into a globally significant net exporter of capital. An interesting structural characteristic of the region's capital outflows is that the public sector accounts for a large share of those outflows. In particular, since around 2000 there has been an explosive growth in developing Asia's foreign exchange reserves, which refer to the foreign currency assets held by central banks to protect a country from shortages of international liquidity. In some cases capital inflows have been an additional source of foreign exchange reserves. To a large extent, the rapid accumulation of reserves reflects the regional central banks' efforts to buildup crisis-preventing war chests of international liquidity. The buildup is therefore partly an understandable reaction to a catastrophic event which has left an indelible scar on the regional psyche.

Policy makers and the general public tend to view the growing reserves favorably as a sign of economic strength and even national pride, all the more so in light of the fact that large reserves are a relatively new phenomenon in developing Asia. At the same time, however, there is also a growing sense that the region's central banks now have more than enough reserves to meet all plausible emergencies and contingencies. This kind of concern is giving rise to the notion that excess reserves—reserves which are above and beyond those required for liquidity purposes—should be actively invested abroad to earn higher risk-adjusted returns. By the same token, there is a growing tendency to view the low rates of return earned by the safe and liquid foreign assets such US government bonds, which are typically held as reserves by central banks, as a waste of valuable national resources. In short, a region-wide consensus is pushing the region's governments toward more active, return-oriented management of their reserves.

---

[1] The views expressed in this paper are those of the authors and do not necessarily reflect the views and policies of the Asian Development Bank (ADB) or its Board of Governors or the governments they represent.

[2] Throughout this chapter, developing Asia refers to the 45 developing member countries (DMCs) of the Asian Development Bank. Please refer to www.adb.org for a full list of those countries.

In principle, earning higher risk-adjusted returns on excess reserves is unambiguously beneficial for developing Asia. In contrast to reserves, the primary social benefit of excess reserves is returns rather than liquidity, so foregoing higher returns by choosing sub-optimal risk profiles or investment horizons entails substantial social costs, especially when excess reserves are large. Regardless of one's views about the excess reserves themselves, it is difficult to see how their earning higher returns can be anything but welfare-enhancing. More specifically, the fiscal dividend from more active management of the region's excess reserves will provide governments with valuable extra resources to tackle the numerous formidable structural obstacles which still stand in the way of growth and development. The strategic shift from passive liquidity management toward active profit-seeking investment, already well underway, thus provides exciting new opportunities for expanding the fiscal space in which the region's governments operate.

In practice, the precise magnitude of the fiscal dividend from excess reserves depends on how good the countries are at actually investing them. In other words, the potential for high returns and the realization of high returns are two different things. In the worst-case scenario, the return from high-risk, high-return foreign assets may be lower than the return from traditional reserve assets, yielding, in effect, a negative fiscal dividend. At a broader level, the state agency in charge of investing excess reserves abroad will be constrained by the external environment in which it operates. That external environment is defined by a mixture of home country, host country, and multilateral factors. For example, the political environment of the home country will influence the state investment agency's transparency, financial protectionism in host countries will limit its investment universe, and lack of well-defined multilateral rules of the game for investments by such agencies may be a deterrent to growth.

The remainder of the chapter is organized as follows. First, we lay out the stylized facts of developing Asia's current reserve accumulation. In particular, we explore the quantitative magnitudes of the accumulation. Second, we investigate the critical issue of whether the reserves have become excessive, using well-established measures of reserve adequacy. Third, we examine the appropriateness of sovereign wealth funds as institutional blueprints for managing the region's excess reserves. Fourth, we outline a number of broad but specific policy lessons which we hope will help the region's policy makers to design and manage SWFs capable of delivering large profits on a sustained basis. Finally, we conclude with some central observations and key messages about developing Asia's strategic shift toward more active managements of its foreign exchange reserves.

17.2 STYLIZED FACTS ABOUT DEVELOPING ASIA'S FOREIGN EXCHANGE RESERVES

Historical data indicate the gradual buildup of foreign exchange reserves in developing Asia from 1990 to 2000 and the accelerated pace of reserve buildup between 2000 and 2010 (Figure 17.1). In particular, foreign exchange reserves grew annually by 13.3% on

Billion US$

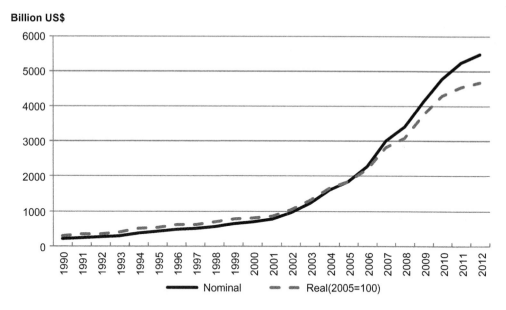

Figure 17.1 Nominal and real foreign exchange reserves of developing Asia (1990–2012). *Source:* Authors' estimates based on data from CEIC Data Company and International Monetary Fund, International Financial Statistics online database (both accessed 23 August 2013).

nominal terms and by 10.2% in real terms between 1990 and 2000. In the following decade, the region's stock of foreign exchange reserves significantly rose, by 21.1% in annual nominal rate and by 18.3% in annual real rate. In value terms, reserves rose from US$202.7 billion in 1990 to US$707.2 billion in 2000. By the end of 2010, the region's stock of reserves was close to US$4.8 trillion.

In 2010–2012, the growth in reserves slowed as a result of weakening external demand. After registering a double-digit annual growth in 2000–2010, the expansion in reserves considerably dropped to just about 6.9% in nominal terms and 4.2% in real terms in 2010–2012. Despite the slower rate of reserve growth, the region's stock of reserves reached US$5.5 trillion by end of 2012.

The steady rise of developing Asia's reserves reflects in part the robust growth of the region's output. It is therefore worthwhile to examine the extent to which the region's reserves have grown relative to its gross domestic product (GDP). The ratio of reserves to GDP shows a modest and steady rise between 1990 and 2000, followed by a sharp increase, and reached a peak of 0.44 in 2009 (Figure 17.2). A slower pace of reserve buildup after that led to a continuous decline in the reserves-to-GDP ratio in 2010–2012, to 0.38 or close to what the ratio was in 2007.

Another important indicator of the size of the region's reserves is the share to global reserves. A rising share to global reserves would lend support to the growing significance of developing Asia's reserve buildup. Figure 17.3 shows that the region's

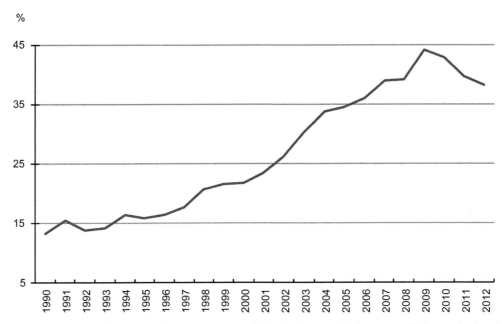

Figure 17.2 Ratio of foreign exchange reserves to GDP, developing Asia (1990–2012). *Source:* Authors' estimates based on data from CEIC Data Company and International Monetary Fund, International Financial Statistics online database (both accessed August 23, 2013).

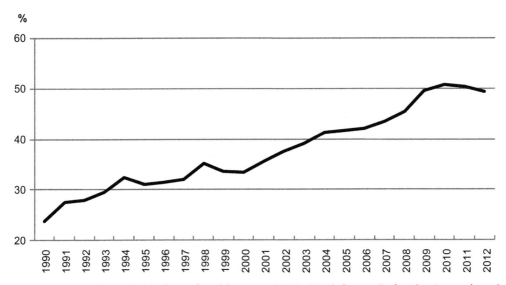

Figure 17.3 Developing Asia's share of world reserves (1990–2012). *Source:* Authors' estimates based on data from CEIC Data Company and International Monetary Fund, International Financial Statistics online database (both accessed 23 August 2013).

Table 17.1 Developing Asia's Top Reserve Holders (As of December 2012)

Rank	Economy	Stock of Foreign Exchange Reserves (Billion US$)	World Ranking in Reserves
1	People's Republic of China	3311.6	1
2	Taipei, China	403.2	6
3	Hong Kong, China	317.2	8
4	Republic of Korea	316.9	9
5	India	261.7	10
6	Singapore	256.8	11
7	Thailand	171.1	14
8	Malaysia	134.9	16
9	Indonesia	105.9	18
10	Philippines	71.7	23

Source: CEIC Data Company and International Monetary Fund, International Financial Statistics Online Database (both accessed 23 August 2013).

share of global reserves rose from 23.8% in 1990 to 33.5% in 2000, and to 49.3% in 2012. This therefore suggests that developing Asia has been accumulating reserves at a significant pace. Further, the large buildup in reserves has occurred among large developing Asian economies, with China now having the most reserves in the region (Table 17.1), as well as in the whole world. Other countries have also substantially accumulated reserves. Thus, five economies in the region were among the world's top 10 reserve holders in 2012.

17.3 INFORMAL EXAMINATION OF THE ADEQUACY OF DEVELOPING ASIA'S FOREIGN EXCHANGE RESERVES

There are well-established measures that examine whether reserves are within their optimal levels (see Edison, 2003; ECB, 2006; Green and Torgerson, 2007). These measures are informal rules of thumb based on general economic intuition rather than on rigorously derived theoretical concepts. Still, they perform quite well in empirical analysis of reserve adequacy and thus can be useful benchmarks. One key rule of thumb is the ratio of reserves to short-term external debt, which is also often used as a measure of an economy's financial vulnerability. According to the so-called Greenspan-Guidotti rule, this ratio should be equal to 1, indicating that a country can service all external debt, having a maturity or one year or less, even during periods of financial crisis. Thus, a value equal or higher than 1 signals financial soundness while a value lower than 1 signals vulnerability to a crisis. Figure 17.4 shows that Asia's top reserve holders have

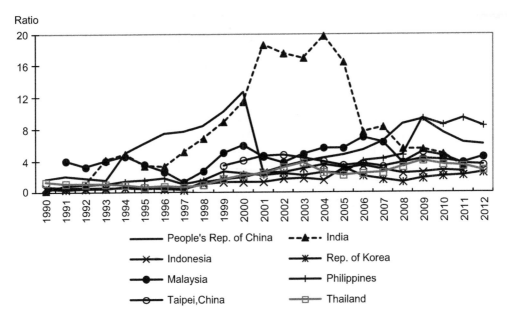

Figure 17.4 Ratio of foreign exchange reserves to short-term external debt in developing Asia's top 10 reserve holders (1990–2012). *Note:* Data not available for Hong Kong and Singapore. *Source:* Authors' estimates based on data from CEIC Data Company, International Monetary Fund, International Financial Statistics online database, and World Bank, World Development Indicators online database (all accessed 23 August 2013).

ratios that are greater than 1 and thus have more than adequate reserves when assessed in terms of the Greenspan–Guidotti rule.

Another relevant measure that is used to examine reserve adequacy is the ratio of reserves to broad money (M2). The higher the ratio, the greater confidence the general public has on the value of the local currency and hence the lower the likelihood of crisis-induced shifts toward other currencies. Figure 17.5 shows that the reserves to M2 ratios of most top reserve holders in the region are higher than the suggested acceptable range of between 0.5 and 0.20. This implies that, based on this measure, countries may have accumulated reserves that are higher than the optimal levels.

A widely used measure of reserve adequacy is the number of months of imports that reserves can sufficiently cover. A large stock of reserves will reduce the vulnerability of a country to adverse current account shocks and limited access to international capital markets. For most countries in Figure 17.6, the number of imports that their reserves can cover ranges between 5 and 20 months. These are higher than the established benchmark of just 3–4 months of imports, which again provides evidence that countries are accumulating huge and excess reserves.

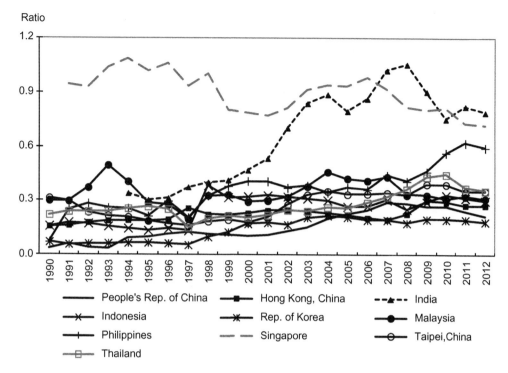

Figure 17.5 Ratio of foreign exchange reserves to M2 in developing Asia's top 10 reserve holders (1990–2012). *Source:* Authors' estimates based on data from CEIC Data Company and International Monetary Fund, International Financial Statistics online database (both accessed 23 August 2013).

Another indicator of reserve adequacy that also appears in the literature is the ratio of foreign exchange reserves to GDP. Unlike the previously discussed measures, this ratio does not reflect external or financial vulnerability, but can nevertheless be a useful measure for comparing reserves across countries and across time. For example, a larger country requires greater reserves compared to smaller ones given the former has greater international capital flows and trade. In a similar vein, a country that has grown through time is also expected to accumulate larger amounts of reserves. Figure 17.7 shows that there has been a steady rise in the reserves-to-GDP ratios across the region. However, these ratios appeared to have reached a peak in 2009 and began to decline somewhat after that in some countries. The highest ratio so far was about 1.2, achieved by Hong Kong, China, and this was followed by Singapore at 1. For China, the peak was equivalent to about half of its GDP.

In summary, the informal tests show that countries have accumulated vast amount of reserves that tend to exceed some optimal levels. Measures that relate reserves to

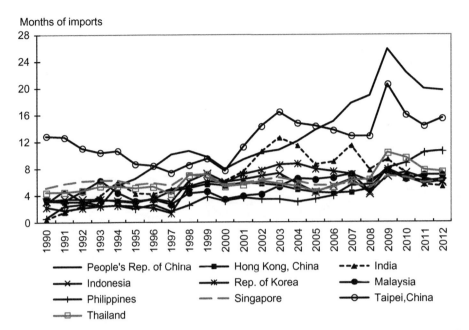

Figure 17.6 Imports covered by foreign exchange reserves in developing Asia's top 10 reserve holders (1990–2012). *Source:* Authors' estimates based on data from CEIC Data Company and International Monetary Fund, International Financial Statistics online database (both accessed 23 August 2013).

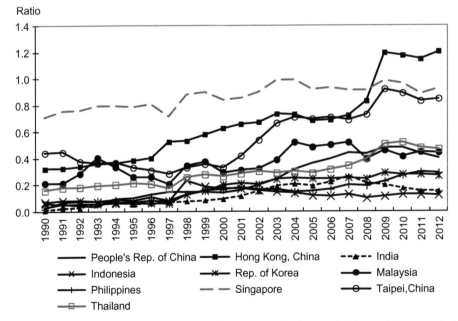

Figure 17.7 Ratio of foreign exchange reserves to GDP in developing Asia's top 10 reserve holders (1990–2012). *Source:* Authors' estimates based on data from CEIC Data Company and International Monetary Fund, International Financial Statistics online database (both accessed 23 August 2013).

short-term external debt, money supply, and monthly imports confirm the conventional wisdom that the region now has excess reserves, or more than that required for precautionary purposes. Since the buildup of excess reserves entails opportunity costs, there is a need to better manage those reserves toward profit-seeking investments.

17.4 SOVEREIGN WEALTH FUNDS AS A BLUEPRINT FOR INVESTING DEVELOPING ASIA'S EXCESS RESERVES

According to informal rules of thumb as well as a growing empirical literature, actual reserves now exceed optimal reserves in developing Asia. Such evidence lends formal support to the conventional wisdom that the region now has too much reserves. Crucially, up until the time of the global financial crisis, those reserves were managed primarily in the form of traditional reserve assets such as US government bonds. More generally, according to conventional wisdom, before the global financial crisis, in most of developing Asia reserve assets were passively managed for precautionary liquidity purposes rather than actively invested for profit maximization. According to the ECB (2006) and Genberg et al. (2005), among others, the stylized facts generally support such conventional wisdom.

The first-best way to address the problem of excess reserves is by not accumulating so much reserves in the first place, for example, by liberalizing restrictions on capital outflows. However, *given* that there is a substantial gap between actual and optimal reserves, the second-best solution is to explicitly convert the excess reserves into investment funds. In short, there is serious intellectual justification for the conventional wisdom that developing Asia should reallocate its reserves from low-risk, low-yielding assets to high-risk, high-yielding assets. Such re-allocation would promote national welfare by generating a fiscal dividend for the government which owns the investment funds.

The conversion of reserves into investment funds logically leads us to a class of state-owned financial institutions known as sovereign wealth funds (henceforth SWFs) which currently have around US$5.8 trillion in assets. The collective volume by Johnson-Calari and Rietveld (2007) provides an in-depth introduction to sovereign wealth funds. Although the term SWF has been first coined only 2 years ago by Rozanov (2005a,b) in 2005, they have actually been around for quite some time. In fact, the oldest fund, the Kuwait Investment Authority (KIA), goes all the way back to 1953. In fact, KIA and most of the world's well-established SWFs started out as investment vehicles for income from natural resources, most often oil and gas. The two striking exceptions are Singapore's Temasek Holdings and Government of Singapore Investment Corporation (GIC). As their name implies, SWFs have two defining qualities—(1) ownership and control by the government and (2) pursuit of high risk-adjusted returns as the central objective. A further common characteristic of the well-established SWFs is that they are based on fiscal reserves derived from government budget surplus, profits of state-owned companies, or other government net income.

A further common characteristic shared by most existing SWFs is a general lack of transparency which makes it difficult to accurately assess their investment strategy, performance, or even overall philosophy. The striking exception in this regard is Norway's Government Pension Fund (GPF), which is characterized by an exceptionally high level of transparency. Partly for this reason and partly due to its good investment track record, the Norwegian fund has become a benchmark model for other resource-rich countries. In developing Asia, Kazakhstan's National Oil Fund and Timor-Leste's Petroleum Fund have explicitly modeled themselves after GPF.

It is easy to see the central relevance of the SWFs in the context of developing Asia's quest to use its reserves more productively. Above all, SWFs fundamentally differ from central banks in that they view foreign exchange as essentially investment funds to be used aggressively for buying high-risk, high-return foreign assets rather than as international liquidity to be conservatively managed for insurance purposes. As such, SWFs fit in perfectly with the strategic and philosophical shift from liquidity to returns currently under way in the region's reserve management. The term SWF also fits in perfectly with the conceptual distinction between reserves and investment funds. It is therefore hardly surprising that the region's policy makers are using SWFs as the new central framework for managing their large excess reserves.

Developing Asia's reserve accumulation is driven mostly by a non-resource current account surplus, sometimes augmented by capital inflows, rather than natural resource revenues. The underlying source of the region's reserves thus has much more in common with Singapore's reserves rather than the reserves of oil exporters such as Norway or the Gulf states. This may be a major reason why the two Singaporean funds are attracting more interest from the regional policy makers than the other existing funds even though Singapore's reserves are fiscal reserves, like those of the oil exporters and unlike those of developing Asia. Indeed Korea's KIC and China's planned CIC, which respectively, are explicitly modeling themselves after GIC and Temasek, respectively. Another reason is that the Singaporean funds are the only well-established SWFs from within the region, and they have relatively long histories and a wealth of experience. However, probably the biggest reason why the Singaporean funds have become the regional model is their excellent investment records.

17.5 POLICY PRESCRIPTIONS FOR DEVELOPING ASIA'S SWFs

Each country faces its own unique set of economic, political, and institutional parameters so it is unlikely that the experiences of a particular SWF, even one which has been highly successful in terms of generating returns, can provide a universally applicable model for other SWFs. Therefore, we must be careful not to make policy prescriptions for developing Asian countries based on the specific experiences of another country, be it Singapore, Norway, or some other country. What is optimal for a Temasek or a GPF may not be optimal for a KIC or a CIC. Nevertheless, we can draw some policy lessons from the experiences of the well-established SWFs which are broad enough to have relevance for a wide range of regional countries yet specific enough to provide useful and practical guidance for regional policy makers. While the below list is hardly an exhaustive list of the dos and don'ts of setting up and running SWFs, it does nevertheless provide a preliminary checklist of best practice principles for policy makers.

By far the biggest policy prescription is the need for operational autonomy and freedom from political interference. Regardless of its specific governance structure, a SWF needs to have complete control over day-to-day investment decision-making if it is to perform successfully. Once government or central bank interferes with how the fund carries out its business, profits will inevitably suffer for the simple reason that motives other than profit maximization will enter the picture. In other words, political interference constitutes a cost of business and a big one at that. The ability to maximize returns subject to manageable risk is inevitably compromised without the autonomy to decide where and how to invest. Of course, operational independence is not a sufficient condition for success but it is a necessary condition without which success will be impossible. Furthermore, independence amounts to very little without accountability. As such, the government should hold the fund strictly accountable for its investment performance. In connection with operational independence, the concept of central bank independence (CBI) provides a potential institutional model for SWFs.

Very much related to the precondition of operational independence is the importance of running the SWF on a purely commercial basis. Since earning the highest risk-adjusted returns or, more simply, making as much money as possible for the government should be the central objective of SWFs; they should not, to the extent possible, be burdened with non-commercial objectives. This also implies that the sole criterion of assessing a fund's performance should be the rate of return. The agency in charge of investing excess reserves should be free from the public interest role of policy-making and market regulations, and it should be managed solely on the basis of commercial criteria without the need to accommodate non-commercial objectives. This has the significant additional benefit of dispelling concerns about non-commercial objectives in host countries.

An important policy lesson is the flip side of the first positive lesson—operational independence. It would be a serious mistake to believe that it is possible to build a Temasek or a GIC overnight. That is, it takes a lot of time and effort to buildup the institutional capacity to make good use of operational independence. Both Temasek and GIC have accumulated a large stock of institutional knowledge and experience from their many years of operations. Furthermore, aside from Hong Kong, Singapore has long been the only major international financial hub in developing Asia. Therefore, unlike the rest of the region, the infrastructure, human capital, and regulatory framework of a sophisticated and well-functioning financial system are all already well in place. It is unrealistic to assume that KIC or CIC already have the capacity to invest competently in areas like private equity, venture capital, and real estate, letting alone equity stakes in start-up companies in emerging industries such as biotech. The practical implication is that a gradualist approach of learning-by-doing is preferable to a cold-turkey approach of a big bang. It is better to start from less risky asset classes and buildup investment management capacity before moving onto more adventurous asset classes. Also, moving into risky assets without adequate institutional capacity may lead to big early losses, which will erode public support for the fund.

There should be a clear-cut separation between liquidity management and excess reserve investment. To the extent possible, the SWF should be free from obligations to provide additional international liquidity to the central bank in case of emergencies such as the Asian crisis. Such concerns should remain solely in the domain of the central bank's reserve management. As long as sovereign wealth remains classified as reserves, it is subject to stringent restrictions in terms of where and how they can be invested. Formal classification aside, as long as there is a mindset of equating reserves and excess reserves, there will be a limit to the returns which the fund can hope to achieve. There is a very real danger that the failure to clearly distinguish between the two will compromise the achievement of both liquidity and return. In this context, there is much to be said for the CIC's plans to issue renminbi-denominated bonds to buy up reserves from the central bank, in effect converting reserves to non-reserve national wealth.

Maximizing returns and wealth over the long run requires adopting a long-term investment horizon as well as taking significant risks. At the most basic level, taking a long-term view allows the sovereign funds to realize substantial premiums for foregoing liquidity. More fundamentally, however, it enables them to ignore short-term volatility and focus on the long-term prospects of their investments rather than change strategy every time there is bad news. We should not underestimate the advantages of a long-term investment horizon. Somewhat related but slightly different from a long-term horizon is the obvious but often neglected dictum that high returns require high risks. And, the experience of the Singaporean SWFs bears this out most emphatically. They have been buying assets which are well outside the tolerance limits of central bank reserve managers, such as private equity, venture capital, and real estate. The Singaporean funds have aggressively taken a lot of risk but have also managed that risk well to deliver premium performance. Besides practicing systematic risk control, risk diversification through extensive diversification of investment portfolio—in terms of geographical location, asset class, and industry—has been an integral part of their investment philosophy.

17.6 CONCLUSION

The rapid accumulation of foreign exchange reserves since 2000 was partly a region-wide response to the devastating Asian crisis of 1997–1998 and has led to reserve levels which are well in excess of all plausible estimates of what developing Asia needs for liquidity purposes. This has led to growing public pressure for a strategic shift in the management of foreign exchange reserves, from passive liquidity management to active profit-seeking investment. The strategic shift is largely taking the form of new sovereign wealth funds, which are being set up across the region by governments eager to earn higher returns on their excess reserves. Although the emergence of new Asian sovereign wealth funds clearly has repercussions on the global financial system, the focus of our chapter is the opportunities and challenges those funds face in the context of the region's growth, development, and welfare. Our discussions yield a number of key messages which will enable the region's policy makers and general public to achieve a more solid and clear understanding of how those funds can contribute to the region's welfare.

First, more active management of excess reserves is unambiguously beneficial for the region. By definition, excess reserves subtract from rather than add to welfare. Since the primary benefit of reserves is liquidity, it is no longer worthwhile for central banks to hold reserves when the additional liquidity they provide is less than their additional cost. At the reserve level where this occurs, return or yield replaces liquidity as the primary benefit from the central bank's foreign exchange holdings. The welfare losses are likely to be substantial in the case of developing Asia, in light of the large and growing levels of excess reserves. The popular view that the region would be better off by re-allocating its excess reserves away from safe and liquid but low-yield assets toward higher-risk, higher-yield assets is thus supported by economic intuition in this case.

Second, it is useful to view excess reserves as a different kind of public sector asset, an asset whose primary benefit is risk-adjusted returns rather than liquidity. For the sake of conceptual clarity, let us refrain from calling this asset reserves at all, but give it an altogether different name—*national wealth*. A clear-cut distinction between the two assets is needed to avoid burdening reserve management with return requirements and national wealth investment with liquidity requirements. Failure to make such a distinction is likely to reduce the liquidity-producing capacity of reserve management and the profit-maximizing capacity of national wealth investment. In this connection, China's plans to issue bonds to buy reserves from the central bank, in effect converting reserves into non-reserve wealth, is a step in the right direction. At an institutional level, the desirability of a clear-cut distinction between liquidity and return favors setting up the sovereign fund as a stand-alone agency rather than as part of the central bank, especially in developing Asia, in light of the relative novelty of excess reserves in the region.

Third, it takes a lot of time and effort to buildup the institutional capacity of effective SWFs which are good at fulfilling their central, purely commercial mandate of generating high returns subject to manageable risk. A region-wide misperception which is as dangerous as the notion that excess reserves are free fiscal assets is the notion that it will not be difficult for the region's new funds to replicate Temasek- or GIC-type investment returns. It is dangerous since such unrealistic expectations may fuel public pressures for unrealistic investment performance. Again, a key policy challenge is to educate the general public. The exceptional rate of return enjoyed by Temasek and GIC is due to their exceptionally high level of institutional capacity, which enables them to take on high risks, manage those risks well, and achieve high returns. The type of high-risk investments they make is not for the faint-hearted and most definitely not for developing Asian countries just moving away from central bank portfolios. This implies that in terms of investment strategy, a gradualist approach of learning-by-doing, starting from less risky asset classes and building up investment management capacity before moving onto more risky asset classes is preferable to trying to become a Temasek overnight. In this sense, there is much to be said for KIC's cautious, go-slow investment strategy despite the widespread criticism it has provoked in Korea. Finally, although we have emphasized operational independence as a precondition for success, the much more urgent task for the region's SWFs is to buildup the institutional capacity which will enable them to take full advantage of operational independence.

In this chapter, we examined an issue of high and growing interest in developing Asia—how to put the region's surging foreign exchange reserves to better use so as to promote the region's growth, development, and welfare. By and large developing Asia's reserve accumulation does not reflect an increase in sovereign net wealth and hence fiscal resources. Policy makers need to effectively educate the public about this inconvenient truth both to temper their expectations and to ultimately induce fiscally responsible use of the reserves. However, the income from the SWFs' investment does augment fiscal resources and thus increases the fiscal space in which the region's governments have to operate. Therefore, to put it in the simplest terms, the SWF's fundamental mission must be to make as much as money possible for the government without taking excessive risks. In the short run, our study yields the loud and clear conclusion that it is feasible and desirable for the region to increase its fiscal space and improve its welfare by strategically shifting its excess reserves from central banks to SWFs, from passive liquidity management to active profit-seeking investment. In the medium run, however, the region's governments should actively pursue liberalization of capital outflows so as to promote the role of the private sector in investing national wealth. In the long run, the region's governments have to address the more structural issue of the region's large and persistent current account surplus, the source of the region's excess reserves. It is worth remembering that accumulating excess reserves on a sustained basis is welfare-reducing although the focus of our study was on how to make best use of them once they had been accumulated.

REFERENCES

Edison, H., 2003. Are foreign reserves in Asia too high? In: World Economic Outlook 2003 Update. International Monetary Fund, Washington, D.C.

European Central Bank, 2006. The accumulation of reserves. ECB, Occasional Paper No. 43, Frankfurt.

Genberg, H., McCauley, R., Park, Y.C., Persaud, A., 2005. Official Reserves and Currency Management in Asia: Myth, Reality and the Future, Geneva Reports on the World Economy 7. International Center for Monetary and Banking Studies (ICMB), Geneva.

Green, R., Torgerson, T., 2007. Are high foreign exchange reserves in emerging markets a blessing or a burden? US Department of the Treasury, Occasional Paper No. 6, March.

Johnson-Calari, J., Rietveld, M. (Eds.), 2007. Sovereign Wealth Management. Central Banking Publications, London.

Rozanov, A., 2005a. Who holds the wealth of nations? Central Banking Journal 15 (4), 52–57.

Rozanov, A., 2005b. From reserves to sovereign wealth management. Central Banking Journal 15 (3), 1–3.

CHAPTER 18

China Investment Corporation: China's Sovereign Wealth Fund

Yuwei Hu

BBVA, 618 Tower 2, Bright China Chang An Building, No. 7, Jianguomen Nei Avenue, Beijing, China

18.1 INTRODUCTION

With the rapid growth of the Chinese economy over the past decades, foreign exchange reserves have accumulated significantly. The latest statistics show that China's forex reserves amounted to approximately USD 3.5 trillion as of June 2013 (SAFE, 2013), which accounted for onethird of global forex reserves. Traditionally, Chinese forex assets are mainly managed by the State Administration of Foreign Exchange (SAFE) under the Chinese central bank; however its performance has been criticized for unsatisfactory returns and opaque operation (Hu, 2010).

With the main objective of diversifying investments of forex reserves and achieving enhanced returns, the Chinese central government established the China Investment Corporation (henceforth, CIC) in September 2007. The initial capital was injected by SAFE with USD 200 billion from forex reserves, which was then swapped with RMB 1.5 trillion special bonds issued by the Ministry of Finance. At the same time the CIC was formed, another major financial institution called Central Huijin was transferred from the SAFE to the CIC as well. As of December 2012 the total asset under management by the CIC was at USD 575 billion.

Since the inception the CIC has received great attention from local and overseas observers. Local observers were not sure whether the CIC could prove itself to be a new, innovative investment channel for China's forex management as expected by the central government, while foreign observers were mainly concerned whether the CIC's investment would be politically driven. The CIC was created only seven years ago and since has grown rapidly. According to the latest statistics (SWF Institute, 2013) it is already ranked in fourth place in global rankings in terms of assets under management (see Figure 18.1 for more details on the top 10 SWFs in the worlds). Furthermore, with such a large amount of cash on hand, governments of countries that have experienced financial crises were in great need of capital and as a consequence the CIC started purchasing global securities which aroused concerns about protectionism of some recipient countries.

Despite great interest in the CIC locally and overseas, studies on this entity have been unfortunately scarce. Over the recent years the CIC witnessed major changes in various aspects; therefore it is necessary to update the literature in this area. While most

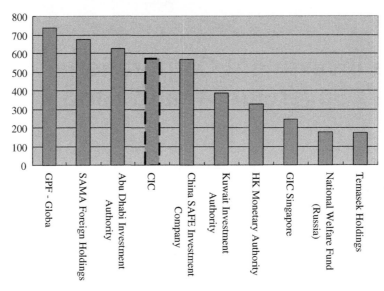

Figure 18.1 The top 10 sovereign wealth funds in the world in USD billion. *Source:* SWF Institute (2013).

of the previous literature focuses on the CIC (or "CIC International": as it is currently called) while leaving out Central Huijin a related and important institution.

In this chapter we first conduct a thorough overview on the structure of the CIC in Section 18.2 and its investment strategy in Section 18.3. In Section 18.4 we seek to identify the problems associated with this institution. In Section 18.5 various reform suggestions are proposed aimed at improving the current setup. Finally, the last section concludes the paper.

18.2 OVERVIEW AND ORGANIZATIONAL STRUCTURE

The CIC is headquartered in Beijing and was established in 2007 by the central government to diversify forex investment. It is considered as a state-owned financial institution equivalent to a ministry-level agency within China's political hierarchical structure. The Chairman of the CIC is nominated and appointed by the State Council, clearly indicating its political affiliation while its organizational structure has been subject to several changes. Based on the current structure, the CIC consists of two independent subsidiary companies, i.e., the CIC International and Central Huijin which enjoys the same hierarchy within the CIC.

18.2.1 CIC International

The CIC International was created in September 2011 as a result of latest internal restructuring. The main mandate of the CIC International is to manage overseas investments, while Central Huijin is in charge of managing local investments in China.

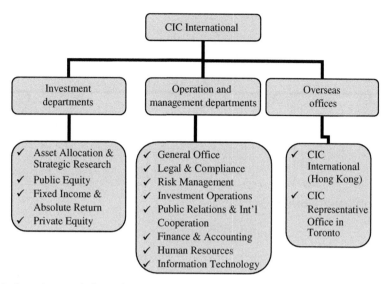

Figure 18.2 Organizational chart of the China Investment Corporation International.

Table 18.1 Staff Composition of CIC International

	Total	Higher Education	Overseas Experience	Overseas Education	Foreign Nationals
2012	443	363	174	250	41
2011	405	334	165	224	44
2010	378	313	154	217	43
2009	246	199	115	132	31
2008	194	184	73	85	18

Source: Annual reports of CIC.

As presented in Figure 18.2 CIC International is composed of three segments, i.e., the front office (investment departments), the back office (operation and management departments), and overseas offices. With regards to overseas offices, CIC International (Hong Kong) was established in November 2010, while the CIC Representative Office in Toronto was set up in January 2011. CIC International (Hong Kong) currently manages such business as global credit products and China concepts shares on behalf of CIC headquarters in Beijing. The CIC Representative Office in Toronto deals with public relations, market research, and local communications in the North America region.

Staff is the key to the success of CIC and since 2008 CIC International has initiated a high-profile global recruitment process, mainly targeting Chinese with overseas (higher) education and work experience. Table 18.1 indicates that more than half of its employees (250 out of 443 as of 2012) have overseas education, while 40% have

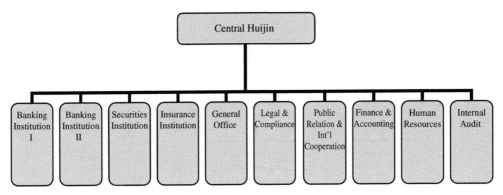

Figure 18.3 Organizational chart of central Huijin.

overseas work experience. The focus of overseas experience is reasonable given CIC International's global investment mandate.

18.2.2 Central Huijin

Central Huijin was established by the central government in December 2003 to help capitalize the fragile banking sector. Although Central Huijin was acquired by the CIC from SAFE in 2007, its mandate remains intact, i.e., serving as a special purchase vehicle by which the central government can operate as a stakeholder for key financial institutions. The main purpose of such management transfers from the SAFE to the CIC was to help enhance the latter's profitability. As noted earlier, the Ministry of Finance issued RMB 1.5 trillion special bonds when CIC was established, while the yield on those special bonds was 4.5% implying huge financial pressure for the CIC. Therefore, the government expected that profits earned from stake holdings in local financial institutions can help the CIC to pay back the dividends in RMB and therefore allowing the CIC to have more freedom to invest abroad.

As demonstrated in Figure 18.3, Central Huijin comprises of nine internal departments, of which two are in charge of matters related to banks, one to securities, and another to insurance companies, while the other departments are back office in nature.

18.3 INVESTMENT STRATEGY

According to the current internal protocol within CIC, the two subsidiary companies (CIC International and Central Huijin) operate in parallel and independently. CIC International is in charge of investing abroad, while Central Huijin focuses on its investment in the local market.

Table 18.2 Breakdown of CIC's Balance Sheet in Percent

	2008	2009	2010	2011	2012
Cash and deposit	16.1	5.6	3.5	4.2	3.9
Financial asset					
Cash management	15.3	6.2	0.8	1.7	1.3
Equity	0.7	12.0	16.0	12.4	15.9
Fixed income	2.8	7.6	8.5	8.0	6.3
Alternative	0.1	2.2	7.1	8.4	9.6
Total-sub	18.8	28.1	32.5	30.5	33.1
Receivables	0.5	0.9	1.0	1.2	0.5
Saleable financial asset	0.0	0.0	0.0	0.0	0.0
Held to maturity investment	5.1	4.3	0.5	0.4	0.1
Long-term equity	57.5	60.6	61.9	63.2	61.9
Deferred tax asset	0.6	0.3	0.3	0.4	0.3
Others	1.3	0.2	0.3	0.1	0.2
Total	100.0	100.0	100.0	100.0	100.0
Total (in USD bn)	297,540	332,394	409,579	482,167	575,178

Source: Annual reports of CIC.

18.3.1 CIC

According to the official statement in the annual reports, CIC "*operates with a clear mandate to diversify China's foreign exchange investments and to seek maximum returns for its shareholder within acceptable risk tolerance*." Under this principle the CIC claims to be a long-term, responsible, and financial investor, while it does not engage in the daily operations of the investee companies, and does not aim to control companies or sectors in which it invests.

Table 18.2 gives detailed information on CIC's financial position over the 5-year period. Among the asset classes, the investment under "financial assets" mainly refers the assets located overseas, therefore as of 2012 one-third of CIC's total assets was allocated abroad and stood at 18.8% in 2008. Overseas investments in cash and deposits witnessed a gradual decline in the portfolio, and its shares dropped from 16.1% in 2008 to 3.9% in 2012. Among the overseas portfolio, a similar trend is discernible whereby cash also decreased from 15.3% in 2008 to 1.3% in 2012. In contrast, asset categories with higher returns have increased their share in the portfolio. For example, equity increased from 0.7% in 2008 to 15.9% in 2012.

Another major asset class in CIC's portfolio is "long-term equity," which mainly refers to the investment by Central Huijin in local financial institutions. As demonstrated in Table 18.2 local assets consistently account for approximately 60% of CIC's total assets during the observation period. Total assets under management of the CIC increased from an initial injection of USD 200 billion in 2007 to USD 575 billion in 2013. However, it is worth mentioning that SAFE made two additional capital injections to the CIC in 2011 and 2012 of USD 30 billion and USD $19 billion, respectively.

18.3.2 CIC International

CIC International mainly focuses on investments abroad and according to current regulations there is no limit of investing in any particular asset class; in other words, the CIC International can invest in whatever it considers appropriate and no quantitative constraints apply. The CIC International's investments have covered traditional assets categories such as stocks, bonds, and alternative investments such as hedge funds, managed futures, venture capital, and private equity. In 2011, in order to better reflect the nature of being a long-term investor the CIC decided to change the performance evaluation horizon from 5 to 10 years. Furthermore, in 2012 the CIC International started to adopt the Yale endowment model of investing abroad. The effect of following this investment strategy remains unclear, however it is expected that such a new approach could help CIC International to enhance returns over the long-run.

In line with the endowment model, CIC International's recent investment activities have paid more attention to direct investments abroad, and particularly those related to natural resources and infrastructure. This point is confirmed by the information in Table 18.3, which presents key direct investments conducted by CIC International in 2012. The investments are either in the natural resources sector (e.g., firms such as Polyus Gold International Russia's largest gold producer) or in infrastructure, (e.g., Heathrow Airport). All investments are below the 10% ownership, which may reflect CIC's intention of not controlling any investee.

As a relatively new SWF, the CIC suffered several major setbacks from its first few overseas investments. For example, in 2007 the CIC purchased 10% of Blackstone's shares with USD 3 billion just before Blackstone's IPO. However, after Blackstone's IPO, the stock price dropped significantly. As of this writing, CIC's investments still

Table 18.3 Selected Direct Investments in 2012

Investee	Country	Sector	In million	Ownership (%)
Thames water	UK	Infrastructure	GBP 276	8.68
EP energy	US	Energy	USD 300	9.90
Polyus gold	Russia	Mining	USD 425	5
Eutelsat communications SA	France	Pan Industry	EUR 386	7
Heathrow Airport Holdings Ltd.	UK	Infrastructure	GBP 450	10
Moscow Exchange	Russia	Pan Industry	USD 187	4.58

Source: CIC annual report 2012.

Table 18.4 Returns of CIC International in Percent

	2008	2009	2010	2011	2012
Annualized	−2.1	4.1	6.4	3.8	5.0
Year-over-year (YoY)	−2.1	11.7	11.7	−4.3	10.6

Source: CIC annual reports. YoY: year-over-year.

Table 18.5 Capital Injection by Central Huijin in USD Billion

2003	2003	2005	2007	2007	2008
BOC	CCB	ICBC	CDB	CEB	ABC
22.5	22.5	15	20	2.6	19

Source: Various. BOC (Bank of China); CCB (China Construction Bank); ICBC (Industrial and Commercial Bank of China); CDB (China Development Bank); CEB (China Everbright Bank); ABC (Agricultural Bank of China).

show a 30% loss in its books, plus an additional investment loss in Morgan Stanley. As a consequence, the CIC become more cautious since the 2008–2009 crisis. In order to achieve better performance the CIC started to outsource investment to external asset managers in 2009 and in 2012 approximately 64% of CIC's International assets were managed by external managers. In terms of performance Table 18.4 shows that year-over-year (YoY) returns were negative in 2008 and 2011, and positive in the other years with an annualized return of 5% over the 5-year period.

18.3.3 Central Huijin

When Central Huijin was established, its capital was used to help write off bad loans/assets of state-owned banks, which was from SAFE's forex. As displayed in Table 18.5 in 2003 Central Huijin injected USD 22.5 billion, respectively, to BOC and CCB, which greatly helped improve the capital base of both banks allowing them get listed on public exchanges. In the following few years, Central Huijin injected capital to four state-owned banks, including ICBC, the largest bank in the world in terms of market capitalization.

Central Huijin plays a crucial role in China's financial system by being the controlling stakeholder of the big four state-owned banks, i.e., ICBC, ABC, BOC, and CCB. Central Huijin also controls several major local insurance companies, securities companies, and other financial institutions, as displayed in Table 18.6. As of 2012 Central Huijin held assets equivalent to RMB 68 trillion, which was approximately half of Chinese financial assets.

Although Central Huijin's investments mainly focus on local Chinese financial institutions, it is interesting to note it has a small stake (14.01%) in UBS Securities (China) which could be interpreted as Central Huijin's intention to expand business scope and invest in non-state-related financial institutions.

Table 18.6 Shareholding in China's Financial Institutions by Central Huijin 2012

China Development Bank	47.63
ICBC	35.46
ABC	40.21
BOC	67.72
CCB	57.21
China Everbright Bank	48.37
China Export & Credit Insurance	73.63
China Reinsurance	84.91
Xinhua Life Insurance	31.23
China Jianyin Investment	100.00
China Galaxy	78.57
Shenyin & Wanguo Securities	55.38
CICC	43.35
China Securities	40.00
China Investment Securities	100.00
UBS Securities (China)	14.01
Everbright China Group	100.00
Jiantou Citic Asset Management	70.00
Guotai & Junan Asset Management	14.54

Source: Huijin annual reports.

18.4 CURRENT PROBLEMS

18.4.1 Ministerial Conflict Between SAFE and the Ministry of Finance

We believe that the current difficulties have caused several secondary problems relating to the ministerial conflict or competition between SAFE and the Ministry of Finance. The capital of the CIC is from SAFE, but it is in the form of forex which was swapped with special bonds issued by the Ministry of Finance. Therefore, in practice the CIC is accountable to the Ministry of Finance, which can be reflected in the makeup of its senior management, namely the Chairman and other senior managers who are often from the Ministry of Finance.

SAFE is the financial source of original funds and reluctant to cooperate with the Ministry of Finance on CIC matters, since they strongly feel that CIC should be accountable to SAFE. Meanwhile, SAFE is concerned that if CIC outperforms well in terms of overseas investments it may further reduce SAFE's influence and power in China's forex management. In this context, Hu (2010) analyzed the competition between SAFE and CIC with evidence demonstrating that SAFE has been gradually moving from conservative investment strategies and has started to engage in higher returns through high-risk asset classes.

18.4.2 Internal Conflict Between CIC International and Central Huijin

CIC International and Central Huijin are the two separate and independent subsidiary companies within the CIC. However, the relationship between both institutions is questionable given their distinct natures. Central Huijin was created by the central government to recapitalize the weak state-owned banks and after the recapitalization and subsequent successful IPOs, as the largest shareholder Central Huijin benefitted significantly from such investments. In fact, the CIC is using profits earned from Central Huijin to account for the losses incurred overseas and disburse the large dividend payments required from the issuance of the RMB 1.5 trillion special bonds.

The CIC started to rethink the efficiency of the internal structure and the rationale was that the close relationship between CIC and Central Huijin was viewed by foreign governments that CIC was not a genuine SWF, but a sovereign vehicle by which the Chinese government could achieve political objectives abroad (Salidjanova, 2011). As a consequence the CIC decided to reorganize and create CIC International as an incorporated company, thus aiming to ease overseas concerns. However, whether such reorganization is able to disperse the concerns of foreign politicians still remains to be seen.

18.4.3 Unsatisfactory Performance of CIC Investments

As previously stated investments by CIC International and Central Huijin are conducted separately and independently. When it comes to CIC International the performance has been unsatisfactory with an average return of 5.5%, just 1% higher than the inflation rate during the period (Table 18.7). This is unfortunate as the CIC aims to become a world-class investment manager in China, but its performance can only slightly outperform the inflation rate. However, when the data are consolidated between CIC International and Central Huijin, it appears that the average return is higher, i.e., 11.8%. This superior performance is due to the large stake holdings in local profitable financial institutions. Even for collection of investments the profitability is not due to Central Huijin's good investment strategy, but rather to the outperforming financial sector in China.

Table 18.7 Returns of CIC vs. Inflation Rate in Percent

	2008	2009	2010	2011	2012	Average
CIC International	−2.1	11.7	11.7	−4.3	10.6	5.5
Total (International + Huijin)	6.8	12.9	13.7	11.4	14.2	11.8
Inflation	5.9	−0.7	3.3	5.4	3.1	3.4

Source: CIC annual reports and national statistics bureau.

18.4.4 The Problematic Financing Mechanism of CIC International

Up until this writing CIC (International) has received capital injections from SAFE in 2007, 2011, and 2012. The first injection at USD 2000 billion was the largest, while the others were at the amount of USD 30 billion and USD 19 billion. However, it has been widely argued that no sustainable financing mechanism is in place between SAFE and CIC. In other words, whenever CIC runs out of money it needs to seek extra capital injection from SAFE and this request is treated each time as a standalone case. Whether such request can be endorsed is at the discretion of SAFE, while no objective approval and evaluation procedures apply. In this context it is not surprising to see that the CIC appealed to the Chinese government for additional capital injections as early as 2009, however this materialized in 2011 and the amount was much less than the original request.

When the CIC was established, an innovative or compromise solution was reached between SAFE and the Ministry of Finance, i.e., USD 2000 billion was swapped with RMB 1.5 trillion between both ministries. However, it resulted in an unavoidable consequence, whereby a huge dividend payment arose from the issuance of RMB 1.5 trillion special bonds yielding between 4.3–4.5%. To further complicate matters, the CIC's liability is in RMB, while its asset is in USD or other foreign currencies resulting in a mis-matching of assets and liabilities. Given that the prime allocation of CIC International assets is based overseas and that the continued RMB appreciation in the foreseeable future (3–5% annually), CIC International would need to earn at least 8% annually abroad so as to meet the domestic annual dividend payment, however, returns at this level have never been attained by the CIC.

18.4.5 Low Transparency of CIC

The CIC claims that it abides by internationally accepted practices and standards related to the global SWFs, notably SWF Santiago Principles—Generally Accepted Principles and Practices (GAPP). However, looking into the details of the SWF Santiago Principles and comparing them with CIC's present situation, it is not difficult to discern that discrepancy still exists. For example, the Santiago Principles state that financial reports should be subject to audits by external, independent, and qualified auditors in accordance with internationally recognized standards. However, as noted in CIC's annual reports, it mentions that financial reports are audited by its own auditors, which implies that reports are not subject to external audits as recommended by the Santiago Principles.

The Chairman and Vice Chairman of the CIC are appointed by the State Council; however no information is disclosed regarding what the selection criteria are among candidates. The background of the current Chairman of the CIC indicates that the political hierarchy may be more important than experience and education.

The above observation is consistent with the transparency index complied by the SWF Institute (2013), which demonstrates that CIC scored 7 out of 10 in the 1–10 scoring system and ranked 24 out of the 48 largest SWFs in the world (with information on transparency). In addition, Truman (2011) also analyzed and compared global SWFs and concluded that CIC scored 57 out of 100 in the SWF Scoreboard.

18.5 POLICY RECOMMENDATIONS

18.5.1 Better Coordination Between SAFE and the Ministry of Finance

The relationship between SAFE and the Ministry of Finance plays a crucial role in the setup and the further development of the CIC. Therefore, it would be important to coordinate the relationship between both institutions in a more efficient manner. A regular coordination mechanism should be in place which could be achieved by either signing a formal memorandum of understanding or via legislation. If there is any specific task involving both parties, then it would be also advisable to form a joint task force to work together. Furthermore, the senior management team at the CIC is still controlled by the Ministry of Finance, for example, both the predecessor and incumbent Chairmen of CIC are from the Ministry of Finance, while SAFE is only represented in CIC with a few independent board directors. Given this observation, it would be helpful if the CIC could give up some power and leave one or two senior executive positions to the discretion of SAFE.

18.5.2 More Sustainable Financing Mechanism

We believe that the current mechanism concerning capital injections to CIC is unsustainable. The question of how much capital injection into the CIC relies at the discretion of SAFE. Therefore, this causes difficulty in planning investment strategies particularly in the long-run. In order to solve this issue, we recommend that the State Council conducts a thorough examination of the current financing arrangement between the CIC and SAFE. Based on the results of the examination, the CIC and SAFE could agree on a feasible and sustainable financing mechanism between them. Only with such a mechanism could CIC anticipate the financial flow in the foreseeable future, thus optimizing its investment portfolio.

18.5.3 Enhance Investment Performance

The performance of CIC investments overseas is still far from satisfactory. There are several reasons: (a) as a new institution, it is less experienced in risk management as well as investing abroad, (b) the investment team is not sufficiently qualified to conduct large investments, and (c) members of the management team are often politicians. In the light of these problems and given CIC's intention of becoming a world-class investment company, it should implement more liberalized HR policy, e.g., offering more competitive remuneration packages to its employees. At the moment, the remuneration system within the CIC still maintains its strong heritage from the old state-owned companies, thus affecting its ability to attract the most qualified professionals from the industry. In addition, the government should attempt to establish a management team which collectively will be equipped with wide relevant professional experience in the investment area, risk management, and accounting, rather than having politicians as part of the management team.

In this context it would be useful if the government, as the owner and sponsor of the CIC sets appropriate evaluation methods to assess the performance of the CIC. Although, the CIC may develop its own evaluation procedures and targets, it may be interpreted as biased and not independent.

18.5.4 Improve Transparency of its Operation

In the first few years of operation, the CIC was subject to much suspicion and concern from abroad due to distrust of its large SWF. As a result of this thinking, the CIC has sought to actively participate in international dialogs such as the International Working Group on SWFs and abide by international best practices. In addition, the CIC's efforts to mitigate foreign concerns have been working to some extent, but have not dispersed the concerns completely, as highlighted by the low score in the SWF Institute's transparency index. As a consequence, the CIC still has a long way to go in terms of improving its transparency. Guidelines and practices as stated in the Santiago Principles are good benchmarks which the CIC can use to compare its internal transparency to international standards. For example, the CIC can consider hiring international auditors to audit annual reports, or disclose its internal protocol, and criteria selection of external asset managers which currently manage over 60% of CIC's international portfolios.

18.5.5 Reorganization of CIC

In order to tackle some intrinsic difficulties relating to CIC's operation, it may be wise to reorganize CIC and re-balance the relationship between SAFE and the Ministry of Finance. In this scenario SAFE would retake back CIC International under its supervision, while Central Huijin still remains with the Ministry of Finance. The immediate benefit of such arrangement is that CIC would be free from the huge financial pressure arising from the dividend payment of the RMB 1.5 trillion special bonds. Secondly, it would automatically solve the problem of capital injection. Given that the current assets under management of SAFE are approximately USD 3.5 trillion, it would not be difficult to inject more capital to the CIC when it is needed. Thirdly, the complete separation between CIC and Central Huijin would greatly enhance CIC's international acceptability and image thus moving potential investment barriers abroad.

Central Huijin is still within the Ministry of Finance and serves as the investment company to achieve state policy objectives such as (a) preserving and enhancing state assets in local financial institutions and (b) help stabilize domestic financial markets when deemed necessary. In this context if capital injection from SAFE is predicted in the future, it would still be still necessary to maintain a well-coordinated relationship between the Ministry of Finance and SAFE.

18.6 CONCLUSION

SWFs today play an important role in global financial markets by providing steady flows of funding and investments. The Chinese government established its own SWF in 2007 and the objective of the China Investment Corporation was the diversification and management of its foreign exchange reserves. In this chapter we conducted a comprehensive review on CIC, CIC International and Central Huijin. We find that CIC suffers from various drawbacks which could hinder its future development with conflicts between SAFE and the Ministry of Finance as well as the poor performance of CIC International. In order to address these problems, we proposed that the following reform options could be considered by the Chinese government:

- The relationship between the Ministry of Finance and SAFE should be better coordinated. Up to now, SAFE has played a minor role in the management of the CIC, which is not consistent with or does not meet the expectations of SAFE which is the main source of funding for CIC.
- A more sustainable financing mechanism for the CIC should be in place. Cooperation from SAFE in this area is important; otherwise CIC may often experience a shortage of funds for investment.
- Investment performance should be enhanced, which may involve changes in the recruitment and HR policies in order attract the best talent and replace politicians with more experienced employees from the financial services industry.
- Transparency is weak in the CIC and this could be addressed by implementing the guidelines and practices as stated in the Santiago Principles.
- A reorganization of the CIC may be worth trying, where CIC International reverts back to the control of SAFE, while Central Huijin remains with the Ministry of Finance.

REFERENCES

Hu, Y., 2010. Management of China's foreign exchange reserves: a case study on the state administration of foreign exchange reserves. European Economy—Economic Papers 421. Directorate General Economic and Monetary Affairs, European Commission, Brussels.

Salidjanova, N., 2011. Going Out: An Overview of China's Outward Foreign Direct Investment. USCC Staff Research Report. US—China Economic & Security Review Commission, Washington, DC.

SAFE, 2013. Foreign Exchange Reserves Database <http://www.safe.gov.cn/> (accessed 10.8.13).

Sovereign Wealth Fund Institute, 2013. Fund Rankings. <http://www.swfinstitute.org/fund-rankings/> (accessed 17.8.13).

Truman, E.M., 2011. Sovereign wealth funds: is Asia different? Working Paper Series WP 11-12. The Peterson Institute for International Economics, Washington, DC.

CHAPTER 19

Portfolio Allocation Dynamics of China Investment Corporation in the Aftermath of the Global Financial Crisis of 2007–2009

Tayyeb Shabbir

Department of Finance, CBAPP, California State University Dominguez Hills, Carson, CA and Department of Finance, Wharton School, University of Pennsylvania, Philadelphia, PA, USA

19.1 INTRODUCTION

The China Investment Corporation (CIC), one of the newest and largest Sovereign Wealth Funds (SWFs) of China, was formally established on September 29, 2007, ostensibly to better manage some of the burgeoning foreign exchange reserves of the country. It is somewhat ironic that CIC was established virtually 1 year prior to the September 15, 2008, bankruptcy of Lehman Brothers which marks the definitive relative peak of the global financial crisis of 2007–2009 since, to many observers, the emergence of SWFs worldwide and this most recent global financial crisis are symbiotically related.[1] At the minimum, the role and the functioning of CIC cannot be effectively understood without appealing to the relevant context of the explosive growth of SWFs in China and elsewhere that have essentially resulted from historically high current account surpluses. While this phenomenon of the growth of SWFs especially as it relates to China's economy will be discussed in this paper, its role will be primarily to provide a context to the genesis of the CIC. The primary focus of this paper will be to critically assess the goals and objectives behind the establishment of CIC as well as analyze the dynamics of its portfolio allocation decisions since its inception. These asset allocation strategies with respect to types of investments, geographical destination of funds, and investment goals of CIC especially as they relate to the global financial crisis of 2007–2009 will be analyzed. Being its largest sovereign wealth investor holding assets of $575 billion as of 2013, CIC's approach to these issues has very significant implications for China's domestic economy as well as the global capital flows, financial stability, and economic growth.

---

[1] The subprime crisis that morphed into the global financial crisis had already started brewing in earnest by the summer of 2007, e.g., as indicated by the liquidity crisis experienced by BNP Paribas on August 7, 2007, when it terminated withdrawals from three hedge funds citing a "complete evaporation of liquidity."

Handbook of Asian Finance, Volume 1
http://dx.doi.org/10.1016/B978-0-12-800982-6.00019-6

The rest of this chapter is organized as follows.

Section 19.2 provides an overview of the SWFs and China's Economic Policy in order to provide an appropriate context for the genesis of CIC. Section 19.3 describes the establishment and objectives of CIC followed by Section 19.4 which describes, analyzes, and critically evaluates the dynamic aspects of the asset allocation strategies (AAS) of CIC in terms of its various dimensions such as the types of investment, geographical destination, relative performance, and relationship to the global financial crisis 2007–2009. Section 19.5 presents a critical assessment of CIC's performance and its role in terms of domestic as well as global implications of its strategy. Section 19.6 consists of concluding remarks.

19.2 SWFs AND CHINA'S ECONOMIC POLICY

19.2.1 Large and Growing FX Reserves of China

In essence, the establishment of CIC was an attempt by China to better manage its growing foreign exchange reserves by setting up this special-purpose SWF. According to the People's Bank of China (PBOC) data, by the end of the second quarter of 2013, the country's foreign exchange reserves had reached a sum of $4.5 trillion. This surpasses the amount accumulated by any other country, and as the following Figure 19.1 exhibits, it reflects a sharp rate of increase since the early 1999—the period closely following the end of the Asian Financial Crisis of 1997–1998. It is often remarked that one of the "lessons" that China may have learned from this crisis was to have "sufficiently large" reserves to withstand speculative onslaught on national currency's exchange rate. For a more detailed analysis, see Klein and Shabbir (2007).

These stockpiles of foreign exchange reserves were a direct result of huge current account surpluses, averaging at approximately $250 billion a year since 2005. China has been able to run since the early 1990s. These surpluses were due to a combination of China's relative cost advantage in production of consumer goods and light manufacturing products and a "stable" (to some, an artificially undervalued) Yuan (or, more formally, renminbi).

Historically, this huge stockpile of FX reserves has meant a high opportunity cost for China since, typically, the Chinese economy has grown faster than the return on these reserves. For instance, during 2003–2006, the years leading up to the formation of CIC, while the Chinese GDP grew on average at 10% p.a., China earned only between 2% and 4% on these FX reserves which at that time were primarily invested in the US Treasury Securities (Cognato (2008, pp. 12–13)). Of course, the onset of the Great Recession (2007–2009) in the USA and the associated easy monetary policy has meant significantly lower returns on the US Treasury Securities, thus only sharpening the opportunity cost burden.

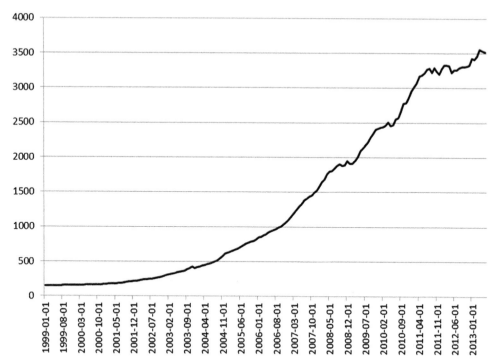

Figure 19.1 Foreign exchange reserves of China 1999–2013 ($ billion). *Data:* FRED (Federal Reserve Bank of St. Louis).

19.2.2 Rising Costs of Sterilization

Besides the sheer size of these accumulated FX reserves, another relevant cost dimension is related to China's preference for relatively fixed or "managed" exchange rate. Maintaining this arrangement can be costly since large and growing current account surpluses may require "sterilization" if exchange rate is to be kept relatively stable. Unlike the "commodity" (mostly oil) exporting countries such as in the Middle East or Norway, China belongs to the group where current account surpluses benefitted from a conscious government economic development strategy comprising of manufacturing sector export orientation supplemented by capital account controls and "managed" foreign exchange rate.[2]

Several critics, with some partial justification, often attribute a significant measure of the success in China's increased exports to an undervalued currency. In any event, China who had kept the US dollar–Yuan rate steady at close to 8 Yuan = $ (during 1997–2005,

---

[2] For other interesting ways in which "commodity" exporting current account surplus countries differ vis-a-vis China, see Koch-Weser and Haacke (2013, pp. 8, 9). Also, see Shabbir (2009) as an illustration of the process of growth of SWFs for oil-exporting Middle Eastern countries.

it was 8.27 Yuan = $1) has steadily let the Yuan appreciate since 2005 such that currently the exchange rate is in the neighborhood of 6 Yuan = $1. Interestingly enough, this gradual appreciation of Yuan has led to increased capital inflows into China as it has raised expectations of future Yuan appreciation. Since PBOC absorbs these growing inflows, its share of the FX reserves has grown from 40% in 2002 to 80% in 2012 (Liu and Spiegel 2012, in Figure 1). These inflows of FX are absorbed by CPOB via the process of "sterilization"—central bank uses Yuans to buy FX from Chinese exporters, and then in order to avoid increasing domestic money supply and thus risking higher inflation, it issues equal value domestic currency bonds to "soak up" or "sterilize" these injections of Yuans into the Chinese economy. The process of sterilization can be profitable or costly depending on the "spread," i.e., the differential between what CPOB earns on its FX reserves (say, on US Treasuries) and the rate it pays on domestic "sterilization" bonds. From 2005 until about the third quarter of 2007, this was a profitable proposition for PBOC; however, by late 2007, the US Treasuries earned less than the interest rate PBOC had to pay on domestic "sterilized" bonds. This negative "spread" only got worse for PBOC as the US Treasuries returns fell sharply with the onset of the Great Recession in the USA (December 2007–June 2009), which necessitated the launch of a radically easy monetary policy by the US FED. Again, the absolute magnitude of the inflow that ended being "sterilized" was also increasing so it was a "double whammy" for PBOC. Thus the 2011 current account surplus, equaling a net inflow of $360 billion, translated into an estimated net PBOC loss of over $10 billion.

Since Yuan's "managed" status was essentially there to stay and yield on foreign Treasuries was exogenous, one way for China to tame the "sterilization" costs was by trying to increase the ROI on FX reserves by investing them into vehicles further along the risk-return spectrum than the US Treasuries.[3]

19.2.3 Quest for Higher Returns

By the start of 2007, in light of the factors discussed in Section 19.2 above, a clear groundswell of policy opinion within China had developed in favor of proactively seeking relatively higher returns on the country's FX reserves. This was motivated by both economic reasoning and political arguments—the central government did not wish to be perceived as by being a bad steward of "nation's wealth" (Cognato, 2008, p. 13).

As of the end of 2006, China already had at least two quasi-SWF entities that had played somewhat limited albeit tentative role in China's previous attempts to improve the ROI of China's FX reserves. Firstly, SAFE Investment Company, established in 1997 in Hong Kong, is one of the four overseas investment arms of State Administration

---

[3] The other possible ways consisted of allowing further Yuan appreciation and/or tolerate a degree of domestic inflation.

of Foreign Exchange (SAFE). It is a branch of PBOC and its primary objective is to preserve the value of China's FX reserves by making portfolio investment overseas. The second such organization was established in 2000 by the State Council and is called National Social Security Fund (NSSF). Its primary objective is to maintain the inflation-adjusted value of China's public pension funds. NSSF is allowed to invest up to 20% of its funds overseas.

19.3 CIC: ESTABLISHMENT AND OBJECTIVES

19.3.1 Immediate Circumstances Leading up to Establishment of CIC

The high opportunity cost of FX reserves, rising "sterilization" costs of maintaining a "managed" exchange rate regime and the need for seeking higher returns, all presented important policy dilemmas for China. Starting with early 2006, in order to pursue a policy of a better management of the country's FX reserves, investments in oil and other real sectors were considered as a part of a diversification strategy. Initially, SAFE played a role in this exercise. Later, Central Huijin Investments, a holding company, which eventually ended up being a part of CIC after its formation, was also considered as a possible platform to diversify and put China's reserves to a more "productive" use (Cognato, 2008, p. 14).

19.3.2 Establishment of CIC: Policy Disputes

While by 2006 there was a widespread agreement over China's need for a new entity that would invest some of the country's vast FX reserves abroad to improve return on investment, there was considerable bureaucratic disagreement as to how best this was to be achieved. The two main contenders vying for control were Ministry of Finance (MOF) and People's Bank of China (PBOC)—China's central bank.

Early speculation was that the new entity will be under PBOC's control, perhaps it would be a repurposed form of its branch, SAFE (State Administration of Foreign Exchange). On the other hand, MOF had contended that it should be entrusted with ownership and management of state assets, while PBOC, being a central bank, should focus its attention on monetary policy alone.

This bureaucratic tug-of-war climaxed during the Central Financial Working Conference in January 2007 where China's top leadership was to consider the relevant proposals. At this moot, MOF made two relevant proposals: (i) formation of a new Chinese SWF to invest some of China's FX reserves globally in search for better returns, and (ii) set up a Financial Assets Commission that would manage the assets of China's state-owned financial institutions.

PBOC vehemently disagreed with both these proposals as the first one would disenfranchise its branch, SAFE, which had traditionally handled some of FX diversification efforts in the past and the second would have replaced another of PBOC branches at the time, Central Huijin, a bank holding company established in 2003, which controlled the largest banking assets in China.

The decision made at the Financial Working Conference in January 2007 seemed to tilt in favor of MOF even though it tried to be "Solomonic" in its approach. While both domestic banks and foreign reserves management were removed from the direct purview of PBOC, they were not formally assigned to MOF but instead entrusted to CIC which was formally placed under the direct control of the State Council. Instead of Financial Assets Commission that would manage the assets of China's state-owned financial institutions as initially proposed by MOF, partly to placate PBOC, Central Huijin was reconfigured and was, in effect, sold for a nominal price of $67 billion to CIC. This has meant that while the initial motivation for the establishment of CIC may have been predominantly management of overseas investment, it has vast role in the domestic banking sector via its control over Central Huijin. In fact, out of its initial financing of $200 billion, $110 was earmarked for the domestic sector and only $90 billion was meant for overseas investments.

19.3.3 CIC: Current Structure

In December 2011, partly to assuage the concerns of Western countries especially the USA, CIC splits its operations more formally into CIC International and Central Huijin Investment so as to put the relationship with the Chinese domestic banking at an arm's length. However, the domestic banking is still under the purview of Central Huijin and it is not clear if the "restructuring" will be able to satisfy the concerns of the foreign host countries where CIC invests (Cai and Clacher, 2013, p. 19). One reason for the need for a more careful analysis of the CIC structure is that even though Central Huijin Investment is ostensibly concerned with only the "domestic sector," it has several indirect routes where it ends up being an international investor. For one, Central Huijin has 100% stake in China Development Bank and its branch, China-Africa Development Bank; the latter has been very active and is playing a growing role in spearheading real sector investments in Africa.

Another indirect route through which CIC is more involved abroad than may be surmised merely from the investment activities of CIC International is the rather symbiotic though somewhat latent relationship that exists between Central Huijin and Chinese state-owned enterprises (SOEs) both in China and those listed abroad especially in Hong Kong. Financial institutions controlled by Central Huijin routinely provide credit to domestic SOEs many of which are involved in foreign investment and trade activities. Perhaps more importantly, CIC International often takes a stake in the SOEs listed in Honk Kong and other international exchanges presumably to support their share price and help them stay well capitalized, for example, share purchase of $100 million in China Railway Group in 2007, $400 million in Longyuan Power Group in 2009, and $250 million in Semiconductor Manufacturing International Corporation in 2011 (Koch-Weser and Haacke, 2013, p. 32). Thus it is important to note that while officially mandated to make outbound investments, CIC is also heavily invested in domestic sector and some of those links may eventually have international connections.

19.3.4 Funding of CIC

The initial financing of CIC amounted to a total of $200 billion with a split of $90 for overseas investments and the rest for the domestic sector including. This initial injection essentially came from the PBOC; however, it was achieved in a rather roundabout fashion. The MOF issued bonds worth Yuan 1.5 trillion bearing interest rates between 4.35% and 4.70%. These bonds were then sold to PBOC for FX reserves to the tune of $200 billion. The sale to PBOC was channeled through Agriculture Bank of China so as to not run afoul of certain legal restrictions. As second injection of $30 billion was made in December 2011 to CIC International[4] which by that time had been created to exclusively handle, at least in theory, CIC's overseas investment transactions. As a matter of fact, as a legacy of the conflict between PBOC and MOF that goes back to the very genesis of CIC and the fact that PBOC nominally is the repository of all of FX reserves, the CIC lacks stable and predictable funding mechanism which is a serious structural flaw (Koch-Weser and Haacke, 2013, p. 17).

19.4 DYNAMICS OF CIC'S INVESTMENT ALLOCATION STRATEGIES

Since its formal inception in 2007, CIC's investment allocation strategies or patterns can be divided into following three time periods:

  (i)   2007 to early 2008.
 (ii)   Mid-2008 to early 2009.
(iii)   2009 to present.

The first phase is characterized by lack of geographical and sectoral diversity as most of the investments are made primarily in the financial sector and in the USA. These investments generally ended in poor outcomes for CIC. The second phase is marked by a period of comparative inactivity most likely as a reaction to the relatively poor experience of the first phase and the need to reassess and consolidate. The third phase is certainly the most interesting and consequential one as it was devised not only in the backdrop of the CIC's past experiences but also to take advantage of the opportunities that may have been presented on account of the global financial crisis that had peaked by 2009. A relatively more detailed discussion and analysis of the above three phases, particularly the third phase, are as follows.

---

[4] By summer of 2013, the capital injection into CIC International may have been as much as $49 billion. Bloomberg (2013) China wealth Fund CIC Posts 10.6% return on Equity. Retrieved from http://www.bloomberg.com/news/print/2013-07-26/china-wealth-fund-reports-10-6-return-amid-global-equity-rally.html.

19.4.1 Phase I: 2007 to Early 2008

When it was established in September 2007, CIC's maiden capitalization comprised of $200 billion as a "loan" from the People's Bank of China (PBOC). Only about $90 billion was earmarked for overseas investments, while the rest was for domestic purposes. The latter was divided roughly equally for recapitalization of domestic financial institutions and purchase of Central Huijin, a state-owned investment company (Wu and Seah, 2008). With little experience to help it allocate the overseas investment budget, CIC generally focused on the US financial sector. A few of the major overseas investments of CIC during Phase I are presented in Table 19.1.

It should be noted that Phase I investments were mostly in the USA and generally in the financial services sector, thus making CIC's initial foray into overseas investments as both geographically and sectorally undiversified. Another factor that made most of these investments relatively high risk was that they fell in one of the three categories: pre-IPO, funds outsourced to external asset management firms, and "bets" on distressed financial firms—all relatively high-risk financial vehicles.

The CIC did not fare well at all in terms of the performance of its Phase I investments. Its three largest investments were made in Morgan Stanley $5.6 billion followed by investments made in two private equity firms—Blackstone Group ($3.0 billion) and J.C. Flowers Fund ($3–4 billion). Neither of these large bets paid off particularly well. The Morgan Stanley investment lost 25% of its value by September 2008, whereas Blackstone Group had lost almost half (46%) of its value by then. Of course, the subprime mortgage crisis that was already starting to brew in the Summer of 2007 was

Table 19.1 Major Investments of CIC During Phase I (2007 to Early 2008)

Investment (Country)	Date	Amount	Sector	Details
Blackstone Group (USA)	May 2007	$3.0 billion	Financial Services	9% pre-IPO
Morgan Stanley (USA)	December 2007	$5.6 billion	Financial Services	9.9% stake, convertible bonds with 9% yield
China Railway Group (Hong Kong)	November 2007	$100 million	Railway Construction	Pre-IPO stake of about 4%
J.C. Flowers Fund	February 2008	$3–4 billion	Financial Services	Private Equity Fund for distressed small financial firms
Visa	March 2008	$100 million	Financial Services	Pre-IPO stake

Source: Author's modification of Table 7 of Wu et al. (2011).

gravely misjudged in its scope and intensity—a hunt for presumably "temporarily" depressed financial assets ended up being a deadly trap by the time Lehman Brothers went bankrupt on September 15, 2008, dooming the USA and soon the global financial sector to a dire and deep distress. By November 2008, Blackstone was trading 82% below CIC's purchase share price of $29.05, while Morgan Stanley's share price of $29.05 had also fallen by a similar percentage. Also, Visa lost about 24% by March 2008. Besides, J.C. Flowers investments lost an undetermined amount, while CIC's investment in Reserve Primary Fund, a money market fund, went belly up too as it became the first such fund to "break the buck" when its NAV went below par of $1.00 (Wu et al., 2011).

These losses provoked a domestic political backlash against CIC which was criticized for wasting "state" resources on foreign ventures who received help when faced with financial distress. Also, charges of "nepotism" were implied since most of Phase I investments in the USA were channeled through Morgan Stanley and Blackstone Group whose executives had personal connections and interlocking business interests intertwined with Chinese bureaucracy's interest (Cognato, 2008, p. 21). In any event, it is clear that Phase I overseas investments of CIC did not prove to be auspicious at all and put CIC and its backers at the defensive within the domestic policy arenas of China.

Clearly, CIC's overseas investments lacked geographical as well as sectoral diversification even though USA was an attractive destination with its relatively well-developed equity markets and the apparent opportunity to purchase a few distressed financial assets. One factor that may also be considered here is an indirect pressure on CIC to take on high-risk (and hopefully high reward) investments since it had a "structural" liability to generate 14% annualized return to repay initial capital to MOF (Wu et al., 2011, p. 125). In any event, CIC's Phase I overseas investments ended poorly.

While the focus of this chapter is on CIC overseas investments, a word about CIC's domestic investments may be in order here. In fact, at least nominally, the bulk of the initial capital of CIC was earmarked for domestic investments ($110 billion). In terms of its domestic investments during Phase I, CIC reportedly invested $47.7 billion in upgrading China's financial sector mostly banks (Monitor Group, 2010, p. 97).

Interestingly enough, while the domestic investment characteristics of CIC did not engender any criticism within China, it raised plenty of eyebrows abroad especially in the USA as this linkage between CIC, a state-owned SWF, and banking system was deemed to be too close for comfort (Martin, 2010, p. 10).

19.4.2 Phase II: Mid-2008 to Early 2009

With the backdrop of significant losses suffered on its Phase I investments, Phase II was marked by great introspection and reorganization on the part of CIC. The following remarks concern the important developments regarding CIC's investment approach during this period.

(i) The bankruptcy of Lehman Brothers on September 15, 2008, unequivocally triggered the definitive stage of the global financial crisis of 2007–2009. CIC realized that the reality had changed and it will need to adjust with it.

(ii) Practically speaking, during this phase, CIC went into an all-cash mode and there was very little investment activity.[5] During this phase, the amount of investment by CIC dropped by one half. The then CIC Chairman, Lou Jiwei best reflected the new cautious outlook toward a previous sector of choice when in December 2008 he said, "Right now we do not have the courage to invest in financial institutions because we do not know what problems they may have" (Wu et al., 2011, p. 128).

(iii) Organizationally, CIC went into a virtual overdrive to restructure and be prepared for post-crisis opportunities. In this respect, it took the following steps:

  (a) CIC beefed up talent by scooping up investment professionals who were displaced due to the global financial upheaval in the months immediately following the Lehman Bankruptcy in September 2008. CIC favored personnel with foreign education and credentials even citizenship so as to buttress its image internationally.

  (b) As it got ready to diversify into energy, real estate, equity, and other financial instruments, CIC structurally reorganized itself by goals rather than bureaucratic departments. Older fixtures such as Fixed Income Investment, Equity Investment, and Alternative Investment were replaced by with new investment divisions such as Public Market Investments, Private Market Investments, and Tactical Investments (Wu et al., 2011, p. 128).

  (c) CIC helped its balance sheet by reaching an agreement with MOF to convert its loan of $200 billion that had initially capitalized CIC into assets. This also removed an artificial expectation from CIC to earn at least 14% in order to be viable. This not only enhanced CIC's autonomy but also not force it into taking unrealistically high risks.

  (d) CIC positioned itself as a "responsible global investor" by working closely with IMF's International Working Group of Sovereign Wealth Funds established in 2008 and by becoming a founding signatory of the Santiago Principles—a good housekeeping seal of SWF corporate governance.

19.4.3 Phase III: 2009 to Present

Starting in the middle of the summer of 2009 and virtually coinciding with the end of the Great Recession[6] in the USA, this post-crisis phase of the CIC investments was

---

[5] CIC was 90% in cash; Wu et al. (2011, p. 128).

[6] The National Bureau of Economic Research, a non-partisan, non-profit academic organization, determined that June 2009 marked the end of the Great Recession in the USA that started on December 2007 at the peak of the sub-prime mortgage crisis.

marked by ambitious expansion and diversification. This diversification occurred in terms of types of investments, by geographical destinations and kinds of sectors. CIC's apparent successful timing of this post-crisis bottom in its assets of interest proved very fortuitous for it. The salient features of CIC's Phase III expansion and diversification drive are detailed below.

By types of investments

During Phase II, CIC had gathered a huge cash hoard. CIC launched Phase III by essentially moving out of a predominantly cash position into equities as well as fixed income assets. As noted in Table 19.2a, CIC increased its exposure to equities by nearly 12-fold—from 3.2% in 2008 to 36% in 2009. At the same time, compared to 2008, CIC increased the fixed income securities part of its global portfolio from 9% to 26%. It is noteworthy that in its bid to put its "cash to work," CIC did not sacrifice the goal of prudent risk management since fixed income securities investment as a category also enjoyed a healthy increase along with the push into equities. Thus this realignment of CIC's global portfolio did not necessarily represent more risk due to a greater percentage holding of equities even though the magnitude of the portfolio risk will be higher only because of the scale of investment effect.

After the end of 2010, CIC changed its Strategic Asset Allocation benchmark from the four categories reported in Table 19.2a and started categorizing it into five classes: Cash, Diversified Public Equities, Fixed Income, Absolute Return Investments, and Long-term Investments. CIC claims that it has switched to this more disaggregated classification in order to "better manage risk." In any event, the important fact that can be clearly noted from Table 19.2b is that the data are consistent with the trends evident from the earlier Table 19.2a despite there being more categories in Table 19.2b. Thus, one can note from Table 19.2b that during 2011 as well as 2012, the cash holdings stayed minimal, while the equities investment share stayed elevated and proportionately more of the investment funds went into Absolute Return Investment which represents investments in hedge funds and some private equity. This is a trend which has been widely noted; for example, see Yang (2013).

Table 19.2a Global Portfolio Distribution by Type of Investment (%) (Old Benchmark—Four Categories; Ended in 2010)

Type of Investment	2008	2009	2010
Equities	3.2	36	48
Fixed Income Securities	9.0	26	27
Cash Funds	87.4	32	4
Alternative Investments	0.4	6	21

Source: CIC Annual Reports (2009, 2010).

Table 19.2b Global Portfolio Distribution by Type of Investment (%) (New Benchmark—Five Categories; Started in 2011)

Type of Investment	2011	2012
Diversified Public Equities	25	32.0
Fixed Income Securities	21	19.1
Cash Funds and Others	11	3.8
Absolute Return Investments	12	12.7
Long-Term Investments	31	32.4

Source: CIC Annual Reports (2011, 2012).

Table 19.3 CIC's Equity Investments by Geographical Distribution (%)

Region	2009	2010	2011	2012
North America	43.0	41.9	43.8	49.2
Asia Pacific	28.4	29.8	29.6	N.A.
Europe	20.5	21.7	20.6	N.A.
Latin America	6.3	5.4	4.7	N.A.
Africa	0.9	1.2	1.3	N.A.

Source: CIC Annual Reports: Various Years.

By geographical destination

As against CIC's concentration of its Phase I and Phase II equity investments in the USA, during Phase III, the geographical destinations became significantly diversified. However, CIC still did not venture much into the relatively riskier geographical destinations in the Emerging Economies until 2012 (Yang, 2013). Thus, once again, CIC signified its gradualist approach to risk-taking. Table 19.3 notes CIC's equity investments since 2009 by region.

In its 2012 Annual Report, CIC changed the classification scheme for reporting the geographical distribution of its equity investment. Instead of the relatively more disaggregated regions, this report presents only three grouping—US (49.2%) and Non-US Advanced Economies (27.8%) and Emerging Markets (23%). Still, it can be surmised that while the share of North America stayed steady, there was an evidently significant increase in investments in Emerging Markets, signifying a shift toward more risk-taking.

By kinds of sectors

Perhaps the most remarkable feature of CIC's Phase III investment was its branching out into real sector in addition to continued investment in the financial sector albeit latter done with a twist. The real sector investments were direct (vs. portfolio) investments and were mainly focused on two sectors—energy/natural resources and real estate.

Table 19.4 CIC's Diversified Investments by Sector in US Billion $ (%)

Sectors	2007–2008	2009 to Early 2010
Financial Markets	14.1 (100%)	3.87 (28%)
Energy and Natural Resources	–	9.58 (70%)
Real Estate	–	0.32 (2%)

Source: Wu et al. (2011).

Table 19.4 presents an estimated distribution of this new configuration of CIC sectoral investment in the aftermath of global financial crisis of 2007–2009 (Wu et al., 2011, p. 132). Starting with 2009–2010 time period, the remarkable shift of CIC's investment focus into the real sector is obvious (see Table 19.6).

Table 19.4 shows the dramatic move of CIC into Energy and Natural Resources sector during 2009 to early 2010 as its investment into this sector went from 0% in 2007–2008 to 70% of its overseas investments, while the Real Sector also enjoyed a push albeit much milder one as its share went from 0% to 2% over the same time periods. Some of the major investments during this period were Teck Resources, JSC KazMunaiGas, and Peace River Oil Partnership in the Energy and Natural Resources Sector, while it was Songbird Estates and Goodman Group in the Real Estate Sector. However, with few exceptions, the direct investments in Energy and Real Estate sectors were spread over many individual entities in the range of $600–$700 million (Eaton and Zhang, 2010, p. 498). Incidentally, later in this paper, Tables 19.7 and 19.8 present more details of CIC's investments in the Energy and Real Estate Sectors arranged by chronological order and updated until 2012. These details essentially show that this transition into the real sectors by CIC during 2009–2010 has been sustained and is expected to do so in the future.

As of the end of 2010, besides Energy and Materials, CIC had diversified further from the financial sector into other real sectors such as Industrials, Information Technology, and Consumer Discretionary. Table 19.5 below presents some of these

Table 19.5 Distribution of Diversified Equities by Sector (%)

Sector	2010	2011	2012
Financials	17	19	22.3
Energy	13	14	10.2
Materials	12	9	6.5
Information Technology	10	10	11.6
Industrials	10	9	9.1
Consumer Discretionary	10	10	10.7
Consumer Staples	9	10	10.4

Source: CIC Annual Reports (2010–2012).

Table 19.6 CIC's Major Investments in the Financial Sector, 2009–2012

Company (Country)	Sector (Sub-Sector)	Date	Type of Investment	Value ($ Billion)	% Ownership
Morgan Stanley (US)	Finance (Banking)	June 2009	Shares	1.21	1.0
Black Rock (US)	Finance (Investment)	Unknown	Shares	0.74	Unknown
Black Rock (US)	Finance (Private Equity)	June 2009	Shares	1.00	3.0
CITIC Capital (HK)	Finance (Banking)	July 2009	Shares	0.25	40.0
Poly Investment (HK)	Finance (Investment Bank)	September 2009	Equity Acquisition	0.05	2.8
Apax Investment (UK)	Finance (Private Equity)	February 2010	Equity Acquisition	0.96	2.3
BTG Pactual (Brazil)	Finance (Investment)	December 2010	Shares	0.30	3.1
VTB Group (Russia)	Finance (Banking)	February 2011	Shares	0.10	5.0
Shanduka Group (S. Africa)	Finance (Investment)	December 2011	Shares	0.24	25.1

Source: Based mainly on Table A-7 Koch-Weser and Haacke (2013).

transitional trends at an aggregative level. As can be seen from this table, while the Financial Sector has continued to enjoy favor by averaging about 19% of the funds over the years 2010–2012, other sectors have grown from being almost non-existent in 2009 to about 8–10% of the CIC's total diversified equities investments overseas.

Let us briefly discuss CIC's post-crisis sectoral allocations.

Financial sector

While the financial sector enjoyed continued favor by CIC even after losses during Phase I, in Phase II, the relevant circumstances as well as CIC's strategy changed. The financial sector was considered as having bottomed out in the aftermath of the crisis and thus could be considered a very "timely bet" for the long run. Rationally, this strategy makes sense since it is impossible to imagine a well-functioning and thriving capitalist system without a recovered financial system. Also, financial instruments are liquid and flexible in terms of providing opportunities to diversify portfolio across sectors via equity positions.

During Phase II, besides garden variety equities, CIC also invested in relatively esoteric financial derivatives, hedge funds, as well as private equity funds. In fact, as

Table 19.5 shows, CIC invested $1.2 billion in Morgan Stanley in June 2009, apparently undaunted by earlier (Phase I) paper losses with the same institution.

Also, note that post-crisis, the relative magnitude of CIC financial investments in Morgan Stanley, Black Rock Inc. and Apax Partners paled in comparison with its pre-crisis investments (presented in Table 19.1) in the financial sector reflecting a measure of prudential risk reassessment.

Spurred on by CIC's new private equity department established in February 2010, CIC's $956 million investment in Apax Partner, a large European private equity fund, also reflected CIC's continued taste for private equity. Since private equity typically operates with longer time horizons, this interest by CIC positively reflects on its preference for long-term investment goals. Another reflection of CIC's prudent risk management was its reliance on professional consultancy firms to ferret out new investments. For example, its private equity investments were advised by Credit Suisse and others, while Paulson & Co was one of the consultants for CIC's hedge fund investments (Wu et al., 2011, p. 135).

Besides reliance on professional advice, even early in Phase III, CIC collaborated in certain investments with other global SWFs, thus engaging in a risk-reward sharing arrangement (Wu et al., 2011, p. 136).

Energy and natural resources sector

One of the most novel and significant aspect of Phase III investments was CIC's push into real sector investments especially in the energy and mineral resources sectors.

The investments into energy sector were significant since China is a net importer of oil and lately even of coal. Given China's growth path, the need for energy is obvious. Thus CIC's energy sector investments would be considered "strategic" investments despite CIC's nominal protestations that such investments are merely being made from a financial standpoint. An additional likely strategic motivation which is still not very pronounced and barely ever acknowledged in Chinese official policy statements is China's widely recognized desire to gradually diversify away from US dollar as the dominant currency in which to hold its state assets and FX reserves. In any event, with its coffers swelling with ready cash, in 2009, CIC made several significant investments in energy and natural resources and in real sector in general which may be considered as being "strategic." Table 19.7 presents a few of the major CIC investments in Energy and Natural Resources for the period 2009–2012.

As can be seen from Table 19.7, the strategic aspects of these investments by CIC are evident since many of these companies either are or could be a part of China's supply chain for commodities. Thus CIC invested in Teck Resources, the largest mining and metallurgical producer in Canada which produces copper, coal, and zinc. Also, these strategic goals explain CIC investment in Russia's Nobel Oil Group. Similarly, JSC KazMunaiGas Exploration Production is Kazakhstan's second largest oil producer and

Table 19.7 CIC's Major Investments in the Energy and Natural Resource Sector, 2009–2012

Company (Country)	Sector (Sub-Sector)	Date	Type of Investment	Value ($ Billion)	% Ownership
Teck Resources (Canada)	Mining (Copper)	July 2009	Shares	1.50	17.2
JSC KazMunaiGas (Kazakhstan)	Energy (Oil & Gas)	July 2009	GDRs	0.94	10.6
PT Bumi Resources (Indonesia)	Energy (Coal)	July 2009	Private Debt	1.9	NA
Nobel Oil Group (Russia)	Energy (Oil)	October 2009	Equity Acquisition	0.27	45.0
Iron Mining International (HK)	Mining (Metals)	October 2009	Loan	0.50	NA
South Gobi Energy (Canada)	Energy (Coal)	October 2009	Conv. Debentures	0.25	13.0
AES (US)	Energy (Electricity)	November 2009	Shares	1.58	15
GCL–Poly Energy Holdings (HK)	Energy (Renewable)	November 2009	Shares	0.72	20.1
Longyuan Power group (HK)	Energy	October 2009	–	0.40	–
CVRD;Vale (Brazil)	Metals (Steel)	December 2009	–	0.50	–
Peace River Oil Partnership (Canada)	Energy (Oil & Gas)	June 2010	–	0.33	–
Chesapeake Energy Corp. (US)	Energy (Oil & Gas)	June 2010	–	0.20	–
GDF Suez	Energy	August 2011	Shares	3.15	30.0
AES–VCM Mong Duong Power Co. (Vietnam)	Energy (Coal)	September 2011	Shares	0.10	19.0
Atlantic LNG Co. (Trinidad)	Energy	November 2011	Shares	0.85	10.0
Sunshine Oilsands (Canada)	Energy	February 2012	Shares	0.15	7.4
Polyus Gold (Russia)	Metals	May 2012	Shares	0.42	5.0
Cheniere Energy	Energy (Oil & Gas)	November 2012	–	0.50	–

Source: Author's reconfigurations of data in Table A–7 Koch–Weser and Haacke (2013).

is crude oil supplier of China. Nobel Group, a diversified supplier of energy and food commodities based in Singapore, is another significant target for CIC investments—Nobel sources commodities globally and ship them for processing and consumption in China; it also deals in energy infrastructure and also manages operations in oil, coal, and ethanol. Still another of CIC's investment was SouthGobi which is based in Canada and it supplies coal to China. SouthGobi is strategic from geographical point of view as well since its main coal mines are located in Mongolia. Geographical proximity also carried significant consideration when CIC invested in PT Bumi Resources—Indonesia's largest coal mining company. Indonesia is world's largest thermal coal exporter and also exports copper and gold.

Besides traditional energy sector investments China has also hastened its pace especially in the last couple of years toward investments in the alternative energy CIC's investments in GLC-Poly (China's lead green energy supplier) and AES (global power generation and distribution), which are two examples in this context.

Table 19.7 also shows that CIC preferred developed country firms compared to firms from Emerging Economies presumably to shelter itself from the vulnerabilities of unpredictable political risks. Also, typically, these acquisitions were vetted through consultations with investment houses such as JP Morgan and Citigroup Global Market Asia (Wu et al., 2011, p. 138). CIC also appointed Blackstone Group as a US-based global fund manager as well as entrusted Morgan Stanley with the task of administering portfolio investments via a fund of funds vehicle.

Real estate

Real Estate is not only location but also timing. If one is apt to believe this dictum, then CIC's foray into real estate in late 2009 was very well timed since real estate sector had bottomed out though not started to rise yet.

CIC bought real estate firms in Australia (Goodman Group, Australia's largest industrial property trust) and in the UK (Song Estates Limited as well as London's Canary Wharf (Wu et al., 2011, p. 139). In 2009 and 2010, CIC acquired 7.6% stake in General Group properties, a US commercial real estate firm. In general, CIC did not buy too many physical real estate assets in the USA; instead, it invested in Mortgage Backed Securities which were being offered at fire sale price and were also receiving financing subsidy from the US government for investors in "toxic" mortgage securities. Also, in 2010, CIC partnered with Blackstone in the purchase of $1 billion Japan property loan portfolio from Morgan Stanley as some green shoots seemed to appear in Japan's real estate market (Wu et al., 2011, p. 140).

Table 19.8 presents the major real estate investments of CIC in the real estate sector during 2009–2012.

As can be seen from Table 19.8, CIC's real estate investments have sustained themselves over time and the geographical destinations are well diversified albeit they are mostly in the developed countries.

Table 19.8 CIC's Major Investments in the Real Estate, 2009–2012

Company (Country)	Sector (Sub-Sector)	Date	Type of Investment	Value ($ Billion)	% Ownership
Songbird Estates (UK)	Real Estate (Property)	August 2009	Shares	0.45	19.0
Goodman Group (Australia)	Real Estate (Property)	August 2009	Shares	1.09	6.9
General Growth Properties (US)	Real Estate (Property)	November 2010	Shares	1.03	7.4
Global Logistic Properties (Japan)	Real Estate (Property)	December 2011	Shares	0.80	50.0
Deutsche Bank (UK)	Real Estate (Property)	November 2012	–	0.40	–
Global Logistics Properties (Brazil)	Real Estate (Property)	November 2012	Shares	0.46	34.5

Source: Author's reconfigurations of data in Table A-7 Koch-Weser and Haacke (2013).

Table 19.9 CIC's Diversified Investments by Sector in US Billion $ (%)

Sectors	2007–2008	2009 to Early 2010	2009–2012
Financial Markets	14.1 (100%)	3.87 (28%)	4.85 (20.78%)
Energy and Natural Resources	–	9.58 (70%)	14.26 (61%)
Real Estate	–	0.32 (2%)	4.23 (18.12%)

Source: For statistics for 2009–2012, author's calculations based on Tables 19.6–19.8 in this paper.

19.4.4 CIC's Aggregated Diversified Investments by Major Sectors (2007–2012)

Table 19.9 is an update of the earlier Table 19.4 in this paper which only extended until early 2010.

As can be seen from Table 19.9, CIC's transition away from solely investing in the financial sector that was jump-started in 2009 sustained itself in the longer run. The process of diversification kept its focus on Energy and Natural Resources sector which claimed 61.5% of the share of investment funds over the 2009–2012 time period with $14.26 billion worth of investment in this sector. The real estate sector attracted even a larger proportionate increase since during the 2009–2012 period, 18.12% of the total funds were invested in this sector—a direct result of the relatively big investments made by CIC in the real estate sector during the end of 2009 and early 2010 based on its determination that real estate markets in many developed countries had bottomed out mid-summer, 2009. It may be noted, however, that diversification into these real sectors did not imply an abandonment of the financial sector—its investment share had stabilized around a lower percentage amount of around 20%.

19.4.5 Relative Investment Performance of the CIC Overseas Portfolio

Table 19.10 presents the Annual Return as well as the Cumulative Annualized Return of the CIC Global or overseas portfolio for the time period 2008–2012.

For 2008, the first full year of CIC's existence, the annual rate of return was −2.1%—this may not seem impressive until one realizes that the other SWFs suffered double digit losses for that year, ranging from −14.40 for Singapore Investment Corporation to −66.70% for Korea Investment Corporation. This was mostly due to the fact that CIC, being a relative newcomer cautiously dipping its toes in the global investment ocean, was not as exposed as were those other older, "well-established," SWFs. During 2009 and 2010, CIC did relatively very well with 11.7% annual rate of return in each of these 2 years on account of what essentially turned out to be an accurate determination made by CIC of the post-crisis bottoming of the real estate and other asset markets. CIC had made a "well-timed" decision to aggressively move into the commodities and real estate sectors as well as distressed financial sector assets during mid-2009 through early 2010. The world economy faced peculiar challenges in 2011 made for an adverse global investment climate. Most notably, these were the deepening Euro-zone crisis moving from the periphery to the core economies, stubbornly elevated unemployment rate in the USA and its credit downgrade in the face of fiscal policy breakdown, and high inflation-low growth environment face by major developing countries. CIC annual rate of return on overseas investments was −4.3% due primarily to a volatile market that saw a decline in commodity and resource prices. However, CIC's cumulative annualized rate (since inception) for its overseas portfolio was 3.8%. Part of the explanation

Table 19.10 Investment Performance of CIC Global Portfolio

Year	Annual Return (%)	Cumulative Annualized Return (%)
2008	−2.1	−2.1
2009	11.7	4.1
2010	11.7	6.4
2011	−4.3	3.8
2012	10.60	5.08

Source: CIC Annual Report (2012 p. 35).

for the relatively low annual return for 2011 was that in January 2011, CIC's Board of Director adopted a 10-year time horizon and CIC needed to rejigger its positions in "non-public market assets, particularly direct investments and private equity investments in such industries as energy, resources, real estate and infrastructure" (CIC Annual Report, 2011, p. 2).

For 2012, the annual return of 10.65% was relatively more auspicious for CIC as it caught the global equities rally during the third quarter of 2012 thanks to FED's QE3 and relative easing of the euro-zone crisis. The cumulative return of 5.08% as of 2012 is claimed to be "above the medium level" among SWFs as reported by Xinhua News Agency in June 2013, citing Gao the then President of CIC.[7]

19.5 CRITICAL ASSESSMENT OF THE ROLE OF CIC

There are several pros as well as cons of the CIC activities both from a home country domestic and from a global perspective. This section presents a critical analysis of CIC's role in this context.

19.5.1 Functioning of CIC: Domestic Implications

Pros (positives)

In China, CIC was expected to meet the expectations that the country's FX reserves can be managed so as to earn a better return than the alternative of US Treasuries. In terms of its relative performance, the overall rates of return garnered by CIC have been reasonably good, with double digit returns in some of the years. While CIC has managed to perform reasonably well so far, it may face domestic as well as foreign challenges in the future. Domestically, it appears that both the public and the policy-makers expect a long-term rate of return in the range of 13–14% which is significantly higher than achieved to date. Also, the bureaucratic strife between different financial ministries and PBOC about CIC may have only gone under the surface making for an uncertain funding mechanism for it. Internationally, the scrutiny of the CIC's "too cozy" a relationship with the domestic banking system and its use of "special-purpose vehicles" and SOE capitalization to make indirect and thus relatively less transparent investments could mean a protectionist pushback from potential host countries which may affect future investment opportunities and rates of returns for CIC (Wu et al., 2011, p. 147).

Overall, besides achieving a respectable cumulative rate of return in its formative years, another positive aspect of CIC from a domestic point of view is that CIC can be a catalyst for institutional reform especially in the financial sector of China.

---

[7] China Wealth Fund CIC Posts 10.6% Return as Equity Rally. *Bloomberg News,* July 26, 2013, available at http://www.bloomberg.com/news/2013-07-26/china-wealth-fund-reports-10-6-return-amid-global-equity-rally.html.

Cons (concerns)

The fortunes of Chinese Communist Party and those of CIC may become too intertwined and there is a realistic fear that CCP may need a superior performance from CIC to sustain the regime especially in light of recent slowing down of the economic growth in China. This undue pressure may not make for sound, rational investment decisions on the part of CIC.

Secondly, since CIC reports directly to State Council, practically speaking, it becomes somewhat "above" the normal regulatory agencies in China which can make for regulatory forbearance.

Thirdly, due to CIC's symbiotic connection with the state, CIC's foreign acquisition targets may get colored by any changes in the geopolitical changing of the environments between China and the prospective host country. For example, in March 2008, CIC apparently abandoned its previously intense efforts to purchase Allianz SE's banking arm, Dresdner Bank, when China-German relations cooled off since China felt offended by the Chancellor Merkel's meeting with Dalai Lama (Cai and Iain (2009), p. 12).

19.5.2 Functioning of CIC: Global Implications

Pros (positives)

Globally, CIC's role is actually or potentially a positive one on the following counts.

Provider of global liquidity

Even at the present early stages of its growth, CIC as a SWF has been a significant provider of investible funds and liquidity to the global financial and investment markets. Liquidity is the lifeblood of investment and thus of economic growth. CIC's willingness to invest China's FX reserves in the overseas equity and projects is to be preferred to the alternative of relatively sterile foreign reserves accumulation. Since its inception, the CIC's overseas investments have been in the \$150–250 billion range depending on whether the activities of indirect subsidiaries such as China Development Fund and China-Africa Development Fund are taken into account. However, this role of CIC will be an unequivocally positive one only if the transactions are conducted in a credibly transparent way and investment decisions are predominantly based on commercial not overtly strategic basis.

A stabilizing force globally

By having a long-run perspective on its investments, unlike the much more leveraged and short-term-oriented hedge funds, CIC and SWFs in general are a source of stability by reducing volatility in the markets. Also, interestingly, by helping China gradually move away from holding its vast FX reserves in the form of US Treasuries, it makes the world safer from financial crises. The reason being that this diversification away from US Treasuries will eventually increase the interest rate in the USA, thus lessening the necessity of investors having to take on ever-more riskier projects to achieve high yields they seek. This relatively risky "yield-seeking" behavior has often been cited as one of the factors that may have precipitated the global financial crisis of 2007–2009.

Cushion in crisis

During the latest period of financial distress on account of the global financial crisis 2008–2009, CIC to some degree and SWFs in general provided a welcome source of emergency liquidity. This role has won the praise of FED Chair Ben Bernanke as well as that of Senator Chris Dodd, Chairman of the Senate Banking Committee, who remarked in the opening statement before the Senate Committee hearing on April 24, 2008, that more than two-thirds of the capital that US Banks raised during the recent credit crisis came from SWFs.

A source of demand for high-quality financial services

CIC has used the services of Morgan Stanley and other high-end professional financial advisory services and fund managers of private equity firms such as Blackstone to manage its investment decisions. Growth in CIC's high-end financial advisory services.

A possible partner with multilateral financial institutions such as IMF, world bank

The CIC and, in general, other SWFs have the potential for working toward the "global financial good" by joining hands with multilateral institutions such as the IMF and the World Bank or regional multilateral institutions such as the African Development Bank to promote anti-poverty schemes or encourage reforms meant to make the developing host countries as open and market-based economies so that they can be poised for self-sustaining economic development.

Cons (concerns)

Generally speaking, the following four different areas are identified as areas of concern in relation to the role of CIC globally.

National security

As a government backed investment fund, it is natural if potential host countries are wary of the CIC activities especially if is perceived as moving into national security sensitive investment projects. It is a rather sensitive matter which raises emotions easily, but in the case of CIC, at least so far, there is little cause for concern. For one thing, the avowed goal of CIC is to make profits which by all indications it needs to pay the financing and operational costs. It is also evident that CIC is viewed as an experiment to "manage FX reserves" better, so CIC will not undertake activities for purely strategic reason and ignore financial loss prospects. What about projects that may be profitable for

CIC yet strategic for the host countries? However, in the USA, for example, there are a number of regulatory safeguards, such as the Committee on Foreign Investment in the United States (CFIUS), that are available even now that screen all foreign investments desiring to enter. While one still needs to monitor the potential influence a large investor such as a SWF can have on the market price and volatility, CIC is on record as to not wishing to acquire control of an overseas investment. In short, these concerns may be overblown and, in any case, continued vigilance would mean that new laws can be written if need to be. A detailed analysis of the regulatory and monitoring issues that may arise in this context of CIC (or similar investments into to the USA) is presented in Koch-Weser and Haacke (2013, pp. 35–43).

Strategically motivated investment

The CIC is set up as a for profit organization with professional management. Its unequivocal assignment is to be profitable so it is likely to stay away from pursuing brazen strategic goals. Other venues that may be available to the state may be preferred by China, and perhaps the SOEs are more effective in achieving such goals or lower profile organizations such as SAFE.

In any event, what is "strategic" is also a matter of definition. Many people, in fact, feel that CIC's relatively aggressive push into the real sectors such as energy and real estate after 2009 is an indication of a "strategic" move. This may be a hard argument to make since these are areas with financial viability. However, it is still true that in the absence of a fool-proof and comprehensive mechanism to prevent a truly "strategic" behavior, a clear and well-defined regulatory framework and a universally agreed upon code of conduct may be needed.

Control over domestic banking system

Besides its mission of managing overseas investments, CIC is also entrusted with the capitalization of the domestic banking and financial system via its control over Central Huijin. This dual role often raises suspicions in the minds of foreign regulators of latent state control of CIC as it may raise the possibility of conflict of interest. Also, via its control of Central Huijin, CIC, undoubtedly, can funnel FX funds through the China Development Fund and China-Africa Development Fund or SOEs listed abroad. In fact, being cognizant of this concern, in December 2011, CIC International was split as the purely overseas investment arm of CIC; however, most observers consider that to be not much more than a cosmetic change (Koch-Weser and Haacke, 2013, p. 19). It is evident that in the long run, governance reforms will have to address this problem of CIC owning and controlling domestic financial institutions.

Lack of transparency in activities, corporate structure, and governance

In general, data on CIC's investment procedures, activities, financial statements, and so on are hard to come by. The CIC's Annual Reports typically are very cryptic and most of the information leaves you wanting many more details and much more depth. In terms of transparency and governance, although Truman Index scores for CIC have improved from a low about 20 at inception to a high of 70 in 2011, there are several outstanding issues that need attention. In particular, there are two—CIC's relationship with the government and its relationship with the "wholly owned subsidiary," Central Huijin, which directly controls and may indirectly control some foreign investments. The financial pro-forma information for Central Huijin is not supplied at all by CIC. Overtime, it will be imperative for CIC to address these concerns and the foreign regulatory and multilateral organizations such as IMF are aware of the need to continue to make progress in this arena (Koch-Weser and Haacke, 2013, pp. 36–40).

19.6 CONCLUSION

Since its inception in 2007, CIC has consolidated its institutional footprint both in China and globally. Though CIC's birth was the result of a "compromise" between contending bureaucracies in China—the MOF and PBOC, the political will that apparently lay behind its formation has endured. CIC has strengthened its institutional fabric by improving its funding mechanism though much still needs to be done in this respect. However, the most remarkable aspect of CIC's growth has been demonstrated by the relative success of its dynamic allocation of its investment funds post-global financial crisis of 2007–2008.

CIC has clearly capitalized on the opportunities presented by this crisis to significantly transform its investment strategy in myriad ways. It has become more diversified by investing in sectors besides financial sector for the USA; instead, it has sizeable and sustained proportions of its investment funds in real sectors such as energy, mining, industrials, consumer discretionary, and real estate. These investments are well diversified geographically as well.

Though many of the sectors that CIC has invested in since the crisis are "strategic" to China's global supply chain, but they are also commercially viable. One sector in particular where CIC invested for purely commercial reasons is real estate and it may stand to gain tremendously from the bet that real estates especially in the USA and the other Advanced Countries may have bottomed out by the end of 2009. CIC is also proving to be farsighted by making considerable investment in green energy and alternative power generation.

CIC has matured and has invested in learning about the regulatory requirements in the USA and other Advanced Countries. In other ways as well, CIC has positioned itself as a responsible investor by making a commitment to adhere to Santiago Principles of Good Governance for SWFs. In fact, compared to 2007, CIC governance score on Truman Index has increased from a low of 20 to a level of 70 in 2011. However, there are still other dimensions related to full disclosure and transparency that call for attention.

For the period 2007–2013, CIC has mostly relied on outside professional managers and advisory services in the USA and Europe. However, it has been focusing on developing in-house talent at a good pace. As noted in its Annual Report, 2012, its current 5-year Talent Development Plan (2012—2016) demonstrates a serious commitment on the part of CIC to become more self-reliant.

Of course, the most significant challenge that CIC faces is to assuage the concerns about its symbiotic relationship with the state. Currently, even though, as of December 2011, CIC International is nominally been made independent of the Central Huijin Investments which generally overseas and capitalizes China's domestic financial institutions as well other state-owned enterprises including those listed abroad in Honk Kong, Singapore, New York, and London, the jury is still out as to how real is this change since there is still much that is interlocking and intertwined between the corporate structure of these two parts of CIC. In the same context, as CIC will continue to assert forth its mission of diversifying into direct investments in Emerging Countries that are rich in mineral resources especially on the African continent, many of the global observers will watch its activities rather warily. Much transparency will be required as to the activities of some of subsidiaries of CIC such as the China Development Fund and China-Africa Development Fund that indirectly partners with CIC in its foreign direct investments. The same goes for CIC's capitalization of SOEs that invest abroad.

Overall, as China's FX reserves continue to grow and the country as a whole continues to move toward its avowed goal to "better manage" them, CIC will be a significant force to reckon with. However, CIC will need to demonstrate its potential for making this process a win–win for the many global stakeholders. It can best do so by consistently having a long time horizon of its investments, following mostly commercial principles, further clarify its relationship with the state and the domestic functions of Central Huijin, being sensitive to the regulatory environment of host countries and temper its enthusiasm so as not to become overly aggressive.

REFERENCES

Cai, C., Clacher, I., 2009. Chinese investment goes global: the China Investment Corporation. Journal of Financial Regulation and Compliance 17 (1), 9–15.

CIC Annual Report, 2009. http://www.china-inv.cn/cicen/include/resources/CIC_2009_annualreport_en.pdf.

CIC Annual Report, 2010. http://www.china-inv.cn/cicen/include/resources/CIC_2010_annualreport_en.pdf.

CIC Annual Report, 2011. http://www.china-inv.cn/cicen/include/resources/CIC_2011_annualreport_en.pdf.

Cognato, M.H., 2008. Understanding China's new Sovereign Wealth Fund. NBR Analysis 19 (1), 9–36.

Eaton, S., Zhang, M., 2010. A principal-agent analysis of China's wealth system: Byzantine by design. Review of International Political Economy 17 (1), 9–15.

Klein, L.R., Shabbir, T., 2007. Asia before and after the financial crisis of 1997–1998: a retrospective essay. In: Klein, L.R., Shabbir, T. (Eds.), Recent Financial Crises: Analysis, Challenges and Implications. Edward Elgar Publishing Ltd, Northampton, MA.

Koch-Weser, I.N., Haacke, O.D., 2013. China Investment Corporation: Recent Developments in Performance, Strategy, and Governance. Congressional Research Service <<www.crs.gov>>.

Liu, Z., Spiegel, , 2012. External shocks and China's monetary policy. FRBSF Economic Letter <<http://www.frbsf.org/economic-research/publications/economic-letter/2012/december/external-shocks-china-monetary-policy/>>.

Martin, M.F., 2010. China's Sovereign Wealth Fund: Developments and Policy Implications. Congressional Research Service. <www.crs.gov>.

Monitor Group, 2010. Back on Course: Sovereign Wealth Fund Activity in 2009. SWF Annual Report 2009.

Shabbir, T., 2009. Role of the Middle Eastern Sovereign Wealth Funds in the current global financial crisis. Topics in Middle Eastern and North African Economies 11 (1), 1–19 <<http://www.luc.edu/orgs/meea/volume11/meea11.html>>.

Wu, F., Seah, A., 2008. The rise of China Investment Corporation: a new member of the Sovereign wealth club. World Economics 9 (2), 45–68.

Wu, F., Goh, C., Hajela, R., 2011. China Investment Corporation's post-crisis investment strategy. World Economics 12 (3), 123–152.

Yang, W., 2013. China Sovereign Wealth Fund's shifting strategy. EconoMonitor <<http://www.econo-monitor.com/blog/2013/04/china-sovereign-wealth-funds-shifting-strategy/>>.

CHAPTER 20

Sovereign Wealth Funds in East Asia: An Update of their Recent Developments

Kin-Yip Ho[a] and Zhaoyong Zhang[b]

[a]The Australian National University, Research School of Finance, Actuarial Studies and Applied Statistics, ANU College of Business and Economics, Canberra, ACT 0200, Australia
[b]Edith Cowan University, Faculty of Business and Law, 270 Joondalup Drive, Joondalup, WA 6027, Australia

20.1 INTRODUCTION

A sovereign wealth fund (SWF) is a state-owned investment fund investing in real and financial assets. Although the term SWF was coined only recently by Rozanov (2005), the first SWF established for a sovereign state goes all the way back to 1953 in Kuwait. There is no single universally accepted definition of SWFs, but they generally share the following characteristics (Elson, 2008; Loh, 2010; Shemirani, 2011): (1) they are owned by a sovereign government; (2) they are usually managed separately from the sovereign central bank, ministry of finance and treasuries; (3) they invest in a portfolio of assets of different risk profiles; (4) they have a long-term investment horizon; (5) unlike pension funds, they usually have no explicit individual liabilities; and (6) in terms of their operations, they can either operate as a legal entity from the government or they can legally be part of the government or central banks. The main objective of these SWFs is usually the desire to get a higher risk-return trade-off for the country's reserves. As such, SWFs perform the function of investing in various asset classes in global markets on behalf of their governments.

Since 2000, the number of sovereign wealth funds has increased dramatically worldwide, but most of the SWFs in the industrialized countries are predominantly from the developing countries and often target acquisitions in industrialized countries (Park, 2008). The recent massive growth of sovereign wealth funds (SWFs) in Asia, coupled with their complex and opaque nature of their investment strategies, has given rise to concern among international organizations, government agencies, and public policy-makers in various countries. As suggested by Shemirani (2011), these Asian SWFs generally share three main features: ownership by sovereign governments, management of portfolios other than official national reserves, and involvement in overseas investments. Due to the substantial accumulation of foreign reserves over the past few decades, it is unsurprising that Asian SWFs are able to dominate the international financial landscape with their overseas investment holdings (Loh, 2010; Lai, 2012). For instance, as of end-October 2012, the official foreign reserves of China and Korea stood at 3.29 trillion and 3.23 billion US dollars, respectively. These reserves are primarily the consequence of the persistent trade and current account surpluses maintained through an export-led development strategy. In a bid to obtain higher investment returns on these reserves, many Asian governments have created SWFs to invest actively in markets abroad, such as purchasing foreign government bonds and private assets.

This aggressive investment strategy abroad has raised alarming concern for those countries on the receiving end of the SWFs' investments, as they are worried about the potentially negative repercussions that these investments have for national ownership, control, and security (Elson, 2008; Mattoo and Subramanian, 2009; Truman, 2011). Given that Asian SWFs are usually not highly transparent, this exacerbates the concern that they could undermine national interests of the countries receiving their investments. In view of these concerns, it seems appropriate to review the background and recent developments of several Asian SWFs: the China Investment Corporation (CIC), the Korea Investment Corporation (KIC), and Vietnam's State Capital Investment Corporation (SCIC). These SWFs are chosen mainly because they are formally established less than ten years ago. Furthermore, these SWFs are loosely modeled after their Singaporean counterparts, Temasek Holdings and Government of Singapore Investment Corporation (Loh, 2010; Kim, 2012; Nguyen et al., 2012). This similarity serves as a starting point to compare and contrast their recent investment decisions. Moreover, literature on these Asian SWFs is relatively small. After discussing the recent developments of these SWFs, this chapter will conclude with some comments on the possible policy implications of their developments.

The remainder of this paper is organized as follows. Section 20.2 provides a brief review of the SWFs. In Section 20.3 we assess the selected Asian SWFs from China, Korea, and Vietnam. Section 20.4 concludes.

20.2 REVIEW OF SWFs

Sovereign wealth funds (SWFs) were introduced in the 1950s but they only came under intense media spotlight in the past few years. In general, SWFs could be considered the brainchild of the British colonial government and were initially set up by commodity-rich countries which had accumulated substantial foreign exchange reserves from commodity exports. As noted by Loh (2010) and Shemirani (2011), the Kuwait Investment Fund was the first SWF set up in 1953 to invest the substantial revenues from its oil industry. Other early examples from commodity-rich countries include the Kiribati Revenue Equalization Reserve Fund and Abu Dhabi Investment Authority. However, over the years, more funds were established using an economy's budget surpluses and foreign exchange reserves, which primarily come from the accumulation of vast current account surpluses. Examples of these non-commodity countries and economies include China, Korea, Taiwan, Hong Kong, and Singapore. These economies are major net exporters and have accumulated vast foreign reserves over the past three decades.

In part, this accumulation was deemed necessary in order to manage their exchange rate systems and defend their currencies from potential speculative attacks. As the level of foreign reserves grew bigger than that required to defend their currencies, the Asian central banks began to shift some of their reserves to SWFs to achieve the objective of reaping potentially higher returns. For instance, the Government of Singapore Investment Corporation (GIC) was set up in 1981 to achieve this objective. Other examples of non-commodity SWFs include China Investment Corporation (CIC), Korea Investment Corporation (KIC), Taiwan National Stabilization Fund (TNSF), and Hong Kong Monetary Authority Investment Portfolio (HKMAIP).

The SWF is characterized by its state-ownership and control, which involves investment in real and financial assets globally, including stocks, bonds, real estate, precious metals, and so on. It is often argued that the SWFs aim to convert physical wealth (often mineral wealth) into financial wealth and preserve such wealth in a trust format for the benefit of multiple generations and manage pools of excess reserves used to support domestic currencies in order to ensure financial stability, as well as provide for some level of fiscal contingency (Lee and Wang, 2011).

SWFs all over the world have grown rapidly in terms of the assets under their management. Since 2000, the number of sovereign wealth funds has increased dramatically. According to the SWF Institute, assets under the management of SWFs reached a record of $5.86 trillion in September 2013. The major funding resources for the SWFs are related to commodities' exports, primarily oil, and gas exports, which account for 59%, while the non-commodity SWFs are mainly funded by transfer of assets from official foreign exchange reserves and in some cases from government budget surpluses and privatization revenue. Of the 70 SWFs listed by the SWF Institute, the top three SWFs, holding SWF assets of US$2.04 trillion, are all associated with commodity-exporting countries, including Norway (Government Pension Fund—Global), Saudi Arabia (SAMA Foreign Holdings), and United Arab Emirates (Abu Dhabi Investment Authority). The rest of the top ten SWFs is mostly dominated by non-commodity SWFs from Asia. It is noted that the two Chinese SWFs for the first time entered the top five (see Table 20.1). As one of the earliest Asian-based SWFs, GIC from Singapore taps on the persistent budget and current account surpluses accumulated over the years to conduct its investments abroad. In fact, many other Asian SWFs, such as CIC (China), HKMAIP (Hong Kong), and KIC (Korea), develop their strategies based on this principle. The rise of these Asian SWFs is the outcome of global imbalances—high balance of payment deficits in developed economies and high balance of payment surpluses in Asia, and a general undervaluation of currencies in Asia. Although the individual sizes of Asian SWFs are still smaller than those of the commodity-based SWFs, it is generally believed that they will play a major role in the fund management industry and could alter the role of government in the private sector in the foreseeable future (Loh, 2010; Chia, 2011; Rozanov, 2011; Truman, 2011).

Table 20.1 Selected SWFs' Ranking and Linaburg-Maduell Transparency Index

Rank	Country	SWF Name	Assets (US$ Billion)	Inception	Origin	LMT Index
1	Norway	Government Pension Fund—Global	737.2	1990	Oil	10
2	Saudi Arabia	SAMA Foreign Holdings	675.9	n/a	Oil	4
3	UAE—Abu Dhabi	Abu Dhabi Investment Authority	627	1976	Oil	5
4	China	China Investment Corporation	575.2	2007	Non-Commodity	7
5	China	SAFE Investment Company	567.9	1997	Non-Commodity	4
6	Kuwait	Kuwait Investment Authority	386	1953	Oil	6
7	China-Hong Kong	Hong Kong Monetary Authority Investment Portfolio	326.7	1993	Non-Commodity	8
8	Singapore	Government of Singapore Investment Corporation	285	1981	Non-Commodity	6
9	Russia	National Welfare Fund	175.5	2008	Oil	5
10	Singapore	Temasek Holdings	173.3	1974	Non-Commodity	10
11	China	National Social Security Fund	160.6	2000	Non-Commodity	5
19	Korea	Korea Investment Corporation	56.6	2005	Non-Commodity	9
47	China	China–Africa Development Fund	5	2007	Non-Commodity	4
59	Vietnam	State Capital Investment Corporation	0.5	2006	Non-Commodity	4

Source: Sovereign Wealth Fund Institute, September 2013.

Note: Rankings are based on assets as in September 2013. LMT Index is the Linaburg-Maduell Transparency Index, which is given to a SWF based on a point system of 1–10 determined by essential principles that depict transparency. A score of 1 in the LMT Index represents complete opaqueness and 10 represents complete transparency. The Sovereign Wealth Fund Institute recommends a minimum rating of 8 in order to claim adequate transparency.

It is observed that the SWFs in Asian countries are mostly based on conventional current account surpluses derived from non-resource exports and their persistent balance of payment surpluses associated with capital inflows, which led to the rapid increase in the region's foreign exchange reserves. The most notable case is China. By June 2013, foreign exchange reserves in China increased to US$35 trillion from a record low of US$2.262 billion in 1980 and US$165.6 billion in 2000 (see Figure 20.1). The reserves are the foreign assets held or controlled by the People's bank of China, the Chinese central bank, and are mostly made of gold, a specific currency (mostly in

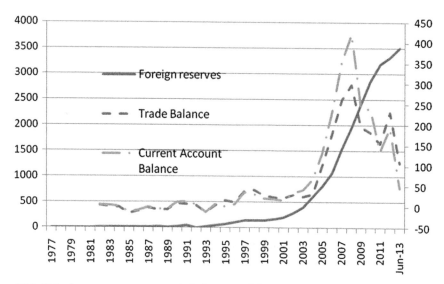

Figure 20.1 China's current account, trade balance, and foreign exchange reserves 1977–June 2013 (billion US dollar). *Note:* Foreign exchange reserves are plotted against the left axis, and the trade balance and current account balance are against the right axis. The sample period for current account balance ranges from 1982 to March 2013, and for foreign exchange reserves and the trade balance until June 2013. Data were adapted from China's State Administration of Foreign Exchange and the Customs of China.

US dollar), and marketable securities denominated in foreign currencies like treasury bills, government bonds, corporate bonds, and equities and foreign currency loans. In 2008 China surpassed Japan and became the biggest foreign creditor of the United States. According to Xinhua News Agency, China held US federal debt with a record of US$1.3 trillion. On the other hand, China's foreign trade has expanded dramatically over the past few decades. In 2009 China surpassed Germany and became the world's number one exporter. As it can be seen in Figure 20.1, because of the global economic turmoil, China's trade surplus fell sharply to US$155 billion in 2011, after the historic peak of about US$300 billion in 2008. The current account balance shows a similar down trend after the global financial crisis in 2008. China's trade balance and current account showed an increasing surplus again in 2012, amounting, respectively, to US$231 billion for the former and US$193 billion for the latter, and will likely maintain the increasing trend in 2013. According to the US Census Bureau, China has surpassed Japan and become the largest contributor to the US trade deficit since 2001. Out of the US record high trade deficits of $816 billion in 2008, China accounted for 33%, and this share rose again to 45% in 2009 before fell to about 36% by April 2010.

Indeed, many of these Asian SWFs were thrust into the media limelight in the wake of the global financial crisis in 2007–2008. They bought stakes in many ailing western financial institutions, and some (such as CIC, GIC, and KIC) were considered rather aggressive in their investment approach. The growing size and aggressiveness of these Asian SWFs have raised several issues. First, would these SWFs use their financial power and clout to advance their political ambitions? As these SWFs have operated in a rather secretive and non-transparent manner with limited disclosure on their strategies, do they have a hidden political agenda? Second, would their investments destabilize international financial markets? Third, would a conflict of interest arise between SWFs and the recipient countries where these funds are invested, since SWF investments could have macroeconomic implications for the local government? Fourth, would the aggressiveness of SWFs create backlash and encourage the rise of protectionism in recipients' countries? Finally, would SWFs lead to state capitalism and undermine the free market system? These remain interesting questions but yet to be resolved.

20.3 ASIAN SWFs: INVESTMENT STRATEGIES AND RECENT DEVELOPMENTS

20.3.1 China Investment Corporation (CIC)

According to the Sovereign Wealth Fund Institute, China now has four SWFs, namely the State Administration of Foreign Exchange Investment Company (SAFEIC) set up in 1997, the National Social Security Fund (NSSF) in 2000, the China Investment Corporation (CIC) in 2007, and the China–Africa Development Fund (CADF) in 2007. By September 2013, total SWF assets held by the four Chinese SWFs were US$1.31 trillion, accounting for 22.4% of the global SWF assets and for 54.3% of global non-commodity SWF assets (see Table 20.1). Of the four SWFs, CIC is the most prominent and also the only officially recognized SWF by the Chinese government.

CIC was established in 2007 as a wholly state-owned company under the Company Law of the People's Republic of China (see Table 20.2). CIC's initial capitalization was US$200 billion and received one additional capital injection worth US$30 billion in 2011 from the People's Bank of China, but experts speculated an additional US$100 billion received by CIC each year (Koch-Weser and Haacker, 2013). At the point of its establishment, it bought out Huijin Investment Ltd., which was set up in 2003 to recapitalize and stabilize China's major state-owned commercial banks. According to Loh (2010), CIC's *modus operandi* is modeled after Singapore's SWF Temasek Holdings, which invests in both domestic and international markets and is accountable to the Ministry of Finance.

CIC's investment strategy in various markets is guided by the following principles (CIC, 2009): (1) as a long-term investor, it focuses on sustainable strategies; (2) CIC is a financial investor and does not aim to gain control of enterprises or sectors through its investments; (3) CIC's investment decisions are driven by research and based on commercial rates of return; and (4) CIC aims to be a socially responsible investor by complying with the laws and regulations of countries that host its investments and avoiding investments in socially undesirable industries (such as tobacco and gaming). As noted

Table 20.2 Major Investments of CIC

Investments	Date	Stake (%)	Cost
Blackstone Group	May 2007	9.9	US$3bn+
China Railway Group	November 2007		US$100m
Morgan Stanley	December 2007	9.9	US$5bn+
KazMunaiGas Exploration Production	September 2009	11	US$939m+
Nobel Oil Group	October 2009	45	US$300m
Goodman Group	August 2009		US$159m
Songbird Estates Ltd.	September 2009	14.7	US$159m
Nobel Group Ltd.	September 2009	14.9	US$858m
Iron Mining International	October 2009		US$500m
AES Corporation	November 2009	15.0	US$1.6bn
South Gobi Energy Resources Ltd.	November 2009		US$500m
GCL-Poly Energy Holdings Ltd.	November 2009	20.1	US$717m
BlackRock Inc.			US$714m
Apax Partners	February 2010	2.3	US$956m
Changsha Zoomlion Heavy Industry Science & Technology Development	March 2010	15.8	US$816m
Penn West Energy Trust	May 2010	45	US$801m
Visa			US$100m
Teck Resources Ltd.		17.2	C$1.74bn+
JC Flower Private Equity Fund			US$4bn+

Sources: CIC Annual Report, various years; Loh (2010) and Liew and He (2012); updated by authors from various news articles.

by Liew and He (2012), these principles are formulated to allay international concerns that there would be undue political influences on CIC's investments. More specifically, the principles are designed to reassure countries receiving CIC's investments that these investments pose no threat to their national security.

In the initial stage of investing abroad, CIC focused on the financial sector. As highlighted by Loh (2010) and Liew and He (2012), by the end of 2008, CIC has made two major investments: US$3 billion and US$5.6 billion in the Blackstone Group and Morgan Stanley, respectively. These investments were justified by the CIC Chairman that unlike a traditional central bank, CIC could not act too conservatively. As a commercial concern, CIC has to be more aggressive and attempt to seek higher profits by taking more risk in the international financial markets.

More recently, CIC has developed a three-layer asset allocation framework comprising strategic asset allocation, policy portfolio, and tactical asset allocation and started to diversify by investing in a wide range of financial products globally, including cash, equities, fixed income, absolute return, and long-term investments. Absolute return investments are primarily hedge funds. Long-term investments include private equity investments, energy, mining, real estate, infrastructure, and others (CIC, 2013). In 2010, CIC purchased a 7.6% interest in General Growth Properties Inc., a company with significant holdings in the US real estate market and joined AREA Real Estate Finance Corp. to jointly acquire a preferred equity stake in a 27-story office building owned by Carlyle Group in Manhattan (Koch-Weser and Haacker, 2013). By seeking overseas investment opportunities in the energy and natural resource sector, CIC can potentially play its part in enhancing China's overall resource security (Loh, 2010; Blanchard, 2011; Liew and He, 2012). For instance, the Chinese government has announced plans to reduce its reliance on the big miners (BHP Billiton, Rio Tinto, and Vale) by 2015 through securing 40% of its iron ore imports from its own mines overseas (de Kretser, 2011). Furthermore, CIC will target emerging economies for investments in their energy and resource sectors (Chen, 2011). These economies are expected to be more receptive to China's capital injections into their energy and resource sectors and to have generally less restrictive controls on inbound direct investments. Furthermore, as they generally lack sufficient domestic savings required for large-scale capital-intensive projects, CIC is able and willing to provide this shortfall. The new asset allocation strategies have resulted in 49.2% of CIC's investment in the US equities, 27.8% in non-US advanced economies equities, and 23% in the emerging market equities as of 31 December 2012 (CIC, 2012). Table 20.3 presents CIC's major investments in Europe and the USA in 2012. These investments are consistent with CIC's new asset allocation plans to creating a long-term asset portfolio. For instance, CIC invested £450 million

Table 20.3 Major CIC Investments in 2012

Company	Closing Date	Country	Sector	Investment Amount (Million)	Initial Ownership
Thames Water	January	UK	Infrastructure	£276	8.68%
EP Energy	May	US	Energy	$300	9.9%
Polyus Gold	May	Russia	Mining	$425	5%—1 share
Eutelsat Communications SA	June	France	Pan Industry	€386	7%
Heathrow Airport Holdings Ltd.	November	UK	Infrastructure	£450	10%
Moscow Exchange	December	Russia	Pan Industry	$187	4.58%

Source: CIC Annual Report 2012.

Table 20.4 Investment Performance on the Global Portfolio

Year	Cumulative Annualized Return (%)	Annual Return (%)
2008	−2.1	−2.1
2009	4.1	11.7
2010	6.4	11.7
2011	3.8	−4.3
2012	5.02	10.60

Source: CIC, Annual Report 2012.
Note: Cumulative annualized returns and the annual return for 2008 are calculated since inception on 29 September 2007.

for a 10% stake in Heathrow Airport Holdings Ltd. in November 2012 as "CIC sees the UK as a destination of choice for long-term investment because of its business-friendly environment and sound legal framework" (CIC, 2012, p. 33).

CIC's higher-risk investment strategy has paid off. In 2012, CIC posted an annualized return of 10.65% on its overseas investment, with cumulative annualized return since its inception reaching 5.02%. Overall, it seems that CIC has performed fairly well since its inception in 2007, registered double-digit gains on its overseas investments in 2009, 2010, and 2012, and two negative returns of 2.1% and 4.3%, respectively, in 2008 and 2011 (see Table 20.4).

However, CIC's low transparency and close relationship with the Chinese government remain the major concerns in countries such as the USA. Of the 25 members of CIC's board and executive committee, only three individuals are not current or former governmental officials (Koch-Weser and Haacker, 2013). CIC's governance raises concerns about its compliance with the Santiago Principles.

20.3.2 Korea Investment Corporation (KIC)

KIC was established in 2005 under the Korean Investment Corporation Act (Truman, 2011). Compared with CIC, KIC is relatively small but with a high-transparency index. As of September 2013 the total assets under KIC's management were US$56.6 billion (see Table 20.1). According to the rankings of the Sovereign Wealth Fund Institute in September 2013, KIC ranks nineteenth worldwide in terms of its total assets and eighth among SWFs with non-commodity origin. As suggested by Kim (2012), KIC is modeled after the Government of Singapore Investment Corporation (GIC), an Asian SWF established in 1981 to manage the country's official foreign reserves. More specifically, the Monetary Authority of Singapore, which has accumulated substantial foreign reserves over the years, transfers a portion of these reserves to GIC so that GIC can invest them in various markets to earn higher risk-adjusted returns in the long-run. This helps to enhance the value of these reserves, which are important for defending the country's managed float exchange rate policy. Based on a mission trip to Singapore, the Korean Ministry of Finance and Economy (MOFE) concluded that the GIC model could help solve the dilemma Korea was facing after the end of the Asian financial crisis in the late 1990s: the appreciation of the Korean Won due to strong capital inflows while facing the potential of deterioration of current account balance.

More specifically, the establishment of KIC was deemed to have the following benefits (Kim, 2012): (1) KIC would allow the government to continue its intervention operations in the foreign exchange market by transferring a significant proportion of foreign reserves to KIC without being labeled as foreign exchange market manipulation; (2) potential economies of scale in overseas investments can be gained; (3) with the KIC focussing on investing overseas, the Korean government could potentially gain better access to high-quality market information; and (4) KIC could potentially spur and enhance the overall development of Korea's asset management industry because the expertise and know-how on overseas investment could be trickled down to other Korean funds.

According to the KIC Annual Report 2012, its investment policy is "to generate consistent and sustainable returns in excess of the benchmark within an appropriate level of risk." Based on this objective, KIC strives to increase returns while (1) diversifying its portfolio to minimize the risks from individual markets and assets and (2) exercising flexibility to seize investment opportunities. Based on an investment management agreement with the Bank of Korea and the Ministry of Strategy and Finance in June and October of 2006, respectively, KIC started its investments out with entrusted assets of USD 20.0 billion. Initially, those investments were concentrated in traditional asset classes such as stocks and fixed-income securities (bonds). However, over the years, the scope of KIC's investment has been broadened to include inflation-linked bonds and commodities as well as private equity, real estate, and hedge funds.

Due to the continued increase in entrusted assets for investments, assets under KIC's management have since grown and stand at USD 56.6 billion as of end-December 2012. In less than ten years after it was established, KIC made it to the top twenty SWF in the world. Actual asset allocations and investment performances are disclosed in various years of KIC's Annual Reports. As it can be seen in Table 20.5, a total of 90.7% of the assets are allocated in traditional assets, with 46.6% in (public) equities. Alternative assets (such as private equity, hedge funds, and real estate) take up 6.1%. Strategic (Special) Investments include KIC's direct exposure to strategically chosen industry sectors, such as mining, energy, raw materials, resource-related services, oil sand, natural gas, and finance. These investments are managed internally rather than outsourced to external managers and could be pursued in partnership with other SWFs and prominent global pension funds. All other alternative asset class investments are carried out by external managers.

Table 20.5 Asset Allocation of KIC as of End-December 2012

Asset Class	Assets Under Management (USD Million)	Weight (%)
Traditional Assets	**51,328**	**90.7**
Equities	25,593	46.6
Bonds	21,988	1.9
Inflation-linked bonds	1582	11.9
Commodities	762	2.3
Cash, other	1403	2.7
Alternative Assets	**3461**	**6.1**
Cash other	131	3.8
Private equity	1088	31.4
Hedge funds	1331	38.5
Real estate	911	26.3
Strategic Investments	**1826**	**3.2**
Total Assets	**56,615**	**100**

Sources: KIC Annual Report, various years; KIC Web site (www.kic.kr/en); and Kim (2012). All figures for Assets Under Management (AUM) are based on Net Asset Value (NAV).

Several aspects of KIC's investment policy deserve mention. First, as part of the strategy of portfolio diversification, KIC has increased their exposure to emerging markets since 2010. Second, decisions related to strategic asset allocation are deliberated by the KIC Steering Committee, which is the highest decision-making body. Third, the investment management agreements signed between KIC and sponsors specify eligible asset classes and benchmark targets, and they serve as the basis for risk management and performance evaluation. KIC pursues benchmark returns (beta) by diversifying investments in the range of currencies and countries as set forth in the investment management guidelines. These benchmark returns differ according to asset classes. For instance, according to the KIC Annual Report 2012, the benchmark for public equities (bonds) is based on a customized version of Morgan Stanley Capital International Index (Barclays Capital Global Aggregate Index). As for the alternative investments, the benchmark is based on the average inflation rates of G7 countries. Fourth, with regard to traditional assets, KIC manages risk using the tracking error from active investing relative to the benchmark. If the weighting of an asset class deviates from a set range relative to the benchmark, adjustments are made so that exposure falls within the set range. The portfolio is rebalanced at predetermined times to maintain policy weightings for each asset class. Fifth, for internal investments, KIC pursues returns slightly in excess of the benchmark (enhanced beta) with a low level of tracking error. For external fund management, however, we adopted an alpha-beta separation strategy in 2009 which seeks greater alpha by employing external managers focusing on specific regions, sectors, and asset classes.

As noted by Kim (2012), KIC's investment performance to date is quite lackluster and unimpressive. Since its inception, KIC's excess return over benchmark is −0.07% (see Table 20.6). The lackluster performance could be attributed to the poor performance of the public equities. As shown in Table 20.6, negative excess returns occurred 5 out of 6 years for the equities portfolio. Furthermore, KIC does not disclose its performance in a transparent manner. First, it is not entirely clear whether the returns are net of fees. Second, KIC does not provide sufficient disclosure on the performance on its alternative investments. Prior to the KIC Annual Report 2012, there is hardly any information on the returns of alternative and special investments. Also, there is no discussion in the annual report on fair value pricing nor any discussion about the level of risk KIC is taking.

Among KIC's Special Investments in recent years, a couple of them deserve mention. The most noteworthy was its US$2 billion acquisition of Merrill Lynch preferred stocks on 15 January 2008. KIC was joined by several other SWFs and institutional investors, including Kuwait Investment Authority, Japan's Mizuho Financial Group, and Temasek Holdings. At that time, many Asian SWFs were betting that the USA would recover quickly from its subprime mortgage crisis, which proved to be wrong. In the case of KIC, it purchased mandatory convertible preferred stocks with a 9% dividend yield that was scheduled to be converted to 38,160,000 shares of common stock on 15 October 2010. KIC projected that the conversion would give KIC a 3% stake in Merrill Lynch. As market conditions worsened, Merrill Lynch continued to take write-downs and losses. According to Kim (2012), this Merrill Lynch deal created approximately a 54.5% loss over a three-year period for KIC. As of December 2010, KIC holds only a 0.61% stake. According to recent reports in August 2013, KIC will still maintain its stake in Bank of America, as KIC views the bank as a proxy for the US economy.

Apart from recent investments in the financial sector, KIC made several cross-border acquisitions in the energy sector in 2010. For example, in June 2010, it made a

Table 20.6 Investment Performance of KIC

Asset Class	2007	2008	2009	2010	2011	2012	Since Inception
(a) Returns							
Fixed Income/Bonds	9.91	3.81	8.56	5.60	3.94	7.76	6.49
Equities	5.19	−41.43	31.96	11.71	−10.26	16.20	−0.94
Traditional Assets	7.40	−13.71	18.67	8.46	−3.32	11.83	4.32
(b) Excess Returns							
Fixed Income/Bonds	0.09	−1.36	1.71	0.35	−0.71	1.24	−0.55
Equities	−1.19	−0.11	−0.23	−0.68	−0.99	0.01	0.15
Traditional Assets	−0.25	−0.66	1.42	0.05	−0.90	0.66	−0.07

Sources: KIC Annual Report, various years; KIC Web site (www.kic.kr/en); and Kim (2012).

US$200 million investment in Chesapeake Energy Co., a US natural gas company. KIC purchased convertible preferred shares jointly with CIC and Temasek Holdings. Additionally, KIC purchased 2.55 million common shares. In November, KIC made a US$99 million investment in Osum Oil Sands Corp., purchasing 7.7 million common shares.

More recently in August 2013, KIC has recently announced plans to spend as much as US$10 billion to triple its allocation to alternative investments. In particular, KIC wants to increase holdings of private equity, real estate, and hedge funds to as much as 20% of its portfolio by 2016 from 6.1% at the end of 2012. Indeed, KIC has already increased its real estate investments in Australia in 2012 by investing in the Queensland-based QIC Property Fund (QPF). It is reported to have committed more than US$200 million in Australian property investments. Apart from increasing alternative investments, it is also reported that KIC plans to expand its investment in China. In 2011, the fund was granted a license from Chinese authorities to invest in the country's stock market under the Qualified Foreign Institutional Investor (QFII) status. Currently, KIC's quota for investing in China is capped at $400 million, with 80% of that amount going to equities and 20% to bonds. As the current quota is less than 1% of assets under KIC's management, KIC plans to expand this quota in future.

20.3.3 Vietnam State Capital Investment Corporation

SCIC was established in 2005, with the primary objective of helping the Vietnamese government make the most of state capital investments in business enterprises under market conditions. Compared with other Asian SWFs, SCIC's size in terms of total assets (US$0.5 billion as of September 2013) is relatively small. As of 31 December 2012, SCIC has 407 portfolio companies with a book value of US$ 710.48 million.

According to Nguyen et al. (2012), SCIC's mandate includes the following requirements: (1) take over state shareholdings and exercise the state's ownership rights in state-invested enterprises (SIEs); (2) conduct investments in key industries domestically and overseas in order to safeguard and develop state capital, use state capital efficiently and improve the operational capacity and competitiveness of SIEs; and (3) provide financial consultancy and advisory services to enterprises. SCIC sees itself as "a strategic investment arm" of the Vietnamese Government, and its executives have often spoken of looking upon Singapore's Temasek Holdings as a role model. SCIC has to grapple with the main challenge of facilitating the "equitization" (that is privatization) of large numbers of state-owned enterprises. As it can be seen in Table 20.7, SCIC has divested in total 579 companies, with 526 companies wholly divested and 53 partly divested by 31 December 2012.

SCIC's recent performance can be evaluated from its investments in several large enterprises (Nguyen et al., 2012). The first is Vinamilk (Vietnam Dairy Products Joint Stock Company), which was first established in 1976 and subsequently equitized

Table 20.7 SCIC's Divestments

Divested Companies	2006–2008	2009	2010	2011	2012	Accumulated by 31/12/2012
Wholly divested	84	219	97	91	35	526
Partly divested	14	19	9	8	3	53
Total no.	98	238	106	99	38	579
Book value (USD million)	10.24	23.24	13.38	20.38	7.24	74.48
Market value (USD million)	29.24	45.24	30.86	37.90	15.14	158.38
Market value/ Book value	2.85	1.94	2.31	1.9	2.1	2.1

Source: SCIC's Web site at http://www.scic.vn.

(privatized) in 2003. As the company's largest investor, SCIC holds 47.6% of Vinamilk's shares (see Table 20.8). Revenues and profits have both been strong and growing, and the rate of return on equity has risen from a healthy 25% in 2006 to 45% in 2010. According to the SCIC report, its return on equity has been consistently high, ranging from 15.8% in 2008 to 18.3% in 2011 (see Table 20.9). According to Nguyen et al. (2012), in just 2010 alone, SCIC received around VND600 billion (US$30 million) in dividends from Vinamilk. Given that Vinamilk is SCIC's star holding, it makes a substantial contribution to SCIC's overall performance. Another major enterprise that SCIC has invested in is Bao Viet Holdings (BVH), which was established in 1964 and then equitized in 2007. As an insurance company, BVH operates mainly in the field of non-life insurance. Nguyen et al. (2012) suggests that BVH's profit levels and rates of return have been good but not as spectacular as Vinamilk's.

In addition to investments in domestic enterprises, SCIC also has joint ventures with overseas SWFs (Nguyen et al., 2012). However, these are overseas ventures are still in their incipient stages. For instance, SCIC has a 25% share in an unlisted joint venture with Oman (with total charter capital of VND80 billion, or US$4 million). In addition, it has been reported that the SWFs of Kuwait and Qatar have entered into (separate) agreements with SCIC to form joint ventures for investment purposes (with total capital of US$1 billion and US$100 million, respectively), but SCIC itself apparently has not reported its holdings in any such joint ventures. In any case, such joint ventures (whenever they do eventuate) will probably serve primarily as vehicles for investing overseas capital in Vietnamese industries.

SCIC has a low-transparency index, with the LMT index scoring only 4 in 2013 (see Table 20.1). Similar to CIC, SCIC's state-ownership and governance remain the underlying concern in line with the Santiago Principle.

Table 20.8 SCIC Holdings in Exchange-Listed Enterprises

Company Name	No. of Shares Owned by SCIC (in Millions)	% of Ownership	Value of Holdings in VND Billion	Value of Holdings in USD Million
Vinamilk	168.6	45.5%	21,755	1044.4
Vietnam Construction and Import–Export Joint Stock Corporation	153.2	51.1%	2236	107.3
Hau Giang Pharmaceutical Joint Stock Company	28.3	43.4%	1713	82.2
Bao Viet Holdings	22.2	3.3%	1595	76.6
FPT Group	13.3	6.2%	699	33.6
Vietnam National Reinsurance Corporation	40.7	40.4%	529	25.4
Vinh Son—Song Hinh Hydropower	49.5	52.4%	515	24.7
Tien Phong Plastic	16.1	37.1%	505	24.2
Baominh Insurance	38.3	50.7%	413	19.8
Binh Minh Plastic	10.4	29.8%	364	17.5
Binh Duong Mineral and Construction (BIMICO)	5.4	50%	268	12.9
Ha Giang Mineral Mechanics	2.9	49%	246	11.8
Traphaco	4.4	35.7%	183	8.8
Thac Ba Hydropower	15.2	24%	178	8.5
H.A.I.	8.7	50%	178	8.5
Domesco Medical Import–Export	6.2	34.7%	150	7.2
Tan Tien Plastic Packaging	4.1	27.3%	126	6.0
Vietnam Electricity Construction	18.9	29.7%	108	5.2
Bac Ninh Agricultural Products	6	13.8%	106	5.1
Southern Logistics	4	47.7%	104	5.0

Sources: SCIC Web site (www.scic.vn); Orient Securities Corporation (OSC) Web site (www.ors.com.vn); Nguyen et al. (2012).

Table 20.9 Performance of Companies Handed Over to SCIC (In USD Million)

Indicators	Time of Handing Over	2008	2009	2010	2011
Revenue	4,477.67	5,495.67	6,178.24	7,235.81	8,042.95
Pre-tax profit	202.52	238.33	468.43	648.05	660.05
Return on equity (ROE)	15.80%	17.50%	17.50%	18.50%	18.30%

Source: SCIC's Web site at http://www.scic.vn.

20.4 CONCLUSION

Due to its state-ownership and control, the SWF and its investment activities have become one of the most controversial issues in international finance. In this paper, we have reviewed the recent developments of three relatively new Asian SWFs, namely CIC, KIC, and SCIC. In terms of overseas investments, it appears that CIC and KIC are much more active compared with their Vietnamese counterpart. Nonetheless, these Asian SWFs are still not very transparent in terms of their actions, with SCIC having the lowest LMT score of 4. These SWFs' low transparency and governance raise questions about their compliance with the Santiago Principles. As it is anticipated that these Asian SWFs have a bigger role to play in future, especially in the Asia-Pacific region, it is suggested that a set of guiding principles on their transparency and accountability be developed. The Santiago Principles (Truman, 2011) is a good starting point, but various Asia-Pacific countries should come together under a multilateral framework to develop these principles.

REFERENCES

Blanchard, J., 2011. China's grand strategy and money muscle: the potentialities and pratfalls of China's sovereign wealth fund and renminbi policies. The Chinese Journal of International Politics 4 (1), 31–53.

Chen, J., 2011. Wealth fund CIC targets emerging economies. China Daily. <http://www.chinadaily.com.cn/cndy/2011-04/22/content_12373920.htm>.

Chia, S., 2011. Comment on are Asian sovereign wealth funds different? Asia Economic Policy Review 6, 269–270.

CIC, 2009. China Investment Corporation Annual Report.

CIC, 2012. China Investment Corporation Annual Report.

CIC, 2013. China Investment Corporation Annual Report.

de Kretser, A., 2011. China seeks control over iron ore. The Australian Financial Review (May 2 2011).

Elson, A., 2008. Sovereign wealth funds and the international monetary system. The Whitehead Journal of Diplomacy and International Relations 9, 71–82.

Kim, W., 2012. Korea investment corporation: its origin and evolution. Journal of the Asia Pacific Economy 17 (2), 208–235.

Koch-Weser, I., Haacker, O.D., 2013. China investment corporation: recent developments in performance, strategy, and governance. U.S.-China Economic and Security Review Commission Report.

Lai, J., 2012. Khazanah Nasional: Malaysia's treasure trove. Journal of the Asia Pacific Economy 17 (2), 236–252.

Lee, B., Wang, H., 2011. Reevaluating the roles of large public surpluses and sovereign wealth funds in Asia. ADBI Working Paper 287, Asian Development Bank Institute, Tokyo.

Liew, L., He, L., 2012. Operating in an inharmonious world: China investment corporation. Journal of the Asia Pacific Economy 17 (2), 253–267.

Loh, L., 2010. Sovereign Wealth Funds: States Buying the World. Talisman Publishing, Singapore.

Mattoo, A., Subramanian, A., 2009. Currency undervaluation and sovereign wealth funds: a new role for the world trade organization. World Economy 32 (8), 1135–1164.

Nguyen, T., Nguyen, P.T., Nguyen, J.D., 2012. Vietnam's SCIC: a gradualist approach to sovereign wealth funds. Journal of the Asia Pacific Economy 17 (2), 268–283.

Park, D., 2008. Developing Asia's new sovereign wealth funds and global financial stability. ADB Briefs October No. 1.

Rozanov, A., 2005. Who holds the wealth of nations? Central Banking Journal 15 (4), 52–57.

Rozanov, A., 2011. Comment on Asian sovereign wealth funds different? Asia Economic Policy Review 6, 271–272.

Shemirani, M., 2011. Sovereign Wealth Funds and International Political Economy. Ashgate Publishing, United Kingdom.

Truman, E., 2011. Are Asian sovereign funds different? Asia Economic Policy Review 6, 249–268.

INDEX

Printed and bound by CPI Group (UK) Ltd, Croydon, CR0 4YY

08/05/2025

01864774-0001